THE YE

THE YELLOWHAMMER WAR

The Civil War and Reconstruction in Alabama

Edited by Kenneth W. Noe

PUBLISHED IN COOPERATION WITH
THE FRANCES S. SUMMERSELL CENTER FOR THE STUDY OF THE SOUTH

THE UNIVERSITY OF ALABAMA PRESS
Tuscaloosa

The University of Alabama Press
Tuscaloosa, Alabama 35487-0380
uapress.ua.edu

Copyright © 2013 by the University of Alabama Press
All rights reserved.

Hardcover edition published 2014.
Paperback edition published 2019.
eBook edition published 2014.

Inquiries about reproducing material from this work should be addressed to the University of Alabama Press.

Typeface: Garamond

Cover photograph: Flag of Rucker's Brigade, Company F, 7th Alabama Cavalry, PN-10171-10173, Cat. No. 86.1876.1, Alabama Department of Archives and History, Montgomery
Cover design: Erin Bradley Dangar / Dangar Design

Paperback ISBN: 978-0-8173-2055-3

A previous edition of this book has been catalogued by the Library of Congress as follows:
Library of Congress Cataloging-in-Publication Data
The yellowhammer war : the Civil War and Reconstruction in Alabama / edited by Kenneth W. Noe.
    pages cm
Includes bibliographical references and index.
ISBN 978-0-8173-1808-6 (hardback)—ISBN 978-0-8173-8704-4 (e book)
1. Alabama—History—Civil War, 1861—1865. 2. Reconstruction (U.S. history, 1865—1877)—Alabama. I. Noe, Kenneth W., 1957— editor.
    E551.Y45 2013
    976.1'05—dc23
          2013017504

Contents

List of Illustrations vii

Acknowledgments ix

Introduction
Kenneth W. Noe 1

1. Precipitating a Revolution: Alabama's Democracy in the Election of 1860
Lonnie A. Burnett 15

2. "The Aggressions of the North Can Be Borne No Longer":
White Alabamian Women during the Secession Crisis and Outbreak of War
Jennifer Ann Newman Treviño 34

3. Confederate Alabama's Finest Hour: The Battle of Salem Church, May 3, 1863
Ben H. Severance 55

4. The Confederate Sun Sets on Selma:
Nathan Bedford Forrest and the Defense of Alabama in 1865
Brian Steel Wills 71

5. Fighting for the Cause? An Examination of the Motivations of Alabama's
Confederate Soldiers from a Class Perspective
Kristopher A. Teters 90

6. Voices from the Margins: Non-Elites in Confederate Alabama
Victoria E. Ott 107

7. Augusta Jane Evans: Alabama's Confederate *Macaria*
Jennifer Lynn Gross 125

8. "The Best Southern Patriots": Jews in Alabama during the Civil War
Patricia A. Hoskins 149

9. Every Man Should Consider His Own Conscience:
Black and White Alabamians' Reactions to the Assassination of Abraham Lincoln
Harriet E. Amos Doss 165

10. Alabama's Reconstruction after 150 Years
Sarah Woolfolk Wiggins   177

11. Of Ambition and Enterprise: The Making of Carpetbagger George E. Spencer
Terry L. Seip   191

12. "He Was Always Preaching the Union":
The Wartime Origins of White Republicanism during Reconstruction
Michael W. Fitzgerald   220

13. Labor, Law, and the Freedmen's Bureau in Alabama, 1865–1867
Jason J. Battles   240

14. Freedom's Church: Sociocultural Construction, Reconstruction, and Post-Reconstruction in Perry County, Alabama's African American Churches
Bertis English   258

Suggestions for Further Reading   281

Contributors   289

Index   291

Illustrations

3.1. Chancellorsville Campaign   57
3.2. Salem Church   61
9.1. Market Street in Montgomery, 1861   166
9.2. Union raids in Alabama during the Civil War   167

Acknowledgments

The idea for this book emerged in 2007 during preliminary discussions about how Alabama should mark the sesquicentennial of the American Civil War. I remain grateful to former Alabama Historical Association president Anne Feathers for her support, as well as to my fellow members of a Civil War committee that she subsequently established: Bob Bradley, Harriet Amos Doss, Bertis English, and George Rable.

Dan Ross of the University of Alabama Press expressed early enthusiasm for the project, and we continued to receive support from his successors and staff in Tuscaloosa, especially Jennifer Backer, Donna Cox Baker, Curtis Clark, Joanna Jacobs, and Dan Waterman. We also are grateful to the anonymous readers who offered tough critiques that in the end made this a stronger volume than it would have been otherwise.

Publishing increasingly is an expensive endeavor, which made a timely subvention from the University of Alabama's Summersell Center for the Study of the South exceedingly welcome. I am especially grateful to the center's director, Joshua Rothman.

Among others deserving mention are Leah Rawls Atkins, Kathryn E. Holland Braund, Gary Burton, Mark Franklin, Keith Hébert, David Hughes, and Charles Israel. All of the contributors stuck with the project even when its prospects appeared slim, but Sarah Wiggins especially became a champion of the book. I am proud of her friendship.

Finally, and most important, I am thankful as always for my wife, Nancy, who rode this literary roller coaster with me from first to last. Proverbs 31 teaches that a good wife is better than rubies, but my spouse is also stronger than the oak trees out on Farmville Road.

Introduction

Kenneth W. Noe

Born in Tennessee in 1833, the Rev. Dr. David Campbell Kelley lived a life full of adventure. After college he took a medical degree and then sailed for China as a Methodist missionary. By the time the Civil War began, however, Kelley was back in America, residing in Huntsville, Alabama. An ardent secessionist, he embraced the Confederate war effort, forming a company of cavalry known variously as the Kelley Rangers or Kelley Troopers. First attached to Col. Nathan Bedford Forrest's 3rd Tennessee Cavalry, the unit shifted at the end of 1862 into the new 4th Alabama Cavalry. "Parson" Kelley and Forrest meanwhile grew close, both in friendship and fierce war-making style. According to one newspaper reporter, Kelley was "a bold, desperate, and notorious partisan" who demonstrated a particular penchant for successfully targeting Union gunboats. After the war, the bold partisan went to seminary, became a minister, participated in the founding of Vanderbilt University, and ran unsuccessfully for the office of governor of Tennessee, all the while singing the praises of his controversial old commander.[1]

Yet as far as most modern Alabamians are concerned, Kelley's importance rests upon a single moment. The tale has been garbled and gilded with the passage of time, but at some point during the winter of 1861–62, Kelley and his Alabamians arrived at Forrest's winter quarters in Hopkinsville, Kentucky, wearing bright new uniforms trimmed in regulation cavalry yellow. Forrest's veteran troopers, their garb in rags, immediately began deriding the spit-and-polished Alabamians. One private in particular, later identified as Will Arnett, cried out to his comrades' amusement, "Yellowhammer, Yellowhammer, flicker flicker!" He referred to a familiar, predominantly yellow and brown woodpecker also known as the Northern Flicker, *Colaptes auratus*. From that point on, the practice of calling Alabama's Confederate soldiers "Yellowhammers" spread rapidly throughout the Southern nation. After the war, Alabama veterans attending reunions proudly wore yellowhammer feathers in their hats or on their lapels. In 1927, almost as an afterthought, the state legislature officially proclaimed Alabama "The Yellowhammer State."[2]

The Yellowhammers and their war remain at center stage a century and a half later, staring out at us from wartime daguerreotypes and as gray-haired men at the reunions. While estimates vary owing to the loss of Confederate records, Alabama sent 90,000 to 120,000 Johnny Rebs to the government in Richmond. Stated differently, out of a total of about 127,000 white men of military age, 70 to 95 percent of them went into uniform, resulting in a massive mobilization. About 9 percent of all Confederate soldiers hailed from Alabama, and a few of those Yellowhammers became legendary. Alabama produced a long list of well-known major generals, including Henry D. Clayton, Evander Law, James Longstreet (appointed to West Point from the state), Robert Rodes, Cadmus Marcellus Wilcox, and Jones Withers. In addition, thirty-six Confederate brigadier generals hailed from Alabama, including Archibald Gracie, Edmund Pettus, and the underrated cavalryman Philip Dale Roddey. William C. Oates led the legendary charge up Little Round Top at Gettysburg, while Raphael Semmes's commerce raiders CSS *Sumter* and CSS *Alabama* terrified Union merchant shipping. John Pelham—"The Gallant Pelham"—became a celebrated Confederate hero well before his death in 1863. And thanks to Josiah Gorgas, the Confederate Army of Northern Virginia may have been hungry at Appomattox, but, as the cliché goes, it never ran out of arms and ammunition. Over the years these men, and those they led, have received attention from Civil War historians, as a nearly constant outpouring of battle narratives, biographies, edited diaries and letters, memoirs, and regimental histories continues to attest.[3]

Nonetheless, at the war's sesquicentennial, there is still much to learn about the Yellowhammers' War. In this volume, for example, Ben H. Severance reexamines one of the major moments in the state's military history, the dramatic if now largely forgotten stand of Cadmus Wilcox's Alabamians at Salem Church during the Battle of Chancellorsville in May 1863. Brian Steel Wills, Nathan Bedford Forrest's principal modern biographer, looks in detail at the clash of arms that took place in Selma early in April 1865, when Maj. Gen. James Wilson's Federal raiders encountered "that Devil Forrest." Wills judges the Confederate defeat that followed as symbolic of the nation's final collapse.

Other scholars take a closer look at the Yellowhammers themselves. Kristopher A. Teters contributes to the exciting current literature regarding the motivations of Confederate soldiers, arguing that class was an important factor in shaping enlistment in Alabama. While men of higher social standing were attracted to the cause because of ideological motivations, poorer men simply wanted to defend their families from Northern invaders and return home in peace. Victoria E. Ott likewise examines military service among similarly non-elite men but instead stresses antebellum ideas of gender and family. In her view, the immediate family functioned as a microcosm of the new nation, and both demanded the allegiance of men and women of all classes.

In their chapters, Terry L. Seip and Michael W. Fitzgerald turn to some of the

Yellowhammers' bitterest enemies: Alabama's Union soldiers. Seip examines the early life and career of George E. Spencer, the Northern-born colonel of the legendary 1st Alabama Cavalry (U.S.), the state's most celebrated Federal unit, while Fitzgerald locates much of the impetus for the state's postwar "scalawag" Unionism in the wartime experiences of the state's persecuted Unionists, men who opposed secession, resisted conscription, and often ended up in Union units.

Like military history, political studies have long been a staple of Civil War historiography. Certainly Alabama politics throughout the secession era, both fascinating and more complicated than many realize, merit attention. Later mythology aside, many state residents opposed secession in 1860, representing a spectrum that ran from the often ignored slave community to white Unconditional Unionists to those who supported secession but not immediately or without coordinated action from the rest of the South. John C. Breckinridge, the presidential standard-bearer of the Southern Democrats in 1860 and the candidate most identified with secession, ultimately won the state's nine electoral votes with 54 percent of the popular vote, but five Alabama counties went to Northern Democrat Stephen A. Douglas, and another five chose Constitutional Unionist John Bell and his poignant pleas for the survival of the Union. After Lincoln's election, the state's divisions only deepened. Secession's opponents elected forty-six "cooperationist" delegates to the state's secession convention, as opposed to fifty-four immediate secessionists who depicted the election as the final straw in a long sectional struggle over slavery and the rights of slaveholding states. Driven by William Lowndes Yancey, the celebrated "Prince of Fire Eaters" and the state's dominant political voice, the convention voted on January 11, 1861, to secede from the Union by a far-from-unanimous vote of 61 to 39. Within a month, the pro-secession majority welcomed the Confederate government to its first capital in Montgomery and cheered the arrival of provisional president Jefferson Davis. Brass bands played "Dixie" while Yancey proclaimed that "the man and the hour have met."[4] In his chapter, Lonnie A. Burnett examines the politics of this critical period while challenging the long-held and still widespread notion that Yancey and his supporters were solely responsible for the breakup of the national Democratic Party and the subsequent election of Republican Abraham Lincoln.

This volume deals with more than military and political history, however. It is impossible to ignore how the conflict's historiography has evolved since the publication of Malcolm C. McMillan's edited collection of contemporary documents, *The Alabama Confederate Reader*, the single most important work on the state's involvement in the war to emerge from the Civil War centennial of a half century ago. McMillan's volume reflected an essential consensus that the war was about "battles and leaders" and paid relatively less attention to the home front and no notice at all to race or Reconstruction. In contrast, this volume is as much about the home front as the battlefield. After the centennial, the rise of the "new social history" slowly led Civil War scholars to pay increasing attention to the majority of Americans who were not soldiers themselves but nonetheless experienced the war. Close to 830,000 Alabama civilians—black and white, slave and free, rich and poor—endured the war at home. In some cases the chapters offered here blur the distinction between these pairs just as the real war did. The chapters by Fitzgerald, Ott, and Teters, as previously noted, are all grounded in soldiers' homes and families. Several of the other chapters maintain as well that those Alabamians' experiences are just as vital for understanding the totality of the conflict as are the marches and battles of the Yellowhammers themselves.

To be sure, Alabama's home-front experience was in many ways unique. Unlike states such as Virginia, the new home of the Confederate government after the commonwealth's secession in the late spring of 1861, most of Alabama largely escaped the hardest hand of war until the bitter end; the major campaigns took place elsewhere. Consequently, with the significant exception of the residents who lived in north Alabama along the Tennessee River, an area occupied by Union forces in 1862, most Alabamians did not face the appearance of Federal forces until the last months of the conflict. Instead, fast-moving, destructive raids largely characterized the Union presence in most of the state. Two were crucial. In May 1864, Maj. Gen. Lovell Rousseau's Union troops, acting in support of Maj. Gen. William Tecumseh Sherman's armies in north Georgia, swept south from Decatur and successfully cut the Montgomery and West Point Railroad east of the capital. Almost a year later, Wilson's cavalry raiders tore the state in half and wrecked its industrial base, the main column leaving a trail of fire and destruction from Florence south to Selma, and then east through Montgomery into Georgia. A secondary column under Brig. Gen. John T. Croxton burned down the University of Alabama before heading east. At roughly the same time that Wilson struck, a third contingent of Union troops under the command of Maj. Gen. E. R. S. Canby completed the occupation of Mobile, already closed off to the rest of the world after the Union Navy "damned the torpedoes" in August 1864 after heavy fighting north of the bay. One of the last Confederate armies still in the field, commanded by Gen. Richard Taylor, finally surrendered near Citronelle on May 4.[5]

Before that Confederate Götterdämmerung, however, Alabamians at even the quietest locations had endured four years of activity, hardships, and heartache. Thanks to the state's relatively safe location away from the major fronts, as well as abundant deposits of iron, Alabama became a center of Confederate industry, with up to ten thousand workers at one point toiling in Selma alone. Other Alabamians, free and enslaved, produced badly needed pig iron at various ironworks near the location of modern Birmingham. Mobile businessmen pioneered the submarine technology that ultimately resulted in the *H. L. Hunley*.[6]

In some respects, to be sure, life went on as before, at least for a while. Historian William Warren Rogers Jr., for example, points out in his well-regarded volume on Montgomery that children still went to school, families attended church, businesses remained open, and residents took full advantage of the city's many entertainment options. The local and state governments continued to operate as well, while the Emancipation Proclamation of 1863 offered hope to the city's slaves. But as the conflict dragged on and the Federal land and sea blockade tightened, the war could not be ignored. Stores and other concerns closed their doors. Confederate hospitals, factories supplying the army, and Confederate government agencies simultaneously offered new sources of income to both workers and the masters of slave labor. In this collection, Patricia A. Hoskins shifts our focus to the state's urban centers in wartime through a survey of the willing contributions to the war effort offered by significant but often forgotten communities within Mobile as well as Montgomery: their Jewish populations.

Women on the home front played roles of vast significance that scholars are only now beginning to elucidate fully. Alabamian schoolchildren once learned the legend of Emma Sansom, the Gadsden teenager who assisted Forrest in his pursuit of Union colonel Abel Streight's "Jackass cavalry" across the northeastern part of the state in May 1863. Another Alabamian woman, largely forgotten today except by scholars but greatly popular in her own time, was the novelist Augusta Jane Evans. She sought to support the Confederacy through her fiction. As Jennifer Lynn Gross maintains in her chapter, Evans not only was willing to sacrifice her own marriage on the altar of her new nation but in her celebrated novel *Macaria* advised other women to follow suit. Sansom and Evans admittedly were exceptions, but many other, lesser-known women contributed to the Confederate cause as well. Indeed, as both Victoria Ott and Jennifer Ann Newman Treviño remind us, white Alabamian women of all classes thoroughly embraced secession, the Confederacy, and "Spartan Motherhood" in 1861. They bowed before Evans's "altars of sacrifice" and gave their husbands, sons, and brothers to the state to become Yellowhammers. They then made uniforms, raised money, managed farms and slaves, and in many other ways contributed greatly to the war effort. Some entered nursing, although never enough to satisfy the state's best-known nurse, Mobile's Kate Cumming. Many became refugees as Union arms advanced, while others stayed at home to protect their property and defy the occupiers. Female slaveholders struggled to control an increasingly restless enslaved population that sensed the dawn of their freedom. Drought, poverty, and inflation took their toll on all Alabamians, notably troubling the destitute "corn women" who wandered from place to place in the Black Belt gleaning fields all but picked clean.[7]

Other difficulties multiplied. Schools and churches in rural areas closed for the war. Federal occupation and strains elsewhere broke down the state's transportation and communication systems, creating pockets of near-famine as well as fear, confusion, and low morale. Policies emanating from Richmond, notably conscription and impressment, led to war-weariness, especially among the poor and yeomen classes, on whom those laws seemed to fall the hardest. Alabamians such as those depicted by Ott and Teters, both in the army and at home, complained increasingly that the conflict had become a "rich man's war and poor man's fight." Enslaved African Americans refused to work (or at least work hard), challenged masters and mistresses, and greeted Union soldiers as liberators.

Meanwhile up to 10,000 Yellowhammers fled Confederate ranks and hid in the north Alabama hills, assisted by a resurgent pro-Union element that supported clandestine groups such as the Peace Society. As Fitzgerald and Seip remind us, up to 3,000 white Alabamians and another 10,000 African American men took the ultimate step and donned Union blue. Urban Unionists in cities such as Montgomery tended to be Northern-born émigrés, but rural adherents to the Union, such as those located in the fabled Unionist enclaves of Winston County, were entirely homegrown. Historian Margaret Storey has estimated that as many as 10 percent of white Alabamians were unconditional Unionists in 1861 and that those sentiments persisted during the war. In this volume, Fitzgerald discusses the difficult wartime experiences of Alabamian Unionists that would cause them to become active state Republicans after the war. But many more white Alabamians simply became weary of the struggle and annoyed with an increasingly intrusive Confederate government. Many of them turned to Thomas Hill Watts, a former Whig and vocal critic of the Jefferson Davis administration despite a brief period when he was a member of it. Elected governor in 1863 by nearly a three-to-one margin, Watts supported Confederate independence but also quietly threw up one roadblock after another against Richmond's policies. Yet the extent of even this war-weariness can be overstated, as many Civil War scholars are beginning to reassert. Clearly large numbers of white Alabamians supported the Confederacy right up to its collapse.[8]

But collapse it did. What followed was Reconstruction, a period ignored by Malcolm McMillan and indeed by the centennial observances as a whole. Sarah Woolfolk Wiggins, the dean of Alabama's Reconstruction scholars, rightly contends that fifty years after the centennial, the Reconstruction era remains misunderstood, ignored, and reviled in the popular mind. Yet those years were just as vital to the history of the state and nation. Though the perceived sharp dividing line between the war and the peace is as much a part of the academic two-semester system as anything else, contemporaries saw no such vivid demarcation, as Harriet E. Amos Doss's chapter in this volume demonstrates through the lens of Alabamians' often contradictory reactions to the assassination of Lincoln and the end of the war in the spring of 1865. Some celebrated, Doss contends, but most Alabamians worried about what it meant for the future. Nor did the white Unionists depicted by Fitzgerald in his chapter experience a clear demarcation between war and peace.

Yet the summer that followed found many of the foundations of antebellum and Confederate Alabama a shambles. Everywhere families mourned their dead; as many as 35,000 Yellowhammers did not survive the war, while many more came home suffering some war-related disability. Often they and more able-bodied veterans found farms, hometowns, and cities desolate and sometimes still smoldering. Much of the state's railroad network lay newly destroyed by Wilson. His Federal raiders had wrecked the state's industrial capacity as well. Hunger and fear stalked much of the state.

Most crucial of all was the end of legal slavery through the Thirteenth Amendment. If Union soldiers often found whites sullen or still defiant, the state's African American population rejoiced at the end of their bondage. Former slaves, now referred to as "freedmen" or "freedpeople," immediately tested their newfound status in various ways. Many walked away from farms, plantations, and plantation labor altogether, heading for urban areas to find better jobs and perhaps to locate lost loved ones torn away by the auctioneer. They began to establish their own churches and schools and to become active politically through the Union League and conventions in which they called for full civil rights and land redistribution. As Bertis English describes it in his chapter, the process of separation went relatively smoothly in the Black Belt's Perry County, but elsewhere black-white relations remained fraught with tension and often violence.[9]

Over the next several years, the Federal government struggled internally and externally to reconstruct Alabama and the rest of the South, both economically and politically. At first the Union occupation force struggled simply to keep the peace. To paraphrase the assassinated president, the occasion was piled high with difficulty. Former secessionists fought Unionists across the state while whites and blacks wrangled over the promises and limits of African American freedom. Labor contracts became a particular bone of contention. Meanwhile, the new Freedmen's Bureau struggled to provide food, fuel, and protection to freedpeople in the face of growing opposition and questionable support from local authorities. Some scholars have criticized the bureau's activities in Alabama as halfhearted, but in this volume Jason J. Battles makes a strong revisionist case that Alabama's assistant commissioner, Brig. Gen. Wager Swayne, not only made a sincere effort to fill his immediate charge but increasingly worked to protect the freedpeople from illegal labor contracts and injustice in the face of disappointment and growing white resistance.[10]

Politically, in the summer of 1865 President Andrew Johnson instituted a period sometimes referred to as Presidential Restoration. As he did elsewhere in the former Confederacy, Johnson appointed a provisional governor, Lewis Parsons, a former congressman and opponent of secession in 1861 who later supported the Confederacy. Johnson also called upon the state's eligible voters to take an oath of allegiance to the Union and elect delegates to a new state constitutional convention. Johnson prohibited the freedmen, those who had held high positions in the Confederacy, and the old planter elite from taking part. Once a constitution had been ratified, voters could elect a new state government and send representatives to Washington. Alabama would be back in the Union.[11]

Nothing went smoothly. Rejecting the president's hope that they would repudiate any right of secession, the convention delegates simply declared the 1861 ordinance null and void. In the elections that followed, Robert M. Patton became governor. Like Parsons, Patton had initially opposed secession only to accept it once the state left the Union. The new legislature soon enacted a "Black Code," laws designed to constrain the rights of African Americans and return them to a life of pseudo-slavery. If more moderate than similar laws of other states, Alabama's code still seemed like a bitter rejection to black Alabamians hoping for real freedom. As Michael Fitzgerald details in his chapter, white Unionists who had suffered during the war, now denigrated by their opponents as "scalawags" for their loyalty to the old flag, were also outraged. And so were Republicans in Washington. Alarmed by the nature of the Southerners who arrived to sit in the new Congress, and thoroughly annoyed with Johnson, the Republican majority refused Southern representatives their seats. A struggle began in 1866 between Congress and the White House for control of Reconstruction. To investigate the perceived failures of Johnson's plan, congressional Republicans established a Joint Committee on Reconstruction. Witnesses testified that the white South remained disloyal and that the blacks were worse off than they had been before the war. In order to protect the freedpeople, Congress enacted the Civil Rights Act of 1866, the nation's first civil rights legislation. It outlawed the Black Code while declaring that former slaves were American citizens, deserving of federal protection. A growing anti-Johnson majority then wrote the new legislation into the Federal Constitution as the Fourteenth Amendment and made its ratification a requirement for representation in Washington. Like all of the ex-Confederate states except Tennessee, Alabama refused to comply.[12]

A new period now began, usually termed Congressional, or Radical, Reconstruction. The Reconstruction Acts of 1867 divided the former Confederacy, minus Tennessee, into five military districts, each supervised by a general. Maj. Gen. John Pope was the first commander of the Third Military District, which contained Georgia and Florida as well as Alabama. His immediate task was to call new constitutional conventions. These new bodies, however, would be far different from those that preceded them. Unless pardoned, former Confederates were ineligible to participate in crafting the new document. "Scalawags," freedmen, and so-called carpetbaggers—northern-born men who had come south after the war—would write the new documents and compose the new governments that followed. They also would eventually make up the South's Republican Party. In Alabama, the three groups that composed the party coexisted uneasily. The issue of race was a major factor in the party's instability, but as Fitzgerald has shown in a larger study of Mobile during Reconstruction, various subgroups also disagreed on policy and vied for control of federal patronage. The Constitutional Convention of 1867 reflected the party's divisions but also revealed additional fissures between more radical state Republicans, white and black, and moderates in Washington, again as demonstrated in Fitzgerald's chapter. The document that resulted from the convention was too conservative for many freedmen and former white Unionists. But, conversely, it was much too radical for the majority of conservative whites who had supported the Confederate experiment. Their opposition became the greatest challenge of all to Republicans and Reconstruction. For example, men such as notorious Tuscaloosa newspaper editor Ryland Randolph rallied anti-Reconstruction Democrats with open racism and appeals to violence. In the end, with Democrats boycotting the polls, a plurality of the remaining electorate approved the new constitution. The new legislature quickly ratified the Fourteenth Amendment, and federal elections followed. Republicans took all six House vacancies as well as both senatorial chairs. As Jason Battles relates, Wager Swayne's hopes for newly elected Governor William Hugh Smith were soon dashed, as he proved to be a conservative with little sympathy for the freedpeople.[13]

Once in power, Republicans embarked on an ambitious campaign of legislative action. The state's modern public school system, for example, has its origins in Reconstruction. The era saw much of the state railroad network rebuilt. But stories of bribery and corruption also emanated from Montgomery. Carpetbaggers like George Spencer, the former commander of the Federal 1st Alabama Cavalry who rose to the U.S. Senate, gained a notorious reputation for unprincipled greed. A more active state government required more taxes. All of this made the Republican government controversial, but the ultimate lightning rod remained the presence of blacks in the halls of power. The Ku Klux Klan rose up to combat Radical Reconstruction and the nascent Republican Party with paramilitary terrorism. Republicans fought back with legislation, calls for Federal protection, and sometimes their own guns. Violence, bloodshed, and a depressed GOP vote marked the 1870 elections, which saw the election of a Democratic governor and gave his party control of the legislature. Congress responded with legislation aimed at destroying the Klan, while many white Alabamians tactically repudiated the Ryland Randolphs of the state. Republicans briefly thus returned to power in 1872, but financial difficulties, reports of corruption, controversial desegregation legislation, and a growing lack of sensitivity to African American Republicans on the part of party leaders all further undermined support for the party. Meanwhile the Democrats grew stronger by attacking the biracial nature of the ruling Republicans and making race the key issue in the forthcoming elections. Fraud, racist rhetoric, the party's repudiation of black support, and a tidal wave of anti-Republican violence committed by successors to the Klan all placed the Democrats back in power at the end of 1874. The Yellowhammers' state, they proclaimed with biblical language, had been redeemed.[14]

Eighty years would pass before what historian C. Vann Woodward called the Second Reconstruction truly began to reverse that Redemption. That series of memorable national events, including the police dogs and fire hoses of Birmingham and the violent confrontation at a Selma bridge named for a Civil War general, took place almost in lockstep with the parades, hoopskirt balls, nascent reenactments, and battle-flag waving marking the Civil War centennial. As historian Robert Cook reminds us, national and state commissions, such as the one in Alabama, organized the massive pageants with both the Cold War and race firmly in mind. Concerned about the increasingly commercial, celebratory, and politicized tone of the event, noted historians such as Bell I. Wiley and T. Harry Williams called instead for a different kind of centennial that would depict the gritty reality of the war through new books, public lectures, the collection and preservation of period documents, and the creation of useful bibliographies. Initially rejected in favor of partisanship and hoopla, new commission leaders Allan Nevins and James I. Robertson finally followed that blueprint after the centennial pageant floundered in South Carolina on the shoals of segregation. McMillan's *Alabama Confederate Reader* was just one important result of the scholarly response.[15]

A half century later, the sesquicentennial of the war is upon us. Much has changed in Alabama in the interim. The current state government is not using the event this time to trumpet states' rights and segregation. Indeed the Becoming Alabama initiative, an informal umbrella group launched by the Alabama Department of Archives and History to mark overlapping anniversaries of the Creek War and civil rights movement as well as the Civil War, is as close as one will get to any official state presence at all. Tellingly, on their official emblem Joe Wheeler gets equal space with the Red Stick leader Menawa and Rosa Parks. Yet other things look vaguely familiar. The Alabama Tourism Department advertises the war's sesquicentennial as a promising—albeit now multicultural—opportunity to attract tourists. Confederate heritage groups marked the celebration's opening in Montgomery with a reenactment of the centennial reenactment of Jefferson Davis's inaugural ceremony, attracting many fewer onlookers to city sidewalks than in 1861 or 1961. Some heritage activists also expressed hope that the sesquicentennial would offer opportunities to propagate what they called a "true history" of the war that would counter "political correctness." Meanwhile, on blogs and Facebook, debates about the war and the legality of secession rage daily. In Selma, a decade-long controversy over a bust of David Kelley's commander, Nathan Bedford Forrest, escalated into open confrontation in the late winter of 2012 when the bronze statue disappeared from a local cemetery. Charges and countercharges followed. Given these conflicting messages, the lack of an overarching official narrative, and contested memories of a war that still elicits passion, what legacy will the sesquicentennial leave? Despite its broader canvas and more modern sensibilities, this volume is offered modestly in the spirit of scholars such as McMillan, who believed that solid scholarship, not profit, pageantry, or the partisan spinning of a usable past, was the best way to mark the anniversary of a bloody and earth-shattering civil war.[16]

Notes

1. John Allan Wyeth, *Life of General Nathan Bedford Forrest* (New York: Harper and Brothers, 1899), 26–27, 30–35, 47, 50, 74, 189, 390, 399, 499, 509–10, 522–23, 547–48, 573, 627–28, 630, 649; Myron J. Smith Jr., *The U.S.S. Carondelet: A Civil War Ironclad on the Western Waters*, foreword by W. Douglas Bell (Jefferson, NC: McFarland, 2020), 252n7; "Confederate Units of Madison County," http://www.oldhuntsville.com/Military/Confederate_Units_of_Madison_County.txt (accessed September 22, 2010).

2. "Official Emblems and Symbols of Alabama, State Bird of Alabama, Yellowhammer," Alabama Department of Archives and History, http://www.archives.state.al.us/emblems/st_bird.html (accessed February 12, 2013).

3. Malcolm C. McMillan, *The Alabama Confederate Reader* (Tuscaloosa: University of Alabama Press, 1963). A brief but useful introduction can be found in the best current history of the state, William Warren Rogers et al., *Alabama: The History of a Deep South State* (Tuscaloosa: University of Alabama Press, 1994), 186–202. Walter Lynwood Fleming, *Civil War and Reconstruction in Alabama* (New York: Columbia University Press, 1905), is a dated account written by a member of the "Dunning School." On numbers and percentages, see also James M. McPherson, *For Cause and Comrades: Why Men Fought in the Civil War* (New York: Oxford University Press, 1997), 179. A bibliography containing all the works written by or about Alabama's soldiers would be book length, but for a few exceptional primary sources, see Ann K. Blomquist and Robert A. Taylor, eds., *This Cruel War: The Civil War Letters of Grant and Malinda Taylor, 1862–1865* (Macon, GA: Mercer University Press, 2000); J. P. Cannon, *Inside of Rebeldom: The Daily Life of a Private in the Confederate Army* (Washington, DC: National Tribune, 1900); Mattie Lou Teague Crow, ed., *The Diary of a Confederate Soldier: John Washington Inzer, 1834–1928* (Huntsville, AL: Strode, 1977); John Kent Folmar, ed., *From That Terrible Field: Civil War Letters of James M. Williams, Twenty-First Alabama Infantry Volunteers* (University: University of Alabama Press, 1981); Lucille Griffith, ed., *Yours Till Death: Civil War Letters of John W. Cotton* (University: University of Alabama Press, 1951); G. Ward Hubbs, ed., *Voices from Company D: Diaries by the Greensboro Guards, Fifth Alabama Infantry Regiment, Army of Northern Virginia* (Athens: University of Georgia Press, 2003); Raphael Semmes, *Service Afloat: The Remarkable Career of the Confederate Cruisers Sumter and Alabama* (Baltimore: Baltimore Publishing, 1887); Jeffrey D. Stocker, ed., *From Huntsville to Appomattox: R. T. Cole's History of the 4th Regiment, Alabama Volunteer Infantry, C. S. A. Army of Northern Virginia* (Knoxville: University of Tennessee Press, 1996); Frank E. Vandiver, ed., *The Civil War Diary of General Josiah Gorgas* (University: University of Alabama Press, 1947); and

Lewis N. Wynne and Robert A. Taylor, eds., *This War So Horrible: The Civil War Diary of Hiram Smith Williams* (Tuscaloosa: University of Alabama Press, 1993). See also the *Alabama Historical Quarterly* and older issues of the *Alabama Review*, as both regularly published edited soldier letters and diaries until recently. For critical secondary works, see G. Ward Hubbs, *Guarding Greensboro: A Confederate Company in the Making of a Southern Community* (Athens: University of Georgia Press, 2003); Charles G. Milham, *Gallant Pelham: American Extraordinary* (Washington, DC: Public Affairs Press, 1959); and Frank E. Vandiver, *Ploughshares into Swords: Josiah Gorgas and Confederate Ordinance* (Austin: University of Texas Press, 1952).

4. On Alabama's secession, see William L. Barney, *The Secessionist Impulse: Alabama and Mississippi in 1860* (Princeton: Princeton University Press, 1974); Lonnie A. Burnett, *The Pen Makes a Good Sword: John Forsyth of the Mobile Register* (Tuscaloosa: University of Alabama Press, 2006); William C. Davis, *"A Government of Our Own": The Making of the Confederacy* (New York: Free Press, 1994); Clarence Phillips Denman, *The Secession Movement in Alabama* (Montgomery: Alabama Department of Archives and History, 1933); Rogers et al., *Alabama*, 181–90; J. Mills Thornton III, *Politics and Power in a Slave Society: Alabama, 1800–1860* (Baton Rouge: Louisiana State University Press, 1978), esp. 343–61; and Eric H. Walther, *William Lowndes Yancey and the Coming of the Civil War* (Chapel Hill: University of North Carolina Press, 2006).

5. Important studies of military operations in the state include George C. Bradley and Richard L. Dahlen, *From Conciliation to Conquest: The Sack of Athens and the Court-Martial of Colonel John B. Turchin* (Tuscaloosa: University of Alabama Press, 2006); David Evans, *Sherman's Horsemen: Union Cavalry Operations in the Atlanta Campaign* (Bloomington: Indiana University Press, 1996), 98–174; James Pickett Jones, *Yankee Blitzkrieg: Wilson's Raid through Alabama and Georgia* (Lexington: University Press of Kentucky, 1976); Sean Michael O'Brien, *Mobile, 1865: Last Stand on the Confederacy* (Westport, CT: Praeger, 2001). For a brief summary, see Rogers et al., *Alabama*, 197, 204–6, 210–13, 214–22.

6. On the war in urban Alabama, see Harriet E. Amos, *Cotton City: Urban Development in Antebellum Mobile* (Tuscaloosa: University of Alabama Press, 1985); Arthur W. Bergeron, *Confederate Mobile* (Jackson: University Press of Mississippi, 1991); Tom Chaffin, *The H. L. Hunley: The Secret Hope of the Confederacy* (New York: Hill and Wang, 2008); Rogers et al., *Alabama*, 195–97; Cullan B. Duke, "The American Civil War, Blockade Running, and Demoralization in Mobile, Alabama" (honors thesis, Auburn University, 2003); and William Warren Rogers Jr., *Confederate Home Front: Montgomery during the Civil War* (Tuscaloosa: University of Alabama Press, 1999).

7. For works focusing on Alabamian women and their families, see Carol Bleser and Frederick Heath, "The Clays of Alabama: The Impact of the Civil War on a Southern Marriage," in *In Joy and in Sorrow: Women, Family, and Marriage in the Victorian South, 1830–1900*, ed. Carol Bleser (New York: Oxford University Press, 1991), 135–53; Kate Cumming, *Kate: The Journal of a Confederate Nurse*, ed. Richard Barksdale Harwell (Baton Rouge: Louisiana State University Press, 1959); Jennifer Ann Newman, "Writing, Religion, and Women's Identity in Civil War Alabama" (PhD diss., Auburn University, 2009); Nancy M. Rohr, ed., *Incidents of the War: The Civil War Journal of Mary Jane Chaddick* (Huntsville, AL: Silver Threads Publishing, 2005); H. E. Sterkx, *Partners in Rebellion: Alabama Women in the Civil War* (Rutherford, NJ: Fairleigh Dickinson University Press, 1970); Henry Walker, "Power, Sex, and Gender Roles: The Transformation of an Alabama Planter Family during the Civil War," in *Southern Families at War: Loyalty and Conflict in the Civil War South*, ed. Catherine Clinton (New York: Oxford University Press, 2000), 175–91; and Sarah Woolfolk Wiggins, "The Marriage of Amelia Gayle and Josiah Gorgas," in *Intimate Strategies of the Civil War: Military Commanders and Their Wives*, ed. Carol K. Bleser and Lesley J. Gordon (New York: Oxford University Press, 2001), 104–19. Stephen Berry tells the fascinating

story of Mary Todd Lincoln's siblings, including the two who spent the war in Selma, in *House of Abraham: Lincoln and the Todds, a Family Divided by War* (New York: Houghton Mifflin, 2007). On Sansom, see her discussion of events in Wyeth, *Forrest*, 210–12.

8. On dissension and Unionism, see Richard Nelson Current, *Lincoln's Loyalists: Union Soldiers from the Confederacy* (New York: Oxford University Press, 1992), 103–7; William Stanley Hoole, *Alabama Tories: The First Alabama Cavalry, U.S.A., 1862–1865* (Tuscaloosa: Confederate Publishing, 1960); Bessie Martin, *Desertion of Alabama Troops from the Confederate Army: A Study in Sectionalism* (New York: Columbia University Press, 1932); William Warren Rogers, "Safety Lies Only in Silence: Secrecy and Subversion in Montgomery's Unionist Community," in *Enemies of the Country: New Perspectives on Unionists in the Civil War South*, ed. John C. Inscoe and Robert C. Kenzer (Athens: University of Georgia Press, 2001), 172–87; Malcolm Cook McMillan, *The Disintegration of a Confederate State: Three Governors and Alabama's Wartime Home Front, 1861–1865* (Macon, GA: Mercer University Press, 1986); Margaret M. Storey, *Loyalty and Loss: Alabama's Unionists in the Civil War and Reconstruction* (Baton Rouge: Louisiana State University Press, 2004); and David Williams, *Rich Man's War: Class, Caste, and Confederate Defeat in the Lower Chattahoochee Valley* (Athens: University of Georgia Press, 1998).

9. The major work on the period remains Eric Foner, *Reconstruction: America's Unfinished Revolution, 1863–1877* (New York: Harper and Row, 1988), see esp. 77–128. See also Michael W. Fitzgerald, *Splendid Failure: Postwar Reconstruction in the American South* (Chicago: Ivan R. Dee, 2007). For a more extensive bibliography on Reconstruction in Alabama, see Wiggins's chapter in this volume. On the end of the war and African American aspirations, see Peter Kolchin, *First Freedom: The Responses of Alabama's Blacks to Emancipation and Reconstruction* (Westport, CT: Greenwood Press, 1972); Rogers et al., *Alabama*, 225–29.

10. On the Freedmen's Bureau in Alabama and its challenges, see Foner, *Reconstruction*, 143, 149, 167; Rogers et al., *Alabama*, 234–40; and Jonathan M. Wiener, *Social Origins of the New South: Alabama, 1860–1885* (Baton Rouge: Louisiana State University Press, 1978).

11. On Presidential Restoration in Alabama, see Foner, *Reconstruction*, 176–84, 187–89, 204, 215; Rogers et al., *Alabama*, 230.

12. On the advent of Congressional Reconstruction in Alabama, see Foner, *Reconstruction* 184–261, 324; Rogers et al., *Alabama*, 232–41; and William Warren Rogers Jr., *Black Belt Scalawag: Charles Hays and the Southern Republicans in the Era of Reconstruction* (Athens: University of Georgia Press, 1993).

13. On the Republican coalition in Alabama, see Richard Bailey, *Neither Carpetbaggers nor Scalawags: Black Officeholders during the Reconstruction of Alabama, 1867–1878* (Montgomery: Richard Bailey, 1991); Foner, *Reconstruction*, 271–345; Rogers et al., *Alabama*, 241–50; Loren Schweninger, *James T. Rapier and Reconstruction* (Chicago: University of Chicago Press, 1978); Sarah W. Wiggins, *The Scalawag in Alabama Politics, 1865–1881* (Tuscaloosa: University of Alabama Press, 1977).

14. Foner, *Reconstruction*, 346–459, 552–53; Rogers et al., *Alabama*, 250–64. On the Klan, see Michael W. Fitzgerald, "Extralegal Violence and the Planter Class: The Ku Klux Klan in the Alabama Black Belt during Reconstruction," in *Local Matters: Race, Crime, and Justice in the Nineteenth-Century South*, ed. Christopher Waldrep and Donald G. Nieman (Athens: University of Georgia Press, 2001), 155–71; Wiener, *Social Origins*, 35–73; Allen W. Trelease, *White Terror: The Ku Klux Klan Conspiracy and Southern Reconstruction* (New York: Harper and Row, 1971). On the widespread national corruption of the era, see Mark Summers, *Railroads, Reconstruction, and the Gospel of Prosperity: Aid under the Radical Republicans, 1865–1877* (Princeton: Princeton University Press, 1984), and Summers, *The Era of Good Stealings* (New York: Oxford University Press,

1993). For Redemption, see Allen Johnston Going, *Bourbon Democracy in Alabama, 1874–1890* (University: University of Alabama Press, 1951).

15. Here I follow Robert Cook, *Troubled Commemoration: The American Civil War Centennial, 1961–1965*, Making the Modern South Series (Baton Rouge: Louisiana State University Press, 2007) and Cook, "Red Termites and Rebel Yells: The Civil War Centennial in Strife-Torn Alabama, 1961–1965," *Alabama Review* 64 (April 2011): 143–67. For Woodward and the "Second Reconstruction," see his *The Strange Career of Jim Crow* (New York: Oxford University Press, 1955), 8–10, 24, 47, 135, 181, 209. I make similar points in "Historians' Forum: The American Civil War's Centennial vs. the Sesquicentennial," *Civil War History* 57 (December 2011): 380–402.

16. Mike Brantley, "Civil War Sesquicentennial Events Planned in Alabama," *Mobile Press-Register*, http://blog.al.com/entertainment-press register/2009/08/civil_war_sesquicentennial_eve.html (accessed September 28, 2010); Steve Murray, "The Becoming Alabama Initiative: Pragmatism to Innovative Partnership," *Alabama Heritage*, http://www.alabamaheritage.com/BecomingAlabama/initiative.htm (accessed September 28, 2010); *Alabama Confederate* (July 2010): 1, 2, 3, 19, 22 (quotation 3); *Alabama Confederate* (October 2010): 4, 16, 18; Robbie Brown, "Bust of Civil War General Stirs Anger in Alabama," *New York Times*, August 24, 2012, http://www.nytimes.com/2012/08/25/us/fight-rages-in-selma-ala-over-a-civil-war-monument.html?_r=0 (accessed February 19, 2013); Noe, "Historians' Forum," esp. 381–98.

I
Precipitating a Revolution
Alabama's Democracy in the Election of 1860

Lonnie A. Burnett

William Lowndes Yancey had a clear view of the future. In 1858, the longtime Alabamian wrote a letter to a young supporter revealing his personal agenda. Yancey expressed a desire to "fire the Southern heart, instruct the Southern mind, give courage to each other, and at the moment, by one organized, concerted action . . . *precipitate the cotton States into a revolution.*"[1] Contemporary critics as well as future historians seized upon this "Scarlet Letter" to positively assign blame for the 1860 split of the national Democratic Party, the subsequent election of Abraham Lincoln, and the resulting secession of the Southern states to Yancey—the "Prince of Secession." Yancey's domination of Alabama's Democratic Party guaranteed that the state would be on the frontline of the most divisive election in American history. Scholars have tended to ignore, however, the role of Yancey's in-state opposition—the moderate wing of Alabama's Democratic Party. This minority, led by editor-politicians such as John Forsyth of the *Mobile Register* and John J. Seibels of the *Montgomery Confederation*, opposed the secessionists at every turn. Supporters of Illinois senator Stephen A. Douglas, this group saw a national, not sectional, party as the only way to keep the federal government out of the hands of the "Black Republicans." Although typically portrayed as falling victim to Yancey's secessionist maneuverings, these veterans of many Democratic battles often took the offensive. At a critical juncture when Yancey appeared to be open to compromise, the "Douglas traitors"—hoping to isolate and destroy the secessionist faction once and for all—worked behind the scenes to make sure the long-threatened convention bolt would indeed transpire. In an August 1860 speech, Huntsville politician Jere Clemens accurately expressed the sentiment of the hour: "This is no holiday occasion. The existence of this republic is at stake."[2]

Yancey was the voice of states' rights and secession in Alabama and perhaps the entire South. The Georgia native gained notoriety as a fire-eater in 1848 with the introduction of the "Alabama Platform."[3] In reaction to the ill-fated Wilmot Proviso (which sought to ban slavery from any territory gained in the Mexican War), Yancey pushed for congressional protection of slave property through a federal slave code. As a delegate to the 1848 national Democratic convention in Baltimore, Yancey led a two-man walkout when the platform committee refused to endorse his position. Concerned that the South was not safe in the national party, in 1850 he helped organize the Southern Rights Party. However, in 1856 Yancey temporarily returned to the Democratic fold. At the Democratic convention in Cincinnati, he went along with a compromise platform that was left intentionally vague so as to be acceptable to both North and South. The 1857 *Dred Scott* decision—in which the Supreme Court ruled that neither Congress nor a territorial legislature could ban slavery in any territory—was a victory for Yancey and his supporters.

Yancey bristled at the suggestion that he was a disunionist. In his mind, secession was a "defensive southern reaction to incendiary revolutionary changes in the North." By refusing to protect slave property in the territories, the North had, in Yancey's words, "in effect, destroyed the Constitutional compact of Union."[4] By the late 1850s, however, Yancey had lost patience with both compromise and moderate Southern Democrats. A broad-based party could not afford to press matters of principle to the extreme and still appeal to a wide-ranging constituency, yet Yancey lamented the fact that political expediency often dictated that Southern interests were sacrificed in the name of party. He also felt this willingness to acquiesce had brought the South little in return. The Compromise of 1850 brought California into the Union as a free state and had abolished the slave trade in the District of Columbia with no compensation to the South. The Fugitive Slave Act of 1850 returned few slaves. The Kansas-Nebraska Act of 1854 ultimately brought no slaves to Kansas. Southern Democrats felt they were losing control of the national party and began to agree with the fire-eaters in much larger numbers.[5]

Stephen A. Douglas meanwhile aspired to lead the national Democratic Party. Douglas had been a member of Congress for many years and was intimately involved in most of the controversial measures of the day. He had played an active role in the final passage of the Compromise of 1850 and, as chairman of the Senate Committee on Territories, had authored the Kansas-Nebraska Act. It was this legislation that forever linked the senator with the doctrine of "popular sovereignty"—a plan whereby the voters in a territory (as opposed to Congress) would decide the fate of slavery. Douglas, the "Little Giant," harbored massive ambition and had set his sights on the nation's highest office. In 1856 he had stepped aside in favor of the nomination of Pennsylvanian James Buchanan. Because Buchanan had pledged to serve only one term, Douglas considered himself the legitimate heir to the 1860 prize.[6]

Although he was the most polarizing figure in the 1860 presidential election process, Douglas had once enjoyed fairly widespread Southern support. He agreed with many Southern leaders on the most important issues, such as the Mexican War and subsequent annexation of territory, opposition to the Wilmot Proviso, and support for the Fugitive Slave Act. The ultimate political pragmatist, the senator viewed the peculiar institution in light of the Constitution and the maintenance of the Union. Thus, said Douglas: "I deal with slavery as a political question involving questions of public policy." Douglas boasted that "I do not admit the fact that there is a better Democrat on earth than I am, or a sounder one on the question of states' rights, and even on the slavery question." Many Northerners lambasted Douglas for his overly *pro-Southern* views. One Chicago editor referred to Douglas as "the most servile tool that has crawled in the slime and scum of slavery at the foot of the slave power." In 1858 one Alabamian editor, who would later side with Yancey, commented that Douglas was "a particular favorite with several of the southern states, and stood a better chance for the Democratic nomination for the contest of 1860 than any other individual."[7]

How then did Douglas come to be regarded as the South's "greatest and most dangerous enemy"? Several of the senator's actions led to his fall from grace. The first would be the fruits of his own Kansas-Nebraska Act. After a period of prolonged violence, the struggle to organize the Kansas Territory returned to the halls of Congress. A constitutional convention of highly questionable legitimacy had met in Lecompton, Kansas, in 1857 and sent a pro-slavery document to Congress for approval. Recognizing the blatant fraud involved in this process, Douglas broke ranks with the Buchanan administration and voted with the majority against the proposed constitution. Alabamian partisans felt that Douglas was turning his back on his own popular sovereignty doctrine in that Congress had thwarted the will of the people in the territory. The Lecompton fiasco led to much more heated debate—now focusing on not just if but when, at what stage, and even how could the inhabitants of a territory legitimately exercise control over slavery. Alabama's judgment of Douglas was severe. Senator Clement C. Clay wrote: "How can any true Southern man maintain that he [Douglas] should have been retained as the exponent of the Democratic Party?"[8]

The *Dred Scott* decision seemed to settle the controversy surrounding the territorial organization procedure. Yanceyites embraced the decision as a repudiation of popular sovereignty and began to aggressively push for a federal slave code. At this point, Douglas once again thrust himself into the center of the national firestorm. At Freeport, Illinois, during the now famous Lincoln-Douglas debates, a relatively unknown Abraham Lincoln asked Douglas if popular sovereignty could survive *Dred Scott*. Douglas responded that a territorial legislature could, in effect, abolish slavery by doing nothing. If local authorities refused to enforce slave laws, slaveholders would be forced to move elsewhere. In this "Freeport Doctrine" Douglas had stripped the South of the victory it felt it had won in the Supreme Court. Negative reaction was such that when Congress convened in December 1859, Southern senators stripped Douglas of his committee chairmanship. Douglas only made matters worse by trying to clarify his position. In a lengthy article he penned for *Harper's*, he set out to explain the historical context of popular sovereignty including a constitutional justification. Douglas abandoned the practical approach and took the debate to the philosophical level. This played into the hands of his opponents, who could now pontificate on the abstract doctrine of states' rights. The ideological differences that had been skillfully hidden at Cincinnati were forced into the open.[9]

Why, then, did a small minority of Alabama's Democrats continue to support Stephen A. Douglas? As is always the case in politics, reasons were sometimes personal. Particularly in the case of Forsyth, a deep animosity toward Buchanan was a factor. Forsyth once remarked that "of all men living he liked Mr. Buchanan the least." Douglas and Forsyth both had well-documented breaks with the administration, and their mutual disdain forged them into a firm alliance. Around the state, similar grudges shook up traditional bonds. The rivalry between Yancey and Douglas advocate Senator Benjamin Fitzpatrick forced many state Democrats to rethink customary power arrangements, as would the 1859 governor's race between secessionist William F. Samford and moderate Andrew B. Moore. Philosophical differences also came into play. Moderates agreed with Douglas's popular sovereignty stance. They could not fathom why avowed Southern rights men would deny the voters of a territory the right to control their own affairs. In a speech before the Alabama House of Representatives, Forsyth noted the irony that an "extreme Southern rights friend claims jurisdiction for Congress over the question of slavery in the territories." Moderates blamed the popular sovereignty confusion on Buchanan's support of the Lecompton constitution, which he had "in an evil hour, thrust upon Congress, and to which he recklessly committed the Democratic Party."[10]

The most important factor, however, was practical politics. Moderates believed the slavery debate was over an abstraction—or what a Northern congressman described as "an imaginary Negro in an impossible place." The editor of the *Gainesville Independent* perhaps explained this best when he wrote, "While we have the abstract right to congressional protection, the assertion of the right ought to be determined by a fair comparison of its advantages and disadvantages. If no particular good is to result from it, it is foolish and wicked to stake the Union and safety of the South on the asserting of this right." Seibels noted that the only important issue for Alabama's Democratic Party was "shall we unite to prevent the election of an abolitionist or shall we aid his election by our supineness?" In an ongoing battle with the Yancey-supporting *Montgomery Advertiser*, Forsyth prophetically warned that if the secessionists did not cease their agitation over the territories, then "as sure as the hand on the dial will travel on to the appointed time, so sure will you have that Black Republican administration. And then, gentlemen, what will become of your claim for protection in the territories?" According to Jere Clemens, the Yancey faction had "dragged the slavery question from the obscure pulpits of a few crazy fanatics and thrust it upon a national theatre."[11] After John Brown's raid in October 1859, the "abstraction" of slavery and abolition became all too concrete. Brown's trial, conviction, execution, and sympathetic Northern reaction would be the backdrop to two critical Alabama events: the opening of the state legislature and the convening of the Democratic State Convention.

The seventh biennial session of the Alabama legislature was gaveled to order in December 1859. Two items of business dominated the assembly. The first involved the election of a U.S. senator. The term of Benjamin Fitzpatrick had two years remaining, but Yancey, who coveted the seat, felt he had the votes needed to unseat his state rival. Yancey attacked Fitzpatrick for his support of the Kansas Conference Bill and other "non-Southern" votes. A *Montgomery Weekly Advertiser* editorial titled "The Treachery of Douglas" took the incumbent to task for his pro-Douglas leanings. After many speeches and behind-the-scenes maneuvers, the vote was called off—a clear defeat for Yancey. The legislature, apparently anticipating future trouble, also began to pass preemptive measures. The lawmakers appropriated $200,000 to equip an eight-thousand-man state militia; authorized the University of Alabama to introduce military training; and chartered the Southern Fire Arms Company to manufacture munitions. Most ominously, both houses passed a resolution calling on Governor Moore to call an election for delegates to a state convention in the event a Republican won the upcoming presidential contest. Although technically the vote was not a call for a secession convention, most viewed it as such.[12]

Official state business soon took a back seat to the second major event: the Alabama Democratic State Convention. With the national debate over slavery and the potential candidacy of Stephen A. Douglas driving state party strategy, even the normally mundane selection of state delegates proved to be contentious. In Montgomery and Mobile, local party meetings split over ideological differences with each side passing resolutions and sending competing delegations to the state meeting.[13] The highly anticipated convention assembled on January 11, 1860, in the House chamber of the Alabama state capitol. Sutton S. Scott, a delegate from Madison County, gave a melancholy description of the opening scene: "A grim sort of quietude and determination were the ruling spirits of the hour. The very atmosphere seemed oppressive with the weight and burden of the issues, the result of which could not be otherwise than far-reaching and enduring." The battle lines were clearly drawn between the Yancey faction and the moderates with the former having a decided majority of the over four hundred delegates in the chamber. Along with Yancey, the Alabama radicals were led by Leroy Pope Walker, Thomas H. Watts, and Francis S. Lyon. Their objective was an affirmation of the Alabama Platform and a determination to bend the national party to their way of thinking. Forsyth, Seibels, and Fitzpatrick were joined by Henry W. Hilliard, John Winston, and Nicholas Davis in advocating a cooperationist stance at the upcoming national meeting.[14]

Day one of the convention was consumed with organizational duties. The body selected Lyon as the convention's presiding officer. This was seen as a victory for Yancey in an early test of strength. More important, the convention selected platform and credentials committees. Yanceyites dominated both groups. The second day began with a wave of resolutions ranging from the amount of time a delegate could speak (no more than thirty minutes on any subject) to a failed preemptive move to put off the adoption of any resolution until after the upcoming Charleston national Democratic Party meeting. In the evening session, the body heard the credentials committee report regarding the contested Montgomery and Mobile County seats. In both cases, the committee, not surprisingly, recommended the acceptance of the pro-Yancey group. The convention concurred with both reports but later allowed both Mobile groups to be seated since several names appeared on both slates.[15]

The entire morning session on the third day was devoted to debate on platform resolutions. Alexander White of Dallas County set the tone with his resolution that "upon the question of slavery in the States and Territories, the South only desires equality and justice, and these she will have peaceably if she can—forcibly if she must." John Forsyth offered a set of moderate resolutions suggesting that Alabama Democrats should "strike hands and lock shields" with their northern and western counterparts in order to defeat the "vandal hordes of Black Republicans." At the Friday evening session, the platform committee presented its long-awaited report. With its twelve resolutions, this report, in retrospect, sealed the fate of the national Democratic Party and of the Union itself. Although much of the document was standard Democratic Party fare, resolutions seven and ten were of particular concern. The seventh resolution stated, in part, that the power to abolish slavery "certainly does not belong to the people of the Territories in any capacity." This not-so-thinly veiled reference was a clear indication that Alabama's delegates to Charleston could not, under any circumstances, support Stephen A. Douglas—the champion of popular sovereignty. The tenth instructed Alabama's Charleston delegation to withdraw if that body did not accept the positions enumerated in the other resolutions. Often overlooked, however, is that Yancey, at this point, insisted that the Charleston delegates have some wiggle room. Perhaps remembering the humiliation of his lonely 1848 walkout, Yancey did not want to go to South Carolina completely handcuffed. Thus the final version of the tenth resolution instructed the delegates to withdraw if the national convention "shall refuse to adopt, *in substance,* the propositions embraced in the preceding resolutions."[16] The addition of this phrase allowed for compromise and ambiguity, as had been the deliberate result of the language used in the 1856 Cincinnati platform.

The last day of the convention witnessed the final vote on the platform. Prior to this vote, Yancey (who, owing to a special exemption, was unencumbered by the thirty-minute rule) delivered a speech in which he tried to debunk his reputation as a disunionist. However, he made it clear that he would "tread a pathway in blood" if the North continued to ignore the rights of the South. All twelve resolutions passed with the support of large majorities. The seventh passed with only three dissenting votes—including Forsyth, who stubbornly insisted that his name be recorded in the minutes as a nay. The convention adjourned with the chair expressing his desire that Alabama would have a harmonious party, but, he boasted, in any event, "we have at least an unterrified Democracy."[17]

The delegates returned home to defend their respective positions. Douglas supporters, who felt Yancey had deliberately orchestrated the future breakup of the national party, argued that "The platform is unwise, impolitic, and absolutely suicidal. It is obviously the progeny of some disunionist per se, and one level of the intended project for precipitating the Southern States into a revolution." Another wrote: "The action of the convention may result in the dissolution or defeat of the Democratic party—in the dissolution of the Union itself." Forsyth and Seibels communicated their opinion to Douglas that the resolutions did not reflect the true sentiment of Alabamians. Seibels felt that "extreme radical views appeared to have considerable sway." The Yanceyites countered by pointing out that the convention included representatives from every county in the state and that most had previously passed similar resolutions. As the Charleston Democratic National Convention neared, the moderates could not help but feel that the state party had "accomplished much mischief and taken a long step forward on the road to revolution."[18]

Few people gave the Charleston convention any chance of success. Robert Barnwell Rhett Jr., the influential editor of the *Charleston Mercury*, penned a pessimistic forecast: "The Democratic party, as a party of principle is dead. It exists now only as a powerful faction. It has not a single principle common to its members North and South." Indeed both sides went to the convention with little thought of compromise. The Northern delegates faced a terrific dilemma regarding the platform. If they abandoned popular sovereignty they could keep the South in the meeting, but their constituents would be bitter because they would be seen as giving in once again to the slave powers. A contemporary noted that if they returned home pledged to support Yancey's plan, they would be viewed as "cheated fools or deliberate traitors." On the other hand, if they rejected the Alabama ultimatum, they would free themselves from the South once and for all but at the cost of a split party. Southern delegates—particularly those from Alabama—faced no less a challenge. After their various state conventions, they felt honor bound to make a stand on principle. The only hope appeared to be an intentionally ambiguous platform, as at Cincinnati. The convention faced a choice between "subterfuge and disruption."[19]

Any compromise on the platform was made more difficult by the prospect of a Douglas nomination. Murat Halstead, a newspaper correspondent from Cincinnati assigned to cover the proceedings, correctly noted that Douglas was "the pivot individual of the Charleston Convention. Every delegate was for or against him, every motion was made to nominate or not to nominate him." Most Alabamians had not softened their opposition to the senator. A week prior to the convention, the *Opelika Weekly Southern Era* stated that "the demagogue of Illinois deserves to perish on the gibbet of Democratic condemnation, and his loathsome carcass to be cast at the gate of the Federal City." A correspondent of Clement C. Clay advised that "if Douglas and disunion were presented as the choice, adopt the latter as the less evil." Moderate Democrats, however, did not weaken in support for their champion. They saw, in Douglas, the only national candidate with a chance to defeat the Republicans in the fall. Forsyth wrote to Douglas, expressing his opinion that "you must be nominated—it will be the very best thing for the Democracy of the South."[20]

The Democratic National Convention opened at Charleston's Institute Hall on April 23, 1860, Stephen A. Douglas's forty-seventh birthday. Caleb Cushing of Massachusetts presided over the gathering as convention president. On day two, the body made the fateful decision to adopt the platform before choosing a nominee. In retrospect, this made a harmonious convention impossible because neither side would budge on the platform as long as the nominee was unknown. Although Northern delegates outnumbered Southern ones in the convention, Southerners controlled the crucial platform committee. On April 27, it returned one majority and two minority platform reports. The majority report was basically an acceptance of the Alabama Platform as it had been espoused in the Alabama state meeting. The first minority report was a pro-Douglas document calling for the reaffirmation of the Cincinnati Platform with the additional guidelines of the *Dred Scott* decision. A second minority report simply called for the readoption of the Cincinnati Platform as written.[21]

During the initial debate on these reports, Yancey addressed the "great heaving volcano of passion and crisis" with a speech he had been rehearsing since 1848. The fire-eater began with a detailed history lesson in which he demonstrated how unchecked anti-slavery sentiment in the North had led to abolitionism and had culminated in John Brown's raid. Yancey then recited a litany of grievances and failed compromises that had left the South in such a tenuous position. During the hour-and-a-half harangue, Yancey lamented, "Ours is the property invaded; ours are the institutions which are at stake; ours is the peace that is to be destroyed; ours is the property that is to be destroyed; ours is the honor at stake." Defeat on principle was preferred over victory "gained by presenting ambiguous issues and cheating the people." Alabama would "yield no position here unless we are convinced we are wrong." Although he again claimed he was not a disunionist, Yancey nonetheless concluded that "there will be disunion if we are defeated." The speech prompted an impassioned response from George E. Pugh of Ohio. Pugh rejected Yancey's demands with the words "Gentlemen of the South—you mistake us—you mistake us—we will not do it!"[22]

The full body rejected both the majority and second minority report. The first minority report was then brought up for consideration. When the popular sovereignty plank was approved, the promised "bolt" occurred. Leroy Pope Walker presented Cushing a written statement reiterating the instructions given the Alabama delegation and his belief that the injustices shown to the South warranted compliance with those instructions. Walker led the withdrawal of Alabama's delegation and was followed by all or large majorities of the delegates from Mississippi, Louisiana, South Carolina, Florida, Texas, Delaware, Arkansas, and (the next day) Georgia. Yancey's long-anticipated disruption had finally transpired. The bolters reassembled in another hall in Charleston and adopted their own platform. They then adjourned with instructions to reconvene in Richmond on June 11. That night, in an impromptu address, a cheerful Yancey stated, "Perhaps even now, the pen of the historian is nibbed to write the story of a new revolution." Meanwhile, back in Institute Hall the chaos continued. Since the body had earlier interpreted the rules in such a way as to require any nominee to get the vote of two-thirds of the *total* delegates—not just those present—to win nomination, Douglas was still short of the required numbers. Two days and fifty-seven ballots later, the hopelessly deadlocked convention adjourned with instructions to reassemble in Baltimore.[23]

Although the final split was still a few weeks away, in Alabama a heated contest to claim the "vacated" seats in the upcoming Baltimore convention began in earnest. The bolters proudly defended their recent actions. Francis Lyon proclaimed that "Alabama has boldly taken her stand in the very van of the Southern States and, God helping her, she will hold it. Let no man call this a 'disunion movement.' It is a movement to uphold the Constitution." As per instructions from the late state convention, the Yancey Democrats called for a meeting to be held on June 4 in Montgomery to chart a course of action. Alabama's Douglas men determined not to let Yancey have another chance at "disruption." Forsyth, through the *Register*, issued a call for another Democratic meeting to convene in Selma (later changed to Montgomery) to select replacement delegates. His political intentions were clear—writing Douglas that "We have just begun to fight [and] mean yet to drive the Yanceyites to the wall. They are very uneasy [and] we shall not spare them. We treat them as aliens—Bolters separated from the Democracy and refuse to join them in the same convention."[24] The moderates drew the unbridled scorn of the bolters, with Forsyth again receiving most of the attention. In an exchange of angry letters between the *Advertiser* and the *Register*, the former singled out the Mobile editor for his "disturber" stand. In mocking tones, the Montgomery editors noted that "he [Forsyth], wrapt in the solitude of his own originality—he had 'squatter' imprinted on his brow." Yancey's nineteenth-century biographer claimed that Forsyth's "self-conceit led him to attempt to overthrow the Democratic party."[25]

The competing state conventions met and selected their respective delegations. The bolters' meeting sent its delegates to Richmond, where they planned to regroup and present themselves for admission at Baltimore. The Douglas group sent Forsyth, Seibels, Winston, and others directly to Baltimore as "replacement" delegates. Regardless of their disdain for this "mongrel crowd of Douglas Democrats," the Yanceyites knew the odds were stacked against them. The *Advertiser* correctly forecasted that "Forsyth will carry his delegation from Selma to Baltimore, and mark this prediction, that if the [Yancey] Montgomery Convention sends a delegation to Baltimore, it will be ruled out by the Baltimore Douglas Convention ... and the Forsyth bogus Douglas delegation under the false name of Democrats will be accepted."[26]

Round two of the national convention took place at Baltimore's Front Street Theatre. After routine business, the convention selected an all-important credentials committee. Several of the states had returned with delegate issues—most notably Louisiana and Alabama, which had come with competing delegations. The pro-Douglas delegations from both states insisted they had fulfilled a request of the Charleston convention to fill vacancies created by the former delegates who had *resigned* their positions. In the case of Alabama, Forsyth pointed out that the Yancey delegation had been empowered to attend a convention in Richmond and, as such, had no legitimacy in Baltimore. Amid wild rumors and speculations—including reports later substantiated that Douglas had offered to withdraw his candidacy—the Credentials Committee presented its report on June 21. Just before the reading of this report—with symbolism that could have only been divinely inspired—the floor of the convention hall literally fell out. One wag joked, "The party suffers from a physically no less than ideologically shaky platform." After hasty repairs, John Krum of Missouri presented the majority report. By a vote of sixteen to nine and fourteen to eleven, respectively, the committee decided to accept the pro-Douglas delegations from Louisiana and Alabama.[27]

Isaac Stevens of Oregon presented the minority report. Solemnly noting that the proper disposition of this issue would determine "whether there shall be a National Democratic party or not," he vehemently denounced the majority decision and particularly touted the legitimacy of Alabama's Yancey delegation. In the view of the minority, the bolters had not resigned but had merely *withdrawn*. In fact, he continued, they could only resign to the body that had originally appointed them—and that body not only had endorsed their late actions but had reappointed them to appear at Baltimore. The second complaint centered on the nature of Forsyth's "call." The notice appeared in only three newspapers and resulted in a convention in which just twenty-eight of the state's fifty-two counties were represented. In addition, Forsyth's appeal to the *people* of Alabama instead of *Democrats* was seen as an attempt to circumvent the state party and establish a rival organization.[28]

When the full body voted on the credentials report, the majority concurred with the majority report. This repudiation of Yancey led to a second bolt of the Southern states. The convention's action was so obviously partisan that a number of Northern delegates joined the walkout, including the chair, Caleb Cushing. With the convention now stacked in his favor, Douglas finally received his party's nomination. In a move designed to neutralize Yancey's Southern support, the convention selected Benjamin Fitzpatrick as its vice-presidential nominee. After receiving floods of advice from Douglas supporters and opponents, Fitzpatrick declined the nomination. Leery of becoming involved in the party's looming destruction, Fitzpatrick wrote that "the distracting differences at present existing in the ranks of the Democratic party were strikingly exemplified at Charleston and at Baltimore, and . . . distinctly admonish me that I should, in no way, contribute to this unfortunate division."[29] With Fitzpatrick out of the picture, the nomination fell to Herschel V. Johnson of Georgia. The bolters reassembled and nominated John C. Breckinridge for president and Joseph Lane for vice president. They also adopted the same platform that had been rejected at Charleston.

Between Democratic conventions, the Republican Party met in Chicago and nominated the relatively unknown Lincoln. A fourth party—the newly organized Constitutional Union—also entered the fray. In June, this upstart band held a state meeting in Selma attended by 204 delegates. Trying to distance themselves from the splintered Democrats, the group advocated "vague tenets" and stressed a strict adherence to the Constitution, enforcement of existing laws, and the preservation of the Union. Most of their statewide support came from former Whigs and from disgruntled Democrats fed up with the party bickering. This group selected Tennessean John Bell as its standard-bearer.[30] Since Lincoln's name did not appear on the ballot in Alabama, the actual campaign centered on which of the remaining parties had the best contingency plan in the event of a Republican victory. The Breckinridge forces felt that such a result would be sufficient cause for secession and the formation of an independent Southern nation, while the Douglas and Bell men took a more cautious approach with the latter being the most hesitant. A vote for Breckinridge was not necessarily a vote for disunion per se but an affirmation that a Republican victory provided justification for such a course.[31]

The highlights of the campaign were the speaking tours undertaken by Yancey and Douglas, both of which would end up in Alabama. Ironically, Yancey would travel to the North preaching disunion while Douglas would go south pleading for patience. Yancey's tour began in Memphis on August 14 and would see him make twenty speeches over the next several weeks. The themes of his talks were, by now, predictable. He steadfastly claimed that the Republicans were the true disunionists. Northern voters must not impose intolerable conditions on the South by electing Lincoln. According to Yancey, the election of Douglas would be no less unacceptable. While in the North, Yancey did not hesitate to play the racial card. He felt that Lincoln wanted to "elevate the Negro by depressing the White man to his level." A Lincoln win would lead to a genocidal race war with former masters becoming the "enemies of that race until we drench the field with the blood of the unfortunate people." Along these lines, Yancey tried to convince his skeptical audiences that slavery was in their own best interests—economically as well as socially—and that they should not object to federal protection for the institution. Returning south, Yancey told a New Orleans gathering that the time had come to "show your love for the Union by preparing ballots" because "after the Lincoln party is elected . . . you will be called to show your love by preparing rifles."[32]

Forsyth and Seibels meanwhile had long been urging Douglas to make a trip to the Deep South. According to Seibels, "Men would listen to you and be converted that could not be induced to read a speech or hear an argument in your defense." On October 8, after receiving the news of Republican gains in key states, Douglas remarked to his private secretary, "Mr. Lincoln is the next president. We must try to save the Union. I will go South." The tour began on October 19 in St. Louis and would take Douglas through Tennessee, North Carolina, Georgia, and, finally, Alabama.[33]

A large crowd welcomed Douglas and his wife, Adele, to Montgomery on November 2. The reception was not entirely favorable, as Douglas's hat was knocked off by a rotten egg and his wife was splattered by several tomatoes. Douglas made a lengthy midday speech from the capitol steps in which he staunchly defended popular sovereignty and urged his listeners not to rush into the secessionist camp. At one point Douglas said, "I know there is a conspiracy on foot to break up the Union." As far as the ascension of Lincoln, he stated that "the election of any man on earth by the American people, according to the Constitution, is no justification to break up the government." Among the throng was Yancey himself—prepared to give a rebuttal address that evening. It is also quite possible that a young actor named John Wilkes Booth—in town with his traveling theatrical company—was in the crowd that afternoon. Douglas could not escape Montgomery without one more platform calamity. While boarding a steamer bound for Selma, the craft's upper deck collapsed under the weight of the crowd with Douglas and Adele falling to the lower level. In considerable pain, Douglas was forced to use a crutch to continue while Adele remained behind in the care of the Seibels family. Five months later, only weeks before his death, Douglas received a bill for the crutch.[34]

Mobile was the final stop. Douglas arrived in the port city on November 5. He was welcomed by Forsyth and Winston and escorted to the Battle House Hotel. That night at 8:00 he was introduced by Forsyth on the steps of the courthouse and proceeded to give a two-hour address. One person in the large crowd reported that Douglas "spoke for hours and all listened with intense interest, as if the exigency of the situation demanded all that could be bestowed upon it."[35] After the speech, a torchlight procession escorted Douglas back to the Battle House, where he retired for the evening. A fireworks display officially ended the 1860 campaign.

Douglas spent Election Day with Forsyth greeting well-wishers and discussing the future. That evening, the two old friends huddled in the offices of the *Register* awaiting any election news that might come across the wire. Forsyth showed Douglas an editorial he had written days earlier that he planned to print in the event of Lincoln's election. The editorial urged the immediate calling of a state convention to decide upon a course of action to meet the current crisis. Douglas strongly objected to the wording and the two had a lengthy and, at times, heated discussion. Unable to sway his loyal yet stubborn supporter, Douglas returned to his room, in the words of his aide, "more hopeless than I had ever before seen him."[36]

Over the next several days, the election results confirmed the worst fears of the South. The split Democratic Party handed Lincoln and the Republicans a solid electoral majority. In Alabama, Douglas finished a distant third, behind Breckinridge and Bell. Mobile was one of only five Alabama counties (and the only one outside the Unionist Tennessee Valley) that produced at least a plurality for the Illinois statesman. Statewide, Breckinridge received 48,671 votes while Bell garnered 27,834 and Douglas amassed 13,613. In some counties, the anti-Douglas vote (if not fraudulent) was staggering. For example, in Barbour County, Breckinridge defeated Douglas 1,715 to 9 while in Coffee County the combined Breckinridge-Bell tally was 1,272 to 2. Perhaps most interesting was Henry County where Douglas was shut out—losing to Breckinridge by a vote of 1,109 to 0, with Bell picking up 317.[37]

As the dust settled, the response to the election galvanized public support for secession. Douglas tried to sound a hopeful tone. After leaving Mobile, he wrote: "Four years will soon pass away when the ballot box will furnish a peaceful, legal, and constitutional remedy to all the evils and grievances with which the country may be affected." In Alabama, no such optimism existed. One Mobile newspaper opined that "the rapid progress of events within the last few weeks leave[s] little ground for hope that the Union can be preserved upon any basis just, equitable, and satisfactory to the Southern people." Many of the moderates closed ranks with the secessionists as the state grappled with the crisis. A correspondent to the *Mobile Daily Advertiser* noted that "Union men, Douglas men, Breckinridge men are alike in the loud denunciation of submission to Lincoln's administration." Across the state the question turned from whether or not to pursue secession to a matter of timing and procedure for the certain event. In a letter to Douglas, Forsyth sadly noted that "with your defeat, the cause of the Union was lost." In a matter of weeks—in the same chamber where the Alabama Democratic State Convention had set the tone for the election of 1860—Alabama would formally secede from the Union.[38]

What, then, in conclusion, was the significance of Alabama's "Democracy" in the revolutionary events of 1860? To fully answer this important question, one must investigate the motivations of both the Yancey and Douglas forces in the nomination and platform adoption processes as well as the legitimacy of Alabama's "replacement" delegation at Baltimore. We turn first to Yancey. It is certainly no secret that the great orator desired a separate Southern nation. Yancey believed that if the South were ever to secede, it would be in response to some egregiously offensive action of the North. The election of a Republican or an unacceptable Northern candidate on a strictly sectional vote would be just such an event. However, a *desire* for something that eventually happens does not necessarily constitute a *cause*. Although Yancey was obviously ready for secession and wanted Alabama to likewise be ready, he did not expect the event to happen in 1860, nor can it be proven that he even desired such an event at that moment. Yancey once stated, "I am a secessionist, and not a revolutionist, and would not precipitate but carefully prepare to meet an inevitable dissolution." Yancey's stand on the withdrawal resolution at the Alabama Democratic State Convention was not an effort at disunion but an attempt to prepare the state should such an event become likely in the future. Likewise, Yancey did not go to the Charleston convention to "precipitate" a revolution but to persuade the national party leadership to openly accept the concept of Southern equality. If the South could not eliminate the national party, Yancey hoped to "elevate and purify" it. It is not unreasonable to believe that Yancey might have eventually compromised as he had done in 1856.[39]

The role of the Douglas men also requires a brief review. In his Montgomery address, Stephen A. Douglas claimed the he "did not desire the Charleston or Baltimore conventions to endorse my opinion or any other person's opinion on popular sovereignty." This statement, however, did not mesh with a private letter in which he wrote, "I do not intend to make peace with my enemies, nor to make a concession on one iota of principle." At the first sign of controversy at Charleston—the adoption of the platform—the Yanceyites were perhaps ready to compromise. Yancey was actually working behind the scenes to find a way to keep Alabama's delegation in the meeting. The minority report, with some adjustment, might have eventually been acceptable to Yancey, but the Douglas supporters refused to seek common ground. Several weeks before the convention, Forsyth sent a letter to Douglas in which he told the senator that their side should "refuse to accept any material interpolations" in the platform as it stood in 1856. In fact, many Douglas supporters wanted to force Yancey to make good on his threatened walkout. Such a withdrawal would achieve two of the national party's objectives: brand Yancey as the disrupter of the party and secure the nomination for Douglas. Before the convention, Forsyth had expressed to Douglas his fear that Yancey would *not* withdraw from the convention. At the moment of Yancey's wavering, Winston insisted that the instructions be carried out because he was determined "to force those who had brought the trouble from Alabama to stand by their work." Overlooked is the fact that a significant portion of the Douglas forces were prepared to withdraw from the convention if the *majority* report was adopted. In addition, everyone involved realized that compromise on the platform was impossible as long as Douglas was the presumed nominee. Wetumpka lawyer Robert S. Thane would later write that the Douglas men must be blamed for "keeping the nominee before the convention, when they must have seen the danger of disruption which such a course involved." If Douglas was sincere in his offer to withdraw his name at Baltimore, the protest of his managers ended such a possibility and guaranteed there would be no compromise for Yancey.[40]

Finally, one must examine the nature of Alabama's "replacement" delegation that appeared at Baltimore. There can be no doubt that the Yancey group had the legitimate claim for the seats vacated at Charleston. This delegation followed the specific instructions given to them by the official state Democratic convention. The Forsyth group, on the other hand, was acting on its own authority without the sanction of any statewide organization. The Baltimore credentials committee accepted the Forsyth group because they knew the Mobile editor and his colleagues would make no trouble regarding the platform, and such an action would serve to punish Yancey for what was perceived as his plan to destroy the national party and promote secession. Many contemporary newspapers assigned blame for the party split to the Douglas forces and the "bogus" Forsyth delegation. One noted that rather than a useful Baltimore convention, "The Douglas Managers determined to carry things with a heavy hand, and they did so. Their tone had become reckless, defiant, domineering. They were evidently determined to exclude the regularly appointed delegates from the southern states and fill these places with creations of their own."[41]

One can only surmise the outcome had the Yancey delegation been seated at Baltimore. Certainly the overall body could have still failed to present an acceptable platform in which case the second walkout would have occurred anyway. However, it would have most likely been to Yancey's advantage to work out some type of compromise—thus being able to claim that he had molded the national party to his own image.[42] The seating of the replacement delegation ended any chance for a solution to the Democratic nomination and platform dilemma. Had Alabama's moderates not led a move after the Charleston breakup to select a pro-Douglas replacement delegation, the Baltimore seats would not have been in question. Without the second "bolt," Douglas still would not have had the numbers necessary for a two-thirds majority. The senator may have then withdrawn his name, which would have pressured Yancey to compromise on the platform. A united Democratic party—while certainly not assured of a victory—would have offered Lincoln a more formidable challenge. While Lincoln most likely would have still received the most electoral votes, he may have been denied a *majority*. Had New York gone for Douglas or if 5 percent of the total vote in California, Ohio, Illinois, and Indiana switched to Douglas, the election would have been thrown into the House of Representatives. The initial political appeal of Douglas was his claim to be the only "national" candidate in the field. As a result of the split party, Douglas lost this status and many Northern votes.

In his masterful study of antebellum Alabama politics, J. Mills Thornton concluded that while Yancey and the fire-eaters usually receive the scorn for the breakup of the Democratic Party and, ultimately, the Union, Senator Douglas and his managers cannot "escape their considerable immediate responsibility for the final disruption which resulted." Roy Franklin Nichols likewise noted that when the Southern Democrats encouraged Douglas to step aside, he was willing but his followers were not. Such managers, he concluded, "forced Douglas to permit the destruction of the Democratic party." As the Baltimore convention prepared to disband, Charles E. Stuart of Michigan admonished the weary delegates to "go into the field where the enemy are and conquer them in a hand to hand fight." The actions of Alabama's leading Democrats—on both the radical and moderate sides—would make Mr. Stuart's words quite prophetic.[43]

Notes

1. William L. Yancey to James Slaughter, June 16, 1858, quoted in Eric H. Walther, *William Lowndes Yancey and the Coming of the Civil War* (Chapel Hill: University of North Carolina Press, 2006), 222, italics added.

2. *Speech of Hon. Jere Clemens, Delivered at Huntsville, Ala., August 6th, 1860*, in Johnson J. Hooper Papers, Alabama Department of Archives and History, Montgomery, Alabama. For a summary of the changing nature of Alabama politics in the 1850s, see J. Mills Thornton III, *Politics and Power in a Slave Society* (Baton Rouge: Louisiana State University Press, 1978), 348–49, 375; Harriet E. Amos, *Cotton City: Urban Development in Antebellum Mobile* (Tuscaloosa: University of Alabama Press, 1985), 222; and Henry M. McKiven Jr., "Secession, War, and Reconstruction," in *Mobile: The New History of Alabama's First City*, ed. Michael V. R. Thomason (Tuscaloosa: University of Alabama Press, 2001), 95–96. In this essay, the term "Democracy" is used in its eighteenth-century context—referring to the Democratic Party.

3. Yancey and his new wife, Sarah Caroline Earle, moved to Alabama in 1837. With little financial success from plantation and newspaper enterprises, Yancey turned his attention to politics. He served in the Alabama legislature and, for a brief time, in the U.S. House of Representatives. For a sympathetic biography of Yancey, see John Witherspoon Dubose, *The Life and Times*

of William Lowndes Yancey, 2 vols. (Birmingham: Roberts and Son, 1892). It has been superseded by Eric Walther's work.

4. Walther, *Yancey and the Coming of the Civil War*, 233; *Charleston Mercury*, July 14, 1859.

5. See George C. Rable, *The Confederate Republic: A Revolution against Politics* (Chapel Hill: University of North Carolina Press, 1994), 11–17; and William W. Freehling, *The Road to Disunion*, vol. 2, *Secessionists Triumphant, 1854–1861* (Oxford: Oxford University Press, 2007), 281–82.

6. See Lonnie A. Burnett, *The Pen Makes a Good Sword: John Forsyth of the Mobile Register* (Tuscaloosa: University of Alabama Press, 2006), 98–102.

7. Robert W. Johannsen, "Stephen A. Douglas and the South," *Journal of Southern History* 33, no. 1 (February 1967): 32; Robert W. Johannsen, *Stephen A. Douglas* (New York: Oxford University Press, 1973), 768; James L. Huston, *Stephen A. Douglas and the Dilemma of Democratic Equality* (Lanham, MD: Rowman and Littlefield, 2007), 143; *Chicago Weekly Citizen*, March 4, 1846; *Greensboro (Alabama) Beacon*, November 26, 1858. It should be noted that at the Cincinnati convention, the Alabama delegation (including Yancey) had cast its votes for Douglas on the first eight ballots.

8. Clement C. Clay to Clement Comer Clay, December 11, 1858, Clement C. Clay Papers, Duke University. For an explanation of the implications of Lecompton, see Freehling, *Road to Disunion*, 277–78.

9. See Sean Wilentz, *The Rise of American Democracy: Jefferson to Lincoln* (New York: Norton, 2005), 755; Huston, *Stephen A. Douglas*, 145; and Johannsen, *Stephen A. Douglas*, 697–710. One must note the irony of supposedly states' rights Democrats upholding assertions of national power in the Supreme Court as well as in calling for a federal slave code.

10. For the political rivalry between Yancey and Benjamin Fitzpatrick, see Thornton, *Politics and Power*, 373–81. *(Mobile) Register*, January 17 and 13, 1860; John Forsyth to William F. Samford, October 5, 1859, in *Letters of Hon. John Forsyth, of Alabama, Late Minister to Mexico, to William F. Samford, Esq. in Defence of Stephen A. Douglas* (Mobile, AL: Lemuel Towers, 1859). For the root of Forsyth's disdain for Buchanan, see Burnett, *The Pen Makes a Good Sword*, 75–96.

11. James G. Blaine, quoted in Roy Morris Jr., *The Long Pursuit: Abraham Lincoln's Thirty-Year Struggle with Stephen A. Douglas for the Heart and Soul of America* (New York: Harper Collins, 2008), 143; *Gainesville (Alabama) Independent*, February 11, 1860; *Montgomery Weekly Confederation*, March 3, 1860; *Mobile Register*, December 9, 1859; *Speech of Hon. Jere Clemens*.

12. *Montgomery Weekly Advertiser*, March 3, 1859; *Journal of the Seventh Biennial Session of the House of Representatives of the State of Alabama, Session of 1859–1860* (Montgomery: Shorter and Hall, 1860), 474; *Journal of the Seventh Biennial Session of the Senate of the State of Alabama, Session of 1859–1860* (Montgomery: Shorter and Hall, 1860), 126–27.

13. For a detailed account of the local meetings prior to the Alabama Democratic State Convention, see *Proceedings of the Democratic State Convention, Held in the City of Montgomery, Commencing Wednesday, January 11, 1860* (Montgomery: Advertiser Book and Job Steam Press, 1860), 11–13, 17–19.

14. Sutton S. Scott, "Recollections of the Alabama Democratic State Convention of 1860," *Transactions of the Alabama Historical Society* 4 (1904): 313–14.

15. *Proceedings of the Democratic State Convention*, 7–10.

16. Ibid., 24–25, 29, italics added. See also Walther, *William Lowndes Yancey*, 238.

17. Walther, *William Lowndes Yancey*, 238; *Proceedings of the Democratic State Convention*, 31–32, 37. The tenth resolution was the closest, but even that passed by a comfortable 374–71 margin.

18. *Gainesville Independent*, February 11, 1860; *Mobile Mercury*, January 18, 1860; Austin L. Venable, "The Conflict between the Douglas and Yancey Forces in the Charleston Convention,"

Journal of Southern History 8, no. 2 (May 1942): 234; James Leonidas Murphy, "Alabama and the Charleston Convention of 1860," *Transactions of the Alabama Historical Society* 4 (1904): 245–46; *Mobile Register*, January 19, 1860.

19. *Charleston Mercury*, April 16, 1860; *Mobile Register*, January 17, 1860; William B. Hesseltine, ed., *Three against Lincoln: Murat Halstead Reports the Caucuses of 1860* (Baton Rouge: Louisiana State University Press, 1960), 40.

20. Hesseltine, *Three against Lincoln*, 3; *Opelika (Alabama) Weekly Southern Era*, April 18, 1860; Hugh Lawson Clay to Clement C. Clay, January 19, 1860, Clement C. Clay Papers, Duke University; John Forsyth to Stephen A. Douglas, February 4, 1860, in Stephen A. Douglas Papers, University of Chicago (hereafter Douglas Papers).

21. Unless otherwise stated, details of the Charleston and Baltimore Conventions are taken from *Official Proceedings of the Democratic National Convention, Held in 1860, at Charleston and Baltimore* (Cleveland: Nevins Print, Plain Dealer Job Office, 1860). The second minority report was offered individually by Benjamin F. Butler.

22. For the text of Yancey's speech, see *Speech of the Hon. William L. Yancey Delivered to the National Democratic Convention* (Charleston: Walker, Evans, and Co., 1860). Hesseltine, *Three against Lincoln*, 53–54; *Charleston Courier*, April 30, 1860; Morris, *The Long Pursuit*, 146–47.

23. Hesseltine, *Three against Lincoln*, 86. For the complete delegation statement, see *Protest of the Alabama Democracy* (Charleston: Walker, Evans, and Co., 1860).

24. *Montgomery Advertiser*, May 16, 1860; John Forsyth to Stephen A. Douglas, May 9, 1860, Douglas Papers. For a text of Forsyth's call, see *Mobile Register*, May 27, 1860.

25. *Montgomery Advertiser*, May 23 and 30, 1860; Dubose, *Life and Times of William Lowndes Yancey*, 475.

26. *Montgomery Weekly Advertiser*, May 23, 1860. For the proceedings of the Douglas state meeting, see *Excerpts from Proceedings of the National Democratic State Convention of Alabama Held in the City of Montgomery, on the 4th Day of June, 1860* (Baltimore: John W. Woods, 1860).

27. Burnett, *The Pen Makes a Good Sword*, 112–13; Freehling, *Road to Disunion*, 319; Hesseltine, *Three against Lincoln*, 215–17.

28. Hesseltine, *Three against Lincoln*, 216.

29. Benjamin Fitzpatrick to William Ludlow of New York and Others in Benjamin Fitzpatrick Papers, Alabama Department of Archives and History, Montgomery.

30. Margaret M. Storey, *Loyalty and Loss: Alabama's Unionists in the Civil War and Reconstruction* (Baton Rouge: Louisiana State University Press, 2004), 23–24; W. Stanley Hoole, *Alias Simon Suggs: The Life and Times of Johnson Jones Hooper* (Tuscaloosa: University of Alabama Press, 1952), 134–35. There was briefly a fifth party—the Southern Rights Oppositionist. This faction held a convention in Selma but then split up with most falling into the Breckinridge camp.

31. Thornton, *Politics and Power*, 402–4.

32. *Wilmington Gazette*, September 28, 1860; Walther, *William Lowndes Yancey*, 262; Freehling, *Road to Disunion*, 340.

33. John J. Seibels to Stephen A. Douglas, August 14, 1860, Douglas Papers; See Johannsen, "Stephen A. Douglas and the South," 46.

34. Johannsen, *Stephen A. Douglas*, 801. For the text of the Montgomery speech, see David R. Barbee and Milledge L Bonham Jr., "The Montgomery Address of Stephen A. Douglas," *Journal of Southern History* 5, no. 4 (November 1939): 527–52.

35. Kate Cumming, *Gleanings from the Southland* (Birmingham: Roberts and Son, 1895), 19–20.

36. Johannsen, *Stephen A. Douglas*, 802–3.

37. For complete county results, see Lewy Dorman, *Party Politics in Alabama from 1850 through 1860* (Tuscaloosa: University of Alabama Press, 1995), 176–77.

38. Stephen A. Douglas to Ninety-six New Orleans Citizens, November 13, 1860, in Robert W. Johannsen, ed., *The Letters of Stephen A. Douglas* (Urbana: University of Illinois Press, 1961), 500–502; *Mobile Daily Advertiser*, December 7, 1860; John Forsyth to Stephen A. Douglas, December 28, 1860, Douglas Papers.

39. See Thornton, *Politics and Power*, 389–91, 382–83; Walther, *William Lowndes Yancey*, 233; Wilentz, *Rise of American Democracy*, 755; and Freehling, *Road to Disunion*, 269.

40. Barbee and Bonham, "Montgomery Address of Stephen A. Douglas," 541; Douglas to James W. Singleton, March 21, 1860, in Johannsen, *Letters of Stephen A. Douglas*, 439; John Forsyth to Stephen A. Douglas, April 5 and February 9, 1860, Douglas Papers; Thornton, *Politics and Power*, 392–93; Storey, *Loyalty and Loss*, 24.

41. Roy Franklin Nichols, *Disruption of American Democracy* (New York: Collier Books, 1940), 313; *Wilmington Journal*, June 28, 1860.

42. For a detailed explanation of this argument, see Thornton, *Politics and Power*, 396–98.

43. Thornton, *Politics and Power*, 396; Nichols, *Disruption of American Democracy*, 320; *Proceedings of the Democratic National Convention*, 181.

2

"The Aggressions of the North Can Be Borne No Longer"

White Alabamian Women during the Secession Crisis and Outbreak of War

Jennifer Ann Newman Treviño

On December 31, 1860, Elizabeth Rhodes of Eufaula penned the following in her diary: "There are dark clouds overspreading our National Horizon and we cannot yet know whether the fringes of prosperity will dispel them and the bright rays of peace and happiness once more [beam] upon us, [or] whether they will grow darker and denser until proved out in wars and bloodshed on our once prosperous and happy nation. Time alone can unfold these things. We can only wait and pray God to overrule all things for His glory and the good of mankind."[1] These words reflected the sentiments of many as 1860 drew to a close. In the few short months between November 1860 and April 1861, as secession and the outbreak of war tore the United States apart, Alabamians such as Rhodes found themselves in a complex situation. Mixed emotions of fear and excitement filled many as the world they knew crumbled around them. Women, who had no political power, were in a unique position and felt especially vulnerable. At the same time, they played a vital role during this period. Many, but not all, Alabamian women supported secession and the newly created Confederacy but worried about the potential consequences of these events. In the uncertainty that surrounded them, they turned to the one constant in their lives: their faith. Ultimately they believed that God controlled everything on earth and had a plan for their lives, and these beliefs became the foundation of their identity as Confederate women.[2]

The events surrounding the secession crisis created turmoil in Alabama. Not all Alabamians supported secession, as historian Margaret Storey demonstrates. Indeed, her argument that 10 to 15 percent of Alabamians were Unionists who never supported the Confederacy sheds light on the complex diversity of opinions surrounding the secession movement.[3] Nonetheless, even taking Storey's analysis into account, it is clear that the majority (85 to 90 percent) of Alabamians supported secession and the creation of the Confederacy. Although many works explore the creation of the Confederacy, none focuses specifically on Alabamian women's religious beliefs and their construction of Confederate identity.[4] The secession crisis and the outbreak of war transformed many middle- and upper-class literate, white,

Protestant Alabamian women into Confederates who would remain loyal to the Confederacy long after its demise in 1865. This process began with the politicization of women, as they wrote in their diaries and letters about national events in the years immediately preceding the war. It continued as they justified the ideological foundation for secession and the creation of the Confederacy throughout the war. Even before the firing on Fort Sumter in April 1861, women encouraged men to defend the South if necessary. Women participated in the process of mobilization by throwing parties and presenting soldiers with banners to carry into battle. The outbreak of war in April 1861 led to an intensification of these activities and others, such as the organization of aid societies to provide for the soldiers' needs. In all of this, religion played an essential role as women developed a new identity as Confederate women.[5]

As dictated by the gender norms of the period, men made the political decision to take Alabama out of the Union, but the women of the state were integral to the process.[6] Alabamian women held their own political opinions, albeit ones that often corresponded with those of their male relatives. The patriarchal hierarchy of the antebellum South identified and defined women within the family and especially in relation to their male relatives—as wife, mother, sister, or daughter. Women were expected to be pure, noble, virtuous, moral, pious, honest, patient, and long-suffering; they were considered more religious and temperate in nature than men, but this did not keep them from developing political opinions.[7] At the same time, the traditional notion that women were weak and subordinate gave them power over their male relatives. It was the duty of Southern men to provide for and protect Southern women. Indeed this was central to upholding Southern manhood. And as historian LeeAnn Whites has argued, many Southern men supported secession and joined the Confederate army to uphold their gendered conception of manhood. Thus during the secession crisis, women's position in society gave them immense power.[8] Had they rejected secession and discouraged men from fighting, the course of history might have proceeded differently.

Their personal writings reveal that they influenced politics more directly and offer significant insight into their feelings and struggles as the country plummeted into disunion and war. With few public outlets for personal expression, many women turned to writing. They wrote in their diaries when there was no one else for them to turn to and recorded their innermost thoughts and feelings, constantly referring to their diaries as an "old friend" or an "old faithful friend" with whom they "communed."[9] The only criterion used for selecting women to include in this study was that they left a written record of their lives. As a result, the women included here range from single girls in their early teens to married women in their sixties; the study includes women from wealthy slaveholding families (one woman's family had as many as eighty slaves) and from families who appear to have owned no slaves; the women lived across the state of Alabama, from Huntsville to Mobile. Although all were white Protestants, their denominational preferences ranged from Baptist to Methodist to Episcopalian.[10] Regardless of their background, all of these women share several traits in common. Given what they wrote, they understood current political events and supported secession.

As women wrote about secession they quickly shifted their loyalties to the newly created Confederate nation and situated themselves within it. Their place embodied antebellum ideals of womanhood, which required sacrifice and submission to God's will despite their concern about the fate of their nation and the safety of their loved ones. Many would take pride in their new nation and go to great lengths to justify its existence. Even before Alabama seceded, one woman anticipated her place as a mother in her new country when she wrote, "the only thing that gives me real pride is that my child may be born in a Southern Republic, and not in the detestable Union."[11]

Throughout the antebellum era women had occasionally written about politics, but after John Brown attempted to lead a slave uprising by raiding Harpers Ferry in 1859, women began focusing on national politics in their personal writings.[12] News of the raid shocked and enraged white Southerners. Sarah Espy, the widow of a Dublin, Alabama, businessman, wrote in her diary about "the abolition riot at Harper's Ferry." She noted that "a great excitement prevails, in some of the Southern states in consequence." She had no use for abolitionists and revealed her utter disdain for them when she exclaimed, "May the Northern assassins be put down with their free-negroes allies." She hoped that peace would follow Brown's hanging and prayed that the "women and children of the South would be saved from their Northern murderers."[13] The manner in which she wrote about Northern abolitionists as a threat to white Southern women and children invoked the familiar image of the weak woman in need of assistance and protection from Southern men, who were honor bound to defend the helpless. As she related her honest fears, she promoted an acceptable image of Southern womanhood as dependent upon men. Espy had just been forced to take over the management of her household and plantation after her husband and two brothers died. Throughout her diary she consistently lamented her new role and wished that she had a male relative to whom she could turn for help. In the absence of this she turned to her one remaining source of strength, and prayed, "May the Lord help us."[14]

Although Brown's raid terrified Southerners, the election of 1860 caused women to focus on national politics to an unprecedented degree. When the Democratic convention met in Charleston, South Carolina, in April, many Southerners supported the Alabama Platform, also known as the Yancey Platform (named for the Alabama radical William Lowndes Yancey). Among many other things, this platform would have constitutionally protected slavery in the United States. After much debate and a rejection of the demands of the Southerners, the Alabama delegation, followed by most other Southerners, walked out of the convention. The delegates agreed to meet again in Baltimore in June, but when they did so most of the Southerners walked out of the convention and the Democratic Party divided. The Northern Democrats nominated Stephen Douglas as their presidential candidate, and the Southern Democrats, who held their own convention a few days later, nominated John C. Breckinridge as their presidential candidate. Meanwhile the Republican Party held their convention in Chicago in May and nominated Abraham Lincoln as their candidate. A fourth party, the Constitutional Union Party, made up of former members of the American Party and the Whig Party, complicated the election even more by nominating John Bell as their candidate.[15]

This election was one of the most intense moments in U.S. history up to that point. Aware that the fate of the Union hung in the balance during the 1860 presidential election, Espy, for example, lamented the "deplorable state" of the country because of the "depredations committed by the Abolitionists" and ardently hoped that the "union loving" Breckinridge would win the election rather than the "black republican," Lincoln. On Election Day, she recorded in her diary, "today the fate of this nation is to be decided by the election of a President." Knowing that she had no power to directly influence the election, she turned to her faith and prayed, "May he who will rule for the general good, be the one chosen, and may peace again bear rule in this glorious land."[16]

When Election Day arrived and the votes were counted, Abraham Lincoln won without a single electoral vote from the South. His name was not even on the ballot in most Southern states. News of Lincoln's election produced outrage throughout the South and caused some women to express a sentiment of unity in favor of immediate secession that did not exist in Alabama or other Southern states. When Espy received word of the outcome of the election, for example, she automatically assumed that the Southern states would withdraw from the Union. She noted that the newspapers were "filled with the [secession] of the South" because "the aggressions of the North can be borne no longer." Upon hearing the same tidings, Margaret Gillis wrote in her diary, "All the Southern states are called on to act together and we are listening for the call, 'to arms' every day." Rhodes likewise adamantly proclaimed that "every true Southerner is for resistance. We feel that we can never never submit to the reign of so great an enemy to our institutions [slavery]. S.C. will secede. Tis hoped that the whole South will be united in this vital matter." The language used indicated an implicit understanding of honor, which was a key factor not only in their support for secession but in the way they viewed themselves and their duty.[17]

Excitement filled the air as women wrote about political meetings held to decide on a course of action for their state. Upon hearing about a mass meeting in

Dublin, Alabama, in November 1860, Espy exclaimed that there was "no doubt that Alabama will withdraw from the Union." After Rhodes's husband, Chauncey, and brother, John, attended a meeting held in Clanton to discuss secession, she likewise noted that "all are more or less excited on the subject of disunion." John was subsequently elected to the state secession convention that met in January 1861, and he supported immediate secession from the Union.[18]

News of South Carolina's secession generated excitement and enthusiasm throughout the South. By the beginning of 1861, talk of secession and Southern rights permeated women's lives and diaries. Twenty-one-year-old Carrie Hunter, who would lose two brothers during the conflict, became caught up in the excitement and enjoyed attending a party for "Southern Rights" held to ring in the new year.[19] By January 7, 1861, when the secession convention convened in Montgomery, Alabama, tensions around the state remained high as the delegates debated the future of the state. News soon reached them that Mississippi and Florida had seceded from the Union. On January 11, Alabama likewise declared independence from the Union and invited the seceded states to hold a convention in Montgomery to determine whether they should unite to form their own country. When this news was announced, many women felt that it was none too soon. Rhodes, for example, "rejoiced to know that we are no longer part of the Union which would make us slaves."[20]

By the beginning of February 1861, the seven Deep South states had declared their independence from the Union. On February 4, 1861, delegates from six of these states met in Montgomery to create the Confederate States of America. Montgomery, which was a relatively young city of almost nine thousand inhabitants, bustled with excitement and energy. Alexander Stephens, the Georgia delegate who would subsequently be elected vice president of the Confederacy, drew up a constitution that was modeled after the U.S. Constitution but that elevated states' rights and enshrined slavery.[21] Jefferson Davis, who had remained at home near Vicksburg, Mississippi, was elected as president of the Confederacy. Several women described these events. After Davis's inauguration, on February 18, 1861, Margaret Gillis wrote that the event marked "quite an era in the history of the Southern Republic." She added that it was "thought there was over ten thousand people there" and a "grand time that was for Montgomery."[22] Elodie Todd Dawson, the half sister of Mary Todd Lincoln, was in Selma visiting her sister Martha Todd White, and both Martha and Elodie attended the festivities surrounding Davis's inauguration. During this period Elodie attracted a lot of male attention and met her future husband, Nathaniel Henry Rhodes Dawson, who fell in love with her at the inaugural ball. As she was preparing to return home to Kentucky, Nathaniel proposed and she accepted. She remained in Selma during the war and corresponded regularly with Nathaniel.[23]

Americans North and South watched anxiously as events unfolded before them. James Buchanan, the lame-duck president of the United States, sent mixed messages to the Confederacy. He openly denied the right to secession but handed over almost every major federal military installation in the South to the Confederacy. By the time of Lincoln's inauguration as U.S. president in March 1861, Fort Sumter, in Charleston, South Carolina, remained one of the last federally controlled forts in the South. Southerners anxiously awaited word of what Lincoln would do. Many expected him to "coerce" the seceding states back into the Union. Like many others, Rhodes placed upon Lincoln, who had "been ever hostile to our dearest institution," the decision to either "command peace or bring war and pestilence upon our once happy people."[24]

Many women had negative things to say about Lincoln and blamed him for what was taking place. Elodie Todd Dawson, who cast her lot with the Confederacy, blamed the present state of affairs on her brother-in-law. She personally attacked his manliness as she wrote, "I do not think of peace and know well Mr Lincoln is not man enough to dare to make it." She judged him to be nothing "but a tool in the hands of his Party" who "would not brave their wrath by such a proposition." He could "redeem himself if he had the courage," but he was "no more fitted for the office than many others who have recently occupied it." The South, according to her, could situate its present trouble from the date when the country allowed the Republican Party to elect a president without regard for his "ability or capacity for it."[25]

When Lincoln decided to resupply Fort Sumter, he forced the Confederacy to fire the first shots of the Civil War. After a thirty-four-hour bombardment, in which over 40,000 shells landed on the fort, Maj. Robert Anderson surrendered the garrison. On April 15, 1861, Lincoln called for 75,000 volunteers to serve for ninety days to preserve the Union.[26] Alabamian women greeted this news with mixed emotions. Even though they had firmly supported secession, they did not desire war. Rhodes, for example, expressed reservations about the outbreak of a war. Dawson likewise hoped that she would receive news that peace was "spreading over the land" as late as July 1861.[27] Schoolgirl Sarah Davis matter-of-factly recorded in her diary on April 15, "And war has commenced. I have heard nothing but war talk for the last week."[28]

Alabamian women anxiously awaited the decision of the eight slave states still in the Union and were thrilled by the news of Virginia's subsequent secession. They felt as though Virginia held physical and symbolic strength because of its historical significance, and many believed it would encourage the rest of the Upper South to follow. When Rhodes heard of Virginia's decision to secede, she exclaimed, "Of course every Southern State will come out with their sister states in the struggle for independence," and turning to her religious beliefs she prayed, "God grant they be victorious."[29] M. E. Thompson, another Southern mother, whose two sons would serve in the Confederate army, likewise wished that all Southern states had the spirit of South Carolina but was concerned that they did not. As she worried, she turned to her faith for assurance and wrote, "I trust an overarching Providence is guiding us."[30]

After the second wave of secession, the border states became a matter of discussion for women. Kentucky, in particular, received notable attention. Many women felt betrayed by the state for its lack of support for the Confederacy. The state's leaders agonized over what to do in the secession crisis and ultimately proclaimed an armed neutrality that lasted until September 1861, when Confederate troops entered the state and pushed Kentucky to remain in the Union. Thompson wrote about Kentucky and the state's inability to remain neutral, noting that she wished that all the Southern states would take up the cause of the Confederacy.[31] Espy lamented that Kentucky had decided to stay in the Union while Dawson noted that people around her believed that Maryland would "soon throw off its chains."[32]

Dawson, who firmly identified herself as a Kentuckian, wrote avidly about the commonwealth's fate. Although she heard no "good news from Kentucky," her faith was "not shaken" and she still hoped Kentucky would join the Confederacy. She was proud that many were "leaving the state to join Companies of others and endeavoring to do what they can, perhaps those remaining will surprise us by doing the same."[33] Throughout the summer, she continued to hope that Kentucky would secede and join the Confederacy, but by September she began to doubt that Kentucky would "act nobly" and join the Confederacy. When news finally reached her that Kentucky would remain in the Union, she exclaimed, "Kentucky with all thy faults I love thee still," but she could not hide her anguish.[34] In a letter to her future husband, she wrote, "You cannot imagine how distressed I was to hear such *terrible* and *disgraceful* news from my birthplace. I had expected better and I almost made myself sick *crying* and bemoaning the fallen condition of my state. I am sorry to have lived to see the day when proud noble old Ky should act in this manner." She was worried about her family living in the state and noted that she could not "hear one word to relieve my anxiety." She lamented, "I cannot imagine now when I shall ever hear or see any of them again." She was proud of some of her family members, such as her youngest brother, Ellick, was doing his "duty" and preparing to defend his rights "or sell his life in the attempt."[35]

～

Throughout their writing, women revealed that they understood the ideological foundation for both secession and the creation of the Confederacy. Honor, slavery, duty, and religion all became wrapped up in Alabamian women's sense of identity with the Confederacy as the new nation was born. The creation of the Confederacy necessitated an expression of its ideological foundation. Southern nationalism became based on a defense of slavery and the intertwined belief that the Confederacy was the true heir of the American Revolution and held the blessing of God. As historian Wayne Flynt has noted, once secession was accomplished, "it was only reasonable" for Alabamians to "help construct a theological foundation for southern nationalism. Confederate nationalism drew almost equally on three intellectual traditions: evangelical Christianity, republican traditions of states' rights, and individualism."[36] Thus many believed that it could not be defeated.[37]

Many women knew that slavery lay at the heart of secession, and although they discussed slavery infrequently, when they did, they made it clear where they stood on the issue.[38] Support for the institution of slavery did not directly correlate to the number of slaves owned. Rhodes, who so adamantly defended "our dearest institution," for example, grew up in a family with multiple slaves, but her husband owned only one slave. South Carolina–born Zillah Brandon of Gaylesville, a mill-owner's wife who owned four slaves, minced no words in her assessment of the causes of secession and the impending war. "The controversy between North and South has been going on for forty years," she wrote. They "never did" and "never can agree" over the issue of slavery. Everything about the North and South was different in her opinion: "their soil is different their interests are conflicting their temperaments and characters are different." The divergence between the North and South stemmed from the South holding "negroes in bondage," which she believed was done "in mercy to them, for could they be freed, they are so improvident that nine tenths would perish, unless they were placed under officers, which would [make] their condition far worse than it now is." When the South could no longer accept Northern infringement on slavery, the natural and logical progression of events led to "a cry for peaceable secession." The North, and particularly "Lincoln, the black republican president," refused to allow Southern states to leave the Union peacefully. As far as she was concerned, if the Confederacy failed, "the last hope for freedom fails."[39] Thompson, who owned two slaves, likewise believed that "it is perfectly evident that the North has for a long time designed to get the Washington government under their control" and when they lost control of the South after secession "they have become furious." Now, she added, "we must defend ourselves or become a thousand times worse slaves than our negroes."[40] Knowing the horrors of slavery made the threat of being enslaved a compelling argument for secession and fighting a war for the survival of the Confederacy.

Many women also stressed the central role of religion in political thought. Throughout her diary, Brandon referred to the Confederacy as a new Israel and believed that its people, "with their chaste glory," would reflect a "brilliance upon them that will ennoble their national name." She was convinced that if the South were to come out of the conflict victorious, it needed to be "consistent in religion." Southerners must constantly "pay our vows to the most High by giving all diligence to make our calling and election sure" and cultivate "those holy principles universally taught by the gospel." She stated that although Southerners were well educated in both political theory and practice, "in God alone we put our trust and humbly pray that He will speak to the north and it will hear." Then she added, "except the Lord of Hosts had left unto us a very small remnant we should have been as Sodom and we should have been like unto Gomorah." <u>The South was being purged by God to create a holier nation.</u> "This war will regenerate the south," she wrote, "and will inspire it from recollections of the past with energy and caution shall guide their steps aright and it will have through coming time a prevailing influence upon nations yet unborn." If the Confederacy sought the divine blessing of God, they would surely succeed. Placing her full trust in God, she turned to Him for comfort and reassurance. She directly petitioned God, "Speak thou the word O Christ our king; and our Confederacy will be unchained, the blockades shattered, and the enemy's army dispersed."[41]

The ideological foundation of the Confederacy encompassed more than slavery and religion. It likewise relied heavily upon the ideas of the American Revolution. In 1862, for example, the Scottish-born Mobilian Kate Cumming wrote, "I am no politician" and admitted that she "must own to ignorance in regard to federal or state rights" but nonetheless asserted, "I think I have a faint idea of the meaning of the word 'union.'. . . according to Webster and other authorities, it is the concord, agreement, and conjunction of mind." Comparing the union to a marriage, she noted that "we all know how little . . . happiness exists in a forced union of man and wife, where there is neither love nor congeniality of feeling." She wondered if the North was "so blind as to think, even if they [succeed], that it can ever bring happiness to them or us? Is it not exactly the same as the case of the marriage state?" If a forced reunion of the North and South occurred, she believed that "they must strike out the word union, and have in its stead monarchy or anarchy; one of these, perhaps, would be better." Cumming further reflected, "grant that we had no lawful right to secede; that I know nothing about, and never was more grieved than when I knew that we had done so . . . [because] united, we were stronger than we would be when separated; and I also feared the bloodshed which might ensue." Yet "if we were sinners" in seceding from the Union, she continued, "what were our forefathers when they claimed the right to secede from the British crown?"[42] In comparing the secession of the Southern states to the thirteen colonies declaring their independence from England in 1776, she claimed historical precedent and authority for the actions taken by the Confederacy.

The outbreak of the war in April 1861 meant that women's rhetorical patriotism would be put to the test. After Fort Sumter women were eager to demonstrate their willingness to bear their Christian burdens without complaint and desire to exhibit their patriotism and loyalty to the new Confederacy. They offered their services to help provide for the soldiers, and many sacrificed their most precious possessions, their male relatives. Indeed, the course of the war would call upon women to live up to their ideal image of the republican mother willing to sacrifice everything for her country.[43]

As various historians have argued, as the early republic developed a political role was created for women that simultaneously elevated them and barred them from active political participation. That role, according to Linda Kerber, "made use of the classic formulation of the Spartan Mother," whose primary responsibility was to raise sons who would be prepared to sacrifice themselves for the good of the polis. As time progressed from the American Revolution through the days of the early republic, women were supposed to play the vital political role of raising sons who would be willing to serve their country. This ideal image appeared in 1861 in various ways ranging from the pulpit to published material.[44] Historian Elizabeth Varon argues that Confederate propagandists, both male and female, stressed the idea that women were somehow "purer patriots than men," as it was not only their duty but their "desire to assume the role of 'Spartan mothers,' accepting the loss of their men in defence of states' rights."[45]

Spartan motherhood did not keep women from worrying about their loved ones as they departed, however. Although they supported secession, many realized that when their loved ones left they could not "expect to see them all again."[46] Espy concluded that she would "have to submit" to the departure of her son Columbus because she knew he was needed by the Confederacy. Less than two years later he was killed.[47] Although they worried about the well-being of their male relatives, women nonetheless encouraged them to join the Confederate army. Hunter, for example, wrote to her brother, "Your home and country may need your aid and protection ere long" even though it was "very sad to think of."[48] Indeed, some were not above pressuring their male relatives and other men into the service of the Confederacy. Thompson wrote to her son that if he desired to win the heart of an attractive girl, he must be a good and faithful soldier because no honorable woman would consider a man who had not proved his devotion to his country. She added that the young men who remained at home were ashamed to even go out in public because they were not doing their duty to the country. Dawson likewise wrote to her fiancé that she never would have considered loving him if he had shirked his duty to his country.[49] Thus in some ways the image of womanhood was used to promote Confederate enlistment.

As the soldiers enlisted and prepared to depart, women continued to encourage and support them by organizing huge parties and elaborate banner presentation ceremonies to send them off to fight the Northerners. Historians William Garrett Piston and Richard W. Hatcher III maintain that one cannot exaggerate the importance of these ceremonies, as they cemented community and company ties. In essence, those presenting the flag promised to care for the families of those leaving, while those departing pledged to uphold the honor of the presenters and the community. In addition, "if the men left their communities to protect their homes, as many of them insisted they did, they brought something of their homes with them into battle. The flag was the physical tie between the homelife they had left and fought for and the war into which they were plunged."[50] This was certainly true for Alabamians.

Presenting men with tokens that they could carry into battle also helped women develop their identity within the Confederacy and its struggle for independence because even though women could not take up arms and fight for the Confederacy, they could take part in the process of sending off their soldiers. Although George Rable has argued that "flag-presentation ceremonies . . . highlighted the contrast between the passive patriotism of women and the active patriotism of men" because women were "supposed to keep quiet on such occasions" and "remain anonymous," this did not prove to be the case for Alabamian women.[51] Indeed, several of the women examined here actively participated in presentation ceremonies and other patriotic events. In doing so, they viewed themselves as being every bit as active and patriotic as their male counterparts. Writing of the departure of two different groups of soldiers, one of which included her two brothers, Hunter expressed the mixture of grief and excitement that accompanied such events. When the soldiers left town carrying their flag, which had been presented amid a host of "fine speeches," Hunter lamented that it was "a strange sad day" and "left many a sad heart in Tuskegee tonight." Although she firmly believed that the soldiers had "enlisted in a noble cause" and had "gone off to fight the fanatical horde that would crush us," she struggled to suppress her fears and turned to her faith for comfort. "God grant that they may be successful," she prayed, adding, "May the Almighty Father watch over and protect them from dangers and death."[52]

Hunter recorded in great detail the preparations for the presentation of a banner she would be presenting. She wrote that she was worried that something would go amiss and became caught up in the process, viewing it as an "all important occasion" in which she would make her "debut in public." At the same time her desires were not simply self-centered. She realized the responsibility placed upon her by the community and wanted to "meet the expectations of my friends," which she successfully accomplished. The day after the presentation she related in her diary her relief that "nothing at all terrible happened to me yesterday as I fully expected it would and I hear nothing but the congratulations of my friends upon having acquitted myself credible on the all important occasion of the presentation. I was not so much discomposed as I expected to be. My horse behaved him self admirably and everything went off well."[53]

Sarah Davis likewise wrote about banner presentation ceremonies. After she attended one in Huntsville at the end of March she wrote, "I think that the banners presented were beautiful and very appropriate," she wrote. But at the same time she was concerned that the preoccupation with the "celebrations" and banner presentations would prevent the girls at her school from studying. At the suggestion of the headmaster of her school, the students presented another banner to the Home Guards.[54] She witnessed an address given to the local Rifle Company that was about to leave to protect the state against an "attack made by the Republicans." She admitted that "it was very touching to see so many young and gallant men preparing to go to war where it is probable they will never return." But, she quickly added, "I hope that will not be the case."[55] Espy also wrote about the departure of volunteers, noting that "a large assemblage of people were there to take leave of them; the scene was most impressive."[56]

In addition to banner presentations and send-off parties, women supported the troops by organizing elaborate soldiers' aid societies, which many saw as an extension of their antebellum charitable practices. They sewed and knit items for the soldiers, made cloth, and coordinated the shipment of goods into the field. By the end of 1861 there were over one thousand aid societies in the Confederacy. The state of Alabama alone had ninety-one registered with the governor's office.[57]

While men sometimes put out calls for women to form these aid societies, women themselves were usually responsible for creating and leading them. Women often took out advertisements in local newspapers announcing the formation of an aid society, called upon women to join, and petitioned others to support their efforts by donating supplies or money. Once they met, women elected leaders, delegated tasks, and scheduled future meetings. Aid societies often attracted large groups; at times as many as fifty women would gather at the local courthouse or church to sew and knit items for soldiers. Many women felt that they were merely continuing their traditional work, but their conception of family expanded from their immediate biological family members to include the broader Confederate nation. Many women believed that it was part of their duty—and in many ways an extension of their religious beliefs as well as an expression of their patriotism—to assist in the war effort in that manner. As Hunter wrote on October 31, 1861, it is "our duty to do everything in our power to make the soldiers life a pleasant one." In actively participating in the Confederacy by providing material assistance to soldiers, women demonstrated an even greater loyalty to the Confederacy.[58] As Thompson wrote to her son in the Confederate army, "The ladies cannot go [fight] but they will provide well for the soldiers."[59]

Overall, then, during this tumultuous period, the literate, white, Protestant women of Alabama supported secession and relied on their faith and sense of identity and duty to see them through their fears and concerns for the safety of their loved ones. The election of 1860 politicized them in a way that previous political events did not. Secession further embroiled them in politics. Although they worried about the consequences of secession and the creation of the Confederacy, many women still became caught up in the excitement of the times and ardently supported the South. As far as these women were concerned, the firing on Fort Sumter followed by Lincoln's call for volunteers sealed their country's fate and forced them into a war with the North. As they wrote about the ideological justification for their newly created country, they drew upon their beliefs in the institution of slavery, that they were God's chosen people, and that their nation was the true heir of the ideals of the American Revolution.[60] When they encouraged men to fight, organized elaborate parties to send off their soldiers laden with the banners presented to them by the women of the town, and formed aid societies designed to supply their soldiers with much-needed supplies, women's sense of identity with the Confederacy became stronger. Women came to see all of these things as part of their personal identity as the secession crisis transformed them into Confederate women. It was an identity that would survive the Confederacy itself. All of this stemmed from their belief in the South and the idea that the South could no longer bear the aggressions of the North.[61]

Notes

1. Elizabeth Rhodes Diary, December 31, 1860, Auburn University Library Special Collections and Archives (hereafter Rhodes Diary; transcripts in author's possession, originals located at the Shorter Museum and Mansion, Eufaula, AL). Carrie Hunter, a Tuskegee diarist in her early twenties who became an ardent Confederate, likewise worried about "the dark cloud that is hovering over us." Carrie Hunter, Tuskegee, to James H. Hunter, New Orleans, January 3, 1861, Cobb and Hunter Family Papers #1745, Southern Historical Collection, Wilson Library, University of North Carolina at Chapel Hill (hereafter SHC-UNC). Hunter was the daughter of a prosperous physician who owned ten slaves in 1860. Both of her two brothers lost their lives while serving in the Confederate army. See 1860 U.S. Census, Tuskegee, Macon, Alabama, found in www.ancestry.com (accessed December 1, 2008); 1860 U.S. Census, Southern Division, Macon, Alabama, Slave Schedule, found at www.ancestry.com (accessed December 2, 2008).

2. Rhodes Diary, November 21, 1860; Zillah Haynie Brandon Diary (hereafter Brandon Diary), October 14, 1860, December 3, 1860, June 7, 1862, January 9, 1863, SPR262, Alabama Department of Archives and History, Montgomery (hereafter ADAH); Margaret Josephine Miles Gillis Diary, February 11, 1861, November 23, 1861, SPR5, ADAH (hereafter Gillis Diary); Sarah Rodgers Rousseau Espy Diary, March 18, 1860, April 3, 1861, June 17, 1861, July 4, 1861, October 11, 1861, May 8, 1862, SPR2, ADAH (hereafter Espy Diary); Sarah Lowe Davis Diary, February 25, 1861, SPR113, ADAH (hereafter Davis Diary); Juliana Dorsey to Lollie, Greensboro, June 2, 1864, Ruffin and Meade Family Papers #642, SHC-UNC; Octavia Wyche Otey Diary, September 25, 27, 28, 1864, October 2, 5, 1864, February 8, 28, 1865, June 3, 1865, Wyche and Otey Family Papers #1608, SHC-UNC (hereafter Otey Diary); Annie Strudwick Diary, January 25, 1862, February 3, 4, 8, 1862, March 6, 10, 24, 25, 1862, May 24, 1862, June 1, 2, 1862, September 8, 11, 1862, October 16, 1862, Annie Strudwick Diary and Letter #1838, SHC-UNC (hereafter Strudwick Diary); Elodie to Dawson, Selma, October 20, 1861, Nathaniel Henry Rhodes Dawson Papers, 1851–1915, #210, SHC-UNC (hereafter Dawson Papers); Carrie Hunter Diary,

October 22, 1861, November 23, 1862, Cobb and Hunter Family Papers #1745, SHC-UNC (hereafter Hunter Diary); M. E. Thompson to Joe Thompson, Marion, December 22, 1861, Benson-Thompson Family Papers, Rare Book, Manuscripts and Special Collections, Nicholas Perkins Library, Duke University (hereafter Benson-Thompson Family Papers). See also Rebecca Vasser Diary, January 7, 1857, Rebecca Vasser Diary, Rare Book, Manuscripts and Special Collections, Nicholas Perkins Library, Duke University (hereafter Vasser Diary); *Montgomery Daily Advertiser*, April 16, 1864; Kate Cumming Diary, April 18, 1862, Kate Cumming, *A Journal of Hospital Life in the Confederate Army of Tennessee from the Battle of Shiloh to the End of the War with Sketches of Life and Character, and Brief Notices of Current Events During that Period* (Louisville: John P. Morton, 1866). There are multiple versions of Kate Cumming's diary. The title given here was the earliest published version. In this chapter the more scholarly edition of her diary will be used. The citation will still include the date of Cumming's diary entries but will include the page numbers on which the entries can be found as well. See Kate Cumming, *Kate: The Journal of a Confederate Nurse*, ed. Richard Barksdale Harwell (Baton Rouge: Louisiana State University Press, 1998), 20. The subject of women's religious beliefs has for many years been relegated to relative unimportance among scholars. Even though attempts to explore the era's social aspects have offered insight into the war, religion still fell by the wayside, as the authors of the groundbreaking *Religion and the American Civil War* pointed out in 1998. Recently historians have begun to focus more on religion and its importance in not only the outbreak of the Civil War but the daily lives of those who lived through it. Yet, overall, more than thirty years after historians have worked to incorporate women into an analysis of the past, it "is still difficult to 'find' women in many books and articles about American religious history," as Catherine Brekus has noted. See Catherine A. Brekus, ed., introduction to *The Religious History of American Women: Reimagining the Past* (Chapel Hill: University of North Carolina Press, 2007), 1; Randall M. Miller, Harry S. Stout, and Charles Reagan Wilson, eds., *Religion and the American Civil War* (New York: Oxford University Press, 1998), 3–18; Edwin S. Gaustad, *Religion in America: History and Historiography* (Washington, DC, 260 AHA Pamphlets, American Historical Association, 1966), 58–59; Harry S. Stout and Christopher Grasso, "Civil War, Religion, and Communications: The Case of Richmond," in *Religion and the American Civil War*, ed. Miller, Stout, and Wilson, 313–59, 313; Eugene D. Genovese, *Consuming Fire: The Fall of the Confederacy in the Mind of the White Christian South* (Athens: University of Georgia Press, 1998); and Mitchell Snay, *Gospel of Disunion: Religious Separatism in the Antebellum South* (Cambridge: Cambridge University Press, 1993). Historians such as Drew Gilpin Faust and George Rable include discussions of women's religious beliefs in their studies of Confederate women. See Drew Gilpin Faust, *Mothers of Invention: Women of the Slaveholding South in the American Civil War* (Chapel Hill: University of North Carolina Press, 1996) and George Rable, *Civil Wars: Women and the Crisis of Southern Nationalism* (Urbana: University of Illinois Press, 1989).

3. Margaret Storey argues that Alabama's Unionists remained loyal to the Union for a variety of reasons, including economics, family ties, conceptions of Southern honor and Southern values. Storey points out that individuals remained Unionists not just out of opposition to the Confederacy but "also out of a deep desire to cleave to something, to consolidate and preserve what they valued in their families, neighborhoods, section, and nation." She further notes that "When these men and women gave their allegiance to the Union in 1860–61, they frequently did so as a matter of obligation. To honor and protect, and not betray, a host of social ties was crucial to their understanding of themselves and their role in their communities." See Margaret M. Storey, *Loyalty and Loss: Alabama's Unionists in the Civil War and Reconstruction* (Baton Rouge: Louisiana State University Press, 2004), 1–17, quotes in note on pp. 4, 5, and Storey, "Civil War

Unionists and the Political Culture of Loyalty in Alabama, 1860–1861," *Journal of Southern History* 69, no. 1 (February 2003): 71–106. See also Daniel W. Crofts, *Reluctant Confederates: Upper South Unionists in the Secession Crisis* (Chapel Hill: University of North Carolina Press, 1989).

4. Drew Gilpin Faust, *The Creation of Confederate Nationalism: Ideology and Identity in the Civil War South* (Baton Rouge: Louisiana State University Press, 1988),

5. M. E. Thompson to her Joe Thompson, Marion, August 30, 1861, Benson-Thompson Family Papers; Rable, *Civil Wars*, 47.

6. Storey, *Loyalty and Loss*, 19. Historians have taken a variety of approaches to understand the events leading up to secession. See William Barney, *The Road to Secession: A New Perspective on the Old South* (New York: Praeger, 1972); Anthony Gene Carey, *Parties, Slavery, and the Union in Antebellum Georgia* (Athens: University of Georgia Press, 1997); Steven A. Channing, *Crisis of Fear: Secession in South Carolina* (New York: Simon and Schuster, 1970); William J. Cooper Jr., *The South and the Politics of Slavery, 1828–1856* (Baton Rouge: Louisiana State University Press, 1978); Eric Foner, *Free Soil, Free Labor, Free Men: The Ideology of the Republican Party before the Civil War* (New York: Oxford University Press, 1970); William W. Freehling, *The Road to Disunion* (New York: Oxford University Press, 1990); William E. Gienapp, *The Origins of the Republican Party, 1852–1856* (New York: Oxford University Press, 1986); William A. Link, *Roots of Secession: Slavery and Politics in Antebellum Virginia* (Chapel Hill: University of North Carolina Press, 2003); Snay, *Gospel of Disunion*; J. Mills Thornton, *Politics and Power in a Slave Society: Alabama, 1800–1860* (Baton Rouge: Louisiana State University Press, 1981); Elizabeth Varon, *We Mean to Be Counted: White Women and Politics in Antebellum Virginia* (Chapel Hill: University of North Carolina Press, 1998); Clarence Phillips Denman, *The Secession Movement in Alabama* (Montgomery: Alabama Department of Archives and History, 1933); Bertram Wyatt-Brown, *Southern Honor: Ethics and Behavior in the Old South* (New York: Oxford University Press, 1982); Wyatt-Brown, *Yankee Saints and Southern Sinners* (Baton Rouge: Louisiana State University Press, 1985); Wyatt-Brown, *Honor and Violence in the Old South* (New York: Oxford University Press, 1986); Wyatt-Brown, *The Shaping of Southern Culture: Honor, Grace, and War, 1760s–1880s* (Chapel Hill: University of North Carolina Press, 2001).

7. Lizzie to Anna Mercur, December 17, 1860, Anna Mercur Papers #751-z, SHC-UNC (hereafter Mercur Papers); Rable, *Civil Wars*, 49; Vasser Diary, November 25, 1856, January 3, 26, 31, 1857, June 11, 1862, September 1, 3, 14, 1862; Elodie to Dawson, Selma, July 7, 1861, April 1, 1862, and Elodie to Dawson, Marengo, August 19, 1861, Dawson Papers; Strudwick Diary, May 27, 1861, September 15, 1861, August 19, 1861, January 13, 1862, March 16, 1862, May 2, 1862; Brandon Diary, December 21, 1860, January 8, 1861, February 1, 1861; Hunter Diary, March 9, 18, 1861, November 20, 1861, January 23, 1862, May 8, 1862, June 30, 1862; Rhodes Diary, November 21, 1860; Gillis Diary, December 31, 1860, July 14, 1861, February 12, 1864; M. E. Thompson to Joe Thompson, Marion, December 22, 1861, and M. E. Thompson to her son, Marion, February 9, 1861, Benson-Thompson Family Papers; Mary Waring Diary, July 26, 31, 1863, August 4, 11, 1863, SPR30, ADAH; Davis Diary, February 13, 1861; *South Western Baptist*, ed. H. E. Taliaferro, Tuskegee, Alabama, January 31, 1861–January 1862, July 25, 1861, August 22, 1861, June 26, 1862, July 3, 1862, December 11, 1862, February 5, 1863, May 26, 1864, Microfilm at Auburn University Library; *Montgomery Daily Mail*, February 11, 1861, October 14, 1862; Elizabeth Fox-Genovese, *Within the Plantation Household: Black and White Women of the Old South* (Chapel Hill: University of North Carolina Press, 1988), 17, 373; Faust, *Mothers of Invention*, 188–92; Emory M. Thomas, *The Confederate Nation: 1861–1865* (New York: Harper and Row, 1979), 22; Sally G. McMillen, *Motherhood in the Old South: Pregnancy, Childbirth, and Infant Rearing* (Baton Rouge: Louisiana State University Press, 1990), 78, 172, 186; Rable, *Civil Wars*, 69; Catherine Clinton, *The Plantation*

Mistress: Woman's World in the Old South (New York: Pantheon Books, 1982), 109, 137, 152–54, 204; Jane Turner Censer, *The Reconstruction of White Southern Womanhood, 1865–1869* (Baton Rouge: LSU Press, 2003), 11–23; Ellen M. Plante, *Women at Home in Victorian America: A Social History* (New York: Facts on File, 1997), 4; Wyatt-Brown, *Shaping of Southern Culture*; Kristina K. Groover, *The Wilderness Within: American Women Writers and Spiritual Quest* (Fayetteville: University of Arkansas Press, 1999), 5; Nancy Chodorow, "Family Structure and Feminine Personality," in *Women, Culture, and Society*, ed. Michelle Zimbalist Rosaldo and Louise Lamphere (Stanford: Stanford University Press, 1974), 43–44; Angela Boswell, *Her Act and Deed: Women's Lives in a Rural Southern County, 1837–1873* (College Station: Texas A&M University Press, 2001), 3; Barbara Welter, *Dimity Convictions: The American Woman in the Nineteenth Century* (Athens: Ohio University Press, 1976), 4; Linda Kerber, "The Republican Mother: Women and the Enlightenment—An American Perspective," *American Quarterly* 28 (Special Issue: An American Enlightenment, 1976): 188, 202; Kerber, "The Limits of Politicization: American Women and the American Revolution," in *The American and European Revolutions, 1776–1848: Sociopolitical and Ideological Aspects*, ed. Jaroslaw Pelenski (Iowa City: University of Iowa Press, 1980), 54–74, 56, 72; Catherine Kerrison, *Claiming the Pen: Women and Intellectual Life in the Early American South* (Ithaca: Cornell University Press, 2006), 11.

8. LeeAnn Whites, *The Civil War as a Crisis in Gender: Augusta, Georgia, 1860–1890* (Athens: University of Georgia Press, 1995); Faust, *Mothers of Invention*, 10; Rable, *Civil Wars*, 2; M. E. Thompson to her son, Marion, January 2, 1861, Benson-Thompson Family Papers; Cumming Diary, May 9, 1862, Cumming, *A Journal of Hospital Life*, 33–34; Faust, *The Creation of Confederate Nationalism*, 21, 84.

9. Davis Diary, April 1–2, 13–25, 1862, September 7, 1862; Vasser Diary, September 24, 1856, June 8, 1862, January 1, 1857, September 3, 1862; Gillis Diary, May 28, 1861, October 1, 1861; Michel Foucault, *The Archaeology of Knowledge: And the Discourse on Language*, trans A. M. Sheridan Smith (New York: Pantheon Books, 1972), 48–49, 107–11, 119–20, 182–84, 216; Joyce Appleby, Lynn Hunt, and Margaret Jacob, *Telling the Truth about History* (New York: Norton, 1994), 214–15; Wyatt-Brown, *Shaping of Southern Culture*, 31–55; Faust, *Mothers of Invention*, 161–66; Hunter Diary, January 7, 1861, February 3, 5, 1862, May 28, 1862, September 28, 1862; Elodie to Dawson, Selma, May 15, 1861, June 16, 1861, August 4, 1861, Dawson Papers; Espy Diary, February 9, 1860; M. E. Thompson to her son, Marion, July 7, 1861, M. E. Thompson to her son Dock, Marion, August 23, 1861, and M. E. Thompson to her son, Marion, September 2, 1861, all in Benson-Thompson Family Papers; Faust, *Mothers of Invention*, 162–64; Fox-Genovese, *Within the Plantation Household*, 346; Clinton, *Plantation Mistress*, 162–63. A few women such as Zillah Brandon and Mary Chestnut did write for posterity. Brandon Diary, August 21, 1861, June 7, 1862. Mary Chestnut, *Mary Chestnut's Civil War*, ed. C. Vann Woodward (New Haven: Yale University Press, 1981) is an example of a diary written and edited for public consumption.

10. See the 1850 and 1860 U.S. Census records found at www.ancestory.com (accessed December 1, 2008). See also Ann Douglas, *The Feminization of American Culture* (New York: Knopf, 1977), 8; Welter, *Dimity Convictions*, 21; and Brandon Diary, January 1, 1861.

11. Lizzie to Anna Mercur, Eufaula, Alabama, December 17, 1860, Mercur Papers. I looked at every wartime diary written by Alabamian women that I could locate and supplemented that research with personal letters, public writing (such as newspapers and advice manuals), and state and church documents. I photographed each document then carefully read, took notes on, and transcribed them. Almost all of the diaries were in bound books. Some were nothing more than notes written in plantation ledgers. None of the diarists was completely consistent in her writing. It seems as though women wrote when they had the chance to do so; sometimes this was

once a day; in other cases weeks and even months lapsed between diary entries. This study will, I hope, provide a model for further study. Looking at the writings of Alabamian women has inherent problems, the most obvious of which is that it limits the findings of this research to literate women, all of whom happened to be Protestant. Despite the shortcomings of this study, it does provide insight into the ways in which one subset of Alabamian women dealt with death and the Civil War.

12. Rable, *Civil Wars*, 39–42; Varon, *We Mean to Be Counted*, 4.

13. Espy Diary, November 26, 1859, December 2, 1859, January 10, 1860, August 31, 1860.

14. Espy Diary, April 27, 1860, July 4–5, 1860; Whites, *The Civil War as a Crisis in Gender*, 3–10, 53, 90.

15. William Warren Rodgers Jr., *Confederate Home Front: Montgomery during the Civil War* (Tuscaloosa: University of Alabama Press, 1999), 12–18; Don E. Fehrenbacher, *The Dred Scott Case: Its Significance in American Law and Politics* (New York: Oxford University Press, 1978).

16. Espy Diary, April 27, 1860, July 4–5, 1860, August 11, 1860, November 6, 7, 1860.

17. Espy Diary, November 14, 25, 27, 1860, December 1, 15, 1860, March 1, 1861; Gillis Diary, November 15, 1860; Denman, *The Secession Movement in Alabama*, 87; Rhodes Diary, November 6, 1860, December 18, 1860; Faust, *Mothers of Invention*, 7, 32; Genovese, *Consuming Fire*, 3, 45; Wyatt-Brown, *Honor and Violence in the Old South*; Wyatt-Brown, *Southern Honor*; Wyatt-Brown, *Shaping of Southern Culture*; Kenneth Greenberg, *Honor and Slavery: Lies, Duels, Noses, Masks, Dressing as a Woman, Gifts, Strangers, Humanitarianism, Death, Slave Rebellions, the Proslavery Argument, Baseball, Hunting, and Gambling in the Old South* (Princeton: Princeton University Press, 1996).

18. Espy Diary, November 27, 1860, December 1, 15, 1860, March 1, 1861; *Southwest Baptist*, January 31, 1861. Rhodes's family also supported secession. She had at least two male relatives (her brother and another relative) who were elected to what she called "secession conventions." Rhodes Diary, November 11, 19, 23, 1860, December 20, 1860. In the official records of the delegates from Barbour County to the secession convention that met in January 1861, J. S. M. Daniel was listed as a delegate. See William R. Smith, *The History of the Convention of the People of Alabama, Begun and held in the City of Montgomery, on the Seventh Day of January, 1861; In which is preserved the speeches of the secret sessions, and many valuable state papers* (Montgomery: White Pfister & Co., 1861), 21. J. W. L. Daniel was listed as a separate state secessionist; he was not a cooperationist. See Denman, *The Secession Movement in Alabama*, 161. For a discussion of the secession commissioners, see Charles B. Dew, *Apostles of Disunion: Southern Secession Commissioners and the Causes of the Civil War* (Charlottesville: University of Virginia Press, 2001). See also, Faust, *Mothers of Invention*, 13–17; Rable, *Civil Wars*, 54; Lizzie to Anna Mercur, Eufaula, Alabama, August 14, 1860, Mercur Papers.

19. Carrie Hunter, Tuskegee, to James H. Hunter, New Orleans, January 3, 1861, Cobb and Hunter Family Papers #1745, SHC-UNC; Lacy K. Ford, *Origins of Southern Radicalism: The South Carolina Upcountry, 1800–1960* (New York: Oxford University Press, 1988).

20. Davis Diary, April 15, 1861, May 9, 16, 1861; Hunter Diary, April 19, 1861; Carrie Hunter to James H. Hunter, January 3, 1861; 1860 U.S. Census, Tuskegee, Macon, Alabama, www.ancestry.com (accessed December 1, 2008); 1860 U.S. Census, Southern Division, Macon, Alabama, Slave Schedule, www.ancestry.com (accessed December 2, 2008); Rhodes Diary, January 7, 11, 1861, January 9, 1861. See also Gillis Diary, January 13, 1861. Alabama seceded on January 11, 1861, by a vote of sixty-one to thirty-nine. See Rodgers, *Confederate Home Front*, 20.

21. There were 8,843 people living in Montgomery (4,341 whites and 4,502 blacks). Free blacks made up around 1 percent of the population. See Rodgers, *Confederate Home Front*, x–9,

22–23 and Denman, *The Secession Movement in Alabama*, 128–46. The dates for the secession of the Deep South states are as follows: South Carolina, December 20, 1860; Mississippi, January 9, 1861; Florida, January 10, 1861; Alabama, January 11, 1861; Georgia, January 19, 1861; Louisiana, January 26, 1861; Texas, February 1, 1861. See Rodgers, *Confederate Home Front*, 19–22; Albert N. Fitts, "The Confederate Convention: 1. The Provisional Constitution," *Alabama Review* 2, no. 2 (April 1949): 83–101; and Fitts, "The Confederate Convention: 2. The Constitutional Debate," *Alabama Review* 2, no. 3 (July 1949): 189–210.

22. Gillis Diary, February 24, 1861; Espy Diary, February 14, 1861, March 19, 1861; Rhodes Diary, March 4, 1861, April 12, 1861.

23. Martha Todd White was the tenth of fourteen Todd children. As a teenager she married Clement White, and by 1861 the couple was living in Selma, Alabama. Elodie was visiting her sister and was ready to return to Kentucky when Nathanial, who had already been married twice and had a daughter by each of his previous wives, proposed. Elodie accepted his offer and decided to stay with her sister in Selma. Throughout this essay (except in the notes) Elodie will be referred to as Dawson to avoid confusion. See Stephen Berry, *House of Abraham: Lincoln and the Todds, a Family Divided by War* (Boston: Houghton Mifflin, 2009), 57–64.

24. Gillis Diary, February 24, 1861; Espy Diary, February 14, 1861, March 19, 1861; Rhodes Diary, March 4, 1861, April 12, 1861.

25. Rhodes Diary, March 4, 1861, April 12, 1861; Elodie to Dawson, Selma, August 4, 1861, Dawson Papers.

26. Rodgers, *Confederate Home Front*, 35–37.

27. Elodie to Dawson, Selma, July 14, 1861, September 22, 1861, Dawson Papers; Faust, *Mothers of Invention*, 13.

28. Rhodes Diary, April 18, 1861; Espy Diary, April 16, 1861; Davis Diary, April 15, 1861; Varon, *We Mean to Be Counted*, 162–63.

29. Rhodes Diary, April 18, 1861.

30. M. E. Thompson to her sons, Marion, September 23, 1861, Benson-Thompson Family Papers. See also Mark S. Schantz, *Awaiting the Heavenly Country: The Civil War and America's Culture of Death* (Ithaca: Cornell University Press, 2008), 209 and Stephanie McCurry, "'The Soldier's Wife': White Women, the State, and the Politics of Protection in the Confederacy," in *Women and the Unstable State in Nineteenth-Century America*, ed. Alison M. Parker and Stephanie Cole (Arlington: Texas A&M University Press, 2000), 15–16, 22–31.

31. M. E. Thompson to her sons, Marion, September 23, 1861; Thomas, *The Confederate Nation*, 88–89, 95.

32. Espy Diary, November 1, 1862; Elodie to Dawson, Selma, September 1, 1861, Dawson Papers.

33. Elodie to Dawson, Selma, November 17, 1861, July 22, 1861, Dawson Papers.

34. Ibid., July 22, 28, 1861, Dawson Papers.

35. Ibid., August 4, 1861, September 15, 22, 1861, November 2, 23, 1861.

36. Wayne Flynt, *Alabama Baptists: Southern Baptists in the Heart of Dixie* (Tuscaloosa: University of Alabama Press, 1998), 122. See also Anne Sarah Rubin, *A Shattered Nation: The Rise and Fall of the Confederacy, 1861–1868* (Chapel Hill: University of North Carolina Press, 2005); Faust, *Mothers of Invention*; Faust, *The Creation of Confederate Nationalism*; Rable, *Civil Wars*; George Rable, *The Confederate Republic: A Revolution against Politics* (Chapel Hill: University of North Carolina Press, 1994); Victoria Ott, *Confederate Daughters: Coming of Age during the Civil War* (Carbondale: Southern Illinois University Press, 2008); and John McCardell, *The Idea of a Southern Nation: Southern Nationalists and Southern Nationalism, 1830–1860* (New York: Norton, 1979).

37. Snay, *Gospel of Disunion*, 184–88, 191–96; Faust, *The Creation of Confederate Nationalism*, 21; Genovese, *Consuming Fire*; Thomas, *The Confederate Nation*, 196, 223, 245–46; Jason Phillips, *Diehard Rebels: The Confederate Culture of Invincibility* (Athens: University of Georgia Press, 2007); Rubin, *A Shattered Nation*.

38. Rhodes Diary, February 22, 1858, April 28, 1860, November 6, 1860; Harry Philpot Owens, "A History of Eufaula, Alabama, 1832–1882" (master's thesis, Auburn University, 1963), 36; *Spirit of the South*, December 22, 1857; population schedules of the eighth census of the United States, 1860, Alabama: (slave) Autauga, Baldwin, Barbour, Bib, Blount, Butler, Calhoun, Microcopy No. M653 Roll No. 27, Auburn University Library; Genovese, *Consuming Fire*, 32; Cumming Diary, November 8, 1863, Cumming, *A Journal of Hospital Life*, 168–69; Brandon Diary, April 25, 1861.

39. Brandon Diary, April 25, 1861, August 21, 1861; 1850 U.S. Census, Seminole, Chattooga, Georgia, www.ancestry.com (accessed December 1, 2008); Otey Diary, September 19, 1864; M. E. Thompson to Joe Thompson, Marion, August 30, 1861, M. E. Thompson to her sons, Marion, January 1, 1862, September 23, 1861, all in Benson-Thompson Family Papers; Espy Diary, December 16, 1859, January 19, 1860, March 18, 1860, August 31, 1860, March 25, 1861, April 26, 1861, May 22, 1861, June 3, 12, 1861, July 11, 13, 1861, March 12, 1862; Martha M. Jones to Samuel H. Jones, Tuscaloosa County, Alabama, May 20, 1860, Martha M. Jones Papers, Rare Book, Manuscripts and Special Collections, Nicholas Perkins Library, Duke University; Lizzie to Anna Mercur, Eufaula, Alabama, December 17, 1860, Mercur Papers; Helen Swift to Anna Mercur, Eufaula, Alabama, March 16, 1861, Mercur Papers; Brandon Diary, September 30, 1860, January 8, 1861, April 25, 1861, August 21, 1861; Elodie to Dawson, Selma, September 22, 1861, December 8, 1861, Dawson Papers; Cumming Diary, October 6, 1863, November 29, 1863, Cumming, *A Journal of Hospital Life*, 146–61, 174–75.

40. M. E. Thompson to Elias Thompson, Marion, July 22, 1861, Benson-Thompson Family Papers.

41. Brandon Diary, April 25, 1861, August 21, 1861, January 11, 1862; Phillips, *Diehard Rebels*, 15, 18–19; Snay, *Gospel of Disunion*, 188.

42. Cumming Diary, May 9, 1862, Cumming, *A Journal of Hospital Life*, 33–34.

43. Drew Gilpin Faust, *This Republic of Suffering: Death and the American Civil War* (New York: Knopf, 2008), xi–xii; Strudwick Diary, June 14, 1862; Hunter Diary, May 28, 1862, October 5, 1862.

44. Kerber, "The Republican Mother," 187–205, 188; Kerber, "The Limits of Politicization," 54–74; Clinton, *Plantation Mistress*, 39–40, 162; Nancy M. Theriot, *Mothers and Daughters in Nineteenth-Century America: The Biosocial Construction of Femininity* (Lexington: University Press of Kentucky, 1996), 2; Hunter Diary, March 18, 1861.

45. Varon, *We Mean to Be Counted*, 4; Rable, *Civil Wars*, 43, 50; M. E. Thompson to her son, Marion, January 2, 1861, Benson-Thompson Family Papers.

46. Quotation from Espy Diary, August 14, 1861. See also Hunter Diary, December 3, 1861; Davis Diary, March 22, 1861, April 15, 1861; M. E. Thompson to her son, Marion, January 14, 1861, Benson-Thompson Family Papers; Espy Diary, July 28, 1861; Hunter Diary, January 7, 1861, February 4, 1864; and Helen Swift to Anna Mercur, Eufaula, Alabama, March 16, 1861, Mercur Papers.

47. Espy Diary, April 19, 1861, November 13, 16, 1861, December 6, 1861, April 6, 1863; Brandon Diary, August 21, 1861, May 29, 1864.

48. Carrie Hunter, Tuskegee, to James H. Hunter, New Orleans, January 3, 1861.

49. M. E. Thompson to her son, Marion, September 2, 1861, Benson-Thompson Family Papers; Elodie to Dawson, Selma, December 22, 1861, Dawson Papers.

50. William Garrett Piston and Richard W. Hatcher III, *Wilson's Creek: The Second Battle of the Civil War and the Men Who Fought It* (Chapel Hill: University of North Carolina Press, 2000), 66–67; Carrie Hunter to James H. Hunter, January 3, 1861. For a discussion of the mobilization of Alabamian troops during the war, see Thomas Alton Smith, "Mobilization of the Army in Alabama, 1859–1865" (master's thesis, Auburn University, 1953).

51. Rable, *Civil Wars*, 47.

52. Hunter Diary, January 7, 1861, May 1, 1861.

53. Ibid., March 11, 18, 21, 1861.

54. Davis Diary, March 25, 1861, April 15, 17, 18, 23, 25, 1861.

55. Ibid., March 22, 1861, April 23, 1861, July 28, 1861; Elodie to Dawson, Selma, July 14, 1861, Dawson Papers.

56. Espy Diary, August 14, 1861.

57. Elodie to Dawson, Selma, August 4, 1861, September 22, 1861, January 12, 1862, April 1, 15, 1862, Dawson Papers; Gillis Diary, August 11, 1861, August 9, 1863; Cumming Diary, July 11, 1862, Cumming, *A Journal of Hospital Life*, 54–55; Brandon Diary, January 1, 1863; Espy Diary, July 9, 1862; M. E. Thompson to her sons, Marion, September 23, 1861, M. E. Thompson to Joe Thompson, Marion, July 22, 1861, August 30, 1861, and M. E. Thompson to her son, Marion, July 7, 1861, all in Benson-Thompson Family Papers. For a discussion of relief efforts in Alabama during the war, see Phyllis LaRue LeGrand, "Destitution and Relief of the Indigent Soldiers' Families of Alabama during the Civil War" (master's thesis, Auburn University, 1964); Faust, *Mothers of Invention*, 24, 40–52; William W. Sweet, *The Story of Religion in America* (Harper and Row, 1930; reprint, Grand Rapids, MI: Baker Book House, 1973), 325; and Edwin C. Bridges, "Juliet Opie Hopkins and Alabama's Civil War Hospitals in Richmond, Virginia," *Alabama Review* 53 (April 2000): 83–111. The more localized aid societies of the South lacked the national organization of Northern aid societies discussed by historians Jeanie Attie and Elizabeth Leonard. Jeanie Attie, *Patriotic Toil: Northern Women and the Civil War* (Ithaca: Cornell University Press, 1998); Elizabeth D. Leonard, *Yankee Women: Gender Battles in the Civil War* (New York: Norton, 1994).

58. Hunter Diary, May 1, 1861, October 22, 31, 1861, August 22, 1862. Most women sent to the front items that ranged from knitted socks and homemade uniforms to blankets (sometimes made out of carpet) and bandages. To support their war work some women also participated in fund-raisers. Others turned to wealthy individuals in the community for support. Many participated in fund-raisers such as concerts even if they did not feel like doing so because, as Dawson wrote, she could not "find it in my heart to refuse when I can do anything of the benefit of the Soldiers." Elodie to Dawson, Selma, September 22, 1861, Dawson Papers. See also Elodie to Dawson, Selma, July 14, 1861, September 1, 1861, December 1, 1861, January 12, 1862, and Elodie to Dawson, Marengo, August 19, 24, 1861, all in Dawson Papers; *Claiborne Southerner*, May 15, 1861, July 3, 10, 31, 1861. Women across the state of Alabama often read the same articles, stories, and governmental proclamations (as was the case before the war). The continuation of this antebellum practice helped create a sense of continuity with the past and promote unity among some Confederate women. "To the Ladies of Alabama," Executive Department, Montgomery, AL, July 20, 1861, also published on July 24, 1861, in the *Mobile Register and Advertiser*; a transcript of this article can be found at http://www.uttyler.edu/vbetts/mobile_reg_and_adv_61-63.htm (accessed February 28, 2013). "Start the Looms and Needles," *Claiborne Southerner*, August 30, 1861; *Dadeville Banner*, October 4, 1861; *Democratic Watchtower*, March 1, 1865; *Montgomery Daily Mail*, October 20, 1862; *Montgomery Daily Advertiser*, December 18, 1862; M. E. Thompson to Joe Thompson, Marion, July 22, 1861, August 30, 1861, M. E. Thompson to her sons, Marion, August 5, 1861, September 23, 1861, M. E. Thompson to her son, Marion, September 26, 1861,

all in Benson-Thompson Family Papers; Gillis Diary, May 5, 1861, August 11, 1861; Mary Waring Diary, April 6, 1865, ADAH; Eliza Corry letter, December 4, 1863, Robert E. Corry Confederate Collection, 1857–1913, RG84, Auburn University; Espy Diary, August 27, 1861; Cumming Diary, May 5, 1862, November 9, 23, 1862, January 14, 1863, March 10, 1863, Cumming, *A Journal of Hospital Life*, 32, 76, 79, 86, 93–94; Faust, *This Republic of Suffering*, 116–17; Rable, *Civil Wars*; Attie, *Patriotic Toil*; Leonard, *Yankee Women*. Word of the war work of Confederate women reached the North. As illustrated by some of the publications of women's Loyal Leagues, formed throughout the North to rally support from the Northern women for the war effort, some Northern women felt the need to justify their method of support for the Union troops while at the same time strongly encouraging women to help with the war effort. These "Ladies National Leagues played a critical role in bridging the gap between Union military policy necessary to Union victory and flagging popular support for the war." LeeAnn Whites, *Gender Matters: Civil War, Reconstruction, and the Making of the New South* (New York: Palgrave MacMillan, 2005), 26–27, 35; "A Few Words in Behalf of the Loyal Women of the United States by one of themselves," Loyal Publication Society, No. 10 (New York: Wm. C. Bryant and Co., Printers, 1863), manuscript at the British Library, London.

59. M. E. Thompson to Joe Thompson, Marion, August 30, 1861, Benson-Thompson Family Papers.

60. Cumming Diary, May 9, 1862, July 11, 1862, September 9, 1863, June 24, 1864, Cumming, *A Journal of Hospital Life*, 33–34, 54–55, 140–41, 207–8; Elodie to Dawson, Selma, August 4, 1861, September 22, 1861, January 12, 1862, April 1, 15, 1862, Dawson Papers; Gillis Diary, August 11, 1861, August 9, 1863; Brandon Diary, January 1, 1863; Espy Diary, July 9, 1862; M. E. Thompson to her sons, Marion, September 23, 1861, M. E. Thompson to Joe Thompson, Marion, July 22, 1861, August 30, 1861, and M. E. Thompson to her son, Marion, July 7, 1861, all in Benson-Thompson Family Papers.

61. Gillis Diary, November 15, 1860. For more on the survival of women's Confederate identities, see Jennifer Ann Newman, "Writing, Religion, and Women's Identity in Civil War Alabama" (PhD diss., Auburn University, 2009), 258–92.

3
Confederate Alabama's Finest Hour
The Battle of Salem Church, May 3, 1863
Ben H. Severance

From about 11:00 in the morning until well into the afternoon on May 3, 1863, Alabamians in Wilcox's Brigade waged a frantic rearguard action, alone, against Union forces ten times their size. Edmund Patterson's memory of the event was that of a race against time. A twenty-three-year-old lieutenant in the 9th Alabama Infantry, Patterson had been on the move for hours: "We had been running until our tongues were hanging out still we saw no escape from capture or death unless we could reach that church before the Yankees did." That church was Salem Church, a Baptist place of worship on the Orange Plank Road. It was located about halfway between Fredericksburg, where the Rebel defenses had recently collapsed, and Chancellorsville, where the bulk of Robert E. Lee's unsuspecting army was grappling with the main body of the Army of the Potomac. Lieut. Elias Davis of the 10th Alabama Infantry also recalled the urgency of the day's movements. "I threw away my knapsack and its contents except my bible," he later wrote his wife, all in an effort to increase speed. Finally, at 4:00 PM, the Alabama Brigade deployed astride the road next to the church and made its stand. Rarely had a tactical objective been clearer: hold the position in order to prevent the enemy from striking the Army of Northern Virginia in the rear. Lee's Alabama boys not only held but successfully counterattacked against heavy odds, thereby making the battle at Salem Church arguably Alabama's finest hour of the war.[1]

Salem Church was one of several bloody engagements during the Battle of Chancellorsville (May 1–5, 1863). Most accounts understandably highlight Stonewall Jackson's famous flanking maneuver that destroyed the Union right wing on the evening of May 2, but many then neglect to emphasize the crucial action at nearby Salem Church the following afternoon. To be fair, plenty of scholars who specialize in the military aspects of the Civil War acknowledge the importance of Salem Church. Park historian Ralph Happel, for instance, describes it as "one of the most brilliant and significant of the subordinate battles of the war." Nevertheless, the larger, more popular story of Chancellorsville continues to be one of Jackson being mortally wounded by friendly fire, Robert E. Lee lamenting the figurative loss of his right arm, and Civil War enthusiasts forever after speculating on whether the South would have won the war had Jackson lived. Lost in this drama is the fact that while Jackson's heroics certainly made Confederate victory possible, it was Rebel success at Salem Church that ultimately secured that outcome.[2]

The complete story is the more compelling one. In April 1863, the Union Army of the Potomac, approximately 130,000 men under Joseph Hooker, initiated a promising offensive against Lee's Army of Northern Virginia with the Confederate capital at Richmond the strategic prize. Only 60,000 strong, Lee's men were still occupying the ground around Fredericksburg where they had defeated a Union incursion the previous December. "Fighting Joe" Hooker's plan was ambitious: 40,000 men under John Sedgwick would contain Lee's forces at Fredericksburg, while 70,000 under Hooker himself would conduct a massive turning movement to the west through the so-called Wilderness. The balance of Hooker's forces stood in reserve at Banks's Ford on the northern side of the Rappahannock River. Hooker was confident his plan would achieve one of two results: either compel the Rebels to beat a hasty retreat to the fortifications around Richmond or trap them in a classic "hammer-and-anvil" battle of annihilation. With characteristic audacity, however, Lee opted for something more daring: he divided his army for a surprise counterattack. Leaving 10,000 men, including Wilcox's Brigade, in the vicinity of Fredericksburg under the overall command of Jubal Early, Lee contested Hooker's advance with 50,000 men on May 1. The Confederates' spirited action that day unnerved Hooker, who halted his advance and thereby forfeited the initiative. The next day, while Lee demonstrated in front of Hooker's army with a scant 20,000 men, the remaining 30,000 under Jackson executed their legendary flank march. Toward evening on May 2, Stonewall struck and threatened to roll up the entire Federal right wing until his accidental wounding. Despite losing Jackson, Lee pressed his advantage with an all-out assault the following morning against Hooker's position around the hamlet of Chancellorsville. Fearing imminent defeat, "Fighting Joe" sent a message to Sedgwick to cross the river at Fredericksburg and come to his rescue.[3]

As these events transpired, Wilcox's Brigade performed security duty at Banks's Ford. It was a boring but important assignment, for an enemy crossing there would bisect the Confederate army. Consisting of 2,000 men distributed among five infantry regiments, the brigade represented all regions of Alabama. From the southern half of the state came the 8th Alabama, a plurality of the male residents of Mobile. The officer in charge was Col. Young Lea Royston, a forty-four-year-old lawyer from Dallas County who at 6'7" inches was an imposing man in uniform. From the other end of the state came the 9th Alabama, made up of yeoman and slaveholders from all over the Tennessee River Valley. The regiment's acting commander was Maj. Jeremiah H. Williams, a thirty-four-year-old civil engineer from Jackson County.

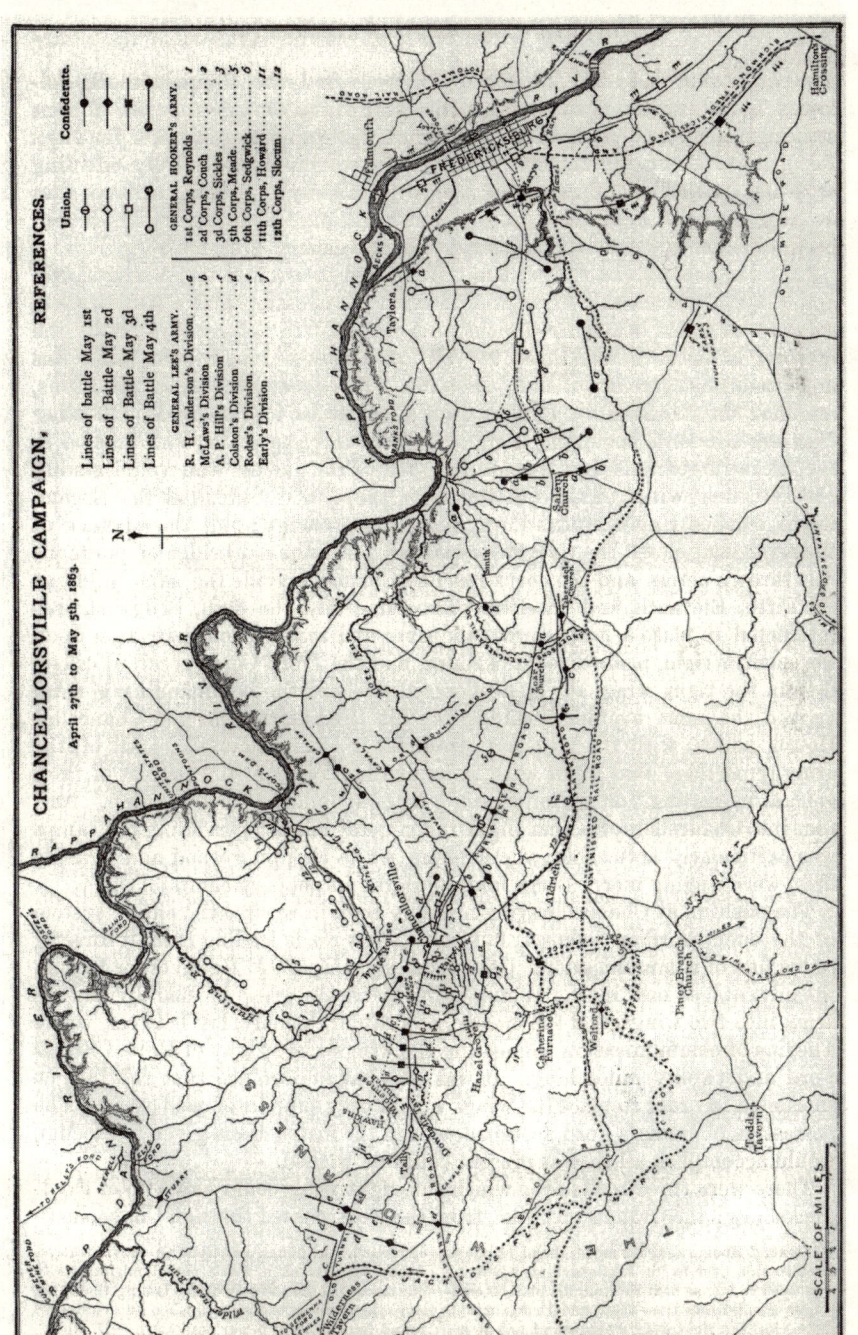

Figure 3.1. "Chancellorsville Campaign." From Robert Underwood Johnston and Clarence Clough Buel, eds., *Battles and Leaders of the Civil War* (New York: Century, 1888), 3:158.

The soldiers in the 10th Alabama hailed from the eastern part of the state and served under forty-year-old Col. William H. Forney, a lawyer from Calhoun County and a Mexican War veteran. Having been wounded in action twice since joining the 10th in 1861, Forney earned a reputation for fearlessness in battle. Rounding out the brigade were the 11th Alabama, its recruits drawn from the western half of the state, and the 14th Alabama, whose companies mustered from the northeastern region. These last two regiments were led by "boy" colonels: respectively, John C. C. Sanders of Tuscaloosa, a twenty-three-year-old former cadet from the University of Alabama, and Lucius Pinckard, age twenty-two, from Macon County. Virtually every soldier in the brigade possessed combat experience, each regiment having seen considerable action since the Peninsula Campaign of early 1862.[4]

At the brigade's helm was Brig. Gen. Cadmus Wilcox, a thirty-nine-year-old Tennessean who in 1861 briefly served as colonel of the 9th Alabama Infantry before receiving a promotion later that same year. A regular army officer, West Point Class of 1846, and a published authority on tactics, Wilcox brought professionalism to his assignment, but he also understood the citizen-soldier mind-set. His Alabama recruits were zealous for the cause of independence, but they resented military regimen. Wilcox adjusted his leadership style accordingly and thereby gained the adoration of his men, who dubbed their general "Old Billy Fixin" on account of his fastidious yet amiable demeanor.[5]

Both general and soldiers chafed at their inactivity during the opening phases of the battle. Other than dispatching various companies to conduct reconnaissance upriver, Wilcox mostly stared at enemy encampments opposite the ford. At least one soldier from the 10th Alabama wiled the time by carving his initials into a tree, the bark of which has been preserved by the National Park Service. The pleasant spring weather, however, along with the blooming dogwoods and chirping redwing blackbirds, belied the tension in the air. At dawn on May 3, John Oden, a forty-year-old lieutenant in the 10th, noted "the firing in front of Chans. was resumed at an early hour this morning very rapid and continuous," adding that "all are anxiously awaiting but sanguine of the results." Around midmorning, Wilcox espied the enemy across the river hurriedly donning their haversacks. He concluded that the Federals were marching west to reinforce Hooker and accordingly readied his own command to move out. Suddenly, he received an urgent dispatch to bring his brigade not to Chancellorsville but to Fredericksburg, where Union forces under John Sedgwick were storming the Confederate position at Marye's Heights. Having already put his men in line of march, Wilcox speedily complied; the 10th Alabama served as the vanguard.[6]

Colonel Forney pushed his 400 men eastward along the River Road and was the first to arrive at a scene of impending disaster. Union forces had broken through the main Confederate line just outside the city. Wilcox assumed that Jubal Early, the

Confederate general whom Lee had tasked with defending the area, would organize a new position and so deployed his brigade into line of battle atop Stansbury's Hill, an eminence that overlooked the roads into Fredericksburg. Unfortunately the brigadier soon received word that Early's forces were retreating south just as a sizable contingent of Federal soldiers was preparing to march west, directly into the rear of Lee's army then still heavily engaged at Chancellorsville less than eight miles away. On his own initiative, Wilcox decided to fall back toward Lee's army. "I felt it my duty to delay the enemy as much as possible in his advance," Wilcox reported, "and to endeavor to check him all that I could should he move forward on the Plank road." It was a gutsy call that pitted his one brigade against an entire corps of more than 20,000 bluecoats.[7]

The sun was shining through clear skies at high noon when Wilcox's Brigade commenced its rearguard action around Stansbury's Hill. The 10th Alabama, with the 11th on its left and the 8th on its right, engaged a strong line of Union soldiers. Simultaneously, Wilcox commandeered a battery of Virginia gunners loitering in the area and added their cannon to his firepower. For the next thirty minutes the Alabamians exchanged volleys with the enemy, who steadily added more weight to their attack. "Their skirmishers kept popping at us and we reciprocated their salutes," Pvt. Bailey McClelen of the 10th later remembered. Fortunately casualties within the brigade were relatively light: the 11th Alabama reported ten wounded and the 8th only three, but notable among the latter was Capt. Robert McCrary, shot dead as he supervised the musketry of Company D.[8]

With a full Union division under John Newton poised to envelop his right flank, Wilcox deftly withdrew his brigade to a new fighting position about a quarter of a mile to the southwest. Thus began a remarkable pattern of reverse leapfrogging. "The brigade would form line every few hundred yards," explained Capt. George Clark of the 11th Alabama, "fight for a short while, and then retire rapidly to escape capture, and then form again and fight." Although the wooded landscape facilitated these tactics, retrograde movements under fire are always complicated and at each stop the brigade did suffer losses, usually stragglers who were scooped up by the Federals. Nonetheless, the Alabamians' performance reflected well on their proficiency and fortitude. Military historian Jay Luvaas comments that "in his delaying operations [Wilcox] did everything prescribed in current army doctrine." As a result, the Union juggernaut lost critical momentum, enabling Wilcox to both notify Lee by courier of the looming threat and identify Salem Church as an appropriate place for his tiring men to make a final stand.[9]

Around 3:00 PM, the Alabama Brigade conducted its last rearguard action around a tollgate where the Orange Plank Road entered more spacious farm country. The Alabamians were pleased to find that a small company of dismounted Virginia cavalrymen were already in position to assist them in their delaying tactics. At that point, a brief lull fell over the battlefield as Union general Sedgwick brought up a fresh division under William "Bully" Brooks to lead his attack. Though both confined by the forest to a column march down the road and frustrated by his foe's dogged resistance, Sedgwick resolved that if he could just get past the Alabamians, a genuine opportunity to win glory awaited him. "We're after Cadmus [Wilcox]," he reportedly told a local civilian, "and we're going to pick him up." But the Yankee commander reasoned without the latest intelligence, for at that moment an officer from Lee's staff raced to Wilcox with word that a Confederate division under Lafayette McLaws was en route as reinforcement. Manifestly delighted by this news, the Rebel general proceeded to withdraw his forces another half mile to Salem Church. "I was almost dead when we got there," recalled Lieut. Edmund Patterson, "and no sooner had we stopped than I fainted." It had been a grueling afternoon of uncertain retreat, but "Old Billy Fixin" was now on ground of his choosing.[10]

The third of May was a Sunday, but it was hardly the Sabbath as Alabamian graybacks tramped through the church lot bordering the south side of the Orange Plank Road. Built in 1844, Salem Church was a plain, two-story, red-brick edifice shaped like a barn but with large windows on all sides. Prior to the war, the Rev. Melzi Chancellor ministered a congregation of some eighty members, including about twenty local slaves. By 1863, however, attendance had dwindled to fewer than fifty, and no parishioners were anywhere in sight on May 3. For several months, in fact, the building had served as a storage warehouse for Fredericksburg refugees, many of whom stashed valuable furniture inside for safekeeping from Yankee foragers. Company G, 9th Alabama occupied the church, and Capt. Thomas Mills ordered his men to make use of the furniture in erecting barricades and firing platforms. A twenty-seven-year-old physician from Butler County, Mills may also have noted how he might use the church as a field hospital. Joining Mills was Capt. John Featherston of Company F, who brought along a few of his Irish recruits because of their reputed expertise with the rifle. A bit farther southeast, Company A, 9th Alabama occupied a small log schoolhouse, which Capt. W. C. Murphy similarly converted into a little fortress. Some men from the 10th also appear to have fought inside the school. These two structures constituted forward redoubts behind which the rest of the brigade deployed.[11]

The Alabama Brigade presented an east-facing line of battle perpendicular to and astride the Orange Plank Road. On the south side of the road, the men of the 10th Alabama assumed a position about sixty yards behind both Salem Church and the schoolhouse. Next to them went the 8th Alabama, which anchored the brigade's right. North of the road, Wilcox deployed his boy colonels with Sanders's 11th nearest the road and Pinckard's 14th guarding the brigade's left flank. The rest of the 9th Alabama stationed itself out of sight behind the 10th, where it served as

Figure 3.2. Salem Church. Photographs of War Scenes, ca. 1870s–1890s, Album 1, p. 53, Duke University Libraries.

the brigade reserve. (A few soldiers, probably from the 9th, also helped local farmer James Orrock hustle his family down into the cellar of their nearby farmhouse.) Lastly, Wilcox's Virginia battery unlimbered on the road and commenced shelling the Federals around the just relinquished tollgate about 1,200 yards distant. Years after the battle, Pvt. Needham Hogan of the 11th Alabama proudly recalled surveying the whole brigade as it completed its formation: "This was the Spartan band of bronzed braves which was to save the rear of Lee's victorious legions."[12]

Regimental dispositions exploited the available terrain features. New-growth trees and bushes were plentiful, but while they provided some concealment they afforded the defenders only minimal cover. Therefore, the brigade began entrenching. "We improvised the best we could," remembered Pvt. Bailey McClelen of the 10th Alabama, "temporary breastworks out of logs, chunks, rocks, or anything we could readily get hold of." Fortunately for the Alabamians, they possessed the higher ground, a barely discernable ridgeline whose slight declivity enabled many of the infantrymen to fire down while lying in the prone position. The two regiments on the north side of the road also enjoyed the relative protection of a brush fence. Much of the ground for nearly a thousand yards to the brigade's front was cleared though badly overgrown with tall weeds and dotted by small copses.[13]

Just before 5:00 PM, Brooks arrayed his division on the fields due east of Salem Church. The Alabama troops undoubtedly breathed a bit easier when units from McLaws's division also started arriving. Wilcox directed their placement: a brigade of Georgians under Paul Semmes tied into the Alabamians' left flank; another of South Carolinians under Joseph Kershaw aligned on their right. Two other brigades, Mahone's and Wofford's, took longer getting into positions farther to the left and right and therefore played only a modest role in the forthcoming action. Either ignorant or contemptuous of the presence of these additional Rebel forces, Brooks launched a frontal attack without waiting for the rest of Sedgwick's corps to arrive. His troops advanced in three lines under a light barrage of artillery fire. Two Union brigades—one entirely of regiments from New Jersey, the other a mix of New Yorkers, Pennsylvanians, and boys from Maine—used the church as a guiding landmark and headed straight for the Alabamians. Portions of a third Union brigade aimed for the Georgians. As Wilcox's skirmishers scampered back to the main line of defense, the general and his men braced for impact. Several Alabamians remembered how their officers paced the lines shouting variants of the famous Revolutionary command "Don't shoot until you see the whites of their eyes." It was a deliberate historical reference suggesting that Salem Church was the Confederacy's Bunker Hill moment. At this crucial juncture, Wilcox received the untimely news that his battery had exhausted its ammunition; the ensuing clash would be purely an infantry fight.[14]

On the brigade right, the 8th Alabama prepared to engage the fast-approaching ranks of the 96th Pennsylvania. Hearing the enemy battle cry, Colonel Royston exhorted his regiment to stand firm. The officer's swaggering 6'7" frame may well have instilled more fear into the men than their charging adversary. Regardless, at eighty yards, the Alabamians unleashed a volley. Dozens of blue-clad men crumpled, but the Pennsylvanians returned fire with deadly effect. Colonel Royston writhed in pain as at least two bullets tore through his left arm, knocking him out of the battle. Instantly, Lieut. Col. Hilary Herbert assumed command and maintained a disciplined rate of fire, one that eventually killed sixteen enemy soldiers and wounded more than fifty more. The Alabamians similarly punished the 5th Maine as that regiment came up alongside the Pennsylvanians' left. Union brigadier Joseph Bartlett blamed the terrain for his men's misfortune. "The woods were thick with harsh, unyielding undergrowth, with little large timber," he complained. "It afforded no protection to our troops from the showers of bullets which were rapidly thinning my ranks, but retarded their advance." When Kershaw's Brigade assembled on the 8th's right, the combined firepower of the Alabamians and the South Carolinians stopped the Union attack altogether on that part of the battlefield.[15]

Next to the 8th, Colonel Forney and his boys in the 10th Alabama blazed away at two enemy regiments of their own: the 23rd New Jersey and the 121st New York. One Alabamian claimed that the 10th fired six aimed volleys into the enemy's ranks, "strewing the sod with his slain." Alabamian sharpshooters inside the schoolhouse and the church added to the Yankees' misery. The two structures acted like breakwaters against the Union tidal wave. A squad of New Yorkers, led by a "sandy whiskered" lieutenant, battered down the door to the schoolhouse. The Union officer reportedly shouted, "Show them no quarter!" but the defenders inside shot him dead. With bluecoats breaking in at other points, however, a fatally wounded Capt. W. C. Murphy surrendered his little garrison. Simultaneously, hundreds of New Jersey boys swarmed around the church. Captain Mills had positioned his best marksmen in the second-floor balcony windows and in the window behind the pulpit. From there, the Alabamians picked off dozens of enemy soldiers. Whereas the schoolhouse had capitulated after a short, sharp fight, the Alabamians inside the church staved off their attackers throughout the battle. At one point, though, some bluecoats penetrated the ground floor, where for several chaotic minutes both sides blasted each other across the pinewood pews. "We had literally converted the House of God into a charnel house," Captain Featherston recalled, "and pushed aside the Book of Life and were using the instruments of death."[16]

Across the road, the 11th and 14th Alabama regiments faced a determined assault by the 1st and 3rd New Jersey but firmly held their ground. Positioned behind a brush fence, the men of the 11th enjoyed an elevated and unobstructed field of fire. Conversely, the Jersey men stumbled through the same thick undergrowth that hindered Union movements elsewhere. Private Hogan of Company A vividly remembered the ensuing melee: "Up this gentle slope approached the dense columns of blue with steady tread, with banners fluttering and shining steel glimmering in the sunlight." The private then explained how at a range of about eighty yards "we rose and poured a deadly hailstorm of lead into it, which was so destructive that our fire was not returned." The Yankees recoiled with one Union officer shot clean off his horse, but the Alabamians did not relent. "Give 'em hell," Capt. John Rains bellowed to his men, "give 'em hell!" Rapidly firing one volley after the next, the 11th Alabama tore the 1st New Jersey to shreds, wounding or killing 106 men. To the 11th's left, the 14th Alabama, assisted by some regiments from the Georgia Brigade, shot to pieces the 3rd New Jersey, which lost 99 men. Success came at a heavy price, however, for the 14th suffered several dozen casualties of its own, including the death of two "very promising young officers," lieutenants Henry Cox from Company K and M. L. Bankston from Company C. The boy colonel Lucius Pinckard also suffered a serious wound.[17]

Despite the losses, Wilcox's Brigade had absorbed the first Yankee onslaught, but Brooks pressed his attack. The 15th New Jersey replaced the spent 1st and 3rd regiments on the north side of the road, where its ranks exchanged volleys with both the Alabamians and their Georgian cohorts in a stand-up fight that quickly shrouded the whole field in thick smoke. On the south side of the road, the 121st New York and 23rd New Jersey redoubled their efforts around the church. Despite having been unhorsed by rifle fire, Col. Emory Upton pitched his New Yorkers into the 10th

Alabama. The Alabamians wavered under a fusillade of close-range musketry. Casualties mounted alarmingly among the regiment's officers, including Capt. Richard Rogan of Company D, wounded, and Capt. Walter Cook of Company E, killed. "We are flanked on the left!" an Alabamian suddenly screamed as soldiers from the 23rd New Jersey clambered up the road and hurled themselves into the 10th as well. Then when Colonel Forney collapsed with a bullet in his leg, the whole regiment broke. The Yankees had momentarily carried the center of Wilcox's line. "They can't stand and face 4 columns of Yankees," Pvt. William McClellan of the 9th Alabama later opined. "The 10th ala is a very good Regt but she always runs," he continued to complain, "the only ala Reg I ever saw to run."[18]

This harsh assessment aside, it was McClellan's regiment that rose to avert the crisis. Shouting "Forward, 9th Alabama!" Maj. Jeremiah Williams led his men straight into the path of the New Yorkers. For the next several minutes, the opposing sides brawled in hand-to-hand fighting. Pvt. Alexander Odom of Company F recalled a bizarre moment during the melee. Evidently his friend and fellow farmer George Stewart was "struck on the head with a Minie ball; and although fired from a gun at short range, his head was so hard that it turned that ball." The ricochet whizzed over Odom's shoulder. The astonished private happily exclaimed, "George, you are all right." The lucky George merely waved his hand in silent gratitude. The outcome was less fortunate for other Alabamians. Company I, led by Lieut. Alex Chisholm, went into the fray with thirty-two men but in quick succession sustained five killed and four wounded.[19]

Upton's breakthrough in the center ironically afforded Hilary Herbert a golden opportunity to deny Union forces any lasting success. With bluecoats streaming past his now exposed left flank, the lieutenant colonel deftly executed a brilliant countermeasure. "The battle seems hanging in the balance," Herbert later recounted in the present tense. "But the 8th Alabama stands fast. The enemy in its front is held at bay, while its three left companies under order make a backward half wheel and fire down the line of the New York regiment." Capt. William Fagan, whose Company K was held back as a regimental reserve for just such a contingency, orchestrated an especially devastating volley. The ensuing enfilade dropped nearly 200 enemy soldiers and utterly shattered the last Federal assault of the afternoon. "No mortal could stay and live where we were," lamented one Union survivor, "the line moved back and retreated in confusion." Herbert's decisive tactics allowed the 9th Alabama to gain the upper hand. In a matter of seconds, the regiment restored the brigade front. "That is the best regiment on the American continent," a jubilant General Wilcox reportedly crowed as he watched the 9th drive the Yankees back. The 10th Alabama also returned to the fight thanks to the quick thinking of Captain Walter Winn, the 11th Alabama's adjutant, who galloped across the road and blocked the flight of infantrymen with his horse. Aided by Colonel Forney, whose wound proved minor, the two officers rallied the entire regiment.[20]

All along the line, the men of Wilcox's Brigade now sensed that the time had come to smash the demoralized Yankees with a general attack of their own. "The brigade leaped forward to charge apparently without orders," Captain Clark of the 11th Alabama later described, "and the chase began." The 14th Alabama could not join the onrush fast enough: "Come on boys," barked twenty-year-old Lieut. Woody Dozier, "we'll get our blankets back." These two regiments, belatedly accompanied by two more from the Georgia Brigade, slammed into the 15th New Jersey. The Union soldiers briefly held their ground, discharging a volley into the 11th that struck down among others Lieut. Osmund Strudwick, "a gallant officer" who perished at the head of his company. But with the 14th Alabama closing in on its flank with fixed bayonets, the New Jersey men started to run. Across the road, Lieutenant Colonel Herbert urged the 8th Alabama forward. "Hold your muskets level," one of his officers laughingly shouted, "and you'll get a Yank!" Union formations there crumbled under the Alabama onslaught. The 8th, 9th, and 10th regiments relieved the beleaguered garrison inside the church and liberated the Alabamians who had surrendered at the schoolhouse. "Old Billy Fixin" himself was seen riding about excitedly, waving his brigade onward; only later did he discover that his uniform had been punctured at four spots by enemy bullets. Everywhere, the bluecoats were in headlong retreat, a "terrible skedipper" according to an officer in the 96th Pennsylvania. "Bully" Brooks desperately threw in his reserves, the 16th New York, but that regiment delivered only a couple of ineffectual volleys before losing 140 men in a rout of its own. The 2nd New Jersey, which had just reassembled after its earlier skirmishing duties, put up some nasty resistance until it, too, got steamrolled just east of the church by a pack of Alabamians shrieking the famous Rebel yell, one that purportedly "made the woods ring."[21]

On reaching the tollgate, Cadmus Wilcox wisely called his brigade to a halt. It was now dusk and his surging regiments were scattered all over the field. That, along with wafting clouds of smoke and the arrival of fresh Union forces, rendered further pursuit foolish. "The rear of our army at Chancellorsville was now secure and free from danger," the general rightly concluded. The Rebels therefore withdrew back to the ridgeline and bivouacked. Besides reveling in their astonishing victory, many Alabamians also foraged the fields for abandoned booty. "I more than got even with the Yankees in the way of baggage," Lieut. Elias Davis of the 10th Alabama chuckled after acquiring two blankets and an enemy officer's sword. "Our army is now better clothed than it has been for sometime."[22]

The next morning, however, the glory gave way to the gore. Hundreds of corpses from both sides littered the field around Salem Church and the Orange Plank Road.

In repulsing the Union attack, the Alabama Brigade lost 495 men. For the whole battle, including the rearguard actions, the 8th regiment suffered 56 casualties, the 9th 113, the 10th 100, the 11th 115, and the 14th 151. In return, the Alabamians, along with their Georgia comrades, inflicted over 1,500 casualties at Salem Church alone, not to mention an indeterminate number of bluecoats during the rearguard actions. Wilcox reported that his men buried 248 Union soldiers, while Lieut. Edmund Patterson of the 9th Alabama recorded in his journal that he escorted 400 prisoners to the provost marshal. "The work of amputation is now fully begun," Lieut. John Oden of the 10th Alabama grimly wrote in his diary as the church switched from fort to hospital. A Georgia soldier described the scene more graphically: "every available foot of space was crowded with wounded and bleeding soldiers. The floor, the benches, even the chancel and pulpit were all packed almost to suffocation. Blood flowed in streams along the aisles . . . screams and groans were heard on all sides, while the surgeons . . . worked with knives, saws, sutures, and bandages." One of the surgeons was a captured Federal doctor whom General Wilcox invited to lend a hand, particularly to the scores of wounded Union prisoners languishing in the churchyard.[23]

Every Confederate involved in the action at Salem Church recognized that they had achieved something extraordinary. Moreover, just about everyone agreed that it was the Alabamians who deserved the most credit. The exception was Paul Semmes, who led the Georgians on Wilcox's left. In his report, Semmes averred that "the brunt of the battle fell upon [my] brigade" and further contended that there was very little combat on the south side of the road, "whilst the roar of musketry raged furiously along my front." To be sure, all of Semmes's men were hotly engaged in support of the Alabamians, but his account grossly distorts the truth. With a dispute over martial honor brewing between Wilcox and Semmes, Robert E. Lee weighed in with a final verdict. Confirming that the Union attack had been "directed mainly against General Wilcox," the commanding general went on to explain how Wilcox and his Alabama boys were "entitled to especial praise for the judgment and bravery displayed in impeding the advance of General Sedgwick toward Chancellorsville, and for the gallant and successful stand at Salem Church." Lee knew that the Alabamians had indeed repelled a mortal threat to his Army of Northern Virginia, just as he knew that their sanguinary performance had nailed down his triumph at Chancellorsville.[24]

Over the next two days, Wilcox's Brigade was tangentially involved in the closing phases of the campaign. After his drubbing at Salem Church, Sedgwick withdrew toward the Rappahannock River, where he endeavored to cross and reunite with Hooker's main body. Ever the aggressor, Lee strived to wipe out Sedgwick's corps while it was still vulnerable. For a variety of reasons, however, his division commanders failed to execute a coordinated attack. For their part, late on May 4, the Alabamians probed Union positions in densely forested terrain a mile north of the church. In the process, the 8th Alabama picked up scores of Yankees floundering in the woods searching for their parent units. Toward midnight, captains M. G. May and Horace King, commanding, respectively, companies C and E of the 9th Alabama, surprised and captured over 150 enemy soldiers in the vicinity of Banks's Ford. These were minor, albeit satisfying, successes. The next day, a heavy rain shower bathed the blood-soaked landscape and allowed Sedgwick to complete his evacuation across the river without further interference. Wilcox and his men returned to their rifle pits at Banks's Ford, having come full circle after forty-eight hours of continuous activity. There they recovered the flag of the 102nd Pennsylvania, floating limply near the southern bank of the Rappahannock. On May 6, the whole Army of the Potomac retreated back to Washington, D.C.; and so the great Battle of Chancellorsville came to an end.[25]

Wilcox's Brigade would earn other combat laurels right up to the final surrender at Appomattox, but nothing quite compared to its unique experience at Salem Church. "It is strange," Needham Hogan of the 11th Alabama commented decades after the war, "that so little attention has been given to this important battle by historians." Perhaps it is not surprising, then, that of all the battles Hilary Herbert talked about in his history of the 8th Alabama, Salem Church was the only one he felt compelled to discuss in great depth. In 1907, veterans from the 23rd New Jersey returned to the church and erected a monument to their own ordeal at that place. Many members of Wilcox's Brigade attended the ceremony. Inscribed on one side of the obelisk was a simple dedication: "To the brave Alabama boys, our opponents on this field of battle, whose memory we honor." Moved by this touching homage from a former enemy, Alexander Odom of the 9th Alabama strolled over to the old church and touched the fresh mortar and plaster that barely hid the pockmarks of the hundreds of bullets that had so rudely smacked its walls that spring day in 1863. "How vastly different the circumstances and emotions," he mused, "more than forty-four years ago!"[26]

The special connection between Salem Church and Alabama can never be overstated. The eminent historian Douglas S. Freeman tried to capture the profound significance of the battle by commenting on the commander. "Cadmus Wilcox," he said, "gave military history an example far outliving his time of the manner in which one brigade, courageously led, can change the course of a battle and retrieve a lost day." The Confederate government eventually promoted Wilcox to the rank of major general, while posterity has made him an honorary Alabamian. For John C. C. Sanders, the boy colonel of the 11th Alabama, Salem Church was all about the soldiers. "Let us not forget to shed tears of deep sorrow," he addressed his regiment mere days after the fight, "over the fresh graves of our comrades, who purchased victory with death." In May 1864, Sanders received promotion to brigadier general and was subsequently killed in action during the Siege of Petersburg. Finally, Hilary Herbert of the 8th Alabama addressed the cause for which the engagement was fought. "It was not any wicked desire to destroy American liberties that prompted Alabamians to do battle that day," he wrote years after the war. "Both armies were fighting for American institutions as they understood them." Present-day attitudes might consider this last remark a soft-pedaling of slavery, but to such men as Herbert the war was indeed a noble conflict over competing ideas of political freedom. Herbert went on to serve as secretary of the navy under President Grover Cleveland. In the end, whether viewed in terms of leadership, sacrifice, or motivation, Alabama's stand at Salem Church was an exemplary display of military prowess, battlefield courage, and patriotic resolve. In short, it was the finest hour in the state's short-lived existence as a member of the Confederacy.[27]

Notes

1. John G. Barrett, ed., *Yankee Rebel: The Civil War Journal of Edmund DeWitt Patterson* (Chapel Hill: University of North Carolina Press, 1966), 100; Elias Davis to G. A. Davis, May 10, 1863, folder 6, BSG024893, Alabama Department of Archives and History, Montgomery (hereafter ADAH).

2. Ralph Happel, *Salem Church Embattled* (Fredericksburg, VA: Eastern National Park and Monument Association, 1980), 61. A recent example of the persistent tendency to brush over events after Stonewall was wounded is James K. Bryant II, *The Chancellorsville Campaign: The Nation's High Water Mark* (Charleston, SC: The History Press, 2009).

3. There are many histories of the Chancellorsville Campaign, but the best are Stephen W. Sears, *Chancellorsville* (Boston: Houghton Mifflin Company, 1998) and Ernest B. Furgurson, *Chancellorsville, 1863: The Souls of the Brave* (New York: Knopf, 1992). Also informative are Edward J. Stackpole, *Chancellorsville: Lee's Greatest Battle* (Harrisburg, PA: Stackpole Books, 1958) and Daniel E. Sutherland, *Fredericksburg and Chancellorsville: The Dare Mark Campaign* (Lincoln: University of Nebraska Press, 1998).

4. Willis Brewer, *Alabama: Her History Resources, War Record, and Public Men* (Montgomery: Barret & Brown, 1872), 600–608, 612–13; Joseph Wheeler, *Confederate Military History, Extended Edition*, vol. 8, *Alabama* (Wilmington, NC: Broadfoot Publishing Company, 1987), 79–93, 99–101, 407–8, 443–44.

5. Gerard A. Patterson, *From Blue to Gray: The Life of Confederate General Cadmus M. Wilcox* (Harrisburg, PA: Stackpole Books, 2001), 26–27.

6. Ira Harrison Weissinger, "The Tenth Alabama Infantry Regiment in the Confederate States Army" (master's thesis, Auburn University, 1961), 123; Ronald G. Griffin, *The 11th Alabama Volunteer Regiment in the Civil War* (Jefferson, NC: McFarland, 2008), 136; Happel, *Salem Church Embattled*, 26; Michael Barton, ed., "The End of Oden's War: A Confederate Captain's Diary," *Alabama Historical Quarterly* 43 (1981): 81; *The War of the Rebellion: A Compilation of the Official Records of the Union and Confederate Armies* [hereafter *O.R.*] (Washington, DC: GPO, 1880–1901), I, 25(1): 855–56.

7. *O.R.*, I, 25(1): 856–57. For Jubal Early's role in the fighting, see Gary W. Gallagher, "East of Chancellorsville: Jubal A. Early at Second Fredericksburg and Salem Church," in *Chancellorsville: The Battle and Its Aftermath*, ed. Gary W. Gallagher (Chapel Hill: University of North Carolina Press, 2008).

8. Griffin, *The 11th Alabama Volunteer Regiment*, 138–39; Hilary A. Herbert, "History of the Eighth Alabama Volunteer Regiment, C.S.A.," *Alabama Historical Quarterly* 39 (1977): 97; *O.R.*, I, 25(1): 884–85; Norman E. Rourke, ed., *I Saw the Elephant: The Civil War Experiences of Bailey George McClelen, Company D, 10th Alabama Infantry Regiment* (Shippensburg, PA: Burd Street Press, 1995), 36; Philip W. Parsons, *The Union Sixth Army Corps in the Chancellorsville Campaign* (Jefferson, NC: McFarland, 2006), 87–89. Parsons's work offers the best coverage of the battle from the Union perspective.

9. George Clark, "Chancellorsville and Salem Church," *Confederate Veteran* 18 (1910): 125; Jay Luvaas and Harold W. Nelson, eds., *The U.S. Army War College Guide to the Battles of Chancellorsville and Fredericksburg* (Carlisle, PA: South Mountain Press, 1988), 135.

10. Sears, *Chancellorsville*, 377; *O.R.*, I, 25(1): 857–58; Patterson, *From Blue to Gray*, 56; Barrett, *Yankee Rebel*, 101.

11. Happel, *Salem Church Embattled*, 13–18; Furguson, *Chancellorsville 1863*, 274; *Supplement to the Official Records of the Union and Confederate Armies*, part II: Record of Events (Wilmington, NC: Broadfoot Publishing Company, 1994), 1:408; James Edmonds Saunders, *Early Settlers of Alabama* (Tuscaloosa: Willo Publishing, 1961); Weissinger, "The Tenth Alabama Infantry Regiment," 130.

12. *O.R.*, I, 25(1): 858; Happel, *Salem Church Embattled*, 39–40; N. B. Hogan, "The Virginia Campaign: A Touching Incident," *Confederate Veteran* 2 (1894): 52.

13. Linda L. Green, *First for the Duration: The Story of the Eighth Alabama Infantry, C.S.A.* (Westminster, MD: Heritage Books, 2008), 51; Rourke, *I Saw the Elephant*, 36; *O.R.*, I, 25(1): 858; Stackpole, *Chancellorsville*, 329–30.

14. *O.R.*, I, 25(1): 568, 858; Parsons, *Union Sixth Army Corps*, 95–96, 98; A. P. Odom, "The Battle of Salem Church," *Confederate Veteran* 16 (1908): 61; Hogan, "The Virginia Campaign," 52; Theodore A. Dodge, *The Campaign of Chancellorsville* (1881; New York: De Capo Press, 1999), 190. Although he became the ranking officer on the field after his arrival, Maj. Gen. Lafayette McLaws appears to have deferred tactical command to Wilcox and then busied himself with bringing up more men and ammunition. *O.R.*, I, 25(1): 827.

15. Herbert, "History of the Eighth Alabama," 101; *O.R.*, I, 25(1): 189, 581, 590; David A. Ward, "Of Battlefields and Bitter Feuds: The 96th Pennsylvania Volunteers," *Civil War Regiments* 3 (1993): 24–25; Parsons, *Union Sixth Army Corps*, 101–2.

16. *The Democratic Watchtower* (Talladega County), July 1, 1863; Rourke, *I Saw the Elephant*, 37; *Supplement*, part II, 1:401; *O.R.*, I, 25(1): 579, 859; Camille Baquet, *History of the First Brigade, New Jersey Volunteers from 1861 to 1865* (Trenton, NJ: MacCrellish & Quigley State Printers, 1910), 276. The historical record contains some confusion as to whether the church changed hands during the battle. Captain Mills, however, states that he and his men left the building only to accompany the Rebel counterattack; Col. E. Burd Grubb, who commanded the 23rd New Jersey, frankly confesses that he utterly failed to dislodge the Alabamians. *Supplement*, part II, 1:408; *O.R.*, I, 25(1): 579.

17. Griffin, *The 11th Alabama Volunteer Regiment*, 141; Hogan, "The Virginia Campaign," 52; *O.R.*, I, 25(1): 576, 578; *Supplement to the Official Records of the Union and Confederate Armies*, part I: Reports (Wilmington, NC: Broadfoot Publishing, 1995), 4:677.

18. *O.R.*, I, 25(1): 572; Salvatore G. Cilella Jr., *Upton's Regulars: The 121st New York Infantry in*

the Civil War (Lawrence: University Press of Kansas, 2009), 168; Rourke, *I Saw the Elephant*, 36; *Democratic Watchtower*, July 1, 1863; Wheeler, *Confederate Military History*, 408; John C. Carter, *Welcome the Hour of Conflict: William Cowan McClellan and the 9th Alabama* (Tuscaloosa: University of Alabama Press, 2007), 227, 229. Because of its temporary rout at the height of the battle, the men of the 10th Alabama endured endless ribbing thereafter from their comrades in the other regiments, the derision typically being an overly dramatic "steady, steady" whenever the 10th was called upon to go into action (Weissinger, "The Tenth Alabama Infantry Regiment," 136–37).

19. Barrett, *Yankee Rebel*, 102; Odom, "Battle of Salem Church," 61; *Supplement*, part II, 1:411.

20. Herbert, "History of the Eighth Alabama," 101; Baquet, *History of the First Brigade*, 243; Cilella, *Upton's Regulars*, 169; Carter, *Welcome the Hour of Conflict*, 229; Sears, *Chancellorsville*, 385; Griffin, *The 11th Alabama Volunteer Regiment*, 142.

21. Clark, "Chancellorsville and Salem Church," 126; *Supplement*, part I, 4:677; Griffin, *The 11th Alabama Volunteer Regiment*, 142, 144; Sears, *Chancellorsville*, 384; Herbert, "History of the Eighth Alabama," 102, 106; Charles Richardson, *The Chancellorsville Campaign: Fredericksburg to Salem Church* (New York: Neale Publishing, 1907), 40; Furguson, *Chancellorsville 1863*, 278; *O.R.*, I, 25(1): 577, 586.

22. *O.R.*, I, 25(1): 859; Elias Davis to G. A. Davis, May 10, 1863, folder 6, BSG024893, ADAH. Two Georgia regiments continued chasing the Yankees for a little while longer before also retiring.

23. *O.R.*, I, 25(1): 189, 854, 861; Barrett, *Yankee Rebel*, 102; Barton, "The End of Oden's War," 82; C. C. Sanders, "Old Salem Church," *Southern Historical Society Papers* 29 (1901): 172; Cilella, *Upton's Regulars*, 178.

24. *O.R.*, I, 25(1): 801, 803, 835. In a fanciful retelling years after the war, an officer from the 50th Georgia presented an image of hapless Alabamians being rescued by Semmes's Brigade, which supposedly not only arrived in the nick of time but almost single-handedly drove the Yankees off the field, inflicting an astounding five thousand casualties in the process. Peter McGlashan, "Battle of Salem Church, May 3, 1863" (addresses delivered before the Confederate Veterans Association of Savannah, GA, 1893).

25. Gallagher, "East of Chancellorsville," 47–53; *O.R.*, I, 25(1): 853, 860; Herbert, "History of the Eighth Alabama," 107; *Supplement*, part II, 1:406.

26. Hogan, "The Virginia Campaign," 52; Herbert, "History of the Eighth Alabama," 98; Baquet, *History of the First Brigade*, 274; Odom, "Battle of Salem Church," 61; Happel, *Salem Church Embattled*, 56–57.

27. Douglas Southall Freeman, *Lee's Lieutenants: A Study in Command*, 3 vols. (New York: Charles Scribner's Sons, 1943), 2:626; Griffin, *The 11th Alabama Volunteer Regiment*, 143; Hilary A. Herbert to E. Burd Grubb, May 18, 1907, folder 6, BSG024892, ADAH. Herbert's letter reflects the spirit of reconciliation that characterized Civil War memory at the turn of the century.

4
The Confederate Sun Sets on Selma
Nathan Bedford Forrest and the Defense of Alabama in 1865
Brian Steel Wills

The year 1864 had proven to be a trying and difficult one for the Confederate States of America. Powerfully constructed twin operations in Virginia and Georgia had seen Robert E. Lee's Army of Northern Virginia driven into increasingly lengthy defenses around Petersburg and nearby Richmond, while Confederate defenders in Georgia had been unable to prevent the penetration of that state, costing the South vital facilities in the area of Rome and the important rail junction of Atlanta. William T. Sherman then pushed toward Savannah, while George Thomas deflected John Bell Hood's efforts to reclaim Tennessee that virtually decimated that state's namesake Confederate army at Franklin and Nashville. Other campaigns brought the destruction of war with them in the Shenandoah Valley of Virginia and elsewhere, while the reelection of Abraham Lincoln offered a renewed sense of purpose for a war-weary populace in the North. Generals Sherman, Thomas, Ulysses Grant, and Philip Sheridan seemed poised to bring about the final collapse of the Confederacy as 1865 dawned. James Harrison Wilson wanted to be among their number.

Bright spots for the Confederate States of America were indeed diminishing, but some significant ones remained. Despite the wave of Union victories that had characterized recent military events, an industrial heartland remained relatively intact and its defenders seemed ready to keep it so. Just a year earlier, in celebrating his achievements as Confederate chief of ordnance, Josiah Gorgas boasted, "I have succeeded beyond my utmost expectations" in creating an infrastructure that would have astonished prewar Southerners with its expansiveness and complexity.[1] Historian Emory Thomas noted such accomplishments as part of the "revolutionary experience" the Confederates had undergone in developing an industrial base to support their war effort. "In Selma, Alabama, besides Gorgas' arsenal," Thomas explained, "was the Naval Iron Foundry, five major iron works, and a huge powder factory, housed in a building which enclosed five acres of land—all of these fashioning the stuff of war."[2] Thousands of individuals found employment in these facilities at the height of their production, advancing the Confederacy's war-making potential significantly.[3] Refugees from other war-torn areas swelled the population as well; the number of residents in Selma was now double what it had been before the war. These developments, the existence of two railroads, and the proximity of the city to the Alabama River turned Selma into a critical center for industrial output and made it a lucrative target for Union forces.[4]

One of the men to whom the defense of the region now fell was Maj. Gen. Nathan Bedford Forrest. He had established a powerful reputation through the earlier course of the conflict. Widely hailed as the "Wizard of the Saddle," and more ominously for Federal opponents as "that Devil Forrest," the Southern horseman had demonstrated his prowess in raids, pursuits, traditional cavalry roles, and departmental operations, rising to general officer ranks from his initial enlistment as a private soldier in 1861. Only a few months earlier a superior had noted regarding Forrest that he was pleased to have an officer under him who was "accustomed to accomplish the very greatest results with small means."[5] Although the circumstances had altered dramatically from the point at which Dabney Maury first offered his assessment, Forrest enjoyed a solid record of besting his opponents.[6]

Forrest's likely adversary in this round, James H. Wilson, had undergone a transition in his own career. After serving as a cavalry commander with General Grant in Virginia with mixed results, he transferred to the Western Theater. Under Gen. George H. Thomas his stint in the saddle had not begun particularly well there. General Forrest had largely outmaneuvered the young Union officer in the lead-up to Franklin and Nashville in John Bell Hood's 1864 Tennessee Campaign. Yet Wilson demonstrated resilience and a willingness and capacity to learn that promised to redound to his credit in a new season of fighting. With the benefit of years of hindsight to refine his viewpoint, Forrest's artillery chief, John Morton, argued that Wilson "had learned enough" in his earlier contacts with Forrest "to enable him to know what he would need" in another clash with the Confederate, and that Wilson had prepared to "cover every possible emergency, every turn and twist" his "wily" opponent might make.[7] Furthermore, Wilson's determination to assemble what he hoped would become an irresistible force of Union cavalry in the aftermath of the decisive victory to which he had contributed at Nashville in December suggested that he would be in a position to make good on the promise of success for Union arms.

Wilson had a great deal of work to do before he could realize his goal of advancing the proficiency of his troops to a level of full combat readiness. The difficult circumstances under which the Union cavalry command had operated required what the general's biographer Edward Longacre termed "its third extensive refit in six weeks." In addition to recouping the human losses sustained in the grueling operations, six thousand horses "had broken down" and would have to be allowed time to recover or be replaced for the next round of campaigning.[8] Hard riding in difficult conditions had taken its toll on men, mounts, and resources throughout the command.

Most of the troops that General Wilson hoped to employ against the Confederates had been pushed to the limits of their endurance in various operations at the end of the year and needed time to recoup themselves. Brig. Gen. Edward McCook had scrambled to react to a raid by Hylan B. Lyon that penetrated Kentucky. Although ultimately successful in decimating that Confederate command, the expedition had proven enormously taxing to the riders and their mounts.[9] Others in Wilson's command had watched their forces simultaneously battle Hood's retreating Southerners and the brutal weather conditions until the bulk of the Army of Tennessee had finally stretched beyond their reach. A correspondent who sought to convey to his readers something of the conditions through which these pursuers maneuvered observed, "It is almost impossible to move. The whole country is one vast sea of mud." Nevertheless, the requirements of the pursuit remained and its effects became tragically obvious. "So violently was our cavalry urged, [that] hundreds of horses perished from exhaustion," while "many of the riders fell off from sheer fatigue."[10]

On January 2, 1865, Wilson was in Huntsville, Alabama, to undertake the task of reconstructing his command. He reflected these challenges in correspondence with his friend Adam Badeau, emphasizing his own desire for action and outlining his efforts to secure the means to refit his command adequately. Poor road conditions and harsh wintry weather, as well as a shortage of mounts and an abundance of unserviceable equipment, remained deterrents to immediate movement. Obstacles to these efforts seemed to occur with daunting regularity and an anxious Wilson chafed at the prospect of delaying active operations any longer than was absolutely necessary.[11]

Conflicting priorities, philosophies, and egos coupled with the effects of weather and refitting complicated matters for the Federals as preparations for renewed campaigning continued. Ulysses Grant had the grand strategic map to consider, while George Thomas grappled with departmental-level demands and James Wilson sought a place for himself in what he saw as the conflict's final chapter. Accordingly, Grant wanted to continue to apply pressure on the Confederates everywhere, and he transferred resources and troops that he considered necessary from one point to another to meet that goal. Thomas remained cognizant of Hood's remnant and aware of his chief's impatience. He had to coordinate efforts for a proposed raid in East Tennessee by George Stoneman, as well as Wilson's potential operation, in addition to meeting the myriad requirements of all of the other troops under his authority. In creating his massive cavalry force, Wilson had multiple motives of his own, as historian John Rowell has observed. Such a command "would play a significant role in closing the war, demonstrate the effectiveness of cavalry when used properly and when operated independently, and establish Wilson's reputation as a great military leader."[12]

One of the elements that favored the Federals was the fact that their opponents were in dire straits themselves. In the aftermath of covering Hood's retreat from Nashville, General Forrest had to turn his attention to replenishing his command and preparing it as much as possible for another heavy season of combat. Given the likelihood of only a brief respite from fighting, the demands of resupplying his troops and recruiting new men to fill empty saddles had to be accelerated at a time when conditions were the least favorable for these crucial activities. Not only was the state of the Confederate nation in crisis, but limited pools of replacements for men, horses, and equipment added measurably to Forrest's command burdens.

Bedford Forrest had always recognized the importance of details as a businessman and a soldier.[13] He took various elements into account that others might have overlooked and not only asked frequent questions but demanded detailed answers. When Richard Taylor took command of the department in which Forrest operated, the men met for the first time. Forrest's approach to this initial encounter between them had taken him aback. "To my surprise, Forrest suggested many difficulties and asked numerous questions," Taylor observed, and the sheer amount of inquiry suggested to the department commander an uncertainty he had not expected in his celebrated subordinate. "I began to think he had no stomach for the work," the department commander admitted, "but at last, having isolated the chances of success from causes of failure with the care of a chemist experimenting in his laboratory," Forrest had leaped into action, calling out orders and seeing that staff members and subordinates took immediate steps to implement them.[14]

Forrest also understood that in the wake of hard fighting and defeat he needed to reinvigorate his men's fighting spirit. He sought to do so by reminding them of past exploits and sacrifices and turning their focus to the renewed demands war was going to impose upon them. In an address delivered in the new year prepared by his staff but reflecting his viewpoint, Forrest exhorted, "Soldiers—The old campaign is ended and your commanding general deems this an appropriate occasion to speak of the steadiness, self-denial, and patriotism with which you have borne the hardships of the past year." Together they had accomplished much, but they must be prepared to build upon a "reputation so nobly won" in facing what lay ahead. "Soldiers! you now rest for a short time from your labors. During the respite prepare for future action. Your commanding general is ready to lead you again in the defense of the common cause." With dramatic allusions to a soldier's "armor" and "a determination to fight," Forrest stoked the rhetorical fires he hoped would motivate his men in the days and months to come.[15]

Richard Taylor saw that his subordinate would have sweeping authority, naming Forrest to lead the cavalry in the Department of Alabama, Mississippi, and East

Louisiana in January. On February 28, 1864, Forrest received promotion to the rank of lieutenant general.[16] Belief in the cavalryman's capabilities was not confined to the top circles of leadership. A newspaper in the Confederate capital captured the essence of this confidence best with an assessment set against the backdrop of the disastrous retreat from Nashville in December: "General Forrest, with his splendid cavalry, have turned up in the right place and put a sudden change upon the aspect of affairs." The result, then, as it would be expected to be in any new phase of combat, was that Forrest would "always make his presence felt."[17]

Wilson matched his adversary in diligence and effort, working to assemble a formidable force in two camps that were now located on the Tennessee River in the northwestern corner of Alabama, at Waterloo and Gravelly Springs. By the time he was ready to commence his expedition into the Confederate heartland, Wilson's force would take on the aspect of a juggernaut. But the inherent delays in action created conditions that were painful reminders of past experiences for some Union officials. George Thomas had undergone tremendous criticism from his superiors prior to the Battle of Nashville over his preference for preparation over aggression. Ulysses Grant had nearly replaced the Virginian twice in command, even venturing in the direction of the Tennessee state capital himself before Thomas's attacks on December 15–16 rendered the matter moot. Union secretary of war Edwin M. Stanton had become enormously frustrated with the state of affairs in Tennessee, lamenting at one point of Thomas's methodical attempts to prepare his cavalry for action, "If he waits for Wilson to get ready, Gabriel will be blowing his last horn."[18]

In the aftermath of the victory at Nashville and the pursuit of Hood's shattered army, the pressure returned, with Ulysses Grant demonstrating increasing irritation at his subordinate's inability to push forward in the field in a manner that the Union commander found acceptable. Thomas tried to offer assurances: "General Wilson has a fine location for thoroughly organizing and disciplining his command, which he can accomplish in a few weeks. He will then have a force which the enemy will be utterly unable to resist." He offered his promise not to delay matters unduly regardless of the conditions "if sufficient horses can be furnished to remount the cavalry."[19]

Thomas's old West Point roommate and immediate superior, William T. Sherman, did not help matters by constantly goading Grant with references to his comrade's "slowness." Grant needed little prodding to reach the same conclusion and began to act on that basis. "Thomas must make a campaign or spare his surplus troops," the Union commander asserted to Henry Halleck.[20] As he assessed the period shortly afterward, Grant noted coldly, "Knowing Thomas to be slow beyond excuse, I depleted his army."[21] Sherman reflected the more aggressive style of field leadership Grant preferred and planned to maintain pressure on the Confederates, in addition to keeping it on his well-meaning but ponderous colleague in Tennessee. For Thomas's piece of the comprehensive campaigning to come, the key effort was meant to be made initially against Selma, Alabama. Sherman wanted the troops assigned to this expedition to do "all the damage possible; burning up Selma, that is the navy yard, the railroad back to the Tombigbee [River], and all iron foundries, mills and factories." For good measure he hoped to dispense with Forrest, too, having the elusive Confederate "hunted down and killed," although Sherman professed to doubt "if we can do that yet."[22]

The circumstances for generating an expedition aimed primarily at Selma remained fluid. Grant seemed to prefer that Thomas support the operations of Edward R. S. Canby against Mobile, including detailing 1,500 of his best mounted troopers under Joseph Knipe for Canby's use. But the departure of these men did not prevent preparations for other operations from continuing in northern Alabama. Biographer Francis McKinney argued that Thomas had evolved in his thinking regarding the use of cavalry for launching major offensive operations. That Thomas recognized the potential of a raid on the scale Wilson was prepared to carry out was apparent, but that he had come to see such a force as a substitute for a larger conventional army is debatable. "It was the culmination of Thomas' vision of a complete, trained and self-sufficient army," McKinney concluded of Wilson's force.[23] As recently as the Atlanta and Nashville campaigns, Thomas had seen how cavalry could be employed, both effectively and ineffectively, but there was no sense that he thought of a command, even one as impressive as Wilson's, as anything more than an extension of his own army.[24]

Wilson was thorough in his preparations. He sought to obtain intelligence from every quarter. He understood how well his opponent gathered and processed information but proclaimed, "My spies and scouts were as good and resourceful as Forrest's."[25] Under the guise of discussing prisoner exchange, he dispatched his provost marshal, Colonel John G. Parkhurst, to meet with General Forrest. Captain Lewis Hosea traveled with Parkhurst, bearing personal instructions from Wilson to "keep his eyes open." Hosea was to take the measure of the man the Federals would oppose shortly and report on conditions as he found them among the Confederates. The Forrest he encountered retained a swagger that reflected the commander's personality but also served to mask the weaknesses in his position that lay behind the confident mien.[26] In making his own assessment of his opponent, Wilson termed his foe "a bold and resolute man, not easily overborne and never rattled."[27]

Delays due to weather conditions continued to plague the Federals. Finally, on March 22, Wilson shook his large and well-appointed mounted command into operation. One anxious Union soldier noted in his journal, "Finally we have started—after so long a time to equip."[28] In addition to 13,000 troopers armed with Spencer carbines, the column had 1,500 teamsters to coax supplies along the Alabama byways when the moment came to advance.[29] The entourage moved toward the Confederate heartland in multiple columns, aided initially by the threat of another expedition that was supposed to have started out northward from Pensacola, Florida. By the time Forrest could determine the veracity of the various rumors and reports, Wilson was several days in the saddle. The Confederate had employed his common practice of spreading his forces so that he could respond as needed, but he now faced the difficult task of consolidating these scattered troops so as to form an adequate defense.

Forrest was not fully informed of Wilson's line of approach until March 26. By the next day, the Union cavalryman was already in Jasper as his Confederate counterpart scrambled to respond to the threat of that advance. Wilson was determined not to experience a recurrence of the experience he had endured opposite Forrest at Spring Hill. He wanted to keep the Southerners as uncertain of his intentions as the presence of large bodies of troops and the fires engulfing destroyed ironworks and other facilities along his line of march would allow. On March 29, Wilson crossed the Black Warrior River and on the following day moved into Elyton (Birmingham), with troops proceeding to wreck the factories in that town.

From Elyton, Wilson detached 1,100 men under Brig. Gen. John T. Croxton to ride for Tuscaloosa. The movement expanded the scope of destruction and disruption while creating another element for the Confederates to take into account. The detachment also took Croxton's command out of the remainder of the campaign for Selma, although the operation played a vital role when Confederate brigadier general William H. "Red" Jackson diverted his force to attack it. "I am closing around him," Jackson informed Forrest on March 31, "with a view of attacking him at daylight in the morning."[30]

Wilson was confident that his movements would continue to enjoy success. In the early morning hours of the same day, the Union cavalryman informed his superior, General Thomas: "I am pushing everything for Selma with all possible speed, and shall reach there in three days, unless the enemy can do more than present appearances seem to indicate." Wilson's command was also fulfilling his intention of continuing to smash Confederate facilities. "We have destroyed several very extensive iron-works and will to-day burn those at Columbiana," he explained.[31]

Confederates under Brigadier Generals James Chalmers and "Red" Jackson remained on the west side of the Cahaba River, while Forrest deployed Brig. Gen. Philip Roddey's cavalry and Brig. Gen. Daniel Adams's Alabama state troops to slow the Union column as it proceeded. These troops proved little more than an annoyance for the lead elements of the Union expedition under Brig. Gen. Emory Upton near Montevallo. The first of these Federal forces reached the town at approximately 1:00 P.M. on March 31, driving their opponents from the scene with relative ease. Only the timely arrival of Col. Edward Crossland's Southern horsemen allowed the situation to stabilize momentarily. Renewed pressure from the Union forces collapsed even that effort, with no less than a hundred of the Confederates killed, wounded, missing, or captured as a result. Forrest's appearance with members of his escort and another two hundred soldiers under Brig. Gen. Frank C. Armstrong prevented the Federals from inflicting worse losses but did nothing substantial to blunt the Union advance.

On April 1, as the Southern cavalry commander neared the community of Randolph, he remained hopeful that circumstances would allow him to concentrate his men and halt the main invading force before it reached Selma. These turned decisively against him when some of Upton's troopers brought in a courier with messages that had been meant to reach Chalmers and Jackson on the opposite side of the Cahaba River. Now Wilson not only understood his enemy's dispositions but also recognized the means of defeating Forrest's intentions. This knowledge would dictate the speed and direction the Union operation would assume for the rest of the campaign.

The intelligence coup offered Wilson the chance to keep Forrest's command divided. Accordingly, Wilson ordered General McCook to locate Croxton if possible but, more important, to drive off the defenders of a crucial bridge crossing at Centreville. The move would not only prevent Southern troops from threatening the flank and rear of his command but leave Forrest in the unenviable position of standing alone with only a portion of his command against the more numerous Union troopers arrayed before them. Forrest's aggressiveness often counted for much when he faced timid opponents, but Wilson understood the strength of his position and was determined to press his advantage accordingly.[32]

Employing the same technique he had perfected in mounting an effective rearguard action to enable the defeated Army of Tennessee to retreat after Nashville, Forrest used Crossland's men to retire by alternate lines before their foes. The Confederate commander established himself in the vicinity of Bogler's Creek, near Ebenezer Church, behind a strong defensive line of rail breastworks. A sharp fight ensued as Brig. Gen. Eli Long's men approached and tested the Southern defenses. A temporary pause for the blue-coated horsemen as they encountered larger numbers than they had anticipated nevertheless yielded positive results when a horse broke from its rider's control and slammed into a piece of Confederate artillery that smashed a wheel on the gun carriage. Horse and rider both perished, but the attack quelled the devastating fire and fractured the Southern position.

Forrest came close to being swept from the fighting himself as the combat swirled around him. Various accounts had the Confederate struggling with opponents, usually against impressive odds, and compelled at least once to leap his horse over an obstructing vehicle to escape. But the most dramatic moment came when a young Union officer singled Forrest out for attack. Slashing vigorously with his saber, the Federal inflicted painful wounds on his opponent's arm and head before the Confederate could turn his pistol and defend himself. Forrest later admitted that he feared the blows "would kill me," before adding dramatically that if his attacker had "known enough" to use the point of the saber rather than slashing with the blade, "I should not have been here to tell you about it."[33] The entire affair was a microcosm of Forrest's personal approach to warfare and an illustration of Richard Taylor's observation, "He was a host in himself, and a dangerous adversary at any reasonable odds."[34]

Additional Union forces arrived, and the weight of numbers and the uncertainty of some of the Confederate defenders began to tell. The state militia units gave way and Forrest had no choice but to retreat to the defensive works surrounding Selma. Wilson could claim a victory over his adversary with a loss inflicted of some three hundred men, while sustaining twelve killed and forty wounded of his own.[35]

As the Federals closed in on the city, panic began to set in for some while others sought to offer comforting platitudes. The *Selma Evening Reporter* provided its readers with a reassuring letter attributed to Forrest. "I am for fighting as long as there is a man left to fight with," the horseman proclaimed.[36] Forrest was prepared to back up the sentiment by pressing into service every able-bodied individual, promising to pitch anyone into the river who would not go into the defensive works.[37] Even with the indifferently armed citizens utilized in the emergency, the three and a half miles of earthworks that were supposed to protect Selma contained only a few thousand defenders. There was no time to prepare a coordinated defense or train civilians who had not expected such duty.

Forrest reached Selma on the morning of April 2 and dutifully reported to his superior, General Richard Taylor, to inform him of the developments that now required a defense of the city itself. Taylor recalled that the celebrated Southern horseman rode up to advise him of the Union advance and to urge him to leave for safety. According to the Confederate commander's recollection, Forrest appeared, "horse and man covered with blood." Taylor remembered that he had "felt anxious" for the wounded subordinate but explained that Forrest had dismissed the concerns, saying that he was "unhurt," pronouncing in his forceful style that he "would cut his way through, as most of his men had done."[38]

Having warned his superior, the Southern cavalryman dashed off to conduct as viable a defense as his limited numbers would permit. Forrest tried to shorten the lines his makeshift force would be called upon to defend by building a second line closer to the city, but Wilson was not going to accommodate the discomfited Confederates to allow them to complete that work. For the moment, Forrest tried to overcome as many adverse factors as he could with the available defenders spread as efficiently and effectively as possible by deploying his best men to cover the most vulnerable areas and dispersing the militia and the impressed civilians between his veterans to provide some sense of stoutness to the part-time soldiery. Troubling gaps remained, but if the defenders could produce enough firepower to thwart the attacks, their actions might buy the time necessary for Forrest's other veteran fighters to reach the scene.

General Wilson's command was in the saddle by 8:00 A.M. on April 2. One participant recalled that destruction continued to mark the progress of the column as it moved toward Selma, including the burning of "a thousand bales of cotton—and a 'gin house' on each plantation." Refugees fled before the wave of blue-coated riders, only to lose the animals that pulled their conveyances to troopers who left them to their own devices to proceed as best they could.[39] By 2:00 P.M. the Union riders began to appear before the lines at Selma, deploying for action, when another important development occurred in their favor. Some of Emory Upton's men brought forward an Englishman who had detailed knowledge of the design of the Selma defenses and agreed to provide a sketch of them that the attackers could use to aid in their assault.[40]

Wilson did not entirely trust his good fortune. He understood the method of planting false deserters as a means of deceiving an opponent. Consequently, as his men prepared for their final push against the Selma defenses, he examined the works personally, hoping to "verify," as much as distance would allow, what he had learned about them. At the end of his hasty reconnaissance, Wilson recorded that the sketch he had obtained, "much to my gratification," turned out to be "surprisingly accurate."[41]

Satisfied that he held as much information as he could get and aware of the lateness of the hour for daylight fighting, Wilson determined to assault the Southern defenses. Yet it was not his actions that precipitated the advance. The impetus came with the appearance at approximately 4:30 P.M. of a portion of James Chalmers's command in the Union rear that offered at least the possibility of a threat to the Union supply train. Forrest had employed such forms of attack before as a way of neutralizing a larger opposing force. This time General Long, like his commander, was in no mood to be deterred from launching the main assault while the viability of such a threat could be substantiated. Without taking the time to dispatch a courier for instructions, Long seized the initiative and accepted responsibility for sending his men forward.

The advance came under heavy fire from the Confederates, but the Union advantages in numbers and armament were too great, and the Federals pushed the defenders out of their works with relative ease. Well-placed shots from the Union artillery and the staggering fire of their carbines caused a wavering in the militia defenders that compromised the entire line. "I knew all was lost," a Southern officer noted as the action unfolded. There were no reserves to plug the gaps and with victorious bluecoats plunging into the works no sense in sacrificing more men in trying to hold them back any longer. By this point, Upton's troops had joined the fray, carrying their portion of the opposing defenses and prying back another part of the Confederate line. Union officer Lewis Hosea remembered, "The conflict on the works was brief. The greater portion of the enemy stampeded in wild confusion."[42]

Wilson came forward to assess the progress of his assaults. The second more compact but incomplete inner line of defensive works closer to the city offered the potential for effective resistance, and he wanted to overcome those positions before the fluid situation coalesced in some sense against his attacks. After regrouping for a final push, the Union assault swept forward once more. Instead of confronting shattered defenders, these Federals encountered substantial enemy fire. One participant observed that "all at once the whole top of the embankment was one sheet of fire, flame and smoke." But the attackers surged on, prompted by Wilson's presence. A wound to the general's charger felled him briefly from the saddle, but neither he nor the men faltered, as Wilson remounted and the bloodied animal carried its rider on into the fight. Reinforcements added their numbers to the crush of Union attackers, and all organized attempts at resistance by the Confederates disintegrated into a series of individual combats and attempts at escape or surrender.[43]

For Forrest, battlefield bravado had its place and applications, but with any semblance of viable defense melting away around him he understood as well as anyone that any further stand would be fruitless.[44] He was also aware that escaping would be no simple matter. Indeed, amid the chaos that now flushed through the streets of Selma, finding safe passage and egress would be an ordeal unto itself. However, it was not in the nature of Nathan Bedford Forrest not to try. The man who had extracted himself from dire circumstances before, most dramatically on the field at Parker's Crossroads in 1862, where he insisted he would "charge 'em both ways" to accomplish the feat, would try to do so again here in order to continue his fight elsewhere. He had the able assistance of his personal escort, the devoted and tightly knit group that he used as a special force to be applied on any occasion. Together they slashed through the darkness and confusion.

By 7:00 Selma was in Union hands and "the town given up to plunder," as one of the occupying soldiers observed.[45] The human toll for the attackers rested at 46 killed, 300 wounded, and 13 missing. But the Confederates, in addition to losing a vital industrial center, had experienced the capture of 2,700 men, in addition to their battlefield casualties and, perhaps most tellingly, the psychological blow of the defeat and dispersal of forces commanded by Gen. N. B. Forrest.[46] Even his prodigious efforts and reputation had not been sufficient to save the city from falling.

However, Forrest's escapades were not at an end. On the circuitous ride away from Selma, Forrest and his personal escort happened upon an isolated Union outpost manned by members of the 4th United States Cavalry. Captured Federal pickets divulged the proximity of a larger body of their comrades. The opportunity now presented itself for retribution against a unit that Forrest's troopers held responsible for the 1863 slaying of their popular comrade Capt. Samuel Freeman while a prisoner, as well as for other misdeeds attributed to them. The Confederates determined to surprise the detachment but refused to go forward unless their general remained behind with the horses to avoid "unnecessary exposure" in a night firefight. An exhausted Forrest, still nursing his wounds from his previous encounters with Wilson's troopers, agreed.[47]

As the Southerners approached, some of the Federals succeeded in firing warning shots and an "animated fight resulted." But the advantages lay with the Confederates, firing from darkness into the light of the campfires or picking off individuals as they tried to slip away. Forrest came up as the firing subsided and the attackers counted thirty-five killed or wounded Federals, while suffering the loss of only one member wounded among their number; five of the bluecoats left the scene as prisoners.[48] The Confederate officer who led the assault in Forrest's stead maintained that "not a single man was killed after he surrendered."[49]

Federal accounts presented the incident in a different light. A Union surgeon asserted, "Forrest, retreating from Selma, came across a party of Federals asleep in a neighboring field, and charged on them, and, refusing to listen to their cries for surrender, killed or wounded the entire party, numbering twenty-five men."[50] Sgt. James Larson of the 4th compared the incident to the more notorious action a year earlier, calling it a "repitition of Ft. Pillow," where Forrest's men were accused of carrying out a massacre of troops after they had ceased to resist.[51] In memoirs that appeared years later, Wilson noted the post-Selma incident and observed that the Confederates had "killed the last one of them," referring to the surprised party of Federals. He concluded, "Such incidents as this were far too frequent with Forrest." Wilson concluded that his former opponent's "ruthless temper . . . impelled him upon every occasion where he had a clear advantage to push his success to a bloody end, and yet he always seemed not only to resent but to have a plausible excuse for the cruel excesses that were charged against him."[52]

The incident bore eerie similarities to the events at Fort Pillow in April 1864, in which some of Forrest's men killed Tennessee Unionist and black garrison members after they had surrendered. The cavalry commander had remained behind when the final assault of that Mississippi River outpost occurred, just as he would do outside Selma, limiting his ability to control affairs once effective Union resistance collapsed. The Confederates, including Forrest, offered a range of explanations for the excesses that had taken place at Fort Pillow, with the same pattern occurring concerning the Selma incident. The cavalryman remained inordinately sensitive to charges that he had perpetrated a "massacre" as the "Butcher of Fort Pillow," yet he took no apparent steps to avoid unnecessary bloodshed in this situation. It is also difficult to assess the degree to which Fort Pillow influenced the surprised Union contingent in continuing to resist longer than they might have otherwise. In any case, as the commander in both instances, the "Wizard of the Saddle" could not escape responsibility for the actions of the men under his command.[53]

Wilson may have understood Forrest's personality as well as anyone, but his own tendency toward hyperbole got the better of him in the aftermath of the battle he had just won. "I regard the capture of Selma [as] the most remarkable achievement in the history of modern cavalry," he observed unabashedly in an after-action report. Nevertheless, the impact of what he and his men had accomplished reflected the harsh reality that was facing the Confederacy. "The capture of Selma having put us in possession of the enemy's greatest depot in the Southwest was a vital blow to their cause."[54] The evacuation of Richmond by the Confederates on the same day overshadowed the events in Alabama, but the loss of Selma to the south nevertheless remained significant. When word of the Union success reached Mobile, the troops there paused in their operations to express their satisfaction at the news. "A saloot of 100 guns was fired on account of the fall of Selma, Ala.," a soldier from Illinois noted in his diary on April 6.[55]

Celebration of achievements would have its day, but in the wake of such a decisive victory, the most pressing concern for the Union commander was to secure the spoils he had obtained and reduce, as much as possible, any potential risk to the integrity of his forces. Bringing the men back under control was a matter of restoring the order and discipline expected of military units and would take place as quickly as roll calls and barking orders could make it so. But Wilson recognized two additional imperatives in the morning after the engagement that had garnered him the city. He still did not know precisely what other hostile forces he faced, and he wanted to begin the process of denying his opponents the resources Selma had previously offered them. Consolidating his command and dispatching scouts into the countryside would help him fulfill one of these objectives, while organizing efforts to deal with the existing military facilities, gathering animal stock, and retrieving abandoned arms and equipment would aid in the other.

Just as had been the case before the city had fallen, no matter proved too small for Wilson's attention. In his assessment of the priorities, the cavalry commander ordered Brig. Gen. Edward F. Winslow to delay the methodical destruction of the Confederate infrastructure briefly, for more practical purposes: "Before burning the arsenal and naval foundry, secure tools, rope, materials, etc.—sufficient to construct a pontoon bridge across the Alabama River."[56]

With the fighting concluded, other Union participants indulged in different impulses. For one Union cavalryman, the routine of duty gave way to curiosity. E. N. Gilpin noted in his journal that he and a companion inspected the works that were supposed to have protected Selma and found them impressive. However, the vastness of the industrial capacity stood out even more. "From the forts we went to the iron foundry," he recorded, and observed there "immense machinery, hundreds of guns of all sizes, some very fine naval guns, and thousands of shot and shell." The next day there was time to visit "the great Selma arsenal," where Gilpin and his friend "looked at the shot and shell piled in great rows, through the long shops," all destined for destruction.[57]

The demolition that followed took days to accomplish. According to their commander's plans, Wilson's men reduced Selma's worth as a center of production capable of supporting the Confederate war effort in methodical fashion. Teams of men, black and white, "disabled" machinery, dumped supplies of all types into the river, and prepared numerous structures for the torch.[58] These ruined elements remained a tangible symbol of the destruction the bluecoats visited upon the city in the aftermath of its capture. Josiah Gorgas, the ordnance chief who had once taken such pride in his nation's efforts at generating war-related manufacturing and production only a year earlier, noted gloomily an assessment three months after Selma's fall. "The aspect of S[elma] is desolate in the extreme," the former official recorded in his diary on July 22, 1865. "I walked up after sunset toward the square where the 'Arsenal' was," he observed ominously. "All vestige of its arrangements had disappeared, except a tall stack; & fragments of gun carriages lay about to show where gun carriages were stored in iron making." The scene had a dampening effect on his spirits, as Gorgas reflected, "It was not thus I had hoped to visit it—one of my principal establishments."[59]

Wilson lingered in Selma for over a week, not only to complete the devastation of the city's war-making production but to allow Croxton to return to the main command with his detached force. In the meantime, as part of his continuing efforts at intelligence gathering, Wilson once again employed the services of Capt. Lewis Hosea. He and a Confederate prisoner selected to accompany him traveled to Cahaba with a communication for Richard Taylor regarding the possible exchange of captives from the recent operations. Hosea accomplished his task of conveying the message and set a meeting between Wilson and Forrest for discussions. Weather prohibited Wilson's attendance on April 7, but on the next day the Union commander traveled to Cahaba for his session with his adversary.

Wilson recalled that the tense atmosphere gave way during the course of a meal, and the antagonists soon "were treating each other like old acquaintances, if not old friends." Despite the limitations of his formal education, Forrest could be companionable and gregarious. In this instance, he was less so because of the recent encounter with his opponent at Selma and the continuing effects of his wounds from the campaign. "Well, General," Forrest admitted quietly, according to Wilson's later account, "you have beaten me badly, and for the first time I am compelled to make such an acknowledgment. I have met many of your men, but never before one I did not get away with first or last." Wilson generously sought to soften the blow. "Our victory was not without cost," he observed. "You put up a stout fight, but we were too many and too fast for you." Forrest accepted the explanation and the verdict of the contest: "Yes, I did my best, but, if I now had your entire force in hand, it would not compensate us for the deadly blow you have inflicted upon our cause by the capture and destruction of . . . Selma."[60] Forrest left the company of his opponent and once more turned to the task of reorganizing the remnants of his command.

Wilson's force had already departed Selma when word filtered to George Thomas of the capture of the city. A report came into Nashville from Huntsville at midmorning on April 11 via a third party and Thomas passed the information along to Henry Halleck in Washington. "I am inclined to believe it," the department commander explained, "although as yet I have received no report direct from General Wilson."[61] Wilson had conveyed the news of Selma's fall in a dispatch dated April 4, but circumstances had prevented its delivery before this point.[62] In any case, the cavalryman renewed his offensive, his extraordinary force proceeding to take the first Confederate capital of Montgomery before targeting Columbus, Georgia. Wilson's final contribution to the Union war effort would be the capture of the Confederate president, Jefferson Davis, and his party in the remote southern portion of the state.[63]

In the wake of the Selma Campaign, Nathan Bedford Forrest never again mounted the kind of operations he had carried out earlier in his career with such success. In his last meeting with Wilson he had appeared worn and dejected but held enough of his old fire to reply staunchly to a comment about his personal safety: "I am much obliged to you, General, but I have no fear! I have faced death on a hundred fields and I am sure the bullet has not been cast which is to kill me."[64] Within a matter of weeks, at Gainesville, Alabama, Forrest surrendered his command after briefly contemplating other options, including heading for Mexico. But Forrest had been too much a soldier to place himself in such an untenable personal position and believed too greatly in having sustained himself honorably in the service of a now lost cause to abandon his men entirely. "Havn't you still a command?" former Tennessee governor Isham Harris had inquired testily before he took the option of flight that Forrest had rejected. "Any man who is in favor of a further prosecution of this war is a fit subject for a lunatic asylum, and ought to be sent there immediately," the cavalryman had responded. Selma was only the final piece of the effort he had undertaken in a war that was now over. Like the men he had encouraged to return to their duties as civilians, with restored allegiance to an old flag and adherence to a newly united nation, he would embrace the peace to come: "Men, you may all do as you damn please, but I'm a-going home."[65]

Selma was left to pick up the pieces Wilson's troopers had left behind. This task would have to be done in the context of a reconstruction of the Union. Wilson and his bluecoats had done their jobs well. A week of systematic effort had reduced the vitals of Confederate industrial facilities and their various ancillary structures to ruins. "What a wreck of a place we have left," one Union soldier noted succinctly.[66] The wreckage was indicative of what the Confederate States of America had become and what even as powerful a force as Nathan Bedford Forrest had proven powerless to prevent. The scene of Union horsemen advancing as the sun was dipping in the western sky over Selma on April 2, 1865, turned out to be symbolic, too, in the larger sense, of the setting of the Confederate sun itself.

Notes

1. "April 8, [1864]," in Josiah Gorgas, *The Journals of Josiah Gorgas 1857–1878*, ed. Sarah Woolfolk Wiggins (Tuscaloosa: University of Alabama Press, 1995), 97–98.

2. Emory M. Thomas, *The Confederacy as a Revolutionary Experience* (Englewood Cliffs, NJ: Prentice-Hall, 1971), 88. See also Richard D. Goff, *Confederate Supply* (Durham: Duke University Press, 1969). Goff examined the efforts of the Confederacy to establish a system of supply for its troops, including the references to Selma (12, 59, 128, 138).

3. Emory M. Thomas, *The Confederate Nation: 1861–1865* (New York: Harper and Row, 1979), 207.

4. James Pickett Jones, *Yankee Blitzkrieg: Wilson's Raid through Alabama and Georgia* (Athens: University of Georgia Press, 1976), 76–79. Jones notes that housing had reached such a critical shortage that one individual slept on a cot in his office at the Nitre Works. Jones and Noah Andre Trudeau have offered the most detailed contemporary examinations of Wilson's preparations for and conduct of the expedition that included Selma. These sources, as well as Wilson's memoir, have provided the base for discussing the campaign in this essay. Noah Andre Trudeau, *Out of the Storm: The End of the Civil War, April–June 1865* (Boston: Little, Brown, 1994); James Harrison Wilson, *Under the Old Flag: Recollections of Military Operations in the War for the Union, the Spanish War, the Boxer Rebellion, etc.*, vol. 2 (New York: D. Appleton, 1912).

5. Dabney Maury to N. B. Forrest, Meridian, August 2, 1864, *The War of the Rebellion: A Compilation of the Official Records of the Union and Confederate Armies*, 128 vols. (Washington, DC: GPO, 1880–1901), series I, 39, pt. 2, 748 (hereafter *OR*; all references are to series I unless otherwise noted).

6. For an account of Forrest's life and wartime career, see Brian Steel Wills, *A Battle from the Start: The Life of Nathan Bedford Forrest* (New York: HarperCollins, 1992).

7. John Watson Morton, *The Artillery of Nathan Bedford Forrest's Cavalry* (Nashville: Publishing House of the M. E. Church South, 1905), 307.

8. Edward Longacre, *From Union Stars to Top Hat: A Biography of the Extraordinary General James Harrison Wilson* (Harrisburg, PA: Stackpole Books, 1972), 195.

9. B. R. Roberson, "The Courthouse Burnin'est General," *Tennessee Historical Quarterly* 23 (December 1964): 372–78. One of McCook's men referred to the pursuit colorfully as a "Lyon hunt." John W. Rowell, *Yankee Artillerymen: Through the Civil War with Eli Lilly's Indiana Battery* (Knoxville: University of Tennessee Press, 1975), 238.

10. Benjamin C. Truman, "The War in Tennessee," *New York Times*, December 20, 1864.

11. Your friend and Left Arm to My Dear Ad, Huntsville, Ala., January 2, 1865, Wilson Papers, Library of Congress. General Thomas concurred with the sentiments of his subordinate. See, for example, Thomas to Wilson, Pulaski, January 1, 1865, 5 P.M., *OR*, 45, pt. 2, 477.

12. Rowell, *Yankee Artillerymen*, 247.

13. See examples in Wills, *Battle from the Start*, of Forrest's attention to detail as a businessman (21–22, 26–27, 29–35, 40–41), with regard to intelligence and information (107, 114, 160), at Brice's Cross Roads (204–5), and in his command (232–35).

14. Richard Taylor, *Destruction and Reconstruction: Personal Experiences of the Late War* (New York: Longmans, Green, 1955), 242–43.

15. Forrest address, n.d., *OR*, 45, pt. 2, 759–60.

16. Thomas Jordan and J. P. Pryor, *The Campaigns of Lieut.-Gen. N. B. Forrest, and of Forrest's Cavalry* (New Orleans: Blelock & Co., 1868), 657.

17. *Daily Dispatch*, December 19, 1864.

18. Stanton to Grant, Washington, December 7, 1864, 10:20 A.M., *OR*, 45, pt. 2, 84.

19. Thomas to Halleck, Eastport, Miss., January 21, 1865, noon, *OR*, 45, pt. 2, 620–21.

20. Grant to Halleck, City Point, Va., January 18, 1865, 9 P.M., *OR*, 45, pt. 2, 609–10.

21. Grant to Sherman, City Point, Va., March 16, 1865, *OR*, 47, pt. 2, 859.

22. Sherman to Thomas, In the Field, Savannah, Ga., January 21, 1865, *OR*, 45, pt. 2, 621–22.

23. Francis F. McKinney, *Education in Violence: The Life of George H. Thomas and the History of the Army of the Cumberland* (Detroit: Wayne State University Press, 1961), 434–35.

24. For an account of the life and career of Thomas, see Brian Steel Wills, *George Henry Thomas: As True as Steel* (Lawrence: University Press of Kansas, 2012).

25. Wilson, *Under the Old Flag*, 2, 183.

26. Ibid., 184–85. Hosea's initial encounter with Forrest impressed the young officer, who left a detailed account of the meeting and his observations. Lewis M. Hosea letter, February 26, 1865, Monroe Cockrell Papers, William R. Perkins Library, Duke University, Durham, NC. See also Lewis M. Hosea, "'The Campaign of Selma,' Read before the Commandery of the Military Order of the Loyal Legion of the United States" (Cincinnati: Peter G. Thompson, 1885), 7.

27. Wilson, *Under the Old Flag*, 2, 208.

28. [March] 22nd [1865], James Nourse Papers, William L. Perkins Library, Duke University, Durham, NC.

29. Rowell, *Yankee Artillerymen*, 249.

30. Jackson to Forrest, James Hill's Sr., March 31, 1865, 8:45 P.M., *OR*, 49, pt. 2, 174.

31. Wilson to Thomas, Cahawba River, March 31, 1865, 6 A.M., *OR*, 49, pt. 2, 154. Thomas did not receive this message until April 12.

32. Wilson to McCook, Randolph, Ala., April 1, 1865, 10 A.M., ibid., 173.

33. Wilson, *Under the Old Flag*, 2, 244. See, for example, Jordan and Pryor, *Campaigns of Forrest*, 668–69 and John Allan Wyeth, *Life of General Nathan Bedford Forrest* (New York: Harper and Brothers, 1899), 600–602.

34. Taylor, *Destruction and Reconstruction*, 268.

35. Wilson reports, May 3, June 29, 1865, *OR*, 49, pt. 1, 351, 361; Long report, April 7, 1865, *OR*, 49, pt. 1, 437; Vail report, April 6, 1865, *OR*, 49, pt. 1, 455–56; Upton report, May 30, 1865, *OR*, 49, pt. 1, 473.

36. Quoted in Pickett, *Yankee Blitzkrieg*, 81.

37. Wyeth, *Life of General Nathan Bedford Forrest*, 603.

38. Taylor, *Destruction and Reconstruction*, 268–69.
39. April 2nd, 1865, James Nourse Papers.
40. Trudeau, *Out of the Storm*, 158.
41. Wilson, *Under the Old Flag*, 2, 225.
42. Hosea, "'The Campaign of Selma,'" 26.
43. Trudeau, *Out of the Storm*, 164. Hosea observed that some of the Confederates "seemed determined to resist to the bitter end" and that there was "a desultory, but vigorous firing." Hosea, "'The Campaign of Selma,'" 27–28.
44. In his memoirs, Dabney Maury placed Forrest in the company of Dan Adams at "the telegraph office" when the city's defense collapsed and related a colorful story of the cavalryman's departure from Selma under duress. Dabney Herndon Maury, *Recollections of a Virginian in the Mexican, Indian, and Civil Wars* (New York: Charles Scribner's Sons, 1894), 218. Jordan and Pryor, whose text Forrest read and generally approved, noted only that the general "had rapidly repaired to the scene where the assault was most strenuous." Jordan and Pryor, *Campaigns of Forrest*, 674–75.
45. April 3, [1865], James Nourse Papers.
46. Wilson, *Under the Old Flag*, 2, 227–36; Wilson reports, May 3, June 29, 1865, *OR*, 49, pt. 1, 351, 361; Long report, April 7, 1865, *OR*, 49, pt. 1, 438–39; Upton report, May 30, 1865, *OR*, 49, pt. 1, 473.
47. Wyeth, *Life of General Nathan Bedford Forrest*, 607.
48. Francis Salter report, n.d., *OR*, 49, pt. 1, 406; Jordan and Pryor, *Campaigns of Forrest*, 676–77.
49. Lieut. George Cowan quoted in Henry, *"First with the Most" Forrest* (Indianapolis: Bobbs-Merrill, 1944), 433.
50. Salter report, n.d., *OR*, 49, pt. 1, 406.
51. Quoted in Pickett, *Yankee Blitzkrieg*, 97.
52. Wilson, *Under the Old Flag*, 240.
53. Union casualties at Fort Pillow, April 12, 1864, amounted to 277–97 deaths or mortal wounds out of a garrison of 585–605. John Cimprich and Robert C. Mainfort Jr., "The Fort Pillow Massacre: A Statistical Note," *Journal of American History* 76 (December 1989): 835–37. See also Wills, *Battle from the Start*, for an assessment of Fort Pillow and Forrest's involvement there (169–96). Jordan and Pryor argued that the Union troops had been engaged in plundering local civilians (*Campaigns of Forrest*, 676–77).
54. Wilson report, June 29, 1865, *OR*, 49, pt. 1, 361.
55. William Wiley, *The Civil War Diary of a Common Soldier: William Wiley of the 77th Illinois Infantry*, ed. Terrence J. Winschel (Baton Rouge: Louisiana State University Press, 2001), 148.
56. Wilson to Winslow, Selma, Ala., April 4, 1865, *OR*, 49, pt. 2, 218.
57. E. N. Gilpin, *The Last Campaign: A Cavalryman's Journal* (Leavenworth, KS: Press of Ketcheson Printing, n.d.), 640–41.
58. Ibid., 342; Wilson, *Under the Old Flag*, 2, 233.
59. "Saturday, [July 22, 1865]," in Gorgas, *Journals*, 183–84.
60. Wilson, *Under the Old Flag*, 2, 240.
61. Thomas to Halleck, Nashville, April 11, 1865, 11:30 PM, *OR*, 49, pt. 2, 318. This communication contained a copy of the one Thomas had received, Granger to Thomas, Huntsville, April 11, 1865, 9 AM, *OR*, 49, pt. 2, 318.
62. Wilson to Thomas, Selma, April 4, 1865, 10 AM, *OR*, 49, pt. 2, 217.

63. For a comprehensive examination of the remainder of Wilson's operations in Alabama and Georgia, see Wilson, *Under the Old Flag*, 2 and Jones, *Yankee Blitzkrieg*.

64. Wilson, *Under the Old Flag*, 2, 245.

65. Jason Niles Diary, Southern Historical Collection, University of North Carolina at Chapel Hill; Dan T. Carter, *When the War Was Over: The Failure of Self-Reconstruction in the South, 1865–1867* (Baton Rouge: Louisiana State University Press, 1985), 9.

66. Quoted in Trudeau, *Out of the Storm*, 180.

5
Fighting for the Cause?
An Examination of the Motivations of Alabama's Confederate Soldiers from a Class Perspective

Kristopher A. Teters

On March 1, 1864, Confederate prisoner of war John Washington Inzer wrote in his diary: "Now fear we will be held as prisoners a long time. Well, we must bear it. Anything for our country. We must never think for one moment of giving up the contest. All we have to do is be true to our cause. We never can be subjugated." Just a few short years before, Inzer had been the youngest representative at Alabama's secession convention, but now he found himself imprisoned on Johnson's Island on the edge of Lake Erie. Despite the terrible conditions, Inzer remained true to the Confederate cause. At about the same time, on February 27, 1864, Pvt. Hiram Smith Williams of the 40th Alabama wrote: "War at best is horrible enough to cause a shudder to chill the heart of all good men, but this [one] so unholy, so bitter . . . so absurd as to the establishment of any great and vital principle, is the worst record upon the pages of modern history." Williams was a recent migrant to the South and part of the Southern middle class. He voiced none of the ideological convictions so ardently expressed by Inzer and painted a very different picture of the war.[1]

These two examples illustrate the contrasting attitudes of Alabama's Confederate soldiers. Although some Alabamian soldiers held strong ideological convictions that motivated them to fight, others expressed hardly any ideological commitment. This distinction largely corresponds to class differences. Alabamian Confederates who were planters, members of planter families, or in some way part of the upper class tended to be much more ideological. For them, the war was a struggle to forge an independent nation and break free from a tyrannical government that threatened their slave property and way of life. On the other hand, Confederates who had been yeomen farmers or were poor whites conveyed much less ideological commitment. Their patriotic feelings, if expressed at all, typically revolved around the defense of their homes and religious faith. Oftentimes Southerners from the lower ranks were just trying to survive and return to their families.

Alabama's soldiers also responded to the war differently over time. Although those of the upper class were more likely to sustain their ideological motivations throughout the war and maintain their morale, those of the lower ranks more often grew disillusioned. These important differences among Alabama's Confederate soldiers point to a Confederate nationalism that was hardly monolithic and whose ideology did not permeate the whole of Southern society.[2]

This essay relies on the 1860 federal census for determining the class of Alabama's Confederates. It uses the value of their total estates or that of their parents if they still resided in their household: $6,882 and above is considered upper class; anything below that number is middle and lower class. Determining the precise cutoff between middle and lower class is not important for the purposes of this essay because both middle- and lower-class soldiers had similar non-ideological motives. Upper-class soldiers often had total estates significantly above the $6,882 figure, and, likewise, middle- and lower-class soldiers usually had estates valued at much less than that number. This places most of these soldiers firmly in their respective classes. When possible, this essay also uses biographical information for verifying the class of soldiers.[3]

Alabama's upper-class Confederates based their ideological motives for enlisting on those of their revolutionary forefathers. Like the revolutionary generation of 1776, they were struggling against an oppressive government that was threatening to destroy their liberty. J. P. Cannon of the 27th Alabama believed that Confederates could endure a long war just as their eighteenth-century ancestors had done: "Our forefathers fought seven years for independence, and we have only fought for three. Can we stand it the other four? Yes, we will never give up as long as we can sustain an army." An Alabamian captain asserted that the wrongs confronted by the Confederates were even more serious than the "trifling" problems faced in 1776. "If the mere imposition of a tax could raise such a tumult what should be the result of the terrible system of oppression instituted by the Yankees," he wondered. Degrees of injustice aside, some Alabamian Confederates considered their fight the "Second American Revolution," a struggle to return to the true vision of the Founders.[4]

Alabamian Confederates from the upper ranks of society also saw the war as a fight for liberty against a despotic government. Nathaniel Dawson, a planter who enlisted in the 4th Alabama, asked his wife, "What would we be without our liberty?" He went on to note that death was better "a thousand times to recognizing once a Black Republican ruler." Adam Henry Whetstone pointed out the sadness of his regiment when they prepared to march off to war and bear years "of suffering and grievous disappointments." He quickly added that this "proves, however, what a people can and will endure when striving for a cause they esteem as dear to them as liberty." Maj. Vincent Elmore of the 1st Alabama Cavalry hoped his brothers would write soon, for "if they cheer his heart and enlighten his spirits . . . they assist in some means to achieve our liberty." The idealistic John Inzer of the 5th Alabama composed a poem in prison: "Man, however vile, whatever his perils, / Whatever his destination, was born / Free and loves Liberty." For some Alabamians, liberty was synonymous with the cause itself, a sacred principle that could be secured and preserved only through great hardship.[5]

In order to secure this liberty, Alabama's Confederates thought it necessary to form a separate nation, and achieving independence was a powerful motivator. Capt. James Williams of the 21st Alabama wrote to his father, "My whole soul is in the success of our struggle for independence; which *sooner or later we will win*." During the battles around Atlanta, another Alabamian soldier mentioned that Gen. A. P. Stewart had produced a circular to inspire the men "to stand by our glorious cause . . . the time has come when we must make a grand struggle for our independence." The whole idea of Southern nationalism inspired James Stephens of the 7th Alabama. Reflecting on the first year of the war, Stephens wrote, "Another year has passed away and within that another new nation has sprung into existence which bids fair to become a great and prosperous nation. I mean our nation the Southern Confederacy."[6]

The Southern Confederacy that upper-class Alabamian Confederates were fighting to establish was a slaveholders' republic. They believed that preserving slavery was central to their cause. Elias Davis of the 8th Alabama wrote that he would be willing "to fight forever, rather than submit to freeing negroes among us." He added that the struggle was for "rights and property bequeathed to us by our ancestors." Lieut. Jake Weil made his feelings clear to his brother when he asserted, "We shall not be deprived of rights or [slave] property without the course of law which our constitution granted."[7]

Some of these soldiers looked at their struggle as a war against abolitionists who threatened to undermine the social and economic fabric of the South. John Taylor Banks of the 6th Alabama noted that he had enlisted because "the Abolitionists occupied Decatur, Ala." James Stephens referred to the Union troops who attacked Harpers Ferry in 1861 as "abolitionists." He rejoiced that "the white livered scoundrels had went there to avenge the death of that old hellion John Brown" and now they "have met the old scoundrel in hell with the halter around his neck and taken up their abode with him in the lowest pit of that doless region." Clearly Stephens made a connection between the Union troops and the abolitionist Brown. James Williams felt optimistic because he believed that Southern men would never "submit to the degrading yoke of a hated abolition master." William Riser in the 10th Alabama also was confident because "all are willing to draw the sword and throw away the scabard until Lincoln's abolition hord shall have been driven back, and our young Republic [established]."[8]

Nothing enraged upper-class Alabamians more than when "Lincoln's abolition hord" began using black troops against the South. This was a direct assault on white supremacy and how white Southerners perceived the natural order of civilization. While a prisoner of war, Col. Daniel Hundley of the 31st Alabama was appalled to see a Union regiment of black troops from a prison window. His mind was quickly transported back three thousand years to the prophet Ezekiel's message of impending destruction for Israel at the hands of a foreign power. At the sight of these black troops, Hundley was filled with an apocalyptic vision that the South would suffer the same kind of destruction. Blacks in blue uniforms made Alabamian soldiers feel that their world was falling apart. Confederates so passionately hated black soldiers that they would not treat them as prisoners of war. An officer in the 9th Alabama, Edmund Patterson, agreed with this policy, declaring, "If we lose everything else, let us preserve our honor." This was echoed by John Inzer, who, after remarking on the use of black troops by the Union, stated, "I live to hate the U.S. Flag. I will marry no woman who has the least respect for it."[9]

For upper-class Alabamian soldiers, no figure represented a greater threat to the institution of slavery and to their liberty than Abraham Lincoln. They both feared and despised him. Some soldiers viewed him as a tyrannical leader unlawfully prosecuting a war against the Southern states. Daniel Hundley compared Lincoln to "the tyrant" King George III and in capital letters proclaimed, "VANDALS AND THE ENEMIES OF ALL FREE GOVERNMENT WERE THE SUPPORTERS OF ABRAHAM LINCOLN." Just as Lincoln began his second year in office, Samuel Pickens of the 5th Alabama commented that Congress "has given him all power of an emperor—a mil. Despot." For many Confederates, Lincoln became the symbol of Northern aggression. James Williams went so far as to call Confederate ammunition "anti-Lincoln pills." These soldiers always feared that Lincoln would oppress and subjugate the South.[10]

Subjugation was a common concern expressed by Alabama's Confederates; they were fighting to avoid this terrible fate. Sgt. Joseph Barnett of the 17th Alabama wrote to a friend back home that "we must with the glittering sword Musket go forth to meet the Mother Vandals and show them That such a Thing as subjugation among the Southern warrior is impossible." Observing the defiant spirit among the people of Decatur when a Union brigade came in sight of the town, John Banks commented, "How can a nation of such people be subjugated? Why it can't be done. No never." Daniel Hundley believed that the North was prosecuting a "barbarous war for the subjugation or extermination of eight millions of the Anglo-Saxon race." He added that future generations would "blush for the vandalism of their sires."[11]

In a more general sense, Hundley expressed another powerful motivator for Alabama's Confederates: a passionate hatred of the North. Northern soldiers were godless creatures who would desecrate their homeland and ravage their women. While passing through Decatur on furlough, John Banks was pleased by the public mood: "I found the people of Decatur doing better than I had ever expected tho they have had the hated foe amongst them for months and had him to desecrate their churches and their parlors and their women insulted by his lawless soldiers."

All of this misbehavior grew out of "the diabolical meanness of a Yankee beast." William Foster, an Alabamian chaplain who suffered through the long siege of Vicksburg, felt "bitter anguish" when the city was surrendered to Union forces. The beautiful country was "now in the possession of a hateful foe, desecrated by the vile footsteps of a heartless, cruel and unprincipled enemy who comes with the felonious purpose of desolating our homes, of spreading the shadow of death over our firesides and of enslaving a free and noble people." Gen. Cullen Battle denounced Gen. Philip Sheridan for "[w]aging war against the defenseless" and making "the Valley of the Shenandoah a desolation." Battle even condemned Confederate general Jubal Early's retaliatory burning of Chambersburg, Pennsylvania, because it "takes from the South the white plume of civilized warfare." The intense hatred of the North fueled the fires of Southern patriotism all the more and made it seem ever more urgent to achieve independence from these uncivilized barbarians.[12]

This anti-Northernism stemmed in no small part from the fact that the North was invading these soldiers' homeland. They were motivated to defend their firesides at all costs. Organizing a company of volunteers, Alabamian lawyer George Miller asserted, "When a Southron's home is threatened, the spirit of resistance is irrepressible." J. P. Cannon remembered that in 1861 the report of a possible Union invasion caused much commotion throughout north Alabama: "The war was coming to our very doors. . . . The time had come for every man to 'shoulder his gun.'" Pvt. Elisha Baker of the 6th Alabama was confident that the Union armies would be devastated when they launched another invasion of the South. "[T]hey will find every hill in the south to be a Gibraltar and every valley a valley of the shadow of death to the invading foe," he contended.[13]

These patriotic Alabamians realized that their fight for freedom and homeland was tied to political developments away from the battlefield. Alabamian soldiers of higher social rank naturally followed politics more closely than their less-educated comrades. James Stephens observed in November 1861 that the Alabama legislature had passed a bill allowing soldiers to vote in presidential and congressional elections. While on active duty in Virginia, Thomas Hubbard Hobbs, a captain in the 9th Alabama, commented on the famous Trent Affair. He attached newspaper articles in his diary that detailed how the two Confederate envoys to England, James Mason and John Slidell, had been arrested and then released by the U.S. government. On January 3, 1862, he noted, "The papers recvd. this morning bring confirmation of the news of yesterday that Slidell + Mason have been surrendered by the Yankee Government. Never was there a more ignominious back-down." Even under the constant stress of campaigning, these soldiers remained conscious of political events occurring far away.[14]

In addition to politics, Alabama's Confederates cared deeply about religion. This was a particularly religious age, and the onset of the war heightened religious sensibilities. Soldiers took Bibles with them when they went off to fight and attended religious services in camp. In his diary, J. P. Cannon discussed the beginning of a revival meeting in August 1863 at which a huge bonfire was lit and hundreds of soldiers converted. Cannon thought that "thousands of Confederate soldiers owe their salvation to the influences brought to bear upon them during their service in the army." Around the same time, D. D. Bonner hoped that the Methodist and Baptist preachers would gain some converts in the camps at Fredericksburg, "for there is an abundance of wickedness in our army that's been the cause of the war (wickedness). The people have gotten above their maker's will."[15]

Religion served many purposes for Alabama's soldiers. Above all else, it helped them cope with the trauma of battle. Despite the fact that many pious men fell in every engagement, some soldiers still believed that God would protect men of faith in battle. An officer in the 4th Alabama, Paul Turner Vaughn, noted that right before a fight, he and his friend prayed together asking God for protection. After barely escaping death during the Vicksburg siege, Chaplain William Foster thanked God for just "gently" striking him with a shell fragment. But the Almighty did more than just shield soldiers in battle; He also steeled their courage. Another Alabamian chaplain, this time at Shiloh, gave his regiment a sermon when they began to waver. "The effect was evident," he stated. "Every man stood to his post, every eye flashed, and every heart beat high with desperate resolve to conquer or die."[16]

After a battle had ended, religion helped men cope with terrible scenes of suffering and death. William Foster tried to console numerous soldiers in the hospital with religion. He averred, "You can almost tell when a child of grace is wounded for they generally bear their pain so meekly, without scarcely a word of complaint." A captain whom Foster visited was not enduring his suffering so meekly, so the chaplain "exhorted him to look up to Christ and trust in him." The captain eventually died wondering in his final moments whether his sins were yet forgiven. After being shot on July 3, 1863, at Gettysburg within fifty yards of the Union line, John Moseley of the 3rd Alabama penned a short note home from the battlefield. He told his mother: "Do not mourn my loss. I had hoped to have been spared, but a righteous God has ordered it otherwise and I feel prepared to trust my case in his hands. Farewell to you all. Pray that God may receive my soul." Religion profoundly influenced many soldiers' lives and was their final refuge in death.[17]

In addition to their religious faith, upper-class Alabamian Confederates held fast to the values of masculinity. In nineteenth-century America, manhood was closely associated with bravery and courage, which could be readily demonstrated in the crucible of war. Alabama's soldiers were eager to prove their manhood to their families and peers. For many, battle was the ultimate test of manhood. James Williams wrote his wife about a possible attack by the Union on Fort Gaines on Dauphin Island. If the attack came, Williams asserted, "I mean to prove myself a man worthy of you my dear wife." One Alabamian woman had to encourage a suitor who was more reluctant than Williams to join the army and prove his manhood. Along with a skirt and petticoat, she sent a message that told him to "wear these or enlist." Most soldiers did not need such a challenge to their manhood to fight for the cause.[18]

Alabama's Confederates, at least those from the upper class, felt they had a duty as men to their cause and country. The idealistic James Branscomb of the 3rd Alabama wrote to his sister, "Leaving home was not near so trying as I thought it would be. I felt that I was doing my duty." Even though this sense of obligation might cost him his life, Branscomb remarked, "it will be only to water the tree of liberty." Branscomb watered that tree when he was killed at Spotsylvania. Samuel Sprott recalled that when he told his brother in the hospital that his wounds were mortal, his brother just said, "I would like to live for the sake of my wife and children. I have tried to do my duty." James Williams told his wife that he wished to leave his record in the history of the war "so that I will have a consciousness of duty well done, and an honorable name to bear away to my peaceful retreat."[19]

Williams alluded to another important value that motivated Alabama's soldiers: honor. During the nineteenth century Southern men were supposed to be honorable, which meant always exhibiting good behavior and judgment, fulfilling assigned social roles, and living by a code of ethics. Maintaining one's honor required demonstrating one's worth and character. Alabamians going off to war wanted to preserve their sense of honor and their reputation by proving themselves good soldiers. James Williams again discussed honor with his wife when he told her that it was noble to die leading men in battle and declared, "when my fate meets me let me hold an honorable post, and die doing it honor!" Heroic death in battle held the "most honor." James Monroe Thompson of the Autauga Rifles and his fellow soldiers paid tribute to fallen comrades in a series of resolutions after the Battle of Antietam. They pledged themselves, if need be, to "go to the same death that has covered the names of our lost with imperishable honor."[20]

Notions of manhood, duty, and honor all shaped the values and worldview of upper-class Confederate soldiers from Alabama. These values combined with an intense desire to create an independent Confederate nation that would protect Southern slavery and liberty motivated these soldiers to fight. Despite the trials of war, upper-class soldiers generally tended to maintain high morale and remained committed to these ideological motives.

The commitment of Alabama's soldiers was all the more remarkable considering the conditions of war. Imprisoned on Johnson's Island, John Inzer remained a diehard Confederate to the last. When Atlanta fell in September 1864, Inzer simply noted in his diary, "Awful blow. We will gain our independence yet." In October that year, Inzer commented on the difficult conditions of the prison but insisted,

"I can endure all for the Southern Cause." Daniel Hundley, also living in the "hell" of Johnson's Island, reacted to the Union capture of Atlanta with regret but added, "I have that confidence in our cause and in the justice of Jehovah that I shall yet expect to see good come of this apparently terrible disaster." When Lincoln was reelected in November, Hundley sounded "indifferent," for "no true believer in a just God can now fear for the result in the four years which are yet to come."[21]

Prisoners of war were not the only ones with staunch faith in the Confederacy. Soldiers in the field also displayed a fervent belief in the cause. James Branscomb constantly tried to lift his sister's spirits when she was downcast about the South's prospects. He encouraged her, "Sister don't be disheartened. We must expect clouds as well sunshine, reverses as well as victories. Be like me, rejoice because you are alive.... We are bound to conquer." Well over a year later, Branscomb was still optimistic. He wrote his sister that even if the Union seized Charleston, "that should not discourage.... It should inspire us with new vigor to prosecute the war." James Williams never expressed discouragement over the course of the war and felt more than content living a soldier's life. In October 1864 he enthusiastically noted, "The best possible condition is that of the soldier.... He is happy and cares for nothing, but the lovely wife and babe far away." These soldiers never became disillusioned with the service or the cause of their country.[22]

The attitudes and motivations of lower-class Confederate soldiers from Alabama differed markedly from those of their upper-class comrades. They were far less ideological and, for the most part, less motivated by ideals of liberty and nation. They almost never mentioned the institution of slavery and its preservation as a reason for enlisting. But slavery was still an important part of the society they were defending and none of them ever disagreed with the institution. The soldiers from the lower ranks of society did share some characteristics with their upper-class counterparts, however. They possessed a strong religious faith, felt a passionate hatred for the North, and believed they needed to defend their homeland against a "foreign" invasion. Some also had a sense of duty and honor. But many simply wanted the war to end so that they and their comrades could live in peace with their families.

During the first months of their service, some lower-class soldiers made a few ideological statements that reflected their early patriotic ardor, but this almost always faded as the realities of war set in. One Alabamian cavalryman who followed this pattern was John Cotton. Enlisting on April 1, 1862, Cotton made some ideological statements in his letters home during his first months as a soldier. Cotton told his wife at the beginning of May that he would be there to see the children right now "if it had not have bee the love I have for them and my country." A few months later Cotton wrote his dear Mariah that "if I get killed just say I dyed in a good cause." "[O]uld abe lincon and his cabinet could not daunt me now," Cotton added. Two days later Cotton penned his most ideological statement of the war: "If it were not for the love of my country and family and the patriotism that bury in my bosom for them I would bee glad to come home and stay there but I no I have as much to fite for as any body else."[23]

Other lower-class Alabamian soldiers expressed ideological commitment during the early stages of their service. A day before Fort Sumter was bombarded, Pvt. Thomas Smyrl of the 34th Alabama declared that the South was "on the Right Side" of the conflict and hoped that God would help them triumph "over the red-nosed tribe of black hearted Black Republicans." In August 1861, J. W. Warner felt his spirits rise when he reflected on "this glorious land of liberty that I am going to fight for." With no money to invest in a Confederate loan, Warner "had nothing to offer but my service to my country." John Davenport, who enlisted on May 14, 1862, in the 23rd Alabama, also talked about the cause of liberty. He told his wife that if he did not come home, "remembe I am fighting for Liberty for you and our Little ones and for the rites and Liberty of others." Serving on picket duty a few months later in the cold, Davenport expressed his intense love for his family and "hopes you and them may yet live to enjoy the rites and liberitys for which I now am freesing all nite on the frosen ground." These Alabamian soldiers were ideologically committed at first, but it did not last. Other soldiers from the lower class expressed no such motives at all.[24]

Lower-class Alabamians did consistently express the ideological motive of defending their homeland. Pvt. H. S. Strom conveyed this in a poem he composed for Mary Loftis. Strom wrote about a friend lost in the war and how "I hope my friend will say / He [Strom] ever at his post did stayed / Ready to defend his Southern Land." John Cotton asked his wife to pray that he would make it safely back to his company "and threw the war til we have moved the yankeys back from our soil and peace is maid." Confederate soldiers constantly referred to Union armies as vandals and invaders that must be resisted. Pvt. Grant Taylor of the 40th Alabama, pining for the days before the war, was "almost axious to be led against this vandal horde, this destroyer of our peace." Henry Bray of the 17th Alabama was "very sorry to hear that the invaders are in owr state it make my blood boil to hear of the deperdations they have done since they landed in owr soil and I hope soon to measure arms with the hireling despradodoes."[25]

Alabama's Confederate soldiers also fought to defend their families. John Davenport tied this motivation together with that of defending the homeland in a poem to his wife: "I take my post on deauty / Whear ever it comes to hand / In protection of my mary / And my dear native land." Samuel King Vann, a private in the 19th Alabama, was also fighting for his beloved at home. He hoped that "this unholy war shall cease so that we can return to those whom we have so long battled for." When his regiment moved from Jackson to Columbus, Mississippi, Grant Taylor wrote his wife, Malinda, "I had rather be here than any place I have been at yet for we are now between the enemy and those I love and it seems more like defending you here than away down at Mobile." Not even two weeks later, Taylor almost got into a battle near Vicksburg. He told Malinda he "did not dread it [the battle]," for it gave him an opportunity "to defend you and the dear little ones." For some Alabamians, their families were more important than any notions of independence or liberty.[26]

A little over three months after Grant Taylor was prepared to defend Malinda at Vicksburg, he wrote to her about Union destruction during the campaign: "They [the Union] burnt up nearly all the houses, corn & steam mills for thirty miles & carried of lots of negroes. I never saw such destruction of property.... I cant believe God will prosper any people that act so." The destruction of Southern property fueled a passionate anti-Northernism that motivated many lower-class soldiers. During Sherman's March to the Sea, John Cotton told his wife how "the yankey are destroying everything before them and ravishing women the citizens are fleeing from them like chaft before the wind." Robert A. Williams, a private in the 34th Alabama, was also disgusted by the way the Union was treating citizens in Georgia. He informed his cousin how much he enjoyed getting into a battle, for "it done me good to poke lead at those who had so cruely treated the fair sex of Ga." Williams boldly added, "I did all I could to avenge them for their conduct although it is writen vengence is mine I will repay sayeth the Lord." Henry Bray also demonstrated a strong anti-Northern feeling when he hoped "to whip the confounded Yankee thieving scoundrels clean out of Dixie and end this evil and barbarous warfare." He would not rest "until the inhuman scoundrels" were driven from the South.[27]

Lower-class Alabamians constantly prayed that they would triumph over the "Yankee barbarians." Religion was central in sustaining these soldiers through the trials of war. Just like their upper-class comrades, lower-class soldiers were frequently exposed to religion in camp. This was particularly true during the revivals of 1863–64. In September 1863, William Thomas Jackson of the 8th Alabama commented on how the soldiers were "hav[ing] A great revival time of it." Jackson said, "We have [a] meeting every day & knight.... & we have had some of the best preaching that I ever heard in my life." The next month, Grant Taylor noted the numerous conversions and extensive preaching in camp. He exclaimed, "Oh how touching it is to see strong men come up with tears streaming down their manly cheeks and tell that they have found the Lord precious to their souls." Taylor hoped that "the good Lord carry on his good work until every soldier shal be converted." Religion continued to spread through Confederate camps after the fall and winter of 1863–64. In April 1864, Thomas Smyrl wrote how "a great many Soldiers are becoming concerned... & some are claiming a place with the Christians telling what the Lord has done for their Souls & being Sprinkled or poured or Baptised by Emersion."[28]

Some soldiers believed it was vital to find God in camp because He would shield them in battle. When Grant Taylor marched to engage the enemy near Vicksburg, he "was not the least excited or scared," for "[m]y prayer to God was . . . for him to cover my head in the hour of battle. . . . I believed it so strong that I was not afraid." Pvt. Thomas Owen of the 11th Alabama worried that he would never see his family again, but he remembered "that ther is on that can save all an I put my self in his hands an pray that the lord ma kepe me from all eavel an harm." Owen's prayers went unanswered as he died just days later at Antietam. William Jackson wrote his wife that a soldier's chance at a fight like Gettysburg was not good, "but the same God that rules over man & prsrves his life in time of peace is able to carry him through the battle field safe."[29]

Daniel Christenberry of the 40th Alabama urged his family to pray to God "to spare my life to see the close of this ware and return home to live to gather." Alabamian soldiers oftentimes prayed that the Lord would not just protect them in battle but bring an end to the war and help them get home. A soldier in the same regiment as Christenberry, Hiram Smith Williams, wrote a poem in which he yearned for God to end the struggle: "Let us pray for the Angel of Mercy [and] Peace / Long banished to come stretch forth his beautiful hand / And dispel the dark clouds that swallow our land / And pronounce that the reign of the Furies is o'er." Grant Taylor wrote to his wife, "This war is a shame, a disgrace to civilization. Oh! would to God it would end." James Pritchett of the 60th Alabama just wished "that the good lord will permit me to pass through this bum pain and see" friends at home again.[30]

These soldiers, however, understood all too well that they might not make it home again. Some took solace in the idea that if they never saw their loved ones again on earth, they would one day meet them in heaven. Grant Taylor tried to reassure his wife that "if there is no more pleasure for us on earth, I feel that there is happiness in store for us beyond this vale of tears in that bright world where wars and parting, sickness, pain and death will be felt and feared no more." John Davenport echoed Taylor when he wrote his wife that if he never saw his family again, "I want to meet you all in haven Whear wores and fightings will be ore / Whear wives and husbands part no more / Whear parance and children each other greete."[31]

As much as some of these soldiers pined to go home, a sense of duty kept them in the ranks. James Moore hoped "they would do the fiting and end the contest." Although, he continued, "I am not keen to get into a fight . . . I am ready when I am called on to do my duty." Writing to his wife, John Davenport asserted, "I have allways filld every post of deauty asined to me to the best of my ability and acknowlege I feal some whot elivated by the chois of my commander when sent as the most srude and relible man in the battalion." Davenport felt that not just he but everyone "boath offersers and men dun ther hole deauty" at the Battle of Chickamauga. Sometimes soldiers coupled this sense of duty with religion. Thomas Smyrl reflected that he was "determined by the Grace of God to change my course & try to Live for God & to do my Duty nearer than I have done." Grant Taylor prayed, "God guide and direct us in the path of duty."[32]

Duty was closely associated with honor, another important motivator for some soldiers. J. E. Bush of the 33rd Alabama told his sister how Jefferson Davis was going to give a medal of some kind to a man in each company for bravery at Chickamauga. He thought that his brother, Dick Bush, who was killed at Chickamauga, would get the medal in his company. This medal would go to the Bush sister. J. E. Bush urged her "to ware it in honor to his name," for "hee has [brought] to him self honor and Relations honor that never will Bee forgotten as long as his name can Bee found on the pages of history." Like Bush, lower-class Alabamian soldiers wanted to be thought of as honorable men. Desertion from the army was considered dishonorable, and many tried to avoid it at all costs. John Cotton said that he was not going to desert because "I dont want it throwed up to my children after I am dead and gone that I was a deserter from the confederate army I dont want to do anything if I no it that will leave a stain on my posterity hereafter." William Thomas Jackson did not want his mother to "be any ways uneasy about my deserting for I decided long since to die in the field rather than bear the name of a deserter."[33]

Many Alabamian soldiers from the lower ranks of society expressed almost no ideology during the war. Sometimes it was just a simple love for their family that sustained them. Pvt. E. W. Treadwell of the 19th Alabama waxed sentimental about his love for his wife: "You Mattie are my jewel more precios than gold—the anchor of my Soul—you are the star by which my life is governed. . . . Tis the one Joyous hope that bears me up." Treadwell wanted to ensure his wife had not forgotten his love for her during the long separation caused by war. Another private, Samuel Vann, repeatedly expressed his deep affection for his "most lovely Lizzie." Vann told Lizzie, "Thou art beautiful, thou art lovely, thou art the fairest of them all. . . . I love thee as I do my own dear life." John Davenport thought of his wife's "image" constantly, comparing her eyes to "electrick *sparkes*. . . . no other eyes how ever fair the heart how ever cind can ever give such joyes to me nor light up my *soul*." Getting home to the women they had left behind was the primary concern of some of Alabama's lowliest soldiers.[34]

Hiram Williams always wanted to just get home. Never filled with patriotic zeal, Williams did not even enlist until May 1862, and then he tried to avoid frontline duty. He stated in May 1864 that "Somehow all that I write, all that I think takes but one channel; one wish—for this war to end. When will it cease? I ask myself that question a score of times a day." Just surviving the war and returning home motivated many Alabamian Confederates. Grant Taylor wrote that the war "is wearing me out. But I feel very thankful that it is no worse. If I can only get home alive I will be thankful." Writing to his friend "Miss Mary," James Woods hoped that "the time is not far distant when we all may return home and spend the remainder of our days with those at home we love." He ended his letter, "I think of the[e] and all most cry." John Cotton declared to his wife, "I hope to god that the thing [war] will soon end and I will get to come home to you and my little ones." In a similar vein, Thomas Smyrl wrote, "Oh Jane . . . will this Cruel War ever stop so that we may yet bee happy again."[35]

Soldiers loved their families and wanted to get back to them, but they were also intensely loyal to their comrades in the army. Many Alabamian soldiers were organized into regiments with men from their hometown. They felt an attachment to these men that came through common sacrifice and courage. Grant Taylor told his wife about his sorrow at the capture of his friend Ide: "Malinda since poor Ide was taken away I have no bosom friend to go to. I am lost. I am like some poor bird that has lost its mate and I must unbosome myself to you." Soldiers oftentimes wrote home about the loss of comrades. During the struggle for Atlanta, Thomas Smyrl informed his wife that "we Lost many of our Brave Companions they fell in the hottest Contest perhaps that history can or will ever record." James Bean of the 15th Alabama noted the loss of many friends and relatives, among them his best friend, Charley: "I was but a few paces from him [Charley] when he fell. I helped to carry him from the field. His kind acts toward me will never be forgotten." On a furlough home with other men from his company, Samuel Vann reflected, "it makes me feel bad to think about how many marched off with the Co. that did not march back with us. O! tis awful to think how many noble-hearted brave men have fallen since our co. left there." Their comrades, both living and dead, inspired Alabamian soldiers to continue the struggle.[36]

Lower-class Alabamian Confederates not only were less driven by ideology but tended to become more disillusioned with the war and experience lower morale than did their upper-class counterparts. By December 1863, John Cotton was "worse out of hart about whipping the yankeys than I have every been there is lots of our men says there is no use to fite them any more." Over a year later, Cotton observed, "it dont look to me like there any use of fiting any longer I think they had better make peace now . . . it looks like we cant whip no where they whip us at every point." Grant Taylor also became demoralized about the war. As early as October 1863 Taylor told his wife, "I sometimes feel almost crazy. I feel like I have sacrificed everything for a phantom." By November 1864 Taylor was merely "languishing out my life in an ungenial clime and hopeless cause." Indeed, Taylor, beginning in the summer of 1862, was willing to pay a high price for another man to join the army as his substitute so that he could go home. A private in the 20th Alabama, W. H. McCullough, wrote that "our Soldiers are all out of heart and runing a way Evry day. . . . the Comfedrecy is out. . . . i hope i will never here another Canon i am getin vary tierd of them."[37]

John Cotton penned his wife, Mariah, that "there is one thing that gives me great consolation you have a plenty to live upon . . . if I were to here that you had nothing to eat I should come home at the risk of my life." Confederate Alabamians followed the status of their families closely, and if they heard they were suffering, it could have a devastating impact on morale. Grant Taylor reminded his wife, "As I have said before I can bear my hardships and hunger if I know you and the children have plenty. I know you have never suffered for the coarser necessities of life yet." In December 1862 John Davenport alluded to the connection between the home front and morale directly when he thought that mail home would be stopped. According to Davenport, this was because "it is feard that solgers famileys will have to suffer and tha ar afraid when the solgers com to know ther condision of ther famileys it will have bad affect or imposible to ceep them emey longer in camps."[38]

Lower-class soldiers had different motives for enlisting and responded to the war differently over time than did upper-class soldiers. But this does not mean they were not fiercely loyal to the Confederacy. Many Alabamian Confederates, of both the upper and lower classes, fought ferociously for Southern independence until the bitter end. However, as this essay has demonstrated, Confederate nationalism was more complex and varied than some historians have acknowledged. Upper-class soldiers were fighting primarily for liberty, slavery, and independence. Securing these ideals meant that they would be forever free from the tyrannical grasp of the North. Religion and notions of duty, honor, and manhood shaped upper-class soldiers' worldview and helped sustain them through the long struggle. Indeed, they generally maintained their ideological commitments until the Southern nation collapsed.[39]

Lower-class soldiers demonstrated a different form of nationalism. Only during the first few months of their enlistments did any lower-class soldiers express anything that was ideologically comparable to what was voiced by the upper class. And most of them never did that. The only ideology many of them had was a desire to defend their homeland against a hated foe. A fervent religious faith and a love for their comrades oftentimes was enough to sustain them through the war, but sometimes it was not. Many lower-class Confederates grew disillusioned and lost faith in the Confederacy. But what is more compelling was that so many from the lower ranks of society stayed in the army despite lacking a strong ideological nationalism. This speaks to the power of motives without a sharp ideological edge, a power that inspired them to bear the brunt of the South's failed struggle for independence.

Notes

1. John Washington Inzer, *The Diary of a Confederate Soldier: John Washington Inzer, 1834–1928*, ed. Mattie Lou Teague Crow (Huntsville, AL: Strode, 1977), 65–66; Hiram Smith Williams, *This War So Horrible: The Civil War Diary of Hiram Smith Williams*, ed. Lewis N. Wynne and Robert A. Taylor (Tuscaloosa: University of Alabama Press, 1993), 33.

2. See James M. McPherson, *For Cause and Comrades: Why Men Fought in the Civil War* (New York: Oxford University Press, 1997), 101, for a brief discussion of the differences in ideological

expressions and commitment among Confederate soldiers of different classes. McPherson notes this general trend in his sample but argues that soldiers were motivated primarily by ideology.

3. The figure of $6,882 was taken from Joseph T. Glatthaar, *General Lee's Army: From Victory to Collapse* (New York: Free Press, 2008), 19.

4. J. P. Cannon, *Bloody Banners and Barefoot Boys: A History of the 27th Regiment Alabama Infantry CSA: The Civil War Memoirs and Diary Entries of J. P. Cannon M.D.*, ed. Noel Crowson and John V. Brogden (Shippensburg, PA: Burd Street Press, 1997), 80; Eugene Blackford to mother, February 22, 1862, cited in McPherson, *For Cause and Comrades*, 105.

5. Nathaniel H. R. Dawson to Elodie Todd Dawson, June 8, 1861, cited in McPherson, *For Cause and Comrades*, 20–21; Adam Henry Whetstone, *History of the Fifty-Third Alabama Volunteer Infantry (Mounted)*, ed. William Stanley Hoole and Martha DuBose Hoole (University, AL: Confederate Publishing, 1985), 11; Vincent M. Elmore to sister, n.d., Wade Hall Collection (unprocessed), W. S. Hoole Special Collections Library, University of Alabama (hereafter UA); Inzer, *Diary of a Confederate Soldier*, 86.

6. James M. Williams, *From That Terrible Field: Civil War Letters of James M. Williams, Twenty-First Alabama Infantry Volunteers*, ed. John Kent Folmer (University: University of Alabama Press, 1981), 102; Cannon, *Bloody Banners and Barefoot Boys*, 87; James P. Stephens, *If I Should Fall in Battle . . . : The Civil War Diary of James P. Stephens, Company C, 7th Alabama Infantry, CSA*, ed. Jack L. Dickinson (Huntington, WV: John Deaver Drinko Academy, 2003), 155.

7. Elias Davis to Mrs. R. L. Lathan, December 10, 1863, cited in McPherson, *For Cause and Comrades*, 107; Jake Weil to Josiah Weil, May 16, 1861, Weil Letter, Alabama Department of Archives and History, Montgomery (hereafter ADAH).

8. "Scriblings of a Private Soldier," John Taylor Banks Diary (no dates), 2, UA; Stephens, *If I Should Fall in Battle*, 79; Williams, *From That Terrible Field*, 90; William E. Riser to Miss Bettie, November 4, 1862, Riser Letter, ADAH.

9. Daniel R. Hundley, *Prison Echoes of the Great Rebellion* (New York: S. W. Green, 1874), 36–42, cited in McPherson, *For Cause and Comrades*, 152; Inzer, *Diary of a Confederate Soldier*, 65.

10. Hundley, *Prison Echoes of the Great Rebellion*, 33–35; G. Ward Hubbs, ed., *Voices from Company D: Diaries by the Greensboro Guards, Fifth Alabama Infantry Regiment, Army of Northern Virginia* (Athens: University of Georgia Press, 2003), 149; Williams, *From That Terrible Field*, 78.

11. Joseph F. Barnett to Mary Allin Loftis, September 25, 1862, Loftis Letters, ADAH; John Taylor Banks Diary, 23–24; Hundley, *Prison Echoes of the Great Rebellion*, 33–34.

12. John Taylor Banks Diary, 22; William Foster to Mildred, June 20, 1863, box 0635, Foster Papers, UA; Cullen Andrews Battle, *Third Alabama!: The Civil War Memoir of Brigadier General Cullen Andrews Battle, CSA*, ed. Brandon H. Beck (Tuscaloosa: University of Alabama Press, 2000), 118–19, 139. See Bell Irwin Wiley, *The Life of Johnny Reb: The Common Soldier of the Confederacy* (Indianapolis: Bobbs-Merrill, 1943), 15–17, for a discussion of hatred for the North as a motivation. Wiley points to this ideological motivation, but generally downplays ideology as a force in the Confederate armies. Indeed, Wiley does not discuss motivations much at all.

13. George K. Miller to Celestine McCann, June 10, 1861, cited in McPherson, *For Cause and Comrades*, 21; Cannon, *Bloody Banners and Barefoot Boys*, 1; Elisha O. Baker to Brother Billy, April 26, 1863, Baker Papers, ADAH; also see D. D. Bonner to Mary Allin Loftis(?), February 1863, Loftis Letters, ADAH.

14. Stephens, *If I Should Fall in Battle*, 125, 159; January 1–3, 1862, Thomas Hubbard Hobbs Diary, UA; Cannon, *Bloody Banners and Barefoot Boys*, 94.

15. McPherson, *For Cause and Comrades*, 63, 67; Cannon, *Bloody Banners and Barefoot Boys*, 41–42; D. D. Bonner to Mary Allin Loftis, August 15, 1863, Loftis Letters, ADAH.

16. Paul Turner Vaughn Diary, April 12, 1863, UA; William Foster to Mildred, June 20, 1863, box 0635, Foster Papers, UA; James I. Robertson Jr., *Soldiers Blue and Gray* (Columbia: University of South Carolina Press, 1988), 180.

17. William Foster to Mildred, June 20, 1863; C. F. Moseley to William W. Moseley, November 10, 1863, cited in Robertson, *Soldiers Blue and Gray*, 226.

18. Williams, *From That Terrible Field*, 34; Robertson, *Soldiers Blue and Gray*, 111.

19. James Branscomb, *Dear Sister: Civil War Letters to a Sister in Alabama*, ed. Frank Anderson Chappell (Huntsville, AL: Branch Springs, 2002), 37; Samuel H. Sprott, *Cush: A Civil War Memoir*, ed. Louis R. Smith Jr. and Andrew Quist (Livingston, AL: Livingston Press, 1999), 106; Williams, *From That Terrible Field*, 104.

20. Williams, *From That Terrible Field*, 34–35; James Monroe Thompson, *Reminiscences of the Autauga Rifles, Co. G, Sixth Alabama Volunteer Regiment, CSA*, ed. William Stanley Hoole (University, AL: Confederate Publishing, 1984), 18–19. See Gerald F. Linderman, *Embattled Courage: The Experience of Combat in the American Civil War* (New York: Free Press, 1987), 7–16 for a detailed discussion of the values of manhood, duty, and honor. For the definition of Southern honor, see Bertram Wyatt-Brown, *Southern Honor: Ethics and Behavior in the Old South* (New York: Oxford University Press, 1982), 14–15.

21. Inzer, *Diary of a Confederate Soldier*, 98, 105; Hundley, *Prison Echoes of the Great Rebellion*, 128, 180.

22. Branscomb, *Dear Sister*, 71, 163; Williams, *From That Terrible Field*, 145–46.

23. John W. Cotton, *Yours Till Death: Civil War Letters of John W. Cotton*, ed. Lucille Griffith (University: University of Alabama Press, 1951), 4, 13, 14.

24. Thomas Smyrl to cousin, April 11, 1861, Smyrl Letters, ADAH; J. W. Warner to Mary Allin Loftis, August 6, 1861, Loftis Letters, ADAH; John F. Davenport to Mary Jane Davenport, August 20, 1862, December 22, 1862, Davenport Letters, ADAH.

25. H. S. Strom to Mary Allin Loftis, January 21, 1862, Loftis Letters, ADAH; Cotton, *Yours Till Death*, 26; Grant Taylor and Malinda Taylor, *This Cruel War: The Civil War Letters of Grant and Malinda Taylor, 1862–1865*, ed. Ann K. Blomquist and Robert A. Taylor (Macon, GA: Mercer University Press, 2000), 106; Henry Bray to Marian Davis, February 19, 1862, Bray Letters, ADAH.

26. John F. Davenport to Mary Jane Davenport, n.d., Davenport Letters, ADAH; Samuel King Vann to Miss N. E. Neel, August 25, 1864, Vann Letters, ADAH; Taylor and Taylor, *This Cruel War*, 138, 146.

27. Taylor and Taylor, *This Cruel War*, 174–75; Cotton, *Yours Till Death*, 120; Robert A. Williams to Mittie Williams, July 2, 1864, Williams Letters, ADAH; Henry Bray to mother, July 3, 1862, Bray Letters, ADAH.

28. William Thomas Jackson, *Kiss Sweet Little Lillah for Me: Civil War Letters of William Thomas Jackson, Company A, Eighth Alabama Infantry Regiment*, ed. Wayne Wood and Mary Virginia Jackson (Birmingham: EBSCO Media, 2000), 47; Taylor and Taylor, *This Cruel War*, 184; Thomas Smyrl to Mary J. Smyrl, April 15, 1864, Smyrl Letters, ADAH.

29. Taylor and Taylor, *This Cruel War*, 148–49; Thomas R. Owen to Reuben Owen, September 2, 1862, Owen Letter, ADAH; Jackson, *Kiss Sweet Little Lillah for Me*, 44.

30. Daniel A. Christenberry to family, May 1, 1864, Christenberry Family Collection, ADAH; Williams, *This War So Horrible*, 44; Taylor and Taylor, *This Cruel War*, 310; James Pritchett to Mary Allin Loftis, August 18, 1862, Loftis Letters, ADAH.

31. Taylor and Taylor, *This Cruel War*, 114–15; John F. Davenport to Mary Jane Davenport, September 7, 1862, Davenport Letters, ADAH.

32. James Moore to Mary Allin Loftis, July [22], 1862, Loftis Letters, ADAH; John F. Davenport to Mary Jane Davenport, n.d., September 26, 1863, Davenport Letters, ADAH; Thomas Smyrl to Mary J. Smyrl, December 27, 1863, Smyrl Letters, ADAH; Taylor and Taylor, *This Cruel War*, 204.

33. J. E. Bush to sister, November 13, 1863, in W. E. Preston Diary and History of the 33rd Alabama, ADAH; Cotton, *Yours Till Death*, 65; Jackson, *Kiss Sweet Little Lillah for Me*, 27.

34. E. W. Treadwell to Mattie Treadwell, April 7, 1863, Treadwell Letters, ADAH; Kenneth W. Noe, *Reluctant Rebels: The Confederates Who Joined the Army after 1861* (Chapel Hill: University of North Carolina Press, 2010), 76; Samuel King Vann to Miss N. E. Neel, February 27, 1864, Vann Letters, ADAH; John F. Davenport to Mary Jane Davenport, April 2, 1864, Davenport Letters, ADAH.

35. Williams, *This War So Horrible*, 54; Noe, *Reluctant Rebels*, 171; Taylor and Taylor, *This Cruel War*, 256; James W. Woods to Mary Allin Loftis, May 22, 1862, Loftis Letters, ADAH; Cotton, *Yours Till Death*, 51; Thomas Smyrl to Mary J. Smyrl, October 17, 1863, Smyrl Letters, ADAH.

36. Taylor and Taylor, *This Cruel War*, 290; Thomas Smyrl to Mary J. Smyrl, July 25, 1864, Smyrl Letters, ADAH; James F. Bean to Mary Allin Loftis, October 11, 1863, Loftis Letters, ADAH; Samuel King Vann to Miss N. E. Neel, October 3, 1864, Vann Letters, ADAH. Kenneth Noe perceptively notes that the camaraderie that existed in regiments oftentimes stemmed from prewar kinship and neighborhood ties. See Noe, *Reluctant Rebels*, 158–60.

37. Cotton, *Yours Till Death*, 98, 126; Taylor and Taylor, *This Cruel War*, 186, 300, 55, 59, 64, 70, 73–75; Noe, *Reluctant Rebels*, 116–17; W. H. McCullough to Martha McCullough, July 24, 1863, McCullough Family Letters, ADAH. In *Embattled Courage*, Linderman argues that Civil War soldiers became disillusioned in the final years of the war but makes no class distinctions in his argument.

38. Cotton, *Yours Till Death*, 60; Taylor and Taylor, *This Cruel War*, 291; John F. Davenport to Mary Jane Davenport, December 22, 1862, Davenport Letters, ADAH.

39. For an excellent discussion of Confederate nationalism, see Gary W. Gallagher, *The Confederate War: How Popular Will, Nationalism, and Military Strategy Could Not Stave Off Defeat* (Cambridge, MA: Harvard University Press, 1997). Gallagher argues that Southerners were unified and strongly committed to the Confederacy throughout the war. Gallagher is right to emphasize the strength of Confederate nationalism, but he ignores class differences. Also see Emory M. Thomas, *The Confederate Nation, 1861–1865* (New York: Harper and Row, 1979) for a general account of the Confederacy that stresses a strong nationalism. For an analysis that emphasizes the weakness of Confederate nationalism, see Richard E. Beringer et al., *Why the South Lost the Civil War* (Athens: University of Georgia Press, 1986), 64–81, 425–29.

6

Voices from the Margins

Non-Elites in Confederate Alabama

Victoria E. Ott

In 1865, John W. Brown returned from service in the Confederate army to discover his wife missing. Having conceived a child with another man, Ellen J. (Vandasdel) Brown had moved out of their residency in Pike County, Missouri, abandoning her marriage to John. The former Confederate soldier subsequently moved to Perry County, Alabama, where he began formal divorce proceedings. The couple had married in 1861, with all hope of beginning a family once he returned from his command in Cockrell's Brigade. In the throes of petitioning for a divorce, during which his wife was mysteriously absent, Brown pointed to his veteran's status to justify severing matrimonial ties, an event often frowned upon in nineteenth-century America. For Brown, his wife's willingness to transgress the boundaries of "proper" female behavior coupled with his service to the cause of Confederate independence was enough to claim power within the Alabama courts. Even Brown's employer, John Bates of Perry County, echoed this sentiment when he proclaimed that "he [Brown] is as virtuous a man as I know and as esteemed by those who know him" and trumpeted that, having met Brown during his military service, believed his "character then was as good as any man's in Alabama." This testimony reveals that ideas of masculine and feminine duty to state and home justified claims of legal, economic, and political power. According to court testimony, Brown had successfully performed his manly duty on the battlefield while his wife failed to maintain her role as a pure and submissive wife on the home front.[1]

John W. Brown's case was the exception rather than the norm for his socioeconomic group. Yet his testimony and that of his neighbors and friends demonstrate that masculine identity and feminine respectability were connected to Confederate patriotism. Although the voices of slaveholding elites are strongest in the canon of historical studies focusing on Confederate supporters, the experiences of those in the economic, political, and social margins of the Old South are worth examining. My focus group of "non-elites" is composed of whites from small, independent landowning families as well as poor, landless whites in Alabama who identified themselves as Confederates. Family and the roles within it—namely those related to parental, marital, and sibling interaction—created an ideological connection to the cause of Southern independence. This link between the personal world of family and the public world of the Confederate cause allowed non-elites to step out of the margins of Southern life and into the mainstream Confederate culture. Family relationships also helped them express their frustration with the war's economic and emotional toll in their daily lives. Using a combination of census and court records, letters, and diaries left by these non-elites, I illuminate the centrality of gender identity and duty rooted in family life to explain how they situated themselves within the Confederate culture and shaped the climate of wartime Alabama.[2]

Personal relationships prove the most powerful lens through which to magnify the common whites' experience, and this thematic approach has proved useful when situating non-elites in the context of the Confederate South. For example, Aaron Sheehan-Dean explores why Virginia soldiers enlisted and fought in a war that seemed to defend an institution so distant from their modest lifestyles. One prominent theme emerging from his study is that of family. Domestic relationships served, in part, as a motivation for enlisting but also for remaining in the military despite growing economic and emotional hardships at home and the constant grief of a combatant's life as the tide of war turned against the Confederates. In situating personal lives within this context, the connection between nationalism and family is clear. Confederate supporters envisioned the family as a microcosm of the infant nation, tying protection of the home to defense of the Southern home front.[3]

The connection between family and nation raises important questions about how the middling and poorer classes situated themselves within the patriotic culture. In conceptualizing the link between family and the Confederacy, how did the language, roles, and images relating to gender contribute to the conceptualization of nationalism? Southerners of all races and classes defined family in terms of male and female duty and familial relations. But how did the war transform ideas of gendered family roles for this group? And, conversely, how did these roles contribute to the creation and continuation of Confederate nationalism? In times when the war seemed too much of a burden to bear and dissent grew, what role did family relations and ideals serve in enabling Alabamians to survive conditions on both the home front and battlefront?

This study of Alabama's common whites from secessionist families demonstrates why Southerners with little economic investment in slavery threw their support behind a nascent Confederacy. Yet placing the domestic circle in the center of the Confederate experience also illustrates the nuances of life in a war-torn region. Familial intimacy allowed "plain folk" to articulate a critical perspective of war. Conditions on the military and home fronts called on all Southerners to sacrifice, and for middling and poor households their preexisting socioeconomic status exacerbated their difficult situation. Living in a culture that privileged the wealth and civic power of the planter elites, this group turned to the ideals and responsibility of family to help endure material privation, emotional turmoil, and physical danger. Family also provided a way to question the war while remaining faithful to the cause of Confederate nationhood.

Alabama is an ideal setting for such a study as its population profile on the eve of and during the Civil War reflected a class and racial diversity common to the Southern states. While plantation districts dominated the central and southern regions of the state, small, independent landowners as well as landless whites comprised the majority of the population. In her study of Alabama's Unionists, historian Margaret Storey notes that most subsistence farming households were in the northern portion of the state, areas termed the Hill and Tennessee Valley countries. Non-elites also lived within the plantation districts of the state but were fewer in number compared to the rest of the state.[4]

Cultural identity in the prewar South emerged from the relationships and responsibilities situated in the family. Intricate kinship ties helped inform the hierarchical power structure that privileged the elite, slaveholding classes. The legitimacy of their community leadership in the world of politics or business was rooted in their ability to provide for the material and physical protection of their families and slaves. Kinship relations also provided the power of family name to buttress community reputation. This culture, which identified the "best men" to lead through a paternalistic lens, placed a great deal of emphasis on traditional family ideals that defined male and female roles in specific, separate terms. Society viewed men as the head of the family who provided for their dependents; women were supportive wives and mothers who maintained the domestic responsibilities of the home. Children were expected to obey their parents but also developed affectionate relationships with them. Brothers and sisters, moreover, mirrored conventional expectations of masculine and feminine behavior in their training to one day assume their place in the adult world. This narrative of traditional family values found in an ideal nuclear structure and functioning on the rhetorical constructions of masculine and feminine identity became the social script elite, white Southerners hoped to perform.[5]

Notions of familial duty and relationships as a source of power and identity also extended beyond the elite classes of the Old South. Whites who found themselves relegated to the margins of a plantation economy and a political structure drew from the gendered language situated within the context of family life to assert the power to enhance and, at times, protect community reputation. By claiming a right to demonstrate the same responsibilities to home and family as did members of the planter class, men and women of the yeomen and poorer socioeconomic classes exhibited a sense of equality in an unequal world. Men demanded the right to perform their masculine duty to provide for the protection and security of their families and made this clear in their daily community transactions. Their concern with their dependents demonstrating proper gendered behavior also illustrated their concern for securing a respectable reputation, something valued in a world deeply immersed in notions of honor and duty. Protecting the family's public image, then, became a means of asserting power in the community. Women, too, found that holding men responsible for fulfilling their paternalistic duties enhanced their domestic power over their husbands, fathers, and brothers. When men shirked their duties, this allowed women to expand the barriers of their world into civic life by demanding protection from the community. The gendered rhetoric emerging from traditional family values that became an important source of power in the Old South therefore extended into the lives of the middling and poorer classes, allowing them to make their claim to the same rights and responsibilities as slaveholding elites.

Plain folks used gendered imagery in the civic world decades before the Civil War commenced. For example, the divorce records found in the Chancery Courts of Alabama counties reveal a willingness on the part of both men and women to defend their character and assert their devotion to Old South ideals of masculine and feminine roles within the context of family. As couples went to court seeking dissolution of their marriage, each stressed that they had performed their duty to the family without failing. Campbell Jefferson of Talladega County, Alabama, for example, testified in 1848 that during his marriage to Lydia Margaret Jefferson he had fulfilled his responsibilities as a dutiful and supportive husband. In 1846 Lydia had abandoned the Jefferson household, leaving Campbell vulnerable to public speculation about his ability to offer a secure, stable family life. Placed on the defensive, he noted that when the couple married in 1844, he entered a "matrimonial alliance" in which he had fulfilled his role "with cheerfulness and affections" and "provided for her comfort and sustenance."[6]

Women likewise attempted to demonstrate to the court their success in performing their marital and maternal duties. Ann M. Brown of Wilcox County filed a bill for divorce on the grounds that she had endured physical and emotional abuse at the hands of her husband, Morgan G. Brown. Ann took great care to express in her testimony that the treatment was unprovoked and undeserving. This was particularly necessary given the nature of the nineteenth-century legal system. Legal authorities typically viewed domestic violence as a private matter, leaving it to members of the household to resolve. A social structure that privileged men as the paternal figure in the home also acknowledged that husbands, at times, would need to punish their dependents, including wives, as long as they refrained from excessive force. When Ann took her case to the court, she assumed the burden of proving that she "had always acted towards him as a kind affectionate and obedient wife" and that Morgan exceeded the limits of patriarchal authority in his physical abuse. Her dependency on Morgan as a provider had left her unable to perform her role as a dutiful mother to their two children. She added to her accusations that, in addition to abuse, Morgan's failure to manage the household finances left the family in such a state of financial destitution that "compelled her to rely for [sic] subsistence."[7]

Conversely, spouses sought to demonstrate how their partner failed in his or her ability to live up to conventional expectations of masculine or feminine duty. In seeking a divorce from his wife, Sarah, in 1849, Malcome A. McKinnon of Talladega County alleged that "he has never been able to have sexual intercourse" since their marriage in 1845 and blamed it on Sarah's "apathy and physical inaptitude for the marriage state." In the paternalistic culture of the Old South, the role of father meant the continuation of family lineage and required men to exercise their role as protector and provider as the head of the household. For those of modest economic means, like Malcome, children also helped expand the labor force on the farm or in a family business. Malcome did not intend to impugn the reputation of his wife but to demonstrate her inability to perform her marital duties. He expressed a deep respect for his wife and remorsefulness over the fact that their lack of intimacy had created a relationship "of gloom . . . without a single hope to light up a dim and cheerless future." Sarah's inability or unwillingness to be intimate with her husband placed social pressure on Malcome to end the marriage.[8]

Ann Brown, however, made the case for her divorce by emphasizing her husband's failures as a husband and father. She portrayed him as a cruel head of home who, in succumbing to alcoholism, hurt rather than cared for his dependents. The original bill of divorce stated that Morgan "had wasted the means of support for his family," leaving Ann to an economic state "approaching want." Ann further asserted that he had failed to act as a sensitive marital companion: "at a time when she most needed his kindness and protection," he "beat bruise[d] and cruelly and inhumanly treat her." Ann punctuated Morgan's dishonorable behavior by bringing to light that he had "expelled her from his house." With Ann gone, he continued to live "a wretched existence, the miserable mark of his folly and intemperance." Morgan, however, attempted to redeem his reputation as a responsible husband. He rebuked her claims that he had forced her to leave the home, testifying that she had left willingly. Morgan accentuated his wife's failure, arguing that she had not performed her role "as a dutiful and loving wife" and that her state of economic dependency was the result of her decision to leave the home. The court, however, believed that there was sufficient evidence of his "cruel and barbarous behavior" and ruled in favor of the divorce.[9]

Gendered rhetoric played a crucial role in claiming power in the civic realm of the Old South. Although both sides in divorce cases often exaggerated declarations of respectability in hopes of winning the case, they certainly reveal the language, images, and symbols used to offer a defense of public reputation. In the era of Confederacy, however, these expressions of masculine and feminine identity and duty took on new meaning. Forced to reconcile the defense of the Confederate cause with the loss of family members, privations, and emotional trials, the "plain folk" refocused the meaning of gender identity and familial responsibility.

Alabamians of the yeomen and poorer socioeconomic classes paid marginal attention to the political climate even as the dark clouds of secession and war loomed ominously over their state. Although they expressed a passing concern with the potential for the election of an "abolitionist" president and talk of secession if a Republican victory occurred, maintaining the comfort and care of the family was the top priority. The diary of Sarah Rodgers Rousseau Espy of Cherokee County reveals the constant struggles of her class group in sustaining the domestic economy. Espy's husband, like many of her class, was a subsistence farmer and raised a modest number of livestock to sell in the community market. The early entries of her diary (beginning in 1858) are primarily concerned with the weather, daily domestic duties, and childcare. After her husband's death in 1860, however, her entries took on a different tone as she struggled to settle his business affairs. Even after she gave power of attorney to a male community member whom she trusted, Sarah recorded a deep concern with her limited means of providing for the family. Although her household included two domestic servants, Espy faced modest financial means at best. Her economic concerns coupled with the emotional stress of losing her husband brought great anxiety about the family's future. She wrote in the summer of 1860 that "we are feeling badly and lonely and destitute . . . for we are weak and look forward to [a] hard struggle with an unfeeling world."[10]

In her diary Zillah Haynie Brandon likewise focused more on the financial and spiritual well-being of her family rather than the political conflict taking shape. Brandon was born in 1801 and lost her parents early in her life. Sent to live with foster parents, Brandon completed one year of formal education before having to turn her energies toward work. Zillah married Francis Lawson Brandon in 1822 and the couple eventually had nine children. By 1851 the couple relocated to Cherokee County, Alabama, where Francis attempted to establish a farm. The couple achieved modest success within a decade, having property valued at $6,300 and five slaves. Zillah kept a diary beginning in 1855, filling the pages with recollections of her life up to that point. She also documented her daily activities in her contemporary life, remarking mainly on the piety of family members, business ventures of her elder sons, and sickness and death of kin. Zillah also intimated the many physical ailments she endured as a woman reaching her sixties. Her other concerns dealt with the weather, in particular a flood, that threatened the state of the farm.[11]

Eventually talk of secession and possible war caused white Alabamians, regardless of their economic station, to take notice. Even as Sarah Espy struggled with the daily tasks of maintaining her household, she eventually recognized the heated struggle between the North and the South and what it could mean for white Southerners. The impending presidential election grabbed her attention and she expressed her support for the Southern candidate John C. Breckinridge, who was the favorite of secessionists. Yet Espy feared for the future of the nation and believed Breckinridge the best candidate to maintain the Union, reasoning that "the country is getting in a deplorable state owing to the depredations committed by the Abolition . . . the safety of the country depend on who is elected to the presidency. May that man be union loving Breckinridge." Espy, like many eventual Confederate supporters, blamed the country's turmoil on outside influences, namely "abolitionist and negroes." When news of Abraham Lincoln's election reached Cherokee County, Espy concluded that it "is the beginning of woe." Zillah Brandon echoed Espy's support of the cause. "We must submit to a cruel and wicked oppressor," she wrote, "of we must be independent by an appeal to arms." She laid blame for the war at the feet of the Federal government: "It is a well authenticated fact . . . that the seceding states sent delegates to adjust an amicable settlement ere this war commenced, but they were spurned."[12]

The politicized culture of the state also brought men to eagerly join in the military in preparation for potential war. For example, the early letters of James Zachariah Branscomb of Union Springs, who kept regular correspondence with his sister Lucinda Branscomb Hunter, reveal his deep support for Alabama's right to secede from the Union in the wake of Lincoln's election. He, along with several of his male neighbors, joined the Southern Rifles in anticipation of going to battle after the state seceded in January 1861. While he acknowledged he was sad to leave Union Springs and his family behind, Branscomb remained in "high glee" as they departed for the new Confederate capital in Montgomery.[13]

At the same time that they articulated a support for the Confederate cause, non-elites questioned what the war could bring in terms of economic security and emotional comfort. Even though Sarah Espy believed that the Confederate cause was just, she feared that the departure of male kin for the front along with the potential for disorder on the home front could cause great distress. "I feel badly," she wrote in March 1861, "for when the war commence when is it to end and what dire consequences will not fall on us! I fear our happy days are all gone."

Emily Moxley of Coffee County likewise spent countless letters reflecting on the emotional toll her husband's absence had on her and their children. Emily and her husband, William, were married in 1853 and eventually had six children. William served as a community physician but made little income in a county composed primarily of small farmers and landless whites. William joined Bullock's Guards in July 1861, which later joined the 18th Alabama Infantry. For Emily, the war and its cause were unwanted intrusions on their personal lives. Her letters lacked the sense that her husband was fulfilling his masculine duty by going to war. Rather she expressed deep sadness over his absence, writing in a September letter that "we are all nearly heart Broken." Zillah Brandon also understood the possible effect war would have as she faced the potential of her five sons enlisting in the Confederate army. When two of her sons, James and Hines, left with a local company for the front, she intimated that their absence "amounted to an agony."[14]

The Confederate patriotism sweeping across the state by early 1861 reached into the personal lives of the yeomen and poor whites of Alabama. Relating the cause of Southern defense against outside intruders to the protection of home and family provided a rhetorical tool in convincing these individuals, consumed with the daily struggles of economic survival, to turn their attention to the civil war taking shape. In particular, the ideal of familial masculine duty helped them reconcile service to the Confederacy with being separated from loved ones and even death. James Branscomb, for instance, wrote frequently to his family members about the pride and sense of honor he felt. In a letter to his sister, James attempted to calm her anxieties about his safety and that of her own children by writing that "if neither of your brothers should never return there should be on[e] consoling thought, that we gave our lives in an honorable cause." James, moreover, reminded Lucinda that she, too, could turn to her family to find solace, citing that "you have some children that I believe will make you happy in after years." Even as hopes of a Confederate victory seemed diminished in 1864, the soldier wrote to his sister that "I am not whipped yet, Sister. I believe I am a patriot, if I do say perhaps who out not to." Southern white men who avoided service were looked upon with contempt and as denying their duty as men. "The son of the south must rally," James wrote to his brother in 1862. "A man that won't fight now has not got a soul." Even as the prospect of death weighed heavy on the members of the Branscomb family, James offered these words of comfort: "I felt that I was doing my duty. I may never return to you all again it is true, but feel assured I will. But if the worst comes to the worst I shall feel contented with my lot. Though I may be reaped at the harvest of death, it will be only to water the tree of liberty." William Moxley likewise called on the notion of masculine duty to help ease his wife's anxieties about their separation and his safety on the battlefront. "But my dear," he wrote to her in September 1861, "if I should be killed, never regret, for it would be the best legacy I could leave you & and my children."[15]

Zillah Brandon relied on conventional notions of Christian motherhood to come to terms with the potential dangers her two soldier sons faced. In one entry, Zillah wrote that although she feared for the life of her son James, she hoped that he would be a positive moral influence in the camps. "I have become better reconciled," she wrote, "knowing that James is a man of God, will speak when moved upon by the Holy Ghost and teach his fellow soldiers to look for the promise of Christ's coming."¹⁶

The language of family life and the roles and relationships within it helped sustain support for the war even as it took an emotional and economic toll on households. Worst still, rising inflation and shortages of supplies placed more pressure on households' already limited means. Knowing their responsibilities to the home and family, non-elite Southerners rationalized enduring hardships on both the military and home fronts wrought by separation, physical dangers, and economic downturns. The gendered expectations of respectable behavior provided a source of stability as well as a close connection to the domestic circle in which members sought solace.

Thoughts of one day returning to the domestic circle proved a powerful symbol in non-elites' quest to survive military dangers and declining conditions on the home front. James Branscomb wrote to his sister in 1863 that having been in the army since the onset of the war, he looked forward to the day when he could "shake hands with you and your children." The prospect of a furlough likewise intensified Branscomb's goal of making it through military engagements to see his family again. "Sister," he wrote Lucinda, "these years absent from those that are so dear him causes a heart to beat as it never did before when he soon expects to meet those dear ones, to meet Father, Mother, Brothers, Sisters after all I have born will be the happiest day of my life." John Wesley Branscomb, the brother of James and Lucinda, echoed the sentiment of reunion in a letter to his sister: "I almost despair when I think childhoods home but the thought of meeting again gives me pleasure. I am not dissatisfied with my home only when I am lonesome."¹⁷

The correspondence between Emily and William Moxley also brings into sharp relief the power of reunion in enduring emotional and economic trials during their separation. William expressed the centrality of family in providing emotional support, writing that letters from home were "a blessing" because they allowed members to "communicate all our thoughts and desires." Emily gave a touching appeal to William that she was in a state of despair over his leaving and that his absence was "the hardest trial I have ever had, by far." Despite the outpouring of emotion that pervaded their letters, both recognized that the prospect of reunion offered a sense of comfort. William wrote to Emily in October 1861 that "I dreamed of you evry night. . . . Some times when I would open my eyes I could hardly believe but you was some where not far from me." Yet William muted the pain of separation by holding onto the prospect of one day seeing his family again. In his estimation, an end to the war was the only means of achieving reunion: "I look forward to that time when I shall be able to see you and all the children togeather at home wonce more, for I believe if I live, & you, and all the children, and we have peace as we desire it, that I shall be as happy as a man can be on this Earth." Emily and William held fast to the hope that they would one day see each other again; it was, at least during the first year of the war, enough to help them navigate the trials of separation.[18]

The continuation of conventional duties also provided a sense of normalcy during wartime disruptions. In particular, those of the yeomen and poorer classes relied on women's traditional roles as a source of continuity with the prewar past. Women were seen as nurturers and caregivers, roles rooted in the domestic circle of family life. During William Moxley's service in the Confederate military, he wrote frequently to his wife about his bouts of illness. She attempted to offer comfort to him, wishing that she could be there to nurse him through his illness. After learning that one spell left him bedridden she responded, "I have not had a night sleep since, but all that I can do is to grieve. I go to bed but not to sleep much but to cry and study about my poor Husband that is lieing on his cot and no one to nurse him as I would do, or at least they would not do it as willingly as I would." William likewise recognized the comforting nature of his wife's care, writing, "[If] every person in the world was present it would [do] me no good if you was not" and "I wanted some of that nursing I always received from your willing hands."[19]

Women also expressed a sense of duty about maintaining their supportive role even in the absence of their husbands. Notions of Confederate womanhood that lauded the willingness of women to extend their domestic roles into the public world of military life touched the lives of those from the yeomen and poorer socioeconomic classes. In their letters and diaries, women used domestic production to help supply their male kin on the military front. Such contributions to the Confederate war effort fit neatly into the confines of women's familial duty to help supply a family that traditionally relied on the labor of women for material support. In her diary, Sarah Rousseau Espy illuminated the invaluable role she played in supplementing the clothing and other supplies of her sons serving in the Confederate army. Rather than begrudge the added burden to her workday, she saw this as a way to ensure the comfort of her sons. Columbus Espy, Sarah's younger son, wrote in September 1861 that he was in need of clothes and she acquiesced. Lucinda Branscomb Hunter also wrote frequently to her brothers on the front asking if they needed homemade supplies, clothing in particular.[20]

Women of the non-elite class used nineteenth-century notions of female piety as an emotional crutch amid the hardships of war. Nineteenth-century women were lauded as moral guardians in the home and encouraged religious devotion among the female population. Turning to notions of divine providence, religious faith, and moral behavior enabled women to endure the emotional and material trials on the home front. Sarah Rousseau Espy, for instance, turned to her religious faith as she faced the prospect of Federal troops entering her community in January 1864, writing that she hoped "the good Lord will not allow them to come, but turn them back to their own country to live in peace." When the enemy finally came that summer, she again turned to her faith. "May the good Lord grant we may never have such another trial pass through," she recorded in her diary, "but may He fight for us against the mighty." Emily Moxley leaned on her religious faith to deal with her separation from her husband, citing that she must "trust in providence for the better." By 1862, Emily relied more on her faith as a source of hope for family reunion, writing to William that "God grant that we may gain the victory and all can go home to familiys in our country now." Similarly, when Zillah Brandon learned in May 1862 that her son James had died in a hospital and then two months later received news that her youngest son, Hines, had died in a hospital in Gainesville, Alabama, she sought to overcome her grief through faith: "Like twin brothers, they were linked by a threefold cord that will ever beautify the Christian name. And as Saul and Jonathan, they were pleasant in life, so they were barely separated in death."[21]

Families remained connected to one another in times of separation during the war as they encouraged each another to uphold the ideals of respectable behavior. Husbands, for example, wrote frequently to their wives directing their conduct in private and community settings. Emily and William Moxley illuminate those concerns in their many letters written during the first two years of the war. When William left for the army, he entrusted Mr. Newton, a male neighbor, with guarding the family finances and ensuring the material comfort of the family. Growing increasingly frustrated with Newton's lack of attention to the family's financial matters and their growing privation, Emily turned to community members to help provide for her dependents. Newton failed to settle debts owed to William and delayed selling land that could have helped supplement the family income, and Emily noted that "he is not willing to do any thing for me and them." Emily revealed to William that she was now at the mercy of a local merchant to provide supplies on credit and was circumventing Newton's authority to oversee her family finances. William deemed Emily's actions as an affront to his ability to provide for his family and implored her to let him procure any necessary supplies. "You know I have always been willing to furnish you with any thing needed I could furnish," he wrote, "if you need any thing let me know it, for [I] expect to furnish it for you."[22]

William also grew increasingly concerned about his wife's personal habits. In particular, William pleaded with his wife in several letters to "quit the use of snuff." Women of the poorer socioeconomic classes commonly used snuff, but William abhorred the thought of his wife using tobacco in his absence and even told her that if she quit he would stop using tobacco until they were reunited. William feared the effect it could have on her health. "My dear, it is for your good that I make the request," he wrote in December 1861, "I would not deny you any thing that would afford you Comfort or Happiness that would not be an injury to you." His insistence that she take his advice, however, illuminates a much deeper concern. In his request he attempted to ensure that his wife followed proper conduct for the wife of a physician, arguing that the practice "was questionable."[23]

Even while serving on the battlefront, men continued to assert their role as provider for and protector of the family. For example, Sarah Rousseau Espy received a letter from one of her sons instructing her how to manage the family's supplies. He was concerned about the growing shortage of food and wrote that she should share her supplies with other members of the family. James Zachariah Branscomb, moreover, attempted to assert his influence in directing his sister Lucinda on how to handle the continual illnesses of her children, especially given her status as a widow. In a letter to his brother William, Daniel Newton Moxley expressed concern that the person in charge of storing William's corn would keep it for himself. To help his brother provide for his family he intervened, writing that "Malloy had githered it all & put it to one crib, & I soposed that he said that you should not have enny of it, but when I went to see him he said that you might have the corn."[24]

Single men found a connection to home by calling on the gendered rituals of courtship. Returning as an honored soldier would enhance their reputation and, in turn, their marital prospects. James Zachariah Branscomb, for example, wrote frequently to his sister asking about the young women in their community and insisted that she speak highly of his military service to them in hopes of securing courtship opportunities when he returned. "I want you to have a sweetheart picked out for me when I get home," he wrote. "Give all the girls my pious regards." In a subsequent letter James charged his sister with finding a "sweetheart . . . tell her about me so she may know what to depend on when I come." The notion of returning to a potential romantic relationship seemed to have lightened James's spirits in his letter to Lucinda: "I am going immediately to courting and I shall you're your judgment. So get to work now and let me know soon who she is so I will know whether to come home like a soldier or like a gentlemen." Charles Thompson Beck wrote to his sister Emily Moxley that she should "write me all the news when writ all about the girls. That is the most interesting of any thing you can write." He also asked her to tell specific women "howdy for me" and "to remember me."[25]

Relationships among male siblings likewise illuminated the solace that familial duty provided during the war. As older brothers left for the front, leaving their younger male kin behind, they felt compelled to offer the traditional brotherly advice often found in their prewar relationships. When James Zachariah Branscomb received word that his brother Louis intended to join the local militia, he advised him against it. "I fear the militia is a bad egg," he wrote. "I will lift you out of the militia when I get home for I have a supreme contempt for it." He based his reasoning on his belief that the local home guard had failed in their responsibility to offer defense to the community. James eventually served with Louis in the Confederate army and wrote home that he was keeping close watch over his safety. In a letter to his sister, he assured her that although Louis appeared "a little homesick" it would "soon wear off." Daniel Newton Moxley likewise wrote his brother William seeking his advice about joining the army as a way to earn money for his family: "you see that if it was to fail, it would be a bad business for me, for it is making a grait sacrifice."[26]

Moral conviction also informed their sense of male respectability and helped men comfort family members on the home front. Stories of drinking, gambling, and prostitution within the camps reached the home front and caused much distress among female kin left to wonder if their men could resist temptation. When it appeared that her younger son Virgil would be drafted into the Confederate army, Sarah Rousseau Espy confided in her diary that she feared "he may be inticed by wicked men into bad habits." However, many men realized they needed to reassure family members that they were staying true to their moral conviction and maintaining their respectable reputation. James Zachariah Branscomb, for example, wrote to his mother that he remained devoted to his religious faith, which helped him through the hardships of military life. "Dear Mother," he wrote, "you can't imagin how I feel when I think of you on your knees at the family altar, supplicating the throne of Grace for me at the hour of retiring . . . but I am glad that I can tell you that I never as yet been out of my place as a soldier." James also reminded his sister of his religious devotion, writing that he attended Sunday services regularly in the camps. In an 1863 letter he boasted to her that there was "good work going on in the regt. Now, we have prayer meeting four times a week. . . . May this good work continue."[27]

By midway through the war, conditions on the home front had grown desperate, particularly for non-elites. In 1864, for example, state officials made an effort to calculate the number of households that received government assistance. Officials reported that the number of indigent families from forty-seven counties totaled 35,393. Even with the assistance now provided by the government, continued separation from male providers who were on the battlefront, growing financial exigencies, and fear of illness and death led non-elites, with less investment in preserving the interests of the wealthy classes, to take a critical approach to the war. The language of gender, situated within the domestic circle, provided them with a voice to express their growing discontent. Declining supplies and increased inflation on the home front in particular magnified class inequities. Sarah Rousseau Espy, for example, confided in her diary her growing concern about the cost of typical household items such as wool. She laid blame for the high prices on "the villainous work of speculators who are taking this time of trouble to enrich themselves." Emily Moxley wrote frequently to her husband about the hardships of acquiring basic necessities for the family. Her writing reflects notions of female dependency rooted in the gendered ideals of the Old South: "I am dependent," she wrote, and punctuated her dependency by explaining how the men of her family and community failed to assist her in properly supplying the home. Emily wrote to William that as the family teetered on the brink of starvation, she would be forced to turn to community assistance: "You don't know how I feel to go any body els for something to eat when I never had it to do in my life. I have all ways had my dear Husband to provide for me and to a head in every thing, and now I have no one that cares for my wellfare that is about here."[28]

Over the course of war, yeomen and poor whites grew increasingly resentful toward the elites on the home front. Those of wealth, for example, found alternatives to staying behind in the face of occupation by relocating to safer ground and possessed more economic resources to weather, at least in appearance, financial downturns. After visiting a wealthy member of her community, Sarah Rousseau Espy reflected on what she believed was a war waged on the backs of "the workingclasses [sic]." When threatened with Federal occupation in December 1863, elite community members possessed the means to retreat from potential danger while those of Espy's class had little choice but to remain. "They are well off," she wrote, "and are going to wealthy friends whereas I, and many others, have no friends and our children even bearly boys, are taken from us and put into the serves. There is a great wrong somewhere." Espy also directed her criticism toward the Confederate government when she wrote about the conscription law that called her son-in-law John to the front, calling the draft policy "as shameful a one as congress ever passed." She criticized Confederate officials for what she believed were self-serving practices that unduly burdened members of her community. "They also passed a law giving themselves $2700 a year," she wrote in August 1862, "and the greater part of the time they are at home attending their business. I look for a rebellion among ourselves at the rate of going on, for the war taxes the people heavy enough."[29]

The material and emotional hardships that Lucinda Branscomb Hunter experienced on Alabama's home front caused her to question her patriotism. In a letter to her brother she expressed her discontent with the continuation of the war after losing her youngest brother to the military front. James attempted to comfort his sister, writing that "the prospect does look a little gloomy, but wait a while and you will hear of another great victory from Genl Lee's army that will cheer every southern heart." Lucinda's brother Louis shared his sister's sentiment about the continuation of the war. "I was sorry to find you so low spirited," he wrote to her in October 1863, "but I can't blame you for you have enough to make you so. I must admit that I am in that line myself." William Moxley's criticism of the war reflected his observations about how the war had disrupted families and he worried that the same fate would befall his domestic circle during his absence: "How dreadful is war. Such as you have witnessed is of evry day accurance some where in consequence of this unholy war, seperating the dearest companions on earth, making widdows & orphans evry day, making the happiest homes desolate, turning joy into mourning."[30] For the Branscomb and Moxley families, the sadness and privation war entailed led them to question the value of its continuation and they situated their doubts within the context of family.

As the war drew to a close, yeomen and poor white families anticipated returning to their former lives. For some, like the Moxleys, the family would resume in a broken state. As early as 1862 William Moxley received the untimely news that his wife, Emily, had died while giving birth to their child. For William, returning home a widower meant a reorientation of household responsibilities and turning to extended female kin for assistance. Death also cast a dark cloud on the Branscomb family household when Louis was killed in battle in late summer 1864. As the other brothers returned from battle, there would be a void in their family. Although Sarah Rousseau Espy's sons survived the war, they returned seriously affected by its harsh conditions. Espy's son Marcelleous, for example, spent time in a Federal prison camp and was released only a month before the close of the war. When he returned home, it was clear to Espy that the conditions her young son had endured had left him in a state of poor health. Yet after families reunited, the prospect of rebuilding life after Confederate defeat provided a way to refocus their energies. Now their daily lives would be filled with recovering from the war.[31]

As the case of *John W. Brown vs. Ellen J. Brown* reveals, gendered notions of familial identity and household roles pervaded the post-Confederate landscape. As a "proper" man who had risked his life to serve the Confederacy, Brown had performed his duty sufficiently to maintain a respectable reputation in the community. When he returned from service to find his wife gone and her reputation tarnished, his own power filtered through Southern masculine honor stood in question. Only through the courts could he publicly declare that he had, in fact, fulfilled his responsibility and therefore deserved to remain in good standing with his community. Alabama's non-elites called on similar notions of family responsibility in the formation and defense of the Confederate nation. As a class relegated to the margins of economic, political, and social life of the prewar South, their support for the war, rooted in notions of family duty and reputation, allowed them to assert public power in the nascent Confederacy. And when material and emotional hardships took a toll on their daily lives, family once again emerged as a key symbol in their struggle to cope with the exigencies of war and even question its continuation without rendering them unpatriotic Confederates. In the aftermath of war, the toll on non-elites was clear. With households in a state of want and family circles broken, they had little choice but to turn once again to the domestic world as a way to rebuild and recover.

Notes

1. *John W. Brown vs. Ellen J. Brown*, Bill of Divorce, Perry County, LGM 249, reel 21, Alabama Department of Archives and History, Montgomery (hereafter ADAH).

2. In selecting my subject group, I chose those with less than $10,000 in personal and real property. To verify their financial status I used the Manuscript Schedules of the Seventh (1850) Census and Eighth (1860) Census of the U.S. Bureau of the Census. I also confirmed their non-slaveholding status using the 1850 and 1860 Slave Schedules of the U.S. Bureau of the Census. For the few who mentioned slave ownership, I confirmed that their holdings were minimal (fewer than ten slaves). I used the editor's information concerning the profile of my subjects in published primary sources to ensure their non-elite status.

3. Charles C. Bolton and Scott P. Culclasure, *The Confessions of Edward Isham* (Athens: University of Georgia Press, 1998); Aaron Sheehan-Dean, *Why Confederates Fought: Family and Nation in Civil War Virginia* (Chapel Hill: University of North Carolina Press, 2007). Works devoted to the lives of non-slaveholding whites were published as early as the 1940s. Frank Owsley, *Plain Folk of the Old South* (Baton Rouge: Louisiana State University Press, 1949), illustrates a more nuanced understanding of the social makeup of the region. Subsequent studies focus on the relationship of non-elites to the planter elites, as well as their economic and cultural contributions to Southern society. See William Harris, *Plain Folk and Gentry in a Slave Society: White Liberty and Black Slavery in Augusta's Hinterlands* (Middletown, CT: Wesleyan University Press, 1985); Bruce Collins, *White Society in the Antebellum South* (New York: Longman, 1985); Charles C. Bolton, *Poor Whites of the Antebellum South: Tenants and Laborers in Central North Carolina and Northeast Mississippi* (Durham: Duke University Press, 1994); and Stephanie McCurry, *Masters of Small Worlds: Yeomen Households, Gender Relations, and the Political Culture of the Antebellum South Carolina Low Country* (New York: Oxford University Press, 1995). Studies relating to the Civil War era tend to focus on reasons why "plain folk" fought and on sources of dissent as wartime conditions worsened. Such studies include Mark V. Wetherington, *Plain Folk's Fight: The Civil War and Reconstruction in Piney Woods Georgia* (Chapel Hill: University of North Carolina Press, 2005) and David Williams, Teresa Crisp Williams, and David Carlson, *Plain Folk in a Rich Man's War: Class and Dissent in Confederate Georgia* (Gainesville: University Press of Florida, 2002).

4. Margaret Storey, *Loyalty and Loss: Alabama's Unionists in the Civil War and Reconstruction* (Baton Rouge: Louisiana State University Press, 2004), 7–11.

5. Craig Thompson Friend and Anya Jabour, eds., *Family Values in the Old South* (Gainesville: University Press of Florida, 2010), 1–8.

6. *Campbell Jefferson vs. Lydia Margaret Jefferson*, Bill of Divorce, Talladega County, LG 4701, ADAH.

7. *Ann M. Brown vs. Morgan G. Brown*, Bill of Divorce, Wilcox County, LG 4012-4069, ADAH. Several historians examine the issue of domestic abuse and the limits of patriarchal power as recognized by Southern courts. For example, see Bertram Wyatt-Brown, *Southern Honor: Ethics and Behavior in the Old South* (New York: Oxford University Press, 1983) and Laura F. Edwards, "Law, Domestic Violence, and the Limits of Patriarchal Authority in the Antebellum South," *Journal of Southern History* 65, no. 4 (1999): 733–70.

8. *Malcome A. McKinnon vs. Sarah M. McKinnon*, Bill of Divorce, Final Record, Chancery Court, Talladega County, LG 4701, ADAH.

9. *Ann M. Brown vs. Morgan G. Brown*, Bill of Divorce. I have chosen to leave misspellings and grammatical errors in the primary sources unedited as they aid in understanding the culture, namely the language, of the era as it pertains to this socioeconomic group.

10. Sarah Rousseau Espy Diary, May 2, July 2–6, and 13, 1860, SPR2, ADAH.

11. U.S. Bureau of the Census, Manuscript Census Schedules, Eighth (1860) Census; U.S. Bureau of the Census, Slave Schedule (1860); Zillah Haynie Brandon Diary, April 28, October 14, and December 3, 1860, February 4, 1861, SPR262, ADAH.

12. Espy Diary, August 11 and September 4, 1860; Brandon Diary, August 21, 1861.

13. James Zachariah Branscomb to Lucinda Branscomb Hunter, January 24, 1861, Branscomb Family Letters, LPR195, ADAH.

14. Espy Diary, March 19, 1860; Thomas Cutrer, ed., *Oh, What a Loansome Time I Had: The Civil War Letters of Major William Morel Moxley, Eighteenth Alabama Infantry and Emily Beck Moxley* (Tuscaloosa: University of Alabama Press, 2002), 1–6, 22. In the case of the Moxley letters, I followed the editor's transcription, which is only the addition of words for readability; Brandon Diary, August 21, 1861.

15. James Zachariah Branscomb to Lucinda Branscomb Hunter, January 11, 1863, January 22, 1864, James Zachariah Branscomb to Louis Branscomb, February 27, 1862, James Zachariah Branscomb to Lucinda Branscomb Hunter, July 27, 1861, all in Branscomb Family Letters; Cutrer, *Oh, What a Loansome Time I Had*, 26.

16. Brandon Diary, August 21, 1861.

17. James Zachariah Branscomb to Lucinda Branscomb Hunter, November 17, 1863, January 22, 1864, John Wesley Branscomb to Lucinda Branscomb Hunter, September 17, 1864, all in Branscomb Family Letters.

18. Cutrer, *Oh, What a Loansome Time I Had*, 25, 41–42, 72.

19. Ibid., 35, 42, 45.

20. Espy Diary, September 27, 1861; James Zachariah Branscomb to Lucinda Branscomb Hunter, August 24, 1861, Branscomb Family Letters.

21. Espy Diary, January 19, June 3, 1864; Cutrer, *Oh, What a Loansome Time I Had*, 23, 128; Brandon Diary, June 7, August 7, 1862.

22. Cutrer, *Oh, What a Loansome Time I Had*, 23, 47, 83, 91.

23. Ibid., 44, 61.

24. Espy Diary, July 10, 1864; James Zachariah Branscomb to Lucinda Branscomb Hunter, December 17, 1861, Branscomb Family Letters; Cutrer, *Oh, What a Loansome Time I Had*, 52.

25. James Zachariah Branscomb to Lucinda Branscomb Hunter, December 17, 1861, January 1, 1863, Branscomb Family Letters; Cutrer, *Oh, What a Loansome Time I Had*, 51.

26. James Zachariah Branscomb to Louis Branscomb, March [n.d.] 1862, James Zachariah Branscomb to Lucinda Branscomb Hunter, May 6, 1862, both in Branscomb Family Letters; Cutrer, *Oh, What a Loansome Time I Had*, 53.

27. Espy Diary, December 31, 1863; James Zachariah Branscomb to Eliza Branscomb, September 11, 1861, James Zachariah Branscomb to Lucinda Branscomb Hunter, July 27, 1861, April [n.d.], 1863, all in Branscomb Family Letters.

28. *Report on Indigent Families*, Public Information subject files, Civil War and Reconstruction Misc., SG 17 131, folder 18, ADAH; Espy Diary, September 5, 1862; Cutrer, *Oh, What a Loansome Time I Had*, 30, 83.

29. Espy Diary, December 18, 1863, August 15, 1862.

30. James Zachariah Branscomb to Lucinda Branscomb Hunter, August 7, 1863, Louis Branscomb to Lucinda Branscomb Hunter, October 25, 1863, both in Branscomb Family Letters; Cutrer, *Oh, What a Loansome Time I Had*, 84.

31. Cutrer, *Oh, What a Loansome Time I Had*, 136–37; John Wesley Branscomb to Lucinda Branscomb Hunter, August 5, 1864, Branscomb Family Letters; Espy Diary, March 21, 1865. For

studies of non-elites after the war, see Wetherington, *Plain Folk's Fight* and Williams, Williams, and Carlson, *Plain Folk in a Rich Man's War*. Historians who have examined Southerners' efforts to rebuild the economic and social structure of their communities amid the climate of Reconstruction include Michael Perman, *Reunion without Compromise: The South and Reconstruction, 1865–1868* (New York: Cambridge University Press, 1973) and Steven Hahn, *The Roots of Southern Populism: Yeomen Farmers and the Transformation of the Georgia Upcountry* (New York: Oxford University Press, 1983).

7
Augusta Jane Evans
Alabama's Confederate *Macaria*
Jennifer Lynn Gross

Augusta Jane Evans (Wilson) was one of the nineteenth-century South's most popular female authors. Born in Columbus, Georgia, on May 8, 1835, Evans spent some of her childhood in San Antonio, Texas, where her father moved the family after he went bankrupt in the early 1840s.[1] By 1849, when many Americans were moving west, Matthew Evans moved his family back east to Mobile, Alabama, to escape the discomfort and uncertainties of life in Texas. It was in Alabama that Augusta Evans lived out her adult life, remaining there until her death from a heart attack 1909.[2] For Evans, Alabama was home, and when Alabama embraced the Confederate cause in 1861, she did too—with gusto. In June 1861, when Evans traveled to Virginia to visit her brothers who had recently been sent there as part of the 3rd Alabama Regiment, Evans encountered the war firsthand as she and her fellow travelers were fired upon by Union soldiers holding Fort Monroe. She wrote to her closest friend, Rachel Lyons, "O! I longed for a Secession flag to shake *defiantly* in their *teeth* at every fire! And my fingers fairly itched to touch off a *red-hot-ball* in answer to their *chivalric civilities*."[3] Only a few months later, far removed from the "action," Evans's ardor had not cooled one bit. Again writing to Lyons, Evans wrote, "How our holy cause brightens as the storm of war thickens around us! Oh Rachel! I thank God that we are both *Southern Women*! My heart swells with exultation, in view of the future of our Young Confederacy! Who shall presume to limit its extent and magnificence!"[4]

As the waves of secession began to flow across the South in 1861, Evans received a letter from an acquaintance, Virginia French, a fellow novelist and the editor of several magazines and newspapers, including, most notably, the *Crusader* and *Ladies' Home*. French wanted Evans to lend her prestige to a "Memorial" that urged Unionism instead of secession, which she intended to present to the Georgia legislature. Evans responded with a resounding "no." In a passionate letter to French dated January 13, 1861, Evans wrote that she had "no sympathy whatever" for the idea of remaining in the Union, asserting that the federal government was "guided by the Demon of fanaticism" and that any effort to delay the dissolution of the

Union was "suicidal." She closed her letter emotionally, mentioning the plight of her father and brothers stationed at Fort Morgan in Mobile and her own work on "*Sand Bags* for the *ramparts* and *cartridges for the cannon*" and asserting that if "the hour arrives when Federal guns pour their fiery hail upon it; I feel that I would infinitely prefer to perish *there* with them, rather than endure the horrors which hundreds of John Browns would inevitably stir up in our midst, sheltered by the protecting mantle of Lincolns Administration." She continued emphatically, "were it my privilege to address my countrymen of Georgia on the 16th, I should point to the flag of Alabama; waving its magnificent folds in the balmy breezes of the Gulf, and with a serene trust in the God of Justice; say triumphantly, 'let the Star of the Empire State blaze with ours along the way to *Freedom*; let us conquer or perish together; delay is ruinous, suicidal—; *the time has come.*'"[5]

While Evans chided French and the other women who signed the "Memorial" for not recognizing the importance of secession, she did so by criticizing them for overstepping the bounds of their gender, arguing, "I think it is an occasion when women should leave matters entirely to the wisdom of our statesmen." Evans herself had no problem commenting publicly and in print on the events of the era, however. In a letter to her cousin in Milledgeville, Georgia's capital, enclosing a copy of French's letter and her response to it, she advised him that she would be happy to address Georgia's esteemed legislators on the merits of secession should they invite her to do so.[6] For Evans, it was not that women should not be involved in public affairs. In an 1860 letter to Lyons, Evans wrote, "I assume that like myself, you are now all absorbed in considering the vital political question of the day. It is an issue of such incalculable solemnity and importance that no true Southern *man* or *woman* can fail to be deeply interested and impressed."[7] It was that women with whom she disagreed, like French and the others who signed the Memorial urging Unionism, should not be involved. Evans had no problem publicly expressing her opinions on secession, the Confederate war effort, and even the Confederate government during the four years the war raged. An 1864 letter to Confederate congressman J. L. M. Curry, congratulating him on the warm reception he received for a speech she helped him write challenging the tendency of President Davis and other politicians of his ilk toward centralization, provides an apt example. Evans, ever verbose, passionately avowed:

> [The] democrats are at present gravitating rapidly toward centralization, consolidation, are quite ready to anathemate [sic] Jefferson as the prince of sophists, and almost prepared to yield allegiance to the dicta of Hamilton. Strange but immemorial paradox! Mankind plunge into cruel wars, into internecine conflicts, in defence of principles, which during the revolution they permit to slip through their fingers. Affrighted by the shadow of Absolutism and

Abolitionism that brooded over Washington, the men of the South flew to arms; but three years of "struggling" have singularly modified their opinions; and I have been pained and astonished to find how many are now willing to glide unhesitatingly into a dictatorship, a military despotism,—even into a state of colonial dependence, with gradual emancipation as a condition of foreign intervention and protection. The original *casus belli* has been lost sight of; hatred of Lincoln, not love of our liberties, principles and institutions now actuates our masses. However humiliating, this is an indisputable phase of popular opinion, which our leaders should gravely ponder, and resolutely oppose.[8]

Clearly Evans did not shy away from giving her opinion on matters of public import.

A prolific author, Evans published nine novels during her career, three of which—*Beulah*, *Macaria*, and *St. Elmo*—emerged in a span of only seven years between 1859 and 1866.[9] While some literary critics like O. J. Victor of the *Cosmopolitan Journal* continually praised Evans's work in reviews and editorials, others routinely panned her writing style as artificial and pretentious. In a letter to a friend regarding an impending visit to New York, Evans wrote of her critics, "Should the critic horde raise the war-whoop with which they invariably welcome me, and fall upon me with 'oot, horse, and dragoon, 'will not your glittering "Excalibar" leap from its scabbard, in defense of that injured innocence, whose scalp has often dangled in imagination from the gory pens, ambushed in the Sanctum of the "Tribune," or the "Times?""" While Evans is clearly aware of her critics' opinions, even her discussions of them illustrate the very criticisms they leveled at her. Despite her critics, or perhaps because of them, her readers responded enthusiastically to her novels. Writing to her friend Rachel Lyons in May 1864, just after the publication of *Macaria*, she wrote, "My new book brings me many letters of congratulations, and I am very much gratified and rejoiced at the flattering criticism upon it. Everyone pronounces it superior to '*Beulah*.'"[10]

At least two of Evans's novels, *Beulah* (1859) and *St. Elmo* (1866), were national best sellers when first published. In fact, other than *Uncle Tom's Cabin* (1852), *St. Elmo* sold more copies than any novel in the nineteenth century.[11] By 1867 *Scott's Monthly* boldly declared, "We venture to place [Evans] at the head of American female novelists. This, if not the decision of contemporary criticism, will be the verdict of posterity."[12] As it turns out, *Scott's Monthly* was quite mistaken about "the verdict of posterity," but Evans was indeed an exceedingly popular author, particularly in the South. As one of the South's leading literary women, Evans had the power to influence Southern society with her pen. Of this power, Evans was keenly aware.

In a letter to General P. G. T. Beauregard, with whom she regularly corresponded, she wrote, "frequently during the last year, I have felt disposed to lament the limited circle of action, the insignificant *role* assigned us, in the mightiest drama that ever riveted the gaze of the civilized world . . . and though debarred from the 'tented field,' the cause of our beloved, struggling Confederacy may yet be advanced through the agency of its' [*sic*] daughters." She continued, "It is not my privilege to enter the ranks, wielding a sword, in my country's cause, but all that my feeble, womanly pen could contribute to the consummation of our freedom, I have humbly, but at least, faithfully and untiringly *endeavored* to achieve."[13]

And achieve it she did. Before the war's end Evans would write numerous newspaper and magazine articles, correspond with several notable Confederate officials, advise a powerful Confederate congressman on the topics of his speeches, and, most important, write the most uncompromisingly pro-Confederate novel to appear during the war. Although many are no longer extant, Evans wrote a number of articles for various Southern newspapers assessing the state of the Southern home front while attempting to bolster Confederate morale. Though she wrote many of these pieces anonymously, she claimed to have done so only to avoid the notoriety associated with people who wrote for newspapers. For example, in response to a letter from Beauregard suggesting that she had authored a recent anonymous piece that had appeared in the paper, she thanked him for his kind words and congratulated him on figuring out it was she who had written the article. In response to his comments, she self-effacingly wrote,

> My desire to remain incognito arose from no reluctance to assume the responsibility of my article, but is attributable solely to my aversion to that species of notoriety, which newspaper contributors so often acquire. To institute reforms in any department of State, is regarded as unsuitable work for womanly hands; and though I have sometimes been impelled to this painful task, by a stern sense of duty to our country, I can not avoid deploring the necessity, and shrinking from the publicity incident to such contributions. Although reluctant to transcend the proper sphere of womanhood, and always fearful of encroaching upon the prerogatives of your sex, I am not to be deterred from fulfilling what I occasionally feel to be a sacred duty,—by fear of the ridicule or wrath of those who contend that women have no interest in matters appertaining to Government errors. Consequently while I am neither ashamed of my opinions, nor *afraid* to *avow* them, I still endeavor to escape all unnecessary notoriety.[14]

As literary scholar Anne Goodwyn Jones, has astutely observed, Evans often explained her controversial behavior away by defining it as a sacrifice.[15] Despite her professed reluctance to get involved in Confederate politics, Evans frequently took pen in hand in the service of that "sacred duty."

While Evans frequently wielded her pen in published forums, she also had the ear of several significant Confederate leaders including Confederate secretary of state Robert Toombs, Confederate diplomat and senator from Georgia William L. Yancey, Confederate senator from Georgia Benjamin Hill, Confederate and Alabama congressman, Baptist minister J. L. M. Curry, Confederate general P. G. T. Beauregard, and Confederate admiral Franklin Buchanan. Though she corresponded at one time or another with all of these men, she had an especially frequent and friendly correspondence with Curry and Beauregard, to whom she "freely and confidently [gave] advice concerning everything from battle plans to government politics."[16]

In her correspondence with Curry, Evans's concern over the state of the home front was paramount. She frequently noted the impact that inflation, deprivation, and war profiteering were having on Confederate morale and suggested actions that should be taken in response. In one letter to Curry, Evans wrote:

> It *chills* the blood in my veins to hear of the degrading and horrible punishments inflicted on *Southern Soldiers*, who plead in palliation of desertion, the cries of hungry wives and starving children. . . . Cursed as is our struggling country by the shameless tribe of speculators and extortioners who swarm in every nook and cranny of the Confederacy battening upon the pittances of families whose providers are toiling in snow, and sleet, and blood, on distant battlefields, or sleeping dreamlessly in nameless martyr-graves, it is not strange that murmurs are swelling ominously; and that disaffection stalks colossal, where cheerful endurance, noble self-abnegation, and sublime fervor of patriotism formerly challenged the admiration of the world, and earned the gratitude of coming generations.[17]

For Evans, the Exemption Bill, which allowed men to avoid military service by paying for a substitute, was an especially troubling matter for Confederate morale. In the same letter, Evans argued against the Exemption Bill, noting that it "offer[ed] premiums for extortion, among all classes of artificers; instead of compelling them either to join the ranks of the army, or furnish such necessities as shoes and meal[s] at reasonable rates." Moreover, the clause exempting those with twenty or more slaves, though designed to guard against slave insurrections, had "resulted most unhappily in the creation of an antislavery element among our soldiers who openly complain that they are torn from their homes, and their families consigned to starvation solely in order that they may protect the property of slaveholders; who are allowed by the '*Bill*' to remain in quiet enjoyment of luxurious ease."[18] By 1863 she was not only calling for the repeal of the Exemption Bill but also challenging the placement of "*Brigades* of *young athletic* bread & butter Captains & Majors" in the "ignominious shelter of Commissary and Quartermaster Dep't's," asserting that they were more needed in "the thin ranks of our noble army."[19]

With General Beauregard, she also discussed the Exemption Bill and other morale issues, but her commentary did not end there. In her letters to Beauregard she also frequently held forth on which generals were superior to others and which should be replaced. She shared Beauregard's disdain for Braxton Bragg, believing many soldiers from the Mobile area to have died as a result of his incompetence in the Western Theater. Evans also freely and routinely criticized Jefferson Davis, even at times suggesting that he was too timid to serve as an effective commander-in-chief.[20] As early as October 1861 she acknowledged her confidence in the Confederate war effort, lauding the "*unequalled* material crowded [into] the ranks of our noble army, and . . . the *skill* and sagacity of our Generals," but asserted that victory would be threatened by the "*inexplicable* policy of the Richmond Cabinet [and] the evident timidity of President Davis."[21]

While Evans certainly tried to impact the Confederate cause through her correspondence with important men and her newspaper articles, it was increasingly clear to her that her greatest contribution of the pen would be made another way—through her novel. Even as she wrote *Macaria*, Evans was keenly aware of the impact it could have on Confederate morale. In a letter to Beauregard Evans tellingly wrote, "I had intended not to publish it [*Macaria*] until the close of the war, but recently circumstances [sagging morale on the home front] have determined me to bring it out, as soon as I can finish copying the *MS*."[22] She reiterated her feeling that it was vitally important her novel be published as soon as possible in a letter to her publishers in 1863. Acknowledging the tedious nature of editing and copying the manuscript, she wrote, "I shall devote my entire time to it until it is accomplished. I fully appreciate the *expediency* of bringing it out as early as practicable, and shall therefore work as rapidly as possible."[23]

In terms of sales at the time of initial publication, *Macaria* was not in the same league as either *Beulah* or *St. Elmo*, but this was largely because it was published during the war. One of the few novels published in the South during the war, there were more than twenty thousand copies of *Macaria* circulating in the region by the end of the conflict. Many in fact recognized it as the most popular book in the Confederacy.[24]

A tome of more than four hundred pages, Evans claimed to have composed *Macaria* on scraps of paper while keeping watch over Confederate soldiers' bedsides at a makeshift Civil War hospital near her Mobile home. Whether the novel was actually written at the bedsides of Confederate soldiers is somewhat debatable. It is clear, however, that she wrote the novel during the first year or so of the war, at the same time that she was engaged in war work including nursing. Regardless of the accuracy of the claim, her target audience ate it up.[25] Indeed, famed Southern diarist Ella Gertrude Clanton Thomas credited her reading of *Macaria* as the reason she began assisting in local hospitals during the war. Given Evans's cachet as one of the most popular Southern writers at the time, Thomas was likely not the only Southern woman Evans inspired, which was exactly what she intended.[26]

Though only the last third of *Macaria* deals with the war directly, Evans wrote the whole of *Macaria* in its context. In fact, it is the novel's use of the war as background that her readers, particularly her Southern readers, probably found the most compelling.[27] *Macaria* had a little something for everyone. The sentimental trappings of the love story in the literary tradition of the domestic novel certainly pleased Evans's female audience. For her male readers, it had a detailed description of Southern heroism in the Confederate victory at first Manassas. In fact, it was General Beauregard himself who assisted Evans with her vivid, if overly flattering, description of Beauregard's victory in that first battle of the war.[28] The purely propagandistic elements decrying the "demagogic" North as the betrayer of the U.S. heritage of democracy undoubtedly appealed to ardent Confederates, but it is possible that even the most tepid of Confederates could relate to these passages. Probably because she intended her novel to appeal to all Southerners no matter where they resided, Evans never locates *Macaria* with any specificity, instead preferring to refer to the nearest town as simply "W____."

Although one scholar asserts that Evans always intended for *Macaria* to find both a Southern and a Northern audience despite the many passages of the novel that are overwhelmingly anti-Union, that is unlikely. As an ardent secessionist and devoted Confederate, Evans had no use for the Union or the Northern states whatsoever. She wrote the book as her contribution to the Confederate cause. Though she certainly expected to be paid for the novel, she did not undertake it explicitly for financial gain. Had she been motivated solely by the lure of a paycheck, she would have tempered some of her anti-Union sentiment in order to render the novel more palatable in the North—something she did in postwar reprints of the novel.[29] If the reaction of Union general George H. Thomas, commander of the Department of the Cumberland in Tennessee, who banned the book in his camp, ordering all copies confiscated and burned, tells us anything, it is that the novel was not likely to receive a warm reception north of the Mason-Dixon Line.[30] And that is likely what Evans intended.

Using the literary technique of creating two parallel, though contrasting, heroines who experience similar dilemmas, Evans brought to life Irene Huntingdon and Electra Grey, neighbors and childhood friends though they were from vastly different backgrounds. Irene was born into a life of wealth and privilege. Her life was not without hardship, however, because she had lost her mother at a young age.

Betrothed at birth to Cousin Hugh in an effort to keep the Huntingdon wealth "in the family," Irene faced a life of comfort but not happiness.[31] Asserting that marriage and a happy home are the loftiest goals to which a woman could aspire, Irene vows never to defile the sacred institution of marriage by agreeing to a loveless marriage with Hugh.

A marriage for love is not completely out of the question for Irene, however, for she devotedly loves the poor but noble Russell Aubrey. Though Irene desperately loves Russell, she refuses his courtship out of loyalty to her father, who forbids the union. To Russell's marriage proposal Irene responds, "Do not urge me; it is useless. Spare me the pain of repeated refusals, and be satisfied with what I have given you. Believe that my heart is, and ever will be, yours entirely, though my hand you can never claim." Eventually Irene's father relents, granting his approval to the young lovers, but it is too late for Irene and Russell. Russell has gone off to war and is killed while fighting for the Confederacy. Thwarted by circumstances beyond her control, Irene vows to remain single and devote herself fully to the "Cause" for which her true love gave his life.[32]

In contrast to Irene, Electra Grey was an orphan raised in the home of her widowed aunt, the mother of Russell Aubrey. Like Irene, Electra loved Russell. Since his heart belonged to Irene, Electra, who excelled as a painter, devoted herself to her art, even to the point of moving to the North to pursue her career under the tutelage of Mr. Clifton, a much older man. Mr. Clifton's intentions toward Electra are simply those of a mentor at first, though eventually he proposes marriage for the sake of convenience and companionship. Electra refuses him, however, because she does not love him and objects to a loveless marriage. Responding to Mr. Clifton's marriage proposal, Electra responds, "Sir, my God never intended me to live on crumbs, and I will not." Continuing emotionally, she cries, "No mess of pottage will I have, in lieu of my birthright. All, or none! Marriage is holy; God in His wisdom, instituted it with the seal of love; but its desecration with counterfeits makes Tophets, Golgothas, instead of Edens." Like Irene, Electra chooses not to enter into a loveless marriage.[33]

In traditional domestic novels, including those written by Evans both before and after *Macaria*, though the heroines regularly endure trials and tribulations as single women, they are always able to overcome them in some manner and are then rewarded with the ultimate prize: marriage.[34] Indeed, in every other novel Evans wrote, her heroines all eventually marry. That is not to say that Evans's heroines are like those created by other authors. In some cases, their ultimate marriage is the only similarity. Literary scholar Nina Baym, has described Evans's heroines as the "strongest, most brilliant, most accomplished . . . [and] most educated" heroines of domestic fiction.[35] Traditionally, the heroines of domestic novels were weak and dependent characters raised to a position of independence by some fateful event or the efforts of an unknown benefactor before they could find true love and be married. Evans's heroines, on the other hand, may begin as weak or dependent characters, but they raise themselves to a position of strength and independence of their own accord before they will marry. In the case of *Macaria*, much of the same theme holds true: both heroines choose to become strong and independent but neither marries because neither can marry for love.

Though twentieth-century critics balked at Evans's "unnatural" marriage of her intelligent and independent heroines in the majority of her books, nineteenth-century readers expected such endings. Indeed, it was this literary twist in *Macaria* that aroused the ire of some critics and longtime fans. For many Southern readers and critics, Evans's decision to keep the heroines of *Macaria* unmarried was not only "improbable," it was offensive.[36] Just as one critic asserted that the novel's conclusion did "no inconsiderable violence to our just expectations," Belle Edmondson, who served the Confederacy as a smuggler and spy throughout the war, "declared herself 'not entirely satisfied with the fate of some of the characters' when she finished reading *Macaria*, although she had been 'delighted' with the book at the outset."[37] Many nineteenth-century readers and reviewers "expected marriage endings in novels and . . . were not yet prepared . . . to imagine a woman's life plot fulfilled outside of marriage."[38] Such critical reception underscores the risk that Evans took as an author to make *Macaria* more than just standard Southern domestic fiction.

While Evans certainly hoped her readers enjoyed her novel, she clearly also hoped they found it instructive and even inspirational.[39] Indeed, all of Evans's novels provide some sort of instruction. In several of her novels, including most notably *Inez*, *Beulah*, and *St. Elmo*, the instruction is decidedly religious in tone. In *Macaria*, however, the instruction is purely secular, focusing specifically on what Southern women could do to aid the Confederate cause and on the long-term ramifications of the Civil War on the South as a whole. It was, as one contemporary reviewer noted, a "quasi-novel—a new experiment in the art of book-making called forth by the times through which we, the citizens of the Southern Confederacy, are now passing."[40]

In her introduction to a reprint of the novel, Drew Gilpin Faust astutely observed that Evans wrote *Macaria* "both as her own contribution to Confederate nationalism and as a narrative that would provide women with models for emulation in their search for 'agency' within the Confederate cause."[41] Indeed, *Macaria* gave Southern women a portrait of exemplary feminine wartime behavior in the character of Irene Huntingdon, who tells the town doctor, "I want to be useful."[42] It is not surprising that Irene's activities in support of the Confederacy mirror much of Evans's own war work. Like Evans, who sewed sandbags to be used in the defense of Fort Morgan in Mobile Bay, Irene initially participates in traditional female activities including sewing uniforms and tents, making regimental flags, and rolling bandages for Confederate hospitals. Also like Evans, who nursed soldiers in a camp hospital near her Mobile home, Irene moves beyond traditional women's wartime activities to the less typical war work of nursing.[43] When telling her family of her decision to become a nurse in Richmond, Irene proudly asserts, "The call is imperative. Mothers and wives are, in most instances, kept at home; but I have nothing to bind me here. I have no ties to prevent me from giving my services in the only way in which I can aid the cause . . . I feel it a sacred duty."[44] Evans provided Confederate women with a model that encouraged social responsibility among Southern women, particularly single women like herself.

It is important to note, however, that it was not just Southern women whom Evans hoped to influence. As literary historian Kathleen Diffley so eloquently put it, "Civil War stories served as exercises in configuration, poised between the action they made meaningful and the reaction they helped to shape."[45] In other words, Evans's *Macaria* was not only an attempt to influence Southern women, especially single Southern women's activities in support of the Confederacy, but it was also meant to influence Southern society in its acceptance of such activities as acceptable for all women and ideal for single women. *Macaria* was a portent of the South's future, painting a vivid picture of what the sacrifice of so many white men would mean for countless Southern women and the region after the war's end. It provided Southerners as a whole with a model of society in which women who could not marry or, in the case of widows, remarry could still be considered "true Southern women" and their contributions to society could be acknowledged and even celebrated. For Evans, the importance was not just in the kinds of work women could do in the context of the war but in the acceptance among her readers that for single women, such work, even beyond the war years, could be fulfilling and make them happy in the same way that marriage and children made other women happy. Evans never saw single womanhood as an opportunity that should be sought out, but she argued that if a woman found herself alone for reasons beyond her control, she should make good use of her life. With the deaths of thousands of men each year during the war, Evans's message most likely resonated deeply with her readers, male and female.

Having experienced the hardships of poverty herself, Evans lamented the conditions that would relegate so many single or widowed women to similar conditions. Most lucrative professions were, of course, closed to women, and those that were not closed were generally male dominated. Evans's message in *Macaria* is clear: better education and training for women was necessary so that those who could not marry or were left widows by the war could support themselves adequately. At the end of *Macaria*, Irene thinks of the "aged wife to be widowed, and the daughter orphaned" by the war and passionately avows, "Our Revolution has beggared thousands, and deprived many of their natural providers; numbers of women in the

Confederacy will be thrown entirely upon their own resources for maintenance. All can not be mantua-makers, milliners, or school-teachers; and in order to open for them new avenues of support, I have determined to establish in W____, a School of Design for women" to improve "the conditions of women, [as] it is advisable to give them the readiest access to independent industrial pursuits, and extend the circle of their appropriate occupations."[46] Evans foresaw a desperate situation in the postwar South in which many women would find themselves alone, like herself, only they would be unprepared to provide for themselves and their families. Thus Evans's vision was not just about expanding the social definition of true Southern womanhood to include widows and other single women who had sacrificed love for the Confederacy. She also wanted to expand the practical definition of what was the appropriate domain of such women. Rather than continuing to limit them to the menial occupations then open to such women, Evans envisioned a world in which they could enjoy access to meaningful work in the public sphere as nurses, educators, artists, authors, and caretakers of the less fortunate—roles she herself relished.[47] In short, they could be useful.

Through Irene and Electra, Evans advocated the expansion of opportunities for single women, not so that they could become an early version of the modern "career woman" but so that they could support themselves independently and contribute to society without feeling pressured to marry solely for economic and social stability. Some readers of *Macaria* found her message compelling. In a letter to Curry, Evans referred to the many letters she had received asking for photos and autographs but also letters from soldiers asking her "to make up schools for their wives."[48]

Macaria was an attempt to deal with an emerging South in which many women would find themselves unable to attain the prescribed goal of marriage and domesticity. In the last chapter Irene avows, "Electra, it is very true that single women have trials for which a thoughtless, happy world has little sympathy. But lonely lives are not necessarily joyless; they should be, of all others, most useful. . . . A wife and mother . . . doubtless she is happier, far happier, than the unmarried woman; but to the last belongs the privilege of carrying light and blessings to many firesides."[49] Recognizing the plight the war had created for countless Southern women (by 1864 nearly half the white male population of the South had been wounded or killed in the war), she suggested a solution: an expansion of the definition of true womanhood to allow women who could never marry or could not remarry after being widowed to find usefulness and social acceptance in their lives as manless women.[50] Ultimately *Macaria* was an acknowledgment that sacrifice would be necessary if the Confederacy were to succeed; for countless Southern women, the sacrifice would be one of love and marriage.

In *Macaria*, Evans recognized a grim future for the postwar South and asserted that when marriage was impossible, as it was for many Southern women during and after the war, women could find happiness, fulfillment, usefulness, and perhaps even glory in their lives as single women. Evans did not advocate the dismantling of Southern gender roles; she was looking only for their modification by the creation of an acceptable place for single womanhood when it was inevitable. Her use of heroines who chose to remain unmarried was a tremendous change for Evans, but it was a reaction born out of her own marital situation and the complexities of the time in which she wrote.

Although none of Evans's books can be considered autobiographical, they all emanated from Evans's life and perception of herself. Every heroine Evans created reflected some aspect of her social, political, or religious belief system. Evans fashioned independent, strong, intelligent heroines who were not afraid to speak their minds because that is how she herself was. Though she was often criticized for her penchant for classical allusions and quotations from works of philosophy, history, and the sciences, Evans was comfortable displaying—her critics might say "showing off"—her intelligence and education through her writing, in both her novels and her personal correspondence, particularly her correspondence with important men.[51] If her characters reflected her perception of herself as an educated and independent woman, so too did the eventual marriage of those characters reflect her desire for her own happy ending. Yet in *Macaria*, she chooses not only to keep her heroines single but to celebrate their manless existence. In a letter to Rachel Lyons she wrote, "I am very glad to hear that you like my Irene. She is the noblest character I ever painted, and is my ideal of *perfect womanhood*."[52]

At the start of the war, Evans was twenty-six years old. Though she was not what most twentieth-century Americans would consider an old maid, for the nineteenth century she was well into her marrying years.[53] She had found love, or at least a marriage proposal, however. James Reed Spaulding, a Northern journalist who expressed admiration for her abilities as a writer, had pursued a friendship with Evans that eventually turned into an informal engagement. In 1860 as the nation teetered on the brink of war, Evans ended the relationship because she believed their opposing political positions would impede any chance for theirs to be a happy marriage.[54] Apparently Spaulding's support of Abraham Lincoln and opposition to both slavery and secession were too much for Evans to overcome.[55] A letter written by Evans to her aunt shortly after Lincoln won the presidency provides a window into Evans's perspective on the end of her engagement. After beginning with the salutation, "It is with a *very sad heart*, that I sit down to write you," Evans goes on to note how though she had confided the news of her engagement to certain family members, she had meant for it to remain a secret from the general public because her engagement was "conditional." Evans provides no explanation for what she meant by this in this letter or anywhere else in her extant papers. Given that she ended the engagement soon after the presidential election, it is possible that for her, it was dependent on whether a Republican won the White House. She continued in her letter, "Two nights ago, we received a letter from a young friend at *College* in *Millegeville* [sic] and in great astonishment he wrote that 'it is *now reported all over town that Miss Augusta is married to the Editor of the World.*'" Clearly distraught, Evans asked her aunt:

> Do you not think I have a *right* to feel *hurt* when I *know* Mr. Benning has said, "*Augusta is going to marry a Mr. Spalding* [sic] *a Black Republican, and the editor of the World*"? *Even if he* had *believed* him to be an abolitionist, was it kind, was it the part of a *friend*, still less of a *relative* to publish his opinion to the world? To put such a report in circulation at such a crisis as this. . . . If he had merely mentioned the possibility of my marriage, and not branded his name as "Black Republican" I would not have been so grieved. To have my name so associated by the members of the Legislature in Millegeville![56]

Although Evans was upset that the news of her engagement had been leaked, her concern seems to have been more about the identification of her suitor as a "Black Republican" and that important people, including Georgia legislators, would associate her with him than about the fact that the engagement, which was now off, had been publicized without her consent. Evans was acutely aware of the role she could play in the Confederate cause, but if she were linked to an abolitionist, her ability to impact policy or mold the hearts and minds of her fellow Southerners would likely be lessened.

Her biographer, William Fidler, assesses *Macaria* and its relationship to this broken engagement as follows: "As viewed in our sober time, Miss Evans's decision to 'sacrifice' her affection for the Yankee journalist and break the engagement may have the appearance of youthful heroics, but few of us can feel the complex tensions of 1860–1861. . . . Those in her confidence undoubtedly read several meanings in the sub-title of her book '*Altars of Sacrifice*.'"[57] Through Irene's last conversation with her beloved Russell, Evans draws a compassionate portrait that likely reflects how she imagined her own break with Spaulding: "*I can give [him] up for the sake of my country.*"[58] In a July 1863 letter to Curry, Evans announced the impending publication of *Macaria*, promising to send him an early copy. She then asked, "What think you of my resurrecting 'Macaria?' The title impresses me as singularly appropriate. In Greek mythology, Macaria saved Athens by offering herself as a human sacrifice to appease the gods who would give Athens a victory over her enemy, Eurystheus."[59]

Writing in the midst of the war and after the end of her engagement, Evans undoubtedly felt that she had sacrificed love and her chance at matrimony for the Confederacy. As the war progressed, the combination of the rising death toll among Southern men and her ever-increasing age must have made her chances for love and matrimony seem increasingly slim.[60] Seeing in her own life fewer and fewer opportunities to marry likely contributed to her choice to buck tradition in *Macaria* by keeping its heroines unmarried. The fact that Irene and Electra are the only characters Evans ever drew who remained unmarried seems to suggest that at the time she was writing *Macaria*, Evans had resigned herself to life as a single woman and envisioned the possibilities for service to her nation within her manlessness. Evans saw herself as the Confederacy's Macaria.

When the Confederacy lost, Evans felt as though she had lost a loved one. After all, she had devoted herself as would a wife to a husband. Writing to a friend in Baltimore, she confided that for her the war was in more ways than one a "melancholy... struggle in which all [her] hopes were involved, and *crushed*."[61] In a letter to a widow who had written Evans thanking her for *Macaria*, Evans offered her condolences, writing, "To know that my ill fated '*Macaria*' furnished even a modicum of consolation to your bereaved heart, is I assure you, a source of profound gratification, and richly compensates for the labor it cost me." She continued, revealing more than just her desire to console this widow:

> All my hopes, aims, aspirations were bound up in the success of our holy precious cause, and its failure has bowed down and crushed my heart, as I thought nothing earthly had power to do. While the majority of persons accept with philosophic serenity the present status of the South and yield gracefully to an imperious necessity, my grief deepens day by day, grows more poignant.... You tell me your noble husband fell at Vicksburg. Ah my stricken friend! would you willingly recall him from the cradling arms of glory;—to live under the hated monstrous despotism which he died to avert! Oh mourn not that your darling was called to his eternal rest, before the land of his birth went down in a starless night of degradation and slavery—but rather thank God that he was spared the humiliation heaped upon us, and sigh that we could not all have perished with him. For affliction such as yours all human sympathy is inadequate and I shall attempt no words of consolation.... God help you and your orphan children, and grant you the grace to be patient and brave under the great curse laid upon us all.

She signed her letter, "Your countrywoman in captivity." Although it is clear Evans intended the letter to be a sympathy note, she seems to equate her own loss—the Confederacy's loss of the war—with the loss of a beloved spouse. When Evans wrote that she could offer no words of consolation, the widow likely agreed.[62] Though Evans's comparison may seem narcissistic to modern readers, her devotion to the Confederacy was unyielding, and she saw herself as its widow. She loved it, promoted it, criticized what she saw as the mismanagement of it, and mourned it when it was gone. In a postwar letter to Curry she wrote, "I feel that I have no country, no house, no hope in coming years, and I brood over our hallowed precious past, with its chrism of martyr blood." She continued emotionally, "God help me to be patient under this course of national trial! Sometimes I shudder at the bitter, bitter feelings I find smoldering in my heart. I believe I love our cause *as a Jesuit his order*, and its utter ruin has saddened and crushed me, as no other event of my life had power to do."[63]

While much of the rest of the South was trying to move on during Andrew Johnson's administration of Reconstruction, Evans declared, "I feel as if my heart were inurned, with my country's flag, and my people's freedom. I am not patient,—I am not reconciled, I am not philosophically, or religiously resigned—and I never shall be!"[64] Evans was so thoroughly distraught by the Confederacy's loss, she even contemplated fleeing her homeland for Europe. In June 1866 she wrote to Curry, "One of the greatest temptations of my life is now set before me; namely to throw down my pen,—leave my work, and all our sorrowful memories behind me, and rest and lose myself among the glories of Europe."[65]

Evans did not go to Europe. Instead she remained in the South and continued supporting the cause long after many others had given it up. To say she was an unreconstructed rebel is an understatement. In postwar letters to friends and professional acquaintances, Evans repeatedly defended the right of secession and the glorious cause. To a friend who had the gall to declare the right of secession settled by the war, Evans wrote, "I do not accept the conclusion of the war, as a test of its [secession's] *legitimacy* or *expediency. Might* often *crushes*—but never makes *right*. Today—the right of Secession is more holy than five years ago,—for now it has been sanctified—baptized anew, with the blood of our Legion of Liberty's Martyrs." She continued passionately, "I have an abiding faith that the cause for which we have suffered so much, will yet triumph, and though I shall perhaps be in my quiet grave, ere it comes, yet: 'Truth crushed to earth will rise again. The eternal years of God—are hers.'"[66]

Evans's devotion to the cause did not waver even to fulfill the request of an old friend from the North. In a letter to William Seaver, the editor of *Harper's New Monthly Magazine*, after she had rejected a meeting with Richard Busteed, to whom Seaver had given a letter of introduction, she responded:

> Officers of high rank have brought me letters of introduction, but I have *invariably refused* to receive the bearers, and have assigned as my reason for doing so, a determination to hold no social intercourse with persons who drew their swords against *a cause*,—for which, I would gladly have sacrificed my

life. Having been an ardent and *conscientious Secessionist*, and *indulging still*, an unwavering faith in the justice and sanctity of the principles for which we fought and prayed so devotedly, I of course could not find it agreeable to associate with those, who were arrayed in arms against my own section and people.

She closed her letter thus: "If you do not promptly write me, I shall fear that you are *displeased with me*, and indeed my dear Sir, it would deeply grieve me to lose your friendship, or alienate your sympathy. Hoping you pardon for pursuing a course, dictated by *mournful memories* of my dead."[67] Seaver apparently did forgive Evans for her treatment of his friend. Ten years after the war's end, Evans wrote Seaver imploring him to use his influence with the other editors of the Harper's publishing company to stop promoting "bitterness, sectional strife, and social hatred,—resorting to every expedient to goad their countrymen into a war of races" with their magazines. She wrote, "Pointing to the myriad graves of our Confederate dead, we ask only for that Peace, which was promised Lee, when he unbuckled and laid down his sword, ten long years ago."[68]

Not long after the close of the war, Evans determined to pick up her pen in the service of the Confederacy once more, this time by writing the history of the Confederacy. To that end, she began soliciting the papers of Confederate politicians and officials, including Beauregard and Curry, of course. In a letter thanking Curry for the use of his congressional documents, she noted, "The truths of history crystallize slowly,—it will be a gigantic task to illuminate these from the *debris* of falsehood and exaggeration in which they are now overwhelmed."[69] Because Evans saw herself as a widow of the cause, she assumed she would be the perfect author to write its history. Moreover, Evans saw her history of the Confederacy as her final and defining work, "My history, I intend to make the *great end of all my labors* in the realm of letters."[70] In an 1865 letter to Alexander Stephens, in which she asked for the use of his papers, she self-deprecatingly wrote:

> With reference to the history of the war (of which Genl Toombs was so kind as to write you,) permit me to say to you candidly, that although I have been repeatedly solicited to undertake it, I doubt my intellectual credentials for this grand mission,—and am haunted by a sceptical dread that *no woman* is capable of the rare critical acumen in military matters,—and of the broad and lofty generalizations absolutely requisite in one who essays to become the historic custodian of our national honor,—and to set us as a people,—crowned, triumphant,—glorified,—before that august tribunal—, that immemorial and infallible assize which Clio decrees for every nation that has waxed and waned since the gray dawn of time.

"Yet," she continued, "Mr. Stephens, my heart vetoes the verdict of my judgment, and prompts me to offer some grateful testimonial, some tribute however inadequate, to the manes of our heroes,—and above all—of our noble unknown dead who have gone down 'unwept, unhonored, and unsung'—in the red burial of battle." Though others may undertake a similar task, Evans declared, "*only one history will live*, . . . *the truth, the whole truth, and nothing but the truth*, is now my sole goal, and to its attainment I desire to dedicate my future years, feeling that my life will not have been spent in vain, if I finally accomplish a historic memorabilia worthy of my matchless theme."[71]

Not long after she sent her letter, she received his response. He was already undertaking just such a history. Though it clearly pained her to do so, she gave up the "holy work."[72] Writing to Beauregard in 1867, she intoned, "Had he not begun the history, I would gladly have dedicated my future years to the successful completion of a work inexpressibly dear to my heart. . . . I confess it cost me a severe struggle to relinquish the fond dream of weaving historic *immortelles* for the tombs of its martyrs,—but able hands snatched it from my weak womanly fingers, and waved me to humbler paths of labor."[73]

By 1866 Evans took on her final work on behalf of the cause, erecting a monument to Confederate soldiers in Mobile. Although she initially "shr[a]nk from the notoriety inevitably consequent upon a compliance with [the] numerous petitions" from men and women in Mobile to take on the task, her "heart turned yearningly to the holy labor of love."[74] In a letter to Curry, Evans revealed her plan for the monument to be a monolith made of "pure-polished Alabama marble," erected on the town square. For Evans, it was vitally important that the monument be made of Alabamian materials or at least materials from another Southern state. She wrote to Curry in 1866, "I should regard it as an *insult* to our Dead, if the cenotaph raised to commemorate their devotion to our hallowed cause,—were bought in Boston,—and chiseled by hands dripping with their precious blood." The monument would include eight marble vases which, she promised Curry, she herself would keep filled with "floral tributes" for as long as she lived. Though seemingly melodramatic, this promise reiterates Evans's sense of loss associated with the war. By promising to keep the vases filled, she was once again declaring herself the Macaria of the Confederacy. Clearly including her own sacrifices with those of soldiers' widows, Evans asserted that at least the women of Athens knew their sacrifices had not been in vain. Southern women "must feel that they have laid *their all* on a crumbling altar, upon which God frowned! and though their quivering lips will whisper, 'Thy will be done';—their aching hearts will not."[75]

In *Macaria*, after her beloved Russell has departed for the battlefield, Irene muses that she is like the Grecian Macaria who sacrificed herself on the altar of the gods to save her city except she had given more than Macaria, who only gave her own life, because she had given her life and her true love for the Confederacy. She cried out, "oh! My lot, and that of thousands of my country-women, is infinitely more bitter than the fate of Macaria!" Irene's thoughts and actions mirrored those of her creator. While writing *Macaria*, Evans undoubtedly felt like Irene. She had, after all, sacrificed a potential husband without knowing that another would be in store for her. She had watched as thousands of men suffered and died while she could do nothing for them. She had thought of the widows and orphans at home who missed the last moments of their loved ones' lives. She had invested her all in a cause that was ultimately lost. Augusta Evans saw herself as the Confederacy's Macaria. Evans did not remain so forever, however. Three years after the war's end, she wed Lorenzo Madison Wilson, a wealthy Mobile businessman twenty-seven years her senior. Though she continued to write, none of her other novels used the war as background. And even *Macaria* underwent significant revisions to make it more palatable to a Northern audience.[76] Though Evans's pro-Confederate sentiment would sometimes reappear in the years following her marriage, for the most part, her days as the Confederate Macaria ended when she became Augusta Evans Wilson.

Notes

1. Unless indicated otherwise, all italicized words and phrases in Evans's writing are hers. Evans, whose childhood began in the lap of luxury, endured poverty for most of her teen years after her father lost his wife's fortune through a series of bad financial decisions. According to her biographer, her childhood experiences left her with such a fear of poverty that as an adult she always carried a hundred dollars with her. William Perry Fidler, *Augusta Evans Wilson, 1835–1909: A Biography* (Tuscaloosa: University of Alabama Press, 1951), 20. Evans's experiences in Texas provided her with the inspiration for her first novel, *Inez: A Tale of the Alamo*. Published anonymously in 1855, *Inez* focused on a young Mexican heiress's efforts to reject an arranged marriage to her cousin. The novel was decidedly anti-Catholic in tone. It was neither a critical nor a financial success. Yet the theme of young women striving to marry for love is one that emerges in all of Evans's novels. While Texas may have served as the initial inspiration for Evans's career as a novelist, her self-professed motivation to begin writing came from a much more practical place, a desire to contribute to her family's financial survival. Although Evans often professed that she began writing to make her father proud of her, one of the themes that resonates through her work is one of patriarchal disappointment. Evans's heroines regularly appear as orphans or young women who have been let down emotionally, socially, or financially by their fathers, echoing Evans's own experience. Anne Riepma has suggested that Evans wrote *Inez* and, to gain her father's approval of it, offered it to him as a gift to augment the family's income. Riepma identifies several instances in Evans's life where she explains what some might see (in the case of *Inez*, her father) as unbecoming behavior by offering it as a gift to that person. Anne Sophie Riepma, *Fire and Fiction: Augusta Jane Evans in Context* (Amsterdam-Atlanta: Rodopi, 2000).

2. For details of Evans's life, see Fidler, *Augusta Evans Wilson* and the introduction to Rebecca Grant Sexton, ed., *A Southern Woman of Letters: The Correspondence of Augusta Jane Evans Wilson* (Columbia: University of South Carolina Press, 2002).

3. Evans to Lyons, June 26, 1861, in Sexton, *Southern Woman of Letters*, 33–34.
4. Evans to Lyons, August 20, 1861, in Sexton, *Southern Woman of Letters*, 36.
5. Evans to Mrs. L. V. French, January 13, 1861, in Sexton, *Southern Woman of Letters*, 28–30.
6. Evans to Hon. H. L. Benning, January 13, 1861, in Sexton, *Southern Woman of Letters*, 27; see Evans to Hon. A. Stephens, November 29, 1865, in Sexton, *Southern Woman of Letters*, 112.
7. Evans to Lyons, November 15, 1860, in Sexton, *Southern Woman of Letters*, 22.
8. Evans to J. L. M. Curry, January 27, 1864, in Sexton, *Southern Woman of Letters*, 91–92.
9. Her works with their publishers and dates of publication are as follows: *Inez: A Tale of the Alamo* (Harpers, 1856); *Beulah* (J. C. Derby, 1859); *Macaria; or, Altars of Sacrifice* (West and Johnson, 1864); *St. Elmo; or, Saved at Last, Vashti; or, Until Death Us Do Part*, and *Infelice* (G. W. Carleton, 1866, 1869, and 1875, respectively); and *At the Mercy of Tiberius, A Speckled Bird*, and *Devota* (Dillingham, 1887, 1902, and 1907, respectively).
10. In a letter to Victor, Evans thanked him for his continual kind words about her novels in the pages of the *Cosmopolitan Journal*. Augusta Jane Evans to Orville James Victor, December 1, 1860, Augusta Jane (Evans) Wilson Papers, University of Virginia; Augusta Evans Wilson to Col. N. A. Seaver, November 20, [1868?], Wilson Papers, University of Virginia Library; Evans to Lyons, May 1, 1864, in Sexton, *Southern Woman of Letters*, 102, 104.
11. *St. Elmo* was so popular that towns, steamboats, and hotels throughout the country were named and even renamed "St. Elmo," and mothers christened countless children "Edna" and "Elmo" after the novel's heroine and hero. Indeed, Eudora Welty may have been a fan of Evans, naming the comic heroine who owned the Beulah Hotel in *The Ponder Heart* Edna Earle Ponder. *St. Elmo* also inspired C. H. (John Paul) Webb to write a parody of it titled "St. Twel'mo," which while poking fun at the book and its author also testified to the book's popularity. G. W. Carleton, Evans's postwar New York publisher, was so sure of Evans's popularity after the publication of *St. Elmo* that they sent her an advance of $25,000 for any novel she had to submit, sight unseen (Sexton, *Southern Woman of Letters*, xxi); Eudora Welty, *The Ponder Heart* (New York, 1953); Drew Gilpin Faust, "A Note on Augusta Jane Evans," in Evans, *Macaria* (Baton Rouge: LSU Press, 1992), x; Augusta Jane Evans Wilson, *St. Elmo; or, Saved at Last*, edited and with an introduction by Diane Roberts (Tuscaloosa: University of Alabama Press, 1992), vi; Frank Luther Mott, *Golden Multitudes: The Story of Best Sellers in the United States* (New York: Macmillan, 1947), 127. See Timothy D. Murray, "G. W. Carleton, G. W. Carleton and Company," in *The Dictionary of Literary Biography, American Literary Publishing Houses*, vol. 49, ed. Peter Dzwonkoski (Detroit: Gale, 1986), 84.
12. Helen Waite Papashvily, *All the Happy Endings: A Study of the Domestic Novel in America, the Women Who Wrote It, the Women Who Read It in the Nineteenth Century* (New York: Harper & Brothers, 1956), 180–83. In *60 Years of Bestsellers, 1895–1955* (New York: R. R. Bowker Company, 1956), Alice Payne Hackett lists *St. Elmo* as an "early best seller" that has "without question sold a total of a million copies or more through the years" (217–19). Frank Mott includes both *Beulah* and *St. Elmo* as best sellers, defining such as a book "believed to have had a total sale equal to one percent of the population of the continental United States . . . for the decade in which it was published." For *Beulah*'s publication in 1859 the figure was 225,000, and for *St. Elmo* it was 300,000. See Mott, *Golden Multitudes*, 303–9. *Scott's Monthly* quoted in Mott, *Golden Multitudes*, 126. Despite the best-selling status and popularity of *Beulah* and *St. Elmo* and the generally prolific nature of Evans's authorship, she is relatively unknown today except among literary scholars. Her third novel, *Macaria*, is the only exception.
13. Evans to General P. G. T. Beauregard, August 4, 1862, in Sexton, *Southern Woman of Letters*, 42. Evans and Beauregard exchanged many letters as well as tokens of friendship. For example, he gave her his pen (mentioned in the letter cited here), and she knitted him a scarf to keep

his neck warm (Evans to Beauregard, November 14, 1863, in Sexton, *Southern Woman of Letters*, 85). He also sent her photographs of Fort Sumter (Evans to Beauregard, December 14, 1863, in Sexton, *Southern Woman of Letters*, 89). For a discussion of women's frustration at not being able to go to war themselves, see Drew Gilpin Faust, *Mothers of Invention: Women of the Slaveholding South in the American Civil War* (New York: Random House, 1996), 20–29.

14. Evans to Beauregard, August 19, 1863, in Sexton, *Southern Woman of Letters*, 72.

15. Anne Goodwyn Jones, *Tomorrow Is Another Day: The Woman Writer in the South, 1859–1936* (Baton Rouge: Louisiana State University Press, 1981), 70.

16. Sexton, *Southern Woman of Letters*, xxix.

17. Evans to J. L. M. Curry December 20, 1862, in Sexton, *Southern Woman of Letters*, 50. Her correspondence with Alabama congressman Curry, who in the postwar period was a zealous advocate for public education in the South, reveals an interesting relationship. She not only reported to him about the hardships of life in wartime Alabama but also advised him on actions to take with regard to morale among the soldiers, inflation, and the Exemption Bill, as well as on which topics to include in his speeches. Although his biographer notes his attendance at a speech given by educational reformer Horace Mann as the motivation behind his postwar work in education, it is possible that his relationship with Evans also played a role. Hugh C. Bailey, "Jabez Lamar Monroe Curry," *Encyclopedia of Alabama*, http://encyclopediaofalabama.org/ (accessed January 25, 2012). The most notable recent study on the Confederate effort to create a national literature independent of Northern publishers and markets is Michael T. Bernath, *Confederate Minds: The Struggle for Intellectual Independence in the Civil War South* (Chapel Hill: University of North Carolina Press, 2010).

18. Evans to Curry, December 20, 1862, in Sexton, *Southern Woman of Letters*, 48–51.

19. Evans to Beauregard, November 14, 1863, in Sexton, *Southern Woman of Letters*, 82–83.

20. See, for example, Evans to Curry, December 20, 1862, in Sexton, *Southern Woman of Letters*, 48–51; Evans to Beauregard, March 17, 1863, in Sexton, *Southern Woman of Letters*, 55; Evans to Beauregard, April 29, 1863, in Sexton, *Southern Woman of Letters*, 62–64; and Evans to Curry, July 15, 1863, in Sexton, *Southern Woman of Letters*, 65–71.

21. Evans to Lyons, October 3, 1861, in Sexton, *Southern Woman of Letters*, 37.

22. Evans to Beauregard, March 17, 1863, in Sexton, *Southern Woman of Letters*, 56.

23. Evans to West and Johnson, February 22, 1863, in Sexton, *Southern Woman of Letters*, 54.

24. Faust, ed., introduction to *Macaria*, xvii.

25. In a letter to one of her closest confidants and friends, Rachel Lyons, dated August 20, 1861, she mentions having sent her "precious MS" to her publisher. Although she does not name the manuscript, it is most likely an early draft of *Macaria*. The final draft of the novel including the copying was completed by February 1863. It would appear that from the beginning of the war, Evans nursed ailing soldiers at Fort Morgan and at a hospital near her home dubbed Camp Beulah by the patients. In 1863, Evans seemed to take a page from *Macaria* when she determined to go to Marietta, Georgia, to work in one of the Confederate hospitals there. Her brothers objected to the venture, so she gave it up and focused on supporting the Confederate cause from Mobile. Though it is possible some work on *Macaria* took place in the hospital, it is more likely that she worked on the novel at the same time that she worked in the hospitals. From her own accounts, writing, editing, and copying her manuscripts could be tedious and necessitated her full attention. For her brothers' objections to her plan to nurse in Marietta, see Augusta Jane Evans to Ella King Newsom, quoted in J. Fraise Richard, *The Florence Nightingale of the Southern Army: Experiences of Mrs. Ella K. Newsom, Confederate Nurse in the Great War of 1861–65* (New York: Broadway Publishing, 1914), 92–94. For the timing of the writing, copying, and printing of the

novels, see Melissa J. Homestead, "The Publishing History of Augusta Jane Evans's Confederate Novel *Macaria*: Unwriting Some Lost Cause Myths," *Mississippi Quarterly* (June 2005), http://digitalcommons.unl.edu/cgi/viewcontent.cgi?article=1072&context=englishfacpubs/ (accessed January 20, 2012). For Evans's claim to have written the novel while nursing, see, among others, Nina Baym, *Feminism and American History: Essays* (New Brunswick, NJ: Rutgers University Press, 1995), 191; Shannon L. Nichols, "Augusta Jane Evans Wilson (1835–1909)," in *Nineteenth-Century American Women Writers: A Bio-Bibliographical Critical Sourcebook*, ed. Denise Knight (Westport, CT: Greenwood, 1997), 479–83; and Elisabeth Muhlenfeld, "The Civil War and Authorship," in *The History of Southern Literature*, ed. Louis Rubin (Baton Rouge: Louisiana State University Press, 1985), 182. For Evans's description of her writing process, see, among other letters, one to Rachel Lyons dated March 20, 1863, in Sexton, *Southern Woman of Letters*, 59.

26. Mary Elizabeth Massey, "The Making of a Feminist," *Journal of Southern History* 39 (February 1973): 11.

27. The war was a central feature of Southerners' experiences during the second half of the nineteenth century. As Mark Twain observed in his autobiography published in 1883: "In the North one seldom hears the recent American civil conflict mentioned, but in the South 'it is very different.' Here, where 'every man you meet was in the war' and 'every lady you meet saw the war,' it is the great chief topic of conversation. To Southerners, the war is in fact what A.D. is elsewhere: they date from it. To grasp the significance of the war, the stranger to the South must realize 'how intimately every individual' Southerner was involved with it." Mark Twain's autobiography, quoted in Lewis P. Simpson, *The Fable of the Southern Writer* (Baton Rouge: Louisiana State University Press, 1994), 74–75.

28. Evans to Beauregard, August 4, 1862 in Sexton, *Southern Woman of Letters*, 41–45. Evans's description glosses over some mistakes made by Beauregard in the battle, portraying him in a very favorable light. Beauregard also shared his battle plans for the Kentucky Campaign, plans that were rejected in favor of another general's ideas, as well as a manual he wrote on military policy. Clearly Beauregard respected her intelligence and her opinions. In recognition of her contribution to the war effort both as a nurse and an author, he awarded her with a citation and gave her his personal writing pen as a gift. William Perry Fidler, "Augusta Evans Wilson as Confederate Propagandist," *Alabama Review* 2 (January 1949): 36–38.

29. Indeed, Evans's strong Southern loyalties contributed to her status among women and men as the South's "most popular and respected woman writer." See Baym, *Feminism and American History: Essays*, 191. By the war's end there were more than twenty thousand copies of *Macaria* circulating in the South as well as a "boot-legged" version in the North. J. C. Derby, *Fifty Years among Authors, Books, and Publishers* (New York: G. W. Carleton & Co., 1884), 394. See also Fidler, *Augusta Evans Wilson*. Although Evans first published *Macaria* in 1864, it continued to be a favorite among Southerners for decades after; G. W. Carleton and various other New York publishers reprinted it seven times in 1867, 1869, 1875, 1887, 1888, 1896, and 1903.

30. For a description of General Thomas's ban, see Muhlenfeld, "The Civil War and Authorship," 182. Melissa Homestead ("The Publishing History of Augusta Jane Evans's Confederate Novel *Macaria*") challenges the idea perpetrated by J. C. Derby, her publisher and friend, that Evans intended the book to be published only in the South. In contrast to Derby's oft-repeated tale that he rescued *Macaria* and thus Evans from the machinations of an unscrupulous publisher who had illegally acquired a copy of the novel and intended to publish it without paying Evans any royalties, and that Evans was completely ignorant of all that went on until after the war, Homestead argues that Evans recognized the likelihood that she could be cheated out of royalties by a Northern publisher because of the weakness of copyright law at that time. Accordingly,

she sought Derby's assistance to publish the book in the North. Thus, according to Homestead, Evans was not some damsel in distress but a savvy businesswoman.

31. Evans, *Macaria*, 196.

32. Ibid., 325. A number of scholars have interpreted Irene's and Electra's decisions to remain unmarried as feminist acts and *Macaria* as a proto-feminist novel, deeming it a forerunner of Kate Chopin's *The Awakening* because of its untraditional, Southern heroines. For example, see Jan Bakker, "Overlooked Progenitors: Independent Women and Southern Renaissance in Augusta Jane Evans Wilson's *Macaria; or, Altars of Sacrifice*," *Southern Quarterly* 25 (Winter 1987): 131–42 and Linda MacDonald, "The Discarded Daughters of the American Revolution: Catharine Sedgewick, E.D.E.N. Southworth, and Augusta Evans Wilson" (PhD diss., University of Colorado, 1992). Such conclusions fail to take into account the context in which Evans wrote *Macaria*.

33. Evans, *Macaria*, 133.

34. Evans, *Macaria*, 277. Indeed one of the "d____d mob of scribbling women" that Nathaniel Hawthorne condemns for contaminating the literary scene with sentimental romances, Evans fits squarely within the genre of domestic fiction, Northern and Southern. There are a number of historical works that discuss traditional Southern womanhood. Some of the best are Elizabeth Fox-Genovese, *Within the Plantation Household: Black and White Women of the Old South* (Chapel Hill: University of North Carolina Press, 1988); Catherine Clinton, *The Plantation Mistress: Woman's World in the Old South* (New York: Pantheon Books, 1982); and Jean E. Friedman, *The Enclosed Garden: Women and Community in the Evangelical South, 1830–1900* (Chapel Hill: University of North Carolina Press, 1985).

35. Nina Baym, *Woman's Fiction: A Guide to Novels by and about Women in America, 1820–70* (Ithaca: Cornell University Press, 1978), 18, 280.

36. Faust, introduction, xxv.

37. D. K. W., "Review" in Faust, introduction, xxiv; Belle Edmondson Diary, June 17 and 20, 1864, Southern Historical Collection, University of North Carolina, Chapel Hill, quoted in Faust, introduction, xxiv.

38. Karen Tracy, *Plots and Proposals: American Women's Fiction, 1850–1890* (Urbana: University of Illinois Press, 1999), 82.

39. "The purpose of literature, Evans had stated explicitly in an 1859 series of articles in the Mobile *Daily Advertiser*, was to provide moral instruction." Faust, introduction, *Macaria*, xvi.

40. Ibid., xxiv.

41. Ibid., xvii.

42. Evans, *Macaria*, 316.

43. Of her own nursing experience, Evans wrote, "For two months past I have been constantly engaged in nursing our poor sick soldiers, keeping vigil by day and night at their bedside; counting pulses, administering medicine, dressing blisters. . . . Oh! My darling if I could tell you of all I have witnessed, and endured since I became a hospital nurse!" See Evans to Lyons, January 22, 1861, in Sexton, *Southern Woman of Letters*, 39; Riepma, *Fire and Fiction*, 94–95.

44. Evans, *Macaria*, 376.

45. Kathleen Diffley, "Where My Heart Is Turning Ever: Civil War Stories and National Stability from Fort Sumter to the Centennial," *American Literary History* 2 (Winter 1990): 629.

46. Evans, *Macaria*, 385, 410, 459.

47. In addition to serving the Confederacy as a nurse and propagandist, Evans also served on the board of an orphanage in Mobile during the 1860s. Riepma, *Fire and Fiction*, 86–87. For evidence of her work for the orphan asylum, see Evans to Curry, October 16, 1863, in Sexton,

Southern Woman of Letters, 77; and Evans to Lyons, May 1, 1864, in Sexton, *Southern Woman of Letters*, 102.

48. Evans to Curry, May 7, 1866, in Sexton, *Southern Woman of Letters*, 120.

49. Evans, *Macaria*, 380, 412–13.

50. Figure for casualties by 1864 from Faust, introduction, *Macaria*, xxi.

51. See Sexton, introduction to *Southern Woman of Letters*, xxv.

52. Evans to Lyons, May 1, 1864, in Sexton, *Southern Woman of Letters*, 102, 104.

53. One scholar suggests that Evans's family's former standing among the elite of the South but financial shortcomings during the years in which she would have been entertaining suitors might have conditioned her to expect a certain kind of suitor that would have been unlikely. See Sexton, *Southern Woman of Letters*, xxii.

54. Interestingly, Evans also ended her friendship with Mary Virginia Terhune, who was an ardent Unionist. See Riepma, *Fire and Fiction*, 90.

55. When gossip about her relationship with the "Black Republican" was spread in Milledgeville, Evans's reaction clearly denotes that it was Spaulding's political views that doomed the relationship. Moreover, she was appalled that misinformation about the status of the affair (she had already broken off the engagement when the gossip spread) had escaped and become public knowledge. See Augusta Jane Evans to her Aunt Mary Howard Jones, November 26, 1860 and December 4, 1860, both in Sexton, *Southern Woman of Letters*, 23–26.

56. Evans to Aunt, November 26, 1860.

57. Fidler, "Confederate Propagandist," 36.

58. Italics mine. Augusta Jane Evans, *Macaria; or Altars of Sacrifice* (Richmond, VA: West and Johnson, 1863), 402.

59. Evans to Curry, July 15, 1863, in Sexton, *Southern Woman of Letters*, 65–71.

60. Faust, *Mothers of Invention*, 172–73.

61. August Jane Evans to Mr. Dawson of Baltimore, June 20, 1866, Papers of Augusta Jane Evans, 1859–1882, University of Virginia. For a similar expression of her feelings, see Evans to Curry, October 7, 1865, in Sexton, *Southern Woman of Letters*, 109. She makes a similar statement in a letter to Alexander Stephens in November 1865. See Evans to Stephens, November 29, 1865, in Sexton, *Southern Woman of Letters*, 112.

62. Evans to Mrs. J. K. Chrisman, February 3, 1866, in Sexton, *Southern Woman of Letters*, 115–16.

63. Evans to Curry, October 7, 1865, in Sexton, *Southern Woman of Letters*, 109.

64. Evans to My dear kind friend (unknown recipient), June 20, 1866, in Sexton, *Southern Woman of Letters*, 124–25.

65. Evans to Curry, June 22, 1866, in Sexton, *Southern Woman of Letters*, 127.

66. Evans to My dear kind friend (unknown), October 23, 1866, in Sexton, *Southern Woman of Letters*, 131–32. See also Evans to Beauregard, March 30, 1867, in Sexton, *Southern Woman of Letters*, 137–40, for another expression of her devotion to the cause even after the war.

67. Evans to Col. Seaver, January 13, 1867, in Sexton, *Southern Woman of Letters*, 136.

68. Evans to Seaver, September 7, 1876, in Sexton, *Southern Woman of Letters*, 158–59.

69. Evans to Curry, October 7, 1865, in Sexton, *Southern Woman of Letters*, 107.

70. Ibid.

71. Evans to Stephens, November 29, 1865, in Sexton, *Southern Woman of Letters*, 112–13.

72. Evans referred to this history as a "holy work" in a letter to Curry. Evans to Curry, October 7, 1865, in Sexton, *Southern Woman of Letters*, 107–9.

73. Evans to Beauregard, November 20, 1867, in Sexton, *Southern Woman of Letters*, 145.
74. Evans to Curry, April 15, 1866, in Sexton, *Southern Woman of Letters*, 117.
75. Evans to Curry, April 15, 1866, in Sexton, *Southern Woman of Letters*, 117–19. In Evans's vision, the thirty-foot-high monument would be erected in Bienville Square in the middle of Mobile "where its pure marble lips will whisper to all passing strangers—*Siste viator*," translated "Be still, traveler." Her desire to erect the monument in the center of town predated by several decades what became common practice: the erection of Confederate monuments on town squares across the South. During the 1860s, most monuments to the Confederate dead were typically raised in cemeteries, not town squares. Evans's request for the monument was granted, despite her fear that the town officials would be "too cowardly to risk giving umbrage to the 'powers that be.'" But when the monument was completed in 1874 without Evans's involvement, it was placed in Magnolia Cemetery rather than Bienville Square, as Evans had intended. See Evans to The Hon. Mayor & Board of Aldermen and Common Council of the City of Mobile, in Sexton, *Southern Woman of Letters*, 123–24 and Evans to Curry, June 22, 1866, in Sexton, *Southern Woman of Letters*, 126–29.
76. For a discussion of Evans's life and career, see Fidler, *August Evans Wilson*; Nichols, "Augusta Jane Evans Wilson (1835–1909)," 479–83. Over the years, and especially in the later editions, *Macaria* was altered to remove the most vitriolic denunciations of the North and some of the more obscure analogies. Throughout the various reprintings, however, Evans's passages about single womanhood and womanhood in general remained unchanged. See the 1896 and 1903 editions in particular. Evans, *Macaria*, xxviii.

8
"The Best Southern Patriots"
Jews in Alabama during the Civil War
Patricia A. Hoskins

On April 26, 1861, two weeks after the firing on Fort Sumter, twenty-six-year-old Solomon Kahn of Montgomery, Alabama, enlisted in the 3rd Alabama Infantry. During the first week of May, the 3rd Alabama became the first Alabama regiment to report to Richmond, Virginia, in defense of the newly formed Confederate States of America. Over the next four years, Kahn and his fellow soldiers in the regiment would participate in many of the bloodiest battles of the war, including Malvern Hill, Fredericksburg, and Chancellorsville. The regiment suffered devastating losses at Gettysburg, and again at the Wilderness, Spotsylvania, and Cold Harbor. Enduring further losses at Petersburg, a little more than forty members of the regiment surrendered with Gen. Robert E. Lee at Appomattox. After the war, Solomon Kahn moved to several different states before finally settling in Dallas, Texas, where, like many of his former comrades, he became an active member of the local camp of the United Confederate Veterans. When he died in 1914, the local newspaper praised him with typical Lost Cause language: "when the tocsin of war sounded he was among the first of the gallant yeomanry of the country to respond to the call of arms and enlisted in an Alabama regiment and served in the Army of Virginia." The newspaper, however, omitted certain information in the obituary. The recently deceased Kahn was not a member of the yeomanry but a Montgomery merchant. He was also Jewish.[1]

Solomon Kahn was just one of the more than 130 Jewish Alabamians who served in the Confederate army during the Civil War. Many more supported the war on the home front, performed diplomatic missions for the Confederacy, or supplied the war effort. Jews played significant roles not just in Alabama but throughout the United States during the war. Of the approximately 150,000 Jews living in the United States in 1860, it is believed that roughly 2,000 Jews fought for the Confederacy, while 7,000 fought for the much more populous Union.

Several Jews held notable positions in the Confederacy. Judah P. Benjamin of Louisiana served in Jefferson Davis's cabinet, first as attorney general, later as secretary of war, and finally as secretary of the treasury. Rabbi M. J. Michelbacher of

Richmond preached one of the most widely circulated printed sermons of the war, titled "A Prayer for the Confederacy." Joshua Moses of South Carolina became the last Jewish soldier to die in the war when he fell at Fort Blakely near Mobile on the same day that Robert E. Lee surrendered at Appomattox. Some of the most notorious acts of the war concern Jews—in particular Gen. Ulysses S. Grant's General Orders No. 11, which expelled the "Jews as a class" from Kentucky, Tennessee, and Mississippi on suspicion of illegal barter.[2]

The history of Jews in the Civil War and in the South in general, however, has received little attention. From the colonial period to the present, Jews have comprised less than 2 percent of the South's population. Yet the first Jewish community in the South developed in Savannah, Georgia, as early as 1733. By 1820 there were 700 Jews in Charleston, South Carolina, giving it the largest Jewish population in the United States at that time. By the time of Fort Sumter, Richmond boasted three synagogues and dozens of Jewish-owned mercantile businesses. Several other cities in Georgia, including Macon, West Point, La Grange, and Atlanta, also included successful Jewish families. Other small communities of Jews could be found in Mississippi, Arkansas, and Texas. Louisiana, and New Orleans in particular, became somewhat of a marvel because of the size of its Jewish population, causing one European visitor to observe, "the Governor [of Louisiana] is supposed to be somewhat under the influence of the Hebrews."[3]

Despite this, the antebellum history of Jews in the South tends to be eclipsed by the larger role they played in the postbellum history of the area. In the late nineteenth and early to mid-twentieth centuries, Jews became objects of scorn and targets of xenophobia in the South, as evinced by the murder of Leo Frank in Georgia in 1915, their status as targets of the Ku Klux Klan in the 1920s, and the bombing of several Jewish synagogues and buildings in the 1950s. In Alabama, the older Jewish communities in Mobile and Montgomery became overshadowed by the larger numbers of Jews who immigrated to the steel capital of Birmingham after 1870. In addition, Jews played significant roles in the tumultuous decades of the civil rights movement, a subject that has received considerable attention.[4]

Yet for all the focus on postbellum Jewish communities, the zenith of Jewish immigration to Alabama occurred during the 1840s and 1850s. Wishing to escape the wars and persecution of the Old World, German and eastern European Ashkenazic Jews flocked to Alabama. Like other Jews in the South, they worked as peddlers, clerks, shopkeepers, tailors, bakers, slave traders and auctioneers, innkeepers, music teachers, grocers, apothecaries, lawyers, and doctors. By 1860 Jews could be found in almost every town and trading post in Alabama. In Claiborne, a tiny community in the southern part of the state along the banks of the Alabama River, fifteen Jewish residents established a Jewish cemetery. In Demopolis, Isaac Marx became one of the wealthiest merchants in the west Alabama Black Belt. In the north Alabama town of Athens, the Rosenau family set up a prosperous clothing store. In Selma, Bavarian immigrant Joseph Seligman and his brothers William and James opened a general merchandise store. In Talladega, the Adler brothers kept a store whose top floor was occupied by three Jewish clerks in their employ.

The largest Jewish communities in antebellum Alabama, however, were in Mobile and Montgomery.[5] In their tendency to settle in towns like Mobile and Montgomery, Alabamian Jews were no different from other Jews in the South. There were few large Jewish planters or landowners in the area during the antebellum period. Jews had traditionally been prohibited from owning land in Europe and thus did not seek to do so in America. They also tended to congregate in urban areas in order to be around fellow Jews. Mobile and Montgomery thus contained large numbers of Jewish merchants who were attracted by the swan song of the cotton boom. On the eve of the Civil War, over five million acres of Alabama land was planted in the prized fiber. By 1860, Mobile was second only to New Orleans in cotton exports, while Montgomery became a commercial trading center for farmers who floated their product down the Alabama River to Mobile. Jewish merchants provided cotton farmers with everything from tools to wholesale items to credit. In addition, the proximity to New Orleans and connections with the numerous Jewish merchants who proliferated in the Big Easy made Mobile and Montgomery an additional haven for Jews. The Civil War would greatly affect these two cities and the Jews who called them home.[6]

Mobile provides a striking example. The first permanent European settlement in Alabama, Mobile was founded by the French in 1702. According to the Code Noir, Jews were forbidden to settle in the new territory. Thus the first Jewish settlers in Mobile did not arrive until the British occupied the city in 1763. The following year three English Jews, Joseph de Palacios, Samuel Israel, and Alexander Solomons, established a merchant trading firm in the city. Jewish immigrants quickly assimilated into Mobile society and often obtained high status in the community. Solomon Mordecai, a physician, came to Mobile in 1823 and was soon followed by the Lazarus brothers, who opened a store and apothecary. The first permanent Jewish community of significance in Mobile, however, did not emerge until the 1830s. One of the Jews who moved to Mobile during this period was George Davis, a popular slave auctioneer. Jacob Cohen moved there in 1839 and was voted city marshal twice in the 1840s. Brothers Solomon and Israel Jones arrived in Mobile from London in the 1830s and became wealthy merchants who both served on the city council. In 1843 Jewish residents constructed their first synagogue in Mobile, Sha'arai Shomayim. By 1860, nearly eighty Jewish families called Mobile home.[7]

Like other Mobilians, the Jews in the port city found themselves in a precarious situation during the Civil War. As one of the major harbors in the Gulf, Mobile was heavily fortified by the state militia at Fort Gaines and Fort Morgan, while additional Confederate troops reinforced the perimeter of the city by digging entrenchments. Despite being blockaded by the Union's Gulf Blockading Squadron, the city would keep up a lively trade via New Orleans until the fall of Mobile Bay in 1864. While all Jewish families felt the sting of war, two Jewish residents of Mobile in particular, Eugenia Levy Phillips and Adolph Proskauer, were greatly affected.[8]

Eugenia Levy Phillips was Alabama's most infamous Jewish woman during the Civil War and gained recognition throughout the Confederacy for her patriotic, if impudent, behavior. Eugenia Levy was born in 1820 in Charleston, South Carolina, to a prominent Jewish family. When Eugenia was sixteen she married Philip Phillips, a member of the South Carolina legislature and successful lawyer from what was considered one of Charleston's best Jewish families. Not long after their wedding in 1836, the Phillipses moved to Mobile, where they became distinguished and respected members of the port city. The Phillipses counted among their close friends future Alabama Supreme Court Justice Edmund S. Durgan and former Alabama governor John Gayle. In addition to his thriving legal practice, which included representing the Bank of Mobile, Phillips continued his foray into Southern politics. In 1844 and 1851 he was elected to the state legislature, and in 1853 was elected to the U.S. House of Representatives. In 1853 the Phillipses and seven of their eventual nine children moved to Washington, D.C. He also served as chair of the Alabama Democratic Party. Phillips served only one term in Congress but chose to remain in the nation's capital and argue cases before the Supreme Court. He did, however, maintain close professional ties to Mobile and Alabama in general.[9]

Following the secession crisis, the Phillips family longed to return to Mobile, but Philip Phillips feared that city's vulnerability to attack. Thus he moved his family to what he considered a safer destination, New Orleans. However, New Orleans would prove to be Phillips's wartime crucible. On April 29, 1862, Union forces captured New Orleans and the city fell under the control of controversial Gen. Benjamin F. Butler. It would not take long for Eugenia Phillips and her vocal opinions to incur his wrath. On June 29, 1862, while standing on her balcony opposite Lafayette Square, Eugenia made the mistake of laughing and jeering at a passing funeral procession for a Union lieutenant. The next day she was arrested. Philip Phillips accompanied his wife to Butler's headquarters, where the Federal officer demanded she explain her actions of the previous day. Eugenia scoffed at the accusations, replying simply, "I was in good spirits that day." The apoplectic general harangued Eugenia for her offense. Outraged at Butler's behavior, Phillips in turn rebuked the general for his "ungentlemanly" behavior. Seething with anger, Butler sat down and wrote Special Order No. 150, which classified Phillips as an "uncommon, bad, and dangerous woman." He further charged her with "stirring up strife and inciting to riot" and "training her children to spit upon officers of the United States." The order sentenced her to Ship Island, a barrier island located off the coast of Gulfport, Mississippi, in the Gulf of Mexico.[10]

After a harrowing three months on Ship Island, Eugenia Phillips was released on October 2. The Phillipses still refused to take the oath of allegiance to the United States and thus were forced to find a new home yet again. The family returned to Mobile for a short period and later settled in La Grange, Georgia. After the war, Philip Phillips, always the moderate voice in his family, returned to pleading cases before the U.S. Supreme Court. His wife, in characteristic fashion, remained an unrepentant rebel, highlighting in her postwar reminiscences that she was "part and parcel of the Southern society, all my sympathies, interests, and affections being with them."[11]

Another Mobile Jew who played a key role in the war was Maj. Adolph Proskauer. He became one of the highest-ranking Jewish Confederate officers in Alabama, and indeed the South. Immigrating to the United States with his father, Julius, sometime in the 1850s, Adolph and his family first settled in Philadelphia and later in Richmond, where they operated a successful mercantile business. Just before the Civil War, Adolph decided to move farther south to Mobile.[12] In May 1861, he enlisted in the Mobile Independent Rifles, which was made up almost entirely of German immigrants, many of whom were Jewish. In July 1861, the Independent Rifles were incorporated into the 12th Alabama Infantry in Richmond, Virginia. It included members from Montgomery, Mobile, Coffee, Coosa, DeKalb, Jackson, Macon, Morgan, and Pike Counties.[13] Several of Proskauer's fellow Jewish Mobilians joined the 12th, including Jules l'Etondal, a successful French-born watchmaker who initially began the war in the Gardes Lafayette, an almost entirely French regiment. Capt. Ernest Karcher, a shoemaker, served throughout the war and "distinguished himself at every battle." After the war he served as lieutenant of police in Mobile. Young Simon Alltemont, an eighteen-year-old Bavarian immigrant and "pickler" before the war, also served in the 12th Alabama as a private.[14]

A handsome, always well-dressed man, Proskauer participated in some of the fiercest battles of the war. For more than a year the regiment saw very little action. Proskauer's first real taste of combat was at the Battle of Seven Pines, where he led a "gallant charge." Promoted to captain, he likewise participated in battles at Gaines Mill, Malvern Hill, and Antietam, where he was wounded in the stomach along the "Bloody Lane." In early 1863, while he was still recovering from wounds, Proskauer applied to become a major. In an apparent case of anti-Semitism, Col. Samuel B. Pickens passed over Proskauer in favor of a junior captain named John W. McNeely. Feeling slighted by Pickens, Proskauer asked an examining committee judge whether he was fit to be major over McNeely. Colonel Pickens persuaded the committee to make the exam overly difficult for Proskauer in the hope that he would fail. Much to Pickens's disappointment, the committee questioned Proskauer on drilling tactics and "army movements suggested by Jomini's tactics" and he "did not fail to answer promptly and accurately every question." Proskauer's promotion was finally confirmed but not until 1864.[15]

In July 1863, Proskauer would face his biggest test of the war. At the Battle of Chancellorsville that May, he had been wounded once again. After recuperating, Proskauer rejoined his regiment and the Army of Northern Virginia as Lee once again attempted to move his army north. Gettysburg would prove to be the highlight of Proskauer's military career. On July 1, Proskauer and his men in Company C joined Col. Edward O'Neal's Alabama Brigade of Maj. Gen. Robert Rodes's division. The 12th Alabama suffered heavy casualties as a result of O'Neal's and Rodes's poor leadership at Oak Ridge, just northeast of Gettysburg. The Alabama Brigade lost 41 percent of its men on the first day of battle. Of Proskauer, one of his men later tellingly recalled that "our gallant Jew major smoked his cigars calmly and coolly during the thickest of the fighting." The next day, Proskauer and his men moved into the tiny Pennsylvania town, hoping the previous day's disaster would not repeat itself. July 2, however, would prove equally devastating as the regiment was ordered to advance on Culp's Hill. The Union held the high ground on Culp's Hill, Cemetery Hill, and Cemetery Ridge. Culp's Hill was critical to the Confederacy's capture of Cemetery Hill. As Proskauer and the 12th began their advance at 4:30 AM, the Union army rained artillery fire upon them. For over seven hours the Confederates made several useless advances up the hill, only to be beaten back at every turn. Devastated, Proskauer and the Confederates withdrew. The next day saw the vainglorious Pickett's Charge, and Lee and the rebels, once again, retreated to Virginia.[16]

The 12th Alabama would participate in further battles of Kelly's Ford and the Wilderness. On May 8, 1864, while fighting at Spotsylvania Courthouse, Major Proskauer received his third and final wound, when a bullet passed through his cheek. He resigned in January 1865 and served out the rest of the war in the Alabama State Reserve Forces in Mobile. After the war Proskauer remained one of the most successful Jews in Alabama and one of the few to actually remain south of the Mason-Dixon Line. He continued to live in Mobile after the war and served in the Alabama legislature before moving to St. Louis in 1895 to serve as president of a cotton exchange. He remained an active and proud member of the Confederate Veterans Association. He died at age sixty-two in St. Louis.[17]

Like Mobile, the capital city of Montgomery was home to many Jews. Indeed, the first Jewish settler in the state established himself around Montgomery. Abraham Mordecai was a Revolutionary War veteran who in the 1790s came from Pennsylvania to the frontier of Alabama, where he set up a trading post and married a Native American woman. As had happened in Mobile, however, most Jews moved to Montgomery during the 1840s. The first Jewish settler in Montgomery was probably Jacob Sacerdote, who reportedly had "a kind of restaurant" on the corner of Court and Montgomery Streets. By 1846, there were enough Jewish families living in Montgomery to establish the first Jewish organization in the city, Chefra Mefacker Cholim, or Society for Relieving the Sick, as well as a Jewish section in Oakwood Cemetery. By the 1850s, Montgomery was becoming a mercantile center for the cotton planters living in the Black Belt, which led to further immigration. By 1850, there were more than thirty Jewish families living in the capital city, which necessitated the founding of the first synagogue, Kahl Montgomery.[18]

Montgomery's Jewish population was well established and close-knit through intermarriage and business dealings by the time the Civil War started. Although it was the original capital of the Confederacy, Montgomery would experience little military turmoil during the first years of the war. As fully integrated members of Montgomery society, most of the city's successful Jewish families would either send their sons off to war or contribute to the war effort at home. One such family that sent loved ones to war were the Weils. The Weil brothers, Josiah, Jacob, and Heinrich, came to Alabama from Germany in the late 1840s to take advantage of the booming cotton trade in and around the Montgomery area. Alabama was good to the Weil brothers, and by 1861 they had successfully established themselves as cotton "factors, buyers, exporters, and ginners" and amassed a fortune of over $180,000 in real and personal income.[19] Jacob had shown his gratitude toward his adopted country by serving in the Mexican War, and by May 1861 he was a lieutenant in the 4th Alabama, assigned to protect the city of Montgomery. In a letter to his brother Joseph, Jacob detailed his thoughts on President Jefferson Davis, whose inauguration he had attended the previous February. Weil found his speech "most impassioned" and the president himself "imposing and impressive," yet he feared the new leader "has not the stomach nor the *verstandt* [experience] to lead us." Weil attempted to explain his Confederate patriotism and devotion to the South to his brother, stating, "This land has been good to us all. We shall not be deprived of rights or property without the course of law which our constitution granted. I shall fight to my last breath and to the full extent of my fortune to defend that which I believe." Weil likewise heavily criticized his Jewish neighbors who did not join the Confederate military effort.[20]

Another family that would contribute to the Confederate war effort was the Abrahams, who sent three sons off to war. By 1861, brothers David, Isaac, and Joseph Abraham had established themselves as merchants worth over $47,000. In March 1861 David and Isaac Abraham joined the Montgomery Mounted Rifles, which joined the 1st Alabama Volunteer Cavalry that November. The regiment was involved in many of the major conflicts in the Western Theater, including Shiloh, Perryville, Murfreesboro, and later the Atlanta Campaign. They surrendered at Salisbury, North Carolina, with fewer than 150 men. Joseph Abraham, however, preferred to stay closer to home. He joined a local Montgomery militia company, the Fireman Guards. Two French Jewish immigrants, Samuel and Leopold Dreyfus, joined Joseph Abraham as local defenders. Two clerks at the Abrahams' store and boarders at Isaac's home, Jacob Cohn and William Colling, enlisted in the 4th Alabama. The Abrahams' neighbor, Elias Blum, a dry goods merchant, also joined the war effort as a member of the 10th Alabama Infantry.[21]

Despite the travails of war, Montgomery's Jewish community remained prosperous enough to purchase land to construct the first physical building for Kahl Montgomery. On March 8, 1862, the wealthiest Jewish families in Montgomery looked on as Rabbi James K. Gutheim of New Orleans conducted the dedication ceremony and delivered "one of the most eloquent sermons heard" in the city. Rabbi Gutheim, however, was not in Montgomery simply to dedicate the synagogue. A leader of a New Orleans synagogue, Temple Sinai, Gutheim was an ardent Confederate supporter. When the city was captured, he refused to take the oath of allegiance and instead fled to Montgomery. The rabbi already had ties to Alabama: his wife, Emilie, was the daughter of Israel I. Jones, one of the wealthiest Jews in Mobile.[22]

From the pulpit in Montgomery, Gutheim prayed "Bless O Father, our efforts in a cause we conceive to be just; the defense of our liberties and rights and independence. May harmony of sentiment . . . animate the people of our beloved Confederate States. Bless and protect the armed hosts that now stand forth in defense of our sacred cause."[23] During the war, Rabbi Gutheim engaged in a spirited debate with Alabama governor Thomas Hill Watts over the role of Montgomery's Jewish community and its support of the Confederacy. In November 1864, in conjunction with President Jefferson's Davis's request that November 16 be set aside as a "day of prayer," Governor Watts called for an additional day of prayer within the state. Watts's proclamation concluded with the statement "at all times it is becoming to a Christian people to bow before the Great Jehovah." Taking great umbrage with Watts's emphasis on "Christian people," Gutheim wrote to Watts, claiming "the Jewish Citizens of Montgomery, during my sojourn here have cheerfully responded to the recommendations to pray by our illustrious President." He respectfully, "in the name of the Jewish citizens of Alabama," asked that the proclamation be amended to address the "whole people" of the state, not just Christians.[24]

Another prominent Jewish family in Montgomery were the Moseses. Various members of the family arrived in the city just before and during the war. Originally some of the earliest Jewish inhabitants of Charleston, South Carolina, brothers Alfred and Moses moved to Montgomery to study law just before the war broke out, while brothers Henry and Mordecai Moses came later to escape the wartime conditions in the Palmetto State. Alfred served as a clerk of court during the war in addition to serving in a home guard unit called the Alabama Rebels along with his brother Henry. Mordecai enlisted as a private in Company E, 46th Alabama. After the war, the Moses brothers stayed in Montgomery and became prominent citizens. Mordecai Moses served three terms as mayor of the city during the late 1870s and early 1880s. In addition, the brothers helped build the largest real estate, insurance, and banking institution in the state, and in 1887 they constructed what was then the largest building in Alabama, the six-story Moses building on Court Square.[25]

Without a doubt, however, the most influential and prosperous Jewish family to emerge from the Civil War in Montgomery was the Lehmans, founders in the last half of the nineteenth century of the legendary financial empire in New York. The first of the Lehman brothers to come to Alabama was Henry Lehman, who immigrated from Rimpar, Bavaria, in 1844. Henry initially peddled goods along the Alabama River before establishing a wholesale grocery that catered to the cotton farmers who came to Montgomery to buy supplies. By 1850, brothers Mayer and Emmanuel Lehman had joined their brother at H. Lehman & Company on Court Street in downtown Montgomery. The brothers soon began dealing in cotton, the business by which they would make their fortune. The cotton farmers who came to Lehman Brothers often paid for goods in cotton. In addition, the brothers extended long-range credit to farmers who had no income until their cotton crop was ready. Eventually they bought cotton outright. Tragedy struck the family in 1855 when Henry Lehman died of yellow fever while on a business trip to New Orleans, leaving behind a wife and four children. It would be brothers Mayer and Emmanuel who would make Lehman a household name in Montgomery. By the late 1850s, the Lehmans were increasingly dealing in cotton, so much so that they established a banking system by which they loaned money to cotton farmers secured by crop liens. The business boomed to such an extent that Emmanuel Lehman moved to New York City to open an office. Mayer, who had much more knowledge of the cotton business, remained in Montgomery.[26]

By 1859 Mayer Lehman and his family were members of the upper echelon of Alabama's Jewish immigrants. They lived in a magnificent home, large enough to house his family and the clerks who worked for him; were respected members of Kahl Montgomery; and were the owners of seven slaves. Mayer was a member of the local Masonic organization and like most of his fellow Southerners was a staunch Democrat. On the eve of the Civil War, life was good for the Lehmans.[27]

After Fort Sumter, Emmanuel and Mayer Lehman faced an uncertain future. From his desk in Manhattan, Emmanuel despaired, scribbling "All is finished!" on business documents in his office. Though he lived in New York, Emmanuel Lehman's allegiance remained with the South. In 1862 he traveled to Europe under the employment of the Confederate government in a futile attempt to sell bonds. After returning to New York for a brief period he went back to Europe in 1863, where he remained till the end of the war. Mayer did not join the Southern war effort like his Jewish neighbors, the Weils and Abrahams, but instead focused on the firm's cotton business in Montgomery.

The growing and selling of cotton became a hotly contested issue in the Confederate states, especially in Alabama. In 1862 the Confederate Congress passed legislation prohibiting the sale of cotton in areas of the South occupied by the Union. With the fall of New Orleans in 1862, the Confederacy lost its busiest and most profitable port. Between 1862 and 1864, a brisk illegal trade developed between Federal-occupied New Orleans and Mobile, with cotton as the main source of barter. To stem the tide of illegal trade and encourage farmers to produce foodstuffs vital to the Confederate army and the Southern population in general, Alabama governor John Gill Shorter presented a series of resolutions in 1862 and 1863 that entreated the people of Alabama to "plant not one seed of cotton . . . but put down your lands in grains and every kind of . . . farm product, and raise every kind of live stock which may contribute to the support of your own families . . . and the grand armies which shall march to achieve your independence." Shorter further stated that farmers who continued to grow their usual mass amounts of cotton would be heavily taxed and have their bales burned.

Mayer Lehman, in the meantime, unable to make a living brokering cotton in Montgomery, briefly moved to New Orleans in 1862 and partnered with his brother-in-law in illegal trade with the occupying Federal army. In 1863, Mayer Lehman and Montgomery merchant John Wesley Durr formed the Alabama Warehouse on the Alabama River waterfront. The warehouse would store cotton until the end of the war, when trade would (they hoped) resume. By 1863, the new governor, Thomas Watts, was hopeful that President Davis would allow Lehman & Durr to ship a thousand bales of cotton through the blockade to Liverpool.[28]

Governor Watts placed a great deal of confidence in Mayer Lehman. In addition to allowing him to store most of the state's cotton in his warehouse, in 1864 Watts chose Lehman for a relief mission for Alabama's soldiers at Elmira prison in New York. Watts's plan was to gain the consent of Union authorities for the sale and shipment of $500,000 worth of cotton stored at Lehman & Durr. The profits would go toward the purchase of clothing, medicine, food, and blankets for the prisoners. In a report to President Davis about his intentions, Watts explained that he chose Lehman because "he is a foreigner, but . . . is thoroughly identified with us" and "one of the best Southern patriots." Lehman, along with Isaac Tichenor of Montgomery, a Baptist minister and fellow Alabamian, traveled to Richmond in January 1865. They twice attempted to meet with Gen. U. S. Grant, who ignored both requests.[29]

By the time Mayer Lehman returned to Montgomery, the war was all but over. In March and April 1865, Union general James H. Wilson led a devastating raid through Alabama, ultimately destroying the state arsenal, munitions works, and niter plant at Selma. Wilson and his men proceeded on to Montgomery, which they by and large spared. One of the few structures Wilson did destroy, however, was the Alabama Warehouse. Lehman & Durr lost most of their assets. After the war, Mayer Lehman focused on rebuilding the firm's cotton business. He was so successful that in 1866 the firm loaned $100,000 to the state of Alabama to settle its wartime debts. The state appointed Lehman Brothers fiscal agent of the state in 1867, authorized to sell bonds, settle debts and interest payments, and oversee other matters. In 1868 Lehman, hoping to escape the strife of Reconstruction in Alabama, moved his family and joined his brother Emmanuel in New York. In 1870, the brothers founded the Cotton Exchange, cementing Lehman Brothers as one of the most successful, yet ultimately doomed, financial companies in the world.[30]

Despite Jews' contributions to the Southern war effort, some Alabamians viewed them with prejudice. As noted earlier, Proskauer's men saw him as a "gallant Jew," while Thomas Watts referred to Mayer Lehman as a "foreigner." In both Mobile and Montgomery, female aid societies refused to accept Jewish members. Jewish women had to form separate societies, often called Hebrew Young Ladies, to contribute to the Confederate war effort. In 1863, Jewish women in Mobile held their own fund-raiser for the 32nd Alabama. In Montgomery, another group of Jewish women, noted in the press as being "composed primarily of Israelites," held a fund-raiser to benefit the refugees of New Orleans.[31] Jewish merchants, however, were frequent targets of anger and scorn. As historian Leonard Dinnerstein explains, the Civil War saw an increase in anti-Semitism across America. Both Northern and Southern Jews were viewed as profiteers who engaged in illegal barter and inflated the price of everyday goods. For example, in a letter to the editor published in the *Montgomery Post* dated August 1861, a member of the Moore Guards praised the work of the ladies of the city, but his praise then turned to indignation: "Mr. Editor, while acknowledging the liberality and patriotism of the ladies of Montgomery, it pains me to say that some of the merchants of your city have not manifested the same spirit. We have found SHYLOCKS among them—men who have shown a disposition to exact to the uttermost farthing of exorbitant and extortionate prices. So far from being liberal and generous to the soldiers they have looked upon them as proper subjects upon which to practice small tricks of petty meanness and extortion." He went on to assert, "I do not say this of all the merchants of the city, but a few types only. These men I understand are Yankees by birth and therefore their want of generosity is not to be so much wondered at." Thus the indignant Moore Guard insulted the merchants twice, once by referring to them as "Shylocks" and second by noting their Yankee birth. A similar letter written after the war again excoriated Southern money lenders and brokers as "blood-sucking Shylocks . . . who during the war, remained at home fattening off the suffering of the people . . . demanding their 'pound of flesh.'"[32]

This show of anti-Semitism was not unique to Alabama. As Gary L. Bunker and John J. Appel point out, existing stereotypes and ethnocentric ideas about Jews on the eve of war made them a visible target for prejudice. From Louisiana to New

York, newspaper cartoons and editorials highlighted an intense bigotry against Jews and an overwhelming belief that Jewish merchants were somehow "unpatriotic." The high prices of food and dry goods resulting from the war often were blamed on Jews, who were painted as price gougers. Even non-Jewish merchants who charged inflationary prices for goods were accused of being greedy and described with terms such as "Shylock." Similar words were used to describe contractors who churned out defective products to the army such as uniforms and guns. Stephen Ash likewise notes that Grant's notorious General Orders No. 11, directed primarily at the Jews in the Mississippi Valley, grew out of a need to scapegoat a minority during the frustration and uncertainty wrought by war. Thus Jewish businessmen in the area, buying and moving cotton up and down the Mississippi River, were singled out as the perpetrators of an illegal trade involving merchants, a majority of whom were non-Jews.[33]

Like many immigrants to the United States, Alabama's Jews participated in the conflict as a way to prove their patriotism and devotion to their adopted homeland. Yet like many Jews throughout the country, Alabamian Jews found themselves fighting two wars: one on the battlefield and one against anti-Semitism. Alabama's Jews, however, never faced the intense prejudice shown to Jews who fell under General Grant's wartime order of expulsion. Indeed, the Lehmans were highly trusted by the governor of Alabama and formed an economic partnership with one of the most respected men in Montgomery. Perhaps this explains why, despite the evidence of anti-Semitism, Jews did not leave Alabama en masse after the war. Indeed, like Mordecai Moses, many served the state during Reconstruction as mayors and bankers. Though Montgomery's and Mobile's Jewish populations dwindled, other Jewish communities popped up in the late nineteenth century to take their place, particularly in Birmingham, Selma, and Huntsville. Even tiny communities such as Anniston saw their Jewish populations increase dramatically as the railroad and steel industries brought new economic opportunities to the state.[34]

In the 1960s, Rubin M. Hanan outlined the accomplishments of Alabama's Jewish men and women: "In Alabama, they have been ardent supporters of the principles of the political and civic order of the South and have been loyal supporters of its *way of life* and its established social institutions." Thus, one hundred years after the Civil War, it seemed that Alabamian Jews' contributions to the war effort had not been forgotten.[35]

Notes

1. U.S. Civil War Soldiers, 1861–1865, http://www.ancestry.com (accessed 2010). On his military record, his last name is misspelled as Cahn. Solomon Kahn Obituary, Temple Beth-El Archives, Fort Worth, Texas. According to the 1900 census, Solomon Kahn emigrated to the United States from Germany in 1859. In 1900 he was living in Dallas with his wife, Anna, four

children, a black servant, and several boarders. He is listed as a "mine owner." The 3rd Alabama holds the unfortunate distinction of losing the largest number of soldiers at the Battle of Malvern Hill. They lost an unimaginable 207 out of 345 men. A sketch of the 3rd Alabama Infantry is located in Willis Brewer, *Alabama: Her History, Resources, War Record, and Public Men* (Tuscaloosa, AL: Willo Publications, 1964). See also Brandon H. Beck, ed., *Third Alabama! The Civil War Memoir of Brigadier General Cullen Andrews Battle, CSA* (Tuscaloosa: University of Alabama Press, 2000).

2. Bertram Wallace Korn, a prominent historian and rabbi, wrote extensively about Judaism in the South. His works include *American Jewry in the Civil War* (Philadelphia: Jewish Publication Society of America, 1951), *The Jews of Mobile Alabama, 1763–1841* (Cincinnati: Hebrew Union College Press, 1970), *Jews and Negro Slavery in the Old South, 1789–1865* (Elkins Park, PA: Reform Congregation Kenesseth Israel, 1961), and *The Early Jews of New Orleans* (Waltham, MA: American Jewish Historical Society, 1969). More recently, Robert Rosen has written about Jews who served in the Confederate army. See Robert Rosen, *The Jewish Confederates* (Columbia: University of South Carolina Press, 2000). In 1895, Simon Wolf published a list of all Jewish soldiers known to have served in the Civil War in *The American Jew as Patriot, Soldier, and Citizen* (Philadelphia: Levytype Company, 1895), 117–409. I have identified almost all of the men listed as serving in Alabama through the National Park Service U.S. Civil Soldiers, 1861–1865, on www.ancestry.com or the Alabama Department of Archives and History's Civil War Soldiers Database. Several rabbis served as chaplains in the Union army, including Isaac Leeser, who served in Philadelphia military hospitals.

3. Rosen, *Jewish Confederates*, 15–34; William Howard Russell, *My Diary North and South* (Boston: TOHP Burnham, 1863), 242.

4. Jack Nelson, *Terror in the Night: The Klan's Campaign against the Jews* (New York: Simon and Schuster, 1993). For a comprehensive work on Jewish life in the New South, see Leonard Dinnerstein and Mary Dale Palsson, eds., *Jews in the South* (Baton Rouge: Louisiana State University Press, 1973). Some of the more recent works that deal with Jews and the civil rights movement are Clive Webb, *Fight against Fear: Southern Jews and Black Civil Rights* (Athens: University of Georgia Press, 2001) and Mark K. Bauman and Berkley Kalin, eds., *The Quiet Voices: Southern Rabbis and Black Civil Rights, 1880–1990s* (Tuscaloosa: University of Alabama Press, 1997).

5. Encyclopedia of Southern Jewish Communities, http://www.isjl.org/history/archive/ (accessed March 2013); Charles R. Geisst, *The Last Partnerships: Inside the Great Wall Street Dynasties* (New York: McGraw Hill, 2001), 43–45. After the war, Joseph and William Seligman founded J. & W. Seligman & Co., one of the wealthiest securities firms in late nineteenth-century America. They invested heavily in railroads, bridges, skyscrapers, steel, and wire, as well as in the Standard Oil Company. Helen Tunnicliff Catterall, *Judicial Cases Concerning American Slavery and the Negro* (Washington, DC: Carnegie Institution of Washington, 1926), 3:210.

6. William Warren Rogers et al., *Alabama: The History of a Deep South State* (Tuscaloosa: University of Alabama Press, 1994), 93–112. See Bertram Wallace Korn, "Jews and Negro Slavery in the Old South, 1789–1865" in Dinnerstein and Palsson, *Jews in the South*, 91–96.

7. Korn, *The Jews of Mobile Alabama, 1763–1841*, 1–60; United States Census, 1850 and 1860, Mobile County, Alabama, http://www.ancestry.com (accessed September 1, 2010).

8. John C. Waugh and Grady McWhiney, *Last Stand at Mobile* (Abilene: McWhiney Foundation Press, 2002); Jack Friend, *West Wind, Flood Tide: The Battle of Mobile Bay* (Annapolis, MD: Naval Institute Press, 2004).

9. Korn, *The Jews of Mobile*, 44–46; Henry Barrett Learned, "The Relation of Philip Phillips to the Repeal of the Missouri Compromise in 1854," *Mississippi Valley Historical Review* 8, no. 4

(March 1921): 303–9; Manuscript autobiography of Philip Phillips, pp. 20–26, Phillips Family Papers, Manuscript Division, Library of Congress, Washington, DC; Jacob R. Marcus, ed., "Eugenia Phillips, Defiant Rebel," in *Memoirs of American Jews, 1775–1865* (Philadelphia: Jewish Publication Society 1955), 3:180–85. Eugenia Phillips's original journal is housed among the Phillips Family Papers. During the war Eugenia's sister, Phoebe Yates Levy Pember, served as the administrator of Richmond's Chimborazo Hospital. Her brother, Samuel Yates Levy, served as a major in the Georgia infantry. In late August 1861, however, the Phillips family home in Washington, D.C., was raided by Federal agents and the family was arrested on suspicion of espionage. Eugenia had been writing back and forth to several of her family members in Alabama, South Carolina, and Georgia, which understandably aroused suspicion.

10. Marcus, "Eugenia Phillips, Defiant Rebel," 184–85; *Official Record of the Union and Confederate Armies*, series I, vol. 15, 510–11 (hereafter *OR*; unless otherwise noted, series I is cited). It is quite possible that General Butler targeted Eugenia Levy Phillips not only for her outspoken pro-Southern views but because she was a Jew. In 1864 Butler publicly targeted Jews as the cause of contraband trade along the Mississippi. In a letter to Myer S. Issacs, publisher of the *Jewish Messenger*, Butler outlined his views of Jews, rebuking them for their tendency to engage as "traders, merchants, and bankers" and their proclivity to aid one another on "all proper and sometimes improper occasions." General Benjamin F. Butler to Myer Issacs, *Jewish Messenger*, February 4, 1864, reprinted in *Publications of the American Jewish Historical Society* 29 (1925): 119–30.

11. Marcus, "Eugenia Phillips, Defiant Rebel," 190–96. Philip Phillips died in 1884; Eugenia Phillips died in 1902.

12. Louis M. Hacker and Mark D. Hirsch, *Proskauer: His Life and Times* (Tuscaloosa: University of Alabama Press, 1978), 1–3. Hacker and Hirsch's book is a biography of Judge Joseph Proskauer of New York, Adolph Proskauer's nephew, who became a lawyer, Democratic Party stalwart, and friend of New York governor Al Smith. The 1860 census lists Julius Proskauer as living in Philadelphia as a "liquor dealer." United States Census, 1860, Philadelphia, Pennsylvania, Ward 7, http://www.ancestry.com (accessed July 21, 2010).

13. Robert Emory Park, *Sketch of the Twelfth Alabama Infantry of Battle's Brigade*, Rodes Division, Early's Corps of the Army of Northern Virginia (Richmond, VA: W. E. Jones, 1906), 1–17. Due to its bustling ports and age, Mobile was the most cosmopolitan city in antebellum Alabama, as evinced by the numerous foreign-born regiments that joined the Confederacy. The 8th Alabama Emerald Guards were just one of the many Irish companies to heed the call of duty, while Company I of the 2nd Alabama boasted another group soldiers from the British Isles, the Scotch Guard. The city also included regiments made up of French, Spanish, and German soldiers. See Ella Lonn, *Foreigners in the Confederacy* (Chapel Hill: University of North Carolina Press, 1940), 95–100.

14. Park rather humorously notes that L'Etondal was a rather heavy man, weighing in at 250 pounds, and was almost killed during the Seven Days Campaign when he led his men into battle holding an umbrella to shield himself from the sun. He resigned his commission in late 1862 for health reasons and died in February 1865 in Mobile. R. A. Brock, ed., *Southern Historical Society Papers* 33 (Richmond, VA: Southern Historical Society, 1905), 198, 201, 228–30.

15. Brock, *Southern Historical Society Papers*, 200.

16. *OR*, vol. 25, part 1, 950–53, 960–61, vol. 27, part 1, 563, vol. 29, part 1, 891–92, vol. 36, part 1, 1083–84; John D. Cox, *Culp's Hill at Gettysburg: The Attack and Defense of the Union Flank, July 2* (Cambridge, MA: Da Capo Press, 2003); James McPherson, *Battle Cry of Freedom: The Civil War Era* (London: Oxford University Press, 1988), 656–62.

Jews in Alabama during the Civil War / 163

17. Proskauer Family Papers, MS 254, box 1, folders 1 and 2, American Jewish Archives, Cincinnati, OH.

18. Leopold Young, "A Sketch of the First Jewish Settlers of Montgomery and a Short History of Kahl Montgomery," Closed Stacks, Alabama Department of Archives and History, Montgomery (hereafter ADAH); Kerry M. Olitsky and Marc Lee Raphael, *The American Synagogue: A Historical Dictionary and Sourcebook* (Westport, CT: Greenwood, 1996), 33–34.

19. United States Federal Census, 1860, Montgomery County, Alabama, http://www.ancestry.com (accessed July 20, 2010).

20. Jacob Weil letter, May 16, 1861, SPR15, ADAH.

21. United States Federal Census, 1860, Montgomery County, Alabama, http://www.ancestry.com (accessed September 2, 2010); Alabama Civil War Service Database, ADAH, http://www.archives.alabama.gov/civilwar/search.cfm (accessed September 2, 2010).

22. See Scott M. Langston, "James K. Gutheim as Southern Reform Rabbi, Community Leader, and Symbol," *Southern Jewish History* 5 (2002): 69–102; Rosen, *Jewish Confederates*, 249; James K. Gutheim Papers, MS-224, American Jewish Archives, Cincinnati, OH. Unlike the Phillips family, Rabbi Gutheim must have realized that fleeing one port city for another was not a wise course of action during the war; thus he moved farther inland to Montgomery. He also served as rabbi in Columbus, Georgia, before returning to New Orleans in 1865.

23. Unknown Montgomery, Alabama, newspaper clipping dated May 16, 1862, M. J. Solomon Scrapbook, 1861–63, Manuscript Department, Perkins Library, Duke University.

24. James K. Gutheim to Governor Thomas H. Watts, November 7, 1864, Governor Thomas H. Watts Papers, Correspondence, 1863–65, SG024, 872, reel 20–23, ADAH.

25. Kenneth Libo, "The Moseses of Montgomery: The Saga of a Jewish Family in the South," *Alabama Heritage* 36 (Spring 1995): 18–25; Michael Feldburg, ed., *Blessings of Freedom: Chapters in American Jewish History* (Hoboken, NJ: American Jewish Historical Society, 2002), 178. After the war, Alfred Moses would invest heavily, and lose mightily, when he single-handedly founded the town of Sheffield along the Tennessee River in northwest Alabama. Moses believed Sheffield would become a booming mining town that would fund Alabama's steel industry. Moses miscalculated the amount of ore located in Sheffield and was forced to leave Alabama for St. Louis, having suffered almost total financial ruin. Alfred Moses's grandson John Loeb, married Frances Lehman, granddaughter of Mayer Lehman.

26. Roland Flade, *The Lehmans: From Rimpar to the New World, a Family History* (Wurzberg, Germany: Konigshausen & Neumann, 1999), 50–67; Elliott Ashkenazi, *The Business of Jews in Louisiana, 1840–1870* (Tuscaloosa: University of Alabama Press, 1988), 109–50; Baker Library Historical Collections, Harvard University, Lehman Brothers Collection–Twentieth Century Business Archives, http://www.library.hbs.edu/hc/lehman/history.html (accessed July 1, 2010).

27. United States Slave Schedules, 1860, Montgomery County, Alabama, http://www.ancestry.com (accessed July 2, 2010). In 2005, Lehman Brothers was involved in a bond issue concerning an expansion project at O'Hare Airport in Chicago that turned into a controversy over slavery. Chicago required all firms desiring contracts with the city to disclose whether their business had ever been involved in slavery. Lehman Brothers provided a receipt showing that Mayer, Henry, and Emmanuel Lehman had purchased a female slave named Martha in 1854. A simple perusal of the U.S. Census Slave Schedules would have proved the brothers had owned seven slaves. In 2005, the firm officially apologized for having owned slaves. See *Chicago Sun Times*, September 12, 2005.

28. Proclamation by the Governor of Alabama, March 1 and April 10, 1862, and March 16,

1862, Governor John Gill Shorter Papers, Administrative Files, SG24, 882, ADAH; Governor Thomas Hill Watts Papers, SG22553, folder 16, ADAH; Walter Lynwood Fleming, *The Civil War and Reconstruction in Alabama* (New York: Columbia University Press, 1905), 189–95; Korn, *American Jewry During the Civil War*, 121–23; Rogers et al., *Alabama*, 186–222. The widespread illegal trade in the Confederacy was due to the Lincoln administration's lax and ill-defined trading policy. The North needed cotton; the South needed merchandise, arms, and medicine. Various government agencies were involved in regulating trade, including the White House, Department of War, Department of Treasury, and individual occupying Union generals. The Boards of Trade and treasury agents were notoriously unscrupulous when it came to issuing trade permits and often pocketed exorbitant amounts of money themselves. Unfortunately Jews, though certainly involved, received the brunt of negative publicity and were accused of illegal trade during the war.

29. *OR*, series II, vol. 7, p. 1223 and vol. 8, pp. 69–70.

30. Flade, *The Lehmans*, 67–68.

31. Women in the Confederacy: Aid Society Notices-General, Civil War and Reconstruction Files, SG11159, folder 12, ADAH.

32. Leonard Dinnerstein, *Anti-Semitism in America* (London: Oxford University Press, 1994), 29–34; *Montgomery Advertiser*, August 1861, Mrs. M. L. Kirkpatrick's Scrapbook, vol. 1, 66, ADAH; *Union Springs Times*, September 26, 1866.

33. Gary L. Bunker and John J. Appel, "'Shoddy' Antisemitism and the Civil War," in *Jews and the Civil War: A Reader*, ed. Jonathan D. Sarna and Adam Mendelsohn (New York: New York University Press, 2010), 311–23 and Stephen V. Ash, "Civil War Exodus: The Jews and Grant's General Order No. 11" in *Jews and the Civil War*, ed. Sarna and Mendelsohn, 363–85. Jonathan D. Sarna's *When General Grant Expelled the Jews* (New York: Schocken Books, 2012) is the most comprehensive work on General Grant's controversial order.

34. Sherry Blanton, "Lives of Quiet Affirmation: The Jewish Women of Early Anniston, Alabama," *Southern Jewish History* 2 (1999): 25–53. Joseph Saks, a cousin to the more famous Saks of department store fame, was one of the most powerful economic and civic leaders in Anniston. He even started his own town outside of Anniston, aptly named Saks.

35. Rubin N. Hanan, "We Too Can Be Proud: Our Jewish American Forefathers," box 2, folder 14, Rubin M. Hanan Collection, Archives and Special Collections, Auburn University-Montgomery Library.

9
Every Man Should Consider His Own Conscience
Black and White Alabamians' Reactions to the Assassination of Abraham Lincoln

Harriet E. Amos Doss

After four grueling years of civil war, by April 1865 Alabamians longed for peace. Union troops captured and occupied places from Huntsville in the north to Blakely in the south. As Confederate general Robert E. Lee was surrendering his army in Virginia, Mayor R. H. Slough of Mobile was surrendering his city to Union generals to protect it from destruction. Just as residents began to adjust to defeat and occupation, they learned of the assassination of Abraham Lincoln. Individually and collectively their reactions varied from shock to celebration.

Indeed, Lincoln's election in November 1860 to his first term as president evoked varied responses among Alabamians, although only the pro-secession views received much public attention. Lincoln's name did not appear on the ballot in Alabama, so voters divided their support among secessionist and moderate candidates. Interior areas more likely voted for Southern Democrat John Breckinridge and urban areas for Constitutional Unionist John Bell or National Democrat Stephen Douglas. After delivering his last speech of his bisectional campaign in Mobile, the state's only seaport, Douglas awaited election returns in the office of John Forsyth, editor of the *Mobile Register*. Douglas won a plurality of Mobile's voters, Bell came in second, and secessionist Breckinridge ran third. Yet Breckinridge carried the state of Alabama. Acting in response to Lincoln's national election, Alabama called a state convention to consider secession from the Union. As they prepared for this convention many Alabamians moved toward support for secession even with its dire consequences. A number of residents lamented, as Sarah R. Espy observed, "There are fearful times in store for us, I greatly fear, for war will be the final result of such withdrawal."[1] On January 11, 1861, a majority of convention delegates voted for Alabama's secession.

Alabamians resented what they called Lincoln's policy of coercion, for they wanted him to acknowledge Southern independence. Despite the general public appearance of support for secession and war, a minority of businessmen, especially Northern-born professionals, and planters in the cotton-producing interior feared war for its destabilization of their national and international commerce. Many

Figure 9.1. Market Street in Montgomery, 1861. From *Harper's Weekly*, February 9, 1861.

nonetheless prepared for war. Expecting to hear a "call to arms any day," Margaret J. Gillis, a minister's wife, reported herself prepared. She observed, "In anticipation of the coming storm I['ve] been practicing shooting, assiduously." Once the war began with the Confederacy firing on Fort Sumter and Lincoln calling for volunteers to defend the Union, residents became more bellicose. As William Howard Russell, correspondent for the *London Times*, observed in May 1861 in Mobile, "The wealth and manhood of the city will be devoted to repel the 'Lincolnite mercenaries' to the last." Confederate defenders faced a daunting challenge.[2]

As the war progressed and the Confederacy's fortunes waned, Alabamians conversed less about Lincoln's administration as what poet Theodore O'Hara called "a direct threat to American Constitutional government." Their statements also included personal hatred of Lincoln himself. Author Augusta Evans advised J. L. M. Curry in 1864, "The original *casus belli* has been lost sight of; hatred of Lincoln, not love of our liberties, principles and institutions now actuates our masses."[3]

Throughout the war many Confederates harbored resentment of Abraham Lincoln; some perhaps even wished him harm. Certainly they did not encourage his continued exercise of power as president of the United States. Alabama's Episcopal bishop Richard Hooker Wilmer advised priests in the state to refrain from praying

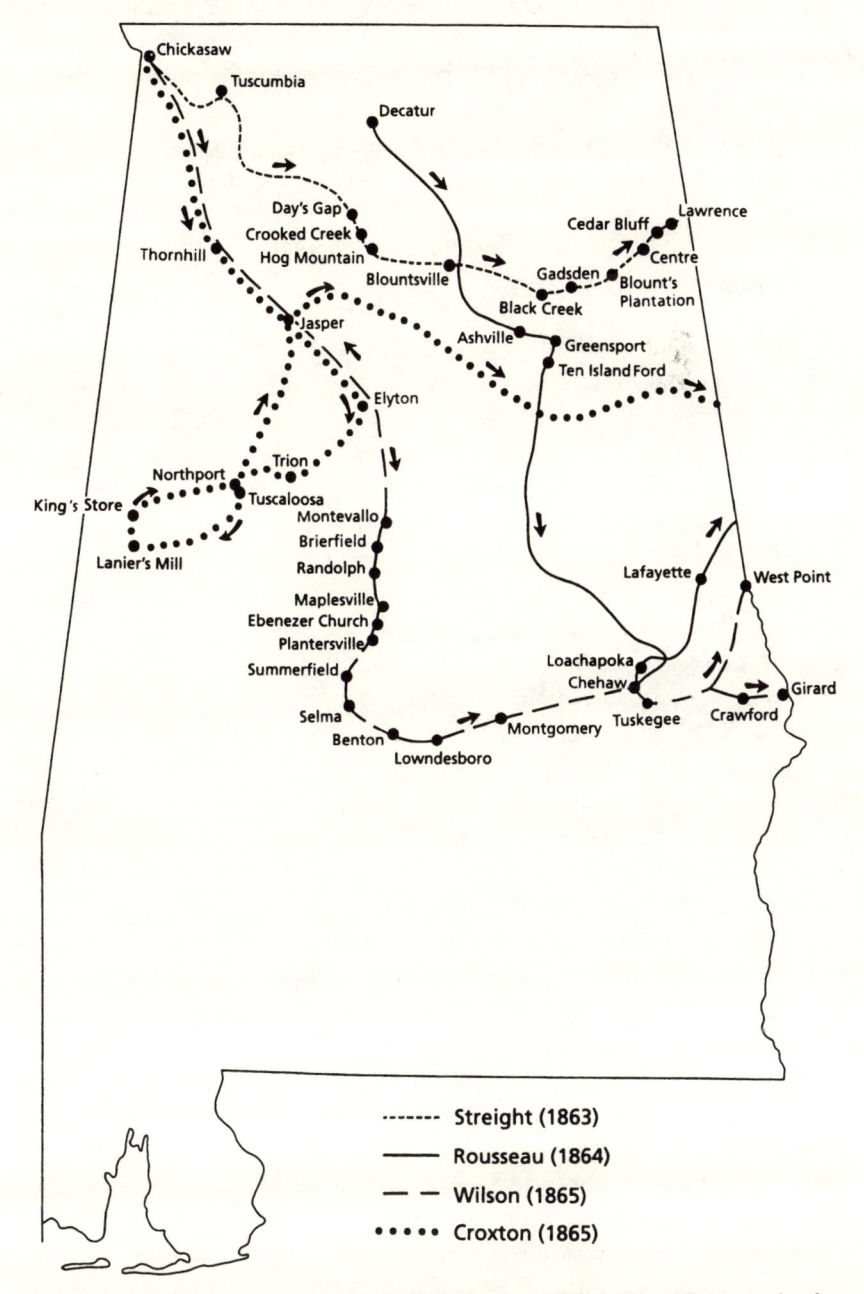

Figure 9.2. Union raids in Alabama during the Civil War. From William Warren Rogers et al., *Alabama: The History of a Deep South State* (Tuscaloosa: University of Alabama Press, 1994), 215.

to God "for the health, prosperity and long life" of the president. Wilmer said this prayer was meant for the safety of civil authority, not for the commander-in-chief of a foreign army. He maintained this ban on prayer for the president for months after the end of the war.

A Unionist Alabamian, however, tried to communicate with President Lincoln directly to promote peace with Southerners. William Bibb of Montgomery, one of perhaps thirty active Unionists in the city, wrote Lincoln on April 12, 1865, "Let me entreat you to be careful of the feelings of the people of the South." As Reconstruction was beginning, Bibb advised Lincoln that if he acted magnanimously and avoided punitive policies he could gain Southerners' goodwill. "We who have borne the heat and burthen of the day," Bibb confided to Lincoln, "are deeply interested in the quiet settlement of this matter."[4] What Bibb could not have known when he wrote this letter was that two days later Lincoln would be fatally shot and then a day later would be dead. But Bibb's deep interest "in the quiet settlement" of the war reflected the views of many Alabamians, whether Confederate or Unionist in their sympathies. Their reactions to news of Lincoln's assassination were inextricably tied to their profound war-weariness.

Records of Alabamians' responses are limited by the circumstances of war-torn areas where local newspapers ceased publication, churches did not hold services or meetings, and residents wrote few diary entries or letters. The thoughts and views of slaves during emancipation received the least documentation. What we are left with are publications of newspapers taken over by Federal troops, the work of some local diarists, and belated recollections of former slaves. The full story of individuals' views remains to be told, but this essay will consider the variety of reactions documented by white and black Alabamians.

In Union-occupied areas of northern Alabama military authorities mourned the assassination of their president in solemn ways and advised local residents against expressing approval for the foul act. News of the assassination reached Decatur and Huntsville first. On April 15, the day Lincoln died, musicians in the 102nd Ohio brass band in Decatur climbed to the roof of the Burleson house to play dirges in his memory.[5]

When residents of occupied Huntsville also learned on April 15 of the assassination, some expressed disbelief while others rejoiced. Local diarist Mary Jane Chadick was "shocked" when the provost marshal told her of Lincoln's murder. She "[f]elt in [her] heart it must be bad news for the South, if Andrew Johnson was to succeed him." Union occupying general R. S. Granger issued an order forbidding residents from showing approval of the assassination "by either word or act." Anyone who expressed "approbation or approval of this most foul . . . shall be immediately arrested and tried by a Military Commission, and if found Guilty they will receive the most Summary punishment," stipulated Granger's general order.

He advised that "such treason shall have no HOME in the District of Northern Alabama." Soldiers took the enforcement of this order quite seriously. They received reports of one Wesley Parkes "standing on the porch of his brother's house, laughing and talking with some young ladies, which excited suspicion they were rejoicing" about Lincoln's death. Soldiers searched his house and moved some of the furniture outside at night, threatening to burn his house. They also arrested Ella Scruggs and Edmonia Toney, ages twenty-two and eighteen, respectively, and presented them "to the Courthouse on a charge of having rejoiced at the late news." Mary Jane Chadick reported that "Col. Horner read them a lecture and dismissed them."[6] Perhaps the colonel's response reflected the young ladies' gender and ages.

Federal authorities in Huntsville observed "a day of mourning for President Lincoln" on April 18, 1865. A cannon was fired at half-hour intervals from early morning until sundown. "All business was suspended, and the business houses draped in mourning," observed Mary Jane Chadick. Schools closed as well, and citizens showed "every mark of respect." "Troops marched through the principal streets with arms reversed, and flags tied with crepe and the band playing a funeral dirge," Chadick added. Several ladies came to her home along the parade route to view the procession.[7]

In Mobile, the state's only seaport, business and political leaders assembled on April 20, 1865, to mark the death of President Lincoln. The *Mobile Daily News* (formerly the *Advertiser and Register*) offered the following editorial opinion: "That the people of a city, which only one short week or so ago, was *in* the Confederacy, *of* the Confederacy, and identified *with* the Confederacy and its Government, should have the realizing sense of the course they ought to pursue, and of the duties devolving upon them . . . and so promptly act on them is creditable to them and gratifying." As residents of a recently conquered city, Mobilians had barely enough time, according to the Unionist *Daily News*, "to realize that they are released from the persecutions of their self-constituted Government, and under the protection of the legitimate government of the United States." When word of the death of Lincoln circulated via the military telegraph from across Mobile Bay and from New Orleans as well, all military departments of the occupying forces suspended business. "[A] general gloom seemed cast over the brave officers who have fought so long and well the battle of the Union," noted the *News*, "by the contemplation of the sad fact that the Chief Magistrate of the nation is no more."[8] These editorial comments, of course, came from the Federals who had taken over the newspaper and reflected the victors' position. Meanwhile the consul of the Netherlands flew the colors in front of his office at half-mast during the day to express condolence "with the people in their national loss." And all vessels in the port raised their flags at half-mast in the morning "as a mark of respect to the memory of the late President of the United States."[9]

Later in the day "the oldest and most prominent citizens of Mobile" filled the Odd Fellows Hall to denounce the murder of President Lincoln: "All differences of political opinion were, for the nonce, buried, and with one accord the people denounced in unmeasured terms the murderer—the dastardly assassin of the President of the United States." Mayor Slough introduced Judge Henry Chamberlain, himself a former mayor, who chaired the meeting. Twenty-four vice presidents and a committee of forty-eight helped draft resolutions. Not only did those assembled condemn the assassination of Lincoln, but they also drafted "a resolution of thanks to the army generally."[10]

Many Federal troops who remained in south Alabama after the Mobile Campaign did not hear the news of Lincoln's assassination until April 26. It enraged many of them toward Southerners, whom they felt had caused his death. Their expressions of shock and anger frightened Confederate soldiers and civilians, who feared Federal retribution against them or fiercer prosecution of the war. Southerners expressed their own regret about Lincoln's death to Federal troops. Charles Musser of the 29th Iowa noted that Confederate civilians and prisoners "are very tired of the war here and all are willing to submit to U.S. authorities." After the Mobile Campaign, Confederate enlisted men and officers captured at Blakely and Spanish Fort were imprisoned at Ship Island south of Biloxi, Mississippi. There they reported much harsher treatment from their guards, men of the 74th U. S. C. T., following receipt on the island of the news of Lincoln's assassination.[11]

Alabamians still in battlefield areas to the north, meanwhile, heard rumors that a rebel soldier had murdered the president, and they realized that Northerners might vent their wrath on them if they said or did the wrong thing. Samuel Pickens of the Greensboro Guards, 5th Alabama, Army of Northern Virginia, was awaiting his parole papers near Point Lookout, Maryland, on April 15 when he saw flags flown at half-mast to mark the death of Lincoln. He and his comrades "were all right uneasy too, lest the Yankees might retaliate on us—as it was said the assassin was thought to be a rebel soldier." As the flag continued to fly at half-mast and guns fired every half hour on April 17, the Greensboro Guard remarked that Lincoln "did not live to enjoy the success which it seems is crowning the efforts of the United States." Defeated Confederates also heard rumors of Yankees "in possession of Mobile, Montgomery & Selma" back in their home state. They soon learned details of James Wilson's raid in Selma and Montgomery.[12]

In Selma, once Union troops returned to occupy the town, leading citizens assembled at a peace meeting called by the mayor to convey thanks to the local commander, Brig. Gen. C. C. Andrews, for his troops' kind and considerate treatment of residents. They resolved "to discountenance and oppose all strife of whatsoever kind between any of our citizens and the United States troops quartered in our midst." Furthermore, they promised to abide by the treaty of peace that would eventually be agreed upon by authorities. Meanwhile, likely in response to the news of Lincoln's assassination, residents of Selma registered their disapproval and condemnation of "all bushwhacking and assassination and other modes of uncivilized warfare." The *Selma Federal Union*, a rare broadside newspaper printed on only one side by Federal troops, provided extensive coverage of residents' endeavors toward peace.[13] Contrary views had already appeared in the *Selma Rebel*, which was published by locals.[14]

Wilson's raiders captured Montgomery so swiftly that the main corps stayed in the first capital of the Confederacy only two days, April 12–13, 1865. Because Montgomery had no strategic value and little military value, it escaped destruction on the scale of Selma. Union forces destroyed the Montgomery arsenal and transportation facilities but generally respected private property. On April 12 Federals held a formal flag-raising at the capitol attended by Montgomery residents, including many blacks. When Union troops passing through Montgomery one week after its surrender heard about Lincoln's assassination, they did not waste the city as they might have done had they not already established good relations with the residents.[15]

News of the assassination reached residents of Montgomery later. Not until April 29, 1865, did the *Montgomery Daily Mail* confirm the fact following receipt of the *Atlanta Intelligencer* for April 25. This newspaper reflected the views of Unionists then in control of the first capital of the Confederacy. According to the *Daily Mail*: "A more appalling tragedy has not transpired in centuries . . . this sad event will cast a universal gloom over the nation, and North and South, this cowardly assassination will excite the most intense indignation." By early May, after further reflection, the editor of the *Daily Mail* observed that "the death of Mr. Lincoln is lamented by the Union men of the South quite as much as those of the North; and it is a calamity in which we of the South are far more deeply interested, even than our fellow-citizens of the Northern States of the Union."[16]

As the last Confederate forces east of the Mississippi surrendered at Citronelle in early May, Alabamians and Mobilians in particular were advised "to accept with becoming spirit, the present situation, and enter the contest in civil life to regain their former happiness and prosperity." The *Mobile Daily News* admonished the state's commercial metropolis, "The merchant should re-open his store, the artisan his shop, the mechanic his avocation, the agriculturist return to his fields and the laborer seek out for honest employment." As for the officers of the occupying forces, the *Mobile Daily News* maintained Alabamians might "safely confide to their forbearance and justice, to their wisdom and their magnanimity."[17]

Alabamians in smaller towns recorded little in newspapers about the assassination, most likely owing to disruptions in publication. Within a few weeks, however, they reported the incident more accurately than had the unverified accounts that circulated initially. For instance, the *Journal* of Clarke County reported matter-of-factly on May 25, 1865, that "President Lincoln was killed in Washington on the 14th of April. J. W. Booth, it is supposed, committed the deed. He was pursued and killed." The writer added that "an unsuccessful effort was made on the same day to take the life of Secretary Seward." After recounting the surrender of the armies of Robert E. Lee, Joseph Johnston, and Richard Taylor, as well as the Confederate fleet, the *Journal*'s editor contended, "The war having thus terminated, we think every citizen should yield to the present situation, and make the best of it.... Obey the laws, be orderly, conciliatory and quiet." The *Journal* added, "By this course everything is to be gained and nothing lost."[18] Confederate soldiers returning to the town of Grove Hill, where the *Journal* was published, were advised to adjust to their circumstances of peace.

In other rural areas in Alabama, farmers who longed for respite from the turmoil of Union raids prayed for peace but remained unsure of what to believe about reports of the death of Lincoln. During the last two weeks of April, for example, James Mallory, who lived near Talladega, commented, "we are kept in alarm every day [by] rumors of the movements of the enemy, all business is suspended, the future is dark, we rely too little on God, our only help." Destruction of the railroad to Selma brought distress in several counties due to shortages of basic supplies. "The Yankees are again in the county 2000 strong," Mallory complained, "all hands are running off to the hills, no forces to meet them." Union troops destroyed public property in Talladega, including cotton factories. "Lord, God Almighty give us peace," Mallory implored. After hearing rumors that Lee had surrendered to Ulysses S. Grant, he wrote, "May God give us peace in some form or another." Only on May 1, 1865, did Mallory receive credible reports of "Lincoln's death and the surrender of Lee's noble veterans with an armistice for the settlement of this war."[19] He said nothing further about Lincoln's demise. His war-weariness mirrored that of many other Alabamians, white and black.

Ex-slaves' reactions to Lincoln's assassination were linked to their own emancipation. They knew that white Southerners had detested Lincoln from the onset of his presidency because they feared that he would end slavery. Some even saw Confederate troops shoot at an effigy of Lincoln before they left for the battlefields. Years later former slaves carefully phrased their comments as they were interviewed by the Federal Writers' Project of the Works Progress Administration during the Great Depression. Several said they did not know anything about Lincoln; others admitted they knew he had set them free. "[T]he Lord had opened a good view to Mr. Lincoln, and he promoted a good idea," recalled Charlie Aarons, an ex-slave from Oak Grove. Former slave Hannah Jones recalled celebrating emancipation with other freedpeople in Greensboro and marching to Prairieville. In other places, such as Eufaula, where Federal troops marched through the town, former slave Gus

Askew was so young at war's end that he recalled that he and other children feared military band music even though the soldiers "had come to set us free."[20]

While some elderly ex-slaves were cautious in discussing Lincoln more than half a century after the end of the war, others reverently praised him. For black Alabamians, as one former slave recalled, "A'ter de Surrender nothin' neber was de same." They knew that Lincoln had set them free. For that, Mary Ella Grandberry of Sheffield observed, "Abe Lincoln was the best president this country ever had." Jim Gillard, who lived in Salem at the end of the war, said, "Mr. Abraham Lincoln died a warrior for this country." As Angie Garrett of Livingston observed, she had never seen Lincoln, but when people told her about him she "thought he was partly God." Mingo White in Burleson in Franklin County was not alone in noting that "Abe Lincoln was as noble [a] man as ever walked." Ties between emancipated slaves and Lincoln ran deep, as White reflected, "The chillun of Is'ael was in bondage one time an' God sent Moses to 'liver 'em. Well I 'spose dat God sent Abe Lincoln to 'liver us."[21]

Alabamians' reactions to Lincoln's death thus reflected their own diversity of opinions about him. Blacks remembered sincerely mourning the death of Lincoln, their Great Emancipator, while some whites celebrated, at least briefly. In the confusion of contradictory news accounts, stories also changed as confirmations were received or newspapers changed publishers. For instance, on April 19 the *Demopolis Herald* ran a story banner titled "GLORIOUS NEWS. Lincoln and Seward Assassinated! LEE DEFEATS GRANT. Andy Johnson Inaugurated President." The *Alabama Beacon* in Greensboro ran the story from Demopolis on April 21, 1865, "with the hope that it may prove true." On May 12, 1865, the *Beacon* ran a front-page story with some corrections obtained from the *Atlanta Intelligencer* of April 21, 1865, titled "DEATH OF LINCOLN. Great Tragedy in Washington."[22] The tone of the later account likely reflects the presence of Federal troops in Greensboro, who might have been able to obtain more accurate reports and mourned the loss of Lincoln. Residents of Greensboro became distressed when they eventually learned that Grant had defeated Lee and Seward had survived the attempt on his life.

Many white Alabamians, like many white Southerners, accepted the Union's victory because it brought peace. They expressed sorrow at Lincoln's assassination partly because they had learned he had a magnanimous spirit but also partly because many feared his successor. A Tennessee Unionist, Andrew Johnson had indicated his seriousness about punishing leading rebels in private and public statements. He even visited Lincoln on Good Friday, April 14, 1865, urging him against a policy of leniency for traitors.[23] One of those "traitors" in the eyes of Johnson was Alabama politician C. C. Clay Jr., former Confederate senator and Confederate agent to Canada, who participated in the evacuation of Richmond at the end of the war. When Clay realized that Lincoln had been murdered he exclaimed, "God help us!... [I]t is the worst blow that has yet been struck at the South!" When reports circulated that Lincoln had been assassinated, one young woman observed, "Some fools laughed and applauded, but wise people looked grave and held their peace.... It is a terrible blow to the South," she added, "for it places that vulgar renegade, Andy Johnson, in power, and will give the Yankees an excuse for charging us with a crime which was in reality only the deed of an irresponsible madman. Our papers ought to reprobate it universally."[24] Newspapers did indeed deplore the assassination of Lincoln, although their reasons for doing so remain murky.

Alabamians were faced with an almost overwhelming number of events in April 1865, including Wilson's and Croxton's raids, the Battle of Blakely on Mobile's eastern shore, and the surrender of Mobile. News of Lincoln's assassination reached people at various times and places, and in various states of veracity. Residents' reactions depended on their affiliation (Confederate or Unionist) and race (white or black). The assassination of the wartime president who was directing early Reconstruction in a generous and magnanimous way created anxiety and confusion for all Southerners. As we study Americans' perceptions and historical memory of the Civil War, we should reconsider the enduring sectional and racial division among Alabamians by examining their recorded reactions to Lincoln's assassination.[25] Alabama's lingering evolution of interpretation about the glory of the Lost Cause began with its initial reaction to the death of the U.S. president who directed the Union victory over the Confederacy.

Notes

1. Harriet E. Amos, *Cotton City: Urban Development in Antebellum Mobile* (Tuscaloosa: University of Alabama Press, 1985), 235; Sarah R. Espy Diary, August 11, 1860, quoted in William L. Barney, *The Secessionist Impulse: Alabama and Mississippi in 1860* (Princeton: Princeton University Press, 1974), 167.

2. William Warren Rogers Jr., "Safety Lies Only in Silence: Secrecy and Subversion in Montgomery's Unionist Community," in *Enemies of the Country: New Perspectives on Unionists in the Civil War South*, ed. John C. Inscoe and Robert C. Kenzer (Athens: University of Georgia Press, 2001), 173; Amos, *Cotton City*, 238; Ray Mathis, *John Horry Dent: South Carolina Aristocrat on the Alabama Frontier* (University: University of Alabama Press for the Historic Chattahoochee Commission, 1979), 195; Margaret J. Gillis Diary, quoted in Barney, *Secessionist Impulse*, 191; William Howard Russell quoted in *Mobile, 1861–1865: Notes and a Bibliography*, ed. Sydney Adair Smith and Carter Smith Jr. (Chicago: Wyvern Press, 1964), 3.

3. Nathaniel Cheairs Hughes Jr. and Thomas Clayton Ware, *Theodore O'Hara: Poet-Soldier of the Old South* (Knoxville: University of Tennessee Press, 1998), 105; Augusta Evans to J. L. M. Curry, January 27, 1864, quoted in Augusta Jane Evans, *A Southern Woman of Letters: The Correspondence of Augusta Jane Evans Wilson*, ed. Rebecca Grant Sexton (Columbia: University of South Carolina Press, 2002), 92.

4. G. Ward Hubbs, *Guarding Greensboro: A Confederate Company in the Making of a South-*

ern Community (Athens: University of Georgia Press, 2003), 203–4; Rogers, "Safety Lies Only in Silence," 184.

5. Robert Dunnavant Jr., *Decatur, Alabama: Yankee Foothold in Dixie, 1861–1865* (Athens, AL: Pea Ridge Press, 1995), 144.

6. Nancy M. Rohr, ed., *Incidents of the War: The Civil War Journal of Mary Jane Chadick* (Huntsville, AL: Silver Threads Publishing, 2005), 287–89. Quotations come from Chadick's diary entries for April 15 and 17, 1865. John W. Horner of the 18th Michigan served as provost marshal in Huntsville; see John Robertson, comp., *Michigan in the War*, rev. ed. (Lansing, MI: W. S. George, 1882), 385–86.

7. Rohr, *Incidents of the War*, 289–90. Diary entry comes from April 18, 1865.

8. *Mobile Daily News*, April 20, 1865.

9. Ibid.

10. Ibid. On Chamberlain, see Willis Brewer, *Alabama: Her History, Resources, War Record and Public Men from 1540 to 1872* (Montgomery: Barrett & Brown, 1872), 346.

11. Charles Musser, quoted in Sean Michael O'Brien, *Mobile, 1865: Last Stand of the Confederacy* (Westport, CT: Praeger, 2001), 216, 228.

12. G. Ward Hubbs, ed., *Voices from Company D: Diaries by the Greensboro Guards, Fifth Alabama Infantry Regiment, Army of Northern Virginia* (Athens: University of Georgia Press, 2003), 372–75. Quotations come from Samuel Pickens diary entries for April 15, 17, 19, 22, 1865.

13. *Selma Federal Union*, May 3, 1865.

14. *Selma Rebel*, April 19, 1865, cited as news source by *Montgomery Daily Mail*, April 24, 1865. The account of Lincoln's death was called "highly romantic and sensational" with "an air of plausibility." The *Mail* expressed hope the story was "a pure fabrication."

15. James Pickett Jones, *Yankee Blitzkrieg: Wilson's Raid through Alabama and Georgia* (Athens: University of Georgia Press, 1976; rpt., 1987), 114–16, 168.

16. *Montgomery Daily Mail*, April 29, May 2, 8, 1865.

17. *Mobile Daily News*, n.d., reprinted in the (Clarke County) *Journal*, May 25, 1865.

18. The (Clarke County) *Journal*, May 25, 1865.

19. Grady McWhiney, Warner O. Moore Jr., and Robert F. Pace, eds., *"Fear God and Walk Humbly": The Agricultural Journal of James Mallory, 1843–1877* (Tuscaloosa: University of Alabama Press, 1997), 348.

20. George P. Rawick, ed., *The American Slave: A Composite Autobiography*, vol. 6, *Alabama and Indiana Narratives* (Westport, CT: Greenwood, 1972), 56, 272, 296, 71, 5 (Aarons quotation), 239–40, 15 (Askew quotation). On the candor of the ex-slaves, especially in response to questions from white interviewers, see Paul D. Escott, *Slavery Remembered: A Record of Twentieth-Century Slave Narratives* (Chapel Hill: University of North Carolina Press, 1979), 6–9.

21. Rawick, *The American Slave*, 163 (Grandberry), 156 (Gillard), 136 (Garrett), 421–22 (White).

22. (Greensboro) *Alabama Beacon*, April 21, May 12, 1865.

23. Rohr, *Incidents of the War*, 287–89; Hans L. Trefousse, *Andrew Johnson: A Biography* (New York: W. W. Norton, 1989), 192.

24. Quoted in Virginia Clay-Clopton, *A Belle of the Fifties: Memoirs of Mrs. Clay of Alabama*, with introduction, annotations, and index to the annotations by Leah Rawls Atkins, Joseph H. Harrison Jr., and Sarah A. Hudson (Tuscaloosa: University of Alabama Press, 1999), 245; Eliza Frances Andrews Papers, typescript of her diary, April 21, 1865, p. 221, Alabama Department of Archives and History, Montgomery, Alabama. Her diary was published under the title *The War-Time Journal of a Georgia Girl, 1864–1865* (1908). The typescript cited here was a galley of the

forthcoming book about which she was corresponding with her publisher from her retirement home on Mildred Street in Montgomery. The quotation from the typescript entry for April 21, 1865, may be found in the published edition on pp. 172–73.

25. See David W. Blight, *Race and Reunion: The Civil War in American Memory* (Cambridge, MA: Belknap Press of Harvard University Press, 2001) and Gaines M. Foster, *Ghosts of the Confederacy: Defeat, the Lost Cause, and the Emergence of the New South, 1865 to 1913* (New York: Oxford University Press, 1987), especially 193–98. Over the course of the war following Lincoln's Emancipation Proclamation, the status of enslaved Alabamians changed to free. Ex-slaves' participation in local ceremonies to honor a slain president often depended on whether their place of residence was then occupied by Federal troops who would protect them in any public notice. The fact that records do not indicate any major observances should not surprise us as the state was in the throes of facing defeat in the war and beginning Reconstruction.

10
Alabama's Reconstruction after 150 Years

Sarah Woolfolk Wiggins

Alabamians, like other Americans, love to celebrate anniversaries, especially those related to the history of our nation. In 1986 it was the centennial of the Statue of Liberty; in 1976 it was the bicentennial of the Declaration of Independence; and in 1961 it was the most elaborate one of all: a four-year-long celebration of the centennial of the Civil War (a celebration that really never ends if one includes the perpetual reenactments of Civil War battles). The number and frequency of these celebrations provoked an outburst in the *New Yorker* in 2009: "Every time you turn around, or, more accurately, turn to face the TV, a big anniversary of some historical or cultural event is being celebrated. Were there always this many anniversaries?"[1]

The answer is, yes, especially regarding the Civil War, because fascination with the war has no end. It is a time our nation cannot forget, as evidenced by the appeal of television productions such as *The Blue and the Gray*, *North and South*, and Ken Burns's Civil War series; of movies such as *Glory* and *Cold Mountain* and the timeless popularity of *Gone with the Wind*; of the plethora of large books analyzing various single Civil War battles; of scholarly conferences that rehash the battles and the politics of the war. (Nobody holds a conference to analyze Reconstruction.) There are two national history journals devoted to the Civil War era, an association of professional historians of the Civil War, and concerts featuring Civil War music, such as that performed by the 5th Alabama Regimental Band with members performing in reproduction Confederate uniforms. No such fascination exists for Reconstruction, and it is now being recognized as part of a sesquicentennial celebration only because this period is also the sesquicentennial of the Civil War.

Reconstruction history has always lived in the shadow of the history of the Civil War, and it has suffered bad press since 1865. While the Civil War is cherished with nostalgia as colorful, romantic, exciting, and glamorous, Reconstruction is branded as a shameful time of defeat, despair, poverty, and upheaval caused by Republicans, who destroyed institutions that had existed for generations. Much of this contempt stems from the conviction that Alabama and the South were treated unfairly during Reconstruction, that ruthless Yankee swindlers preyed upon Southern economic misfortune, that illiterate freed slaves dominated the white population, that the region awoke from its broken dreams of independence to find itself occupied by a Yankee oppressor in the form of a conquering army—an experience that remains unique in American history and for many Southerners remains unforgivable.[2] It is understandable that with their physical world in ruins around them and their regional psyche bleeding, Southerners prefer to talk about and to take pride in a prosperous and glorious past. Whatever went wrong during Reconstruction is blamed on the Yankee Republican Party. Although it is fashionable in the twenty-first century in Alabama to be a Republican, these same Republicans blanch at the idea of acknowledging that one of their ancestors was a Republican during Reconstruction.

Since the surrender of the Confederacy, Southerners have attempted to rationalize secession by insisting that the South fought to protect states' rights (one of which was the right to own slaves), to explain Confederate defeat, and to denounce Reconstruction as evil. This effort has created an enduring legend, the myth of the Lost Cause, the myth of the glorious South crushed under the heel of Yankee Reconstruction. The actual outcome of the war cannot be changed, but catastrophic events can be reinterpreted to ease the pain of defeat. Reconstruction is a period where North and South have greatly misunderstood each other. Northerners have never understood that Southerners were sorry about having lost the war but were not sorry about having started it. Southerners, on the other hand, have refused to acknowledge what they do not wish to see: that the South *lost* a civil war that had grown increasingly unpopular with Confederates.[3]

The image of Reconstruction with which many Alabamians are most comfortable is that presented in Walter Lynwood Fleming's *Civil War and Reconstruction in Alabama*, published in 1905.[4] Fleming's work was the first scholarly study of Alabama's Reconstruction based on the manuscripts, newspapers, and government documents available at that time. In the century that has passed since Fleming's work, tons of new sources of information have become available. Equally important is the fact that racial attitudes have changed dramatically, affecting the context through which we read sources to understand and interpret events. Fleming's book is satisfying to those who want a text with which to blame an outside force, a Yankee oppressor, for what they believe was a period of unmitigated evil. Fleming grouped his chapters on congressional Reconstruction as "Carpet-bag and Negro Rule" and labeled Republicans a "motley crew—white, yellow, and black." Native whites (scalawags) were men "utterly unknown" to their contemporaries, and carpetbaggers were men who favored social equality but "thought it more important that spoils be procured first."[5] This book created stereotypes that have remained indelibly embedded in many Southern minds, and it has been recommended as "an authoritative report of the Carpetbag Rule which was backed up for 12 years by Yankee troops occupying the South" (never mind that Reconstruction in Alabama lasted only from 1865 into 1874). Scholars whose work revises that of Fleming have been dismissed as "radical faculty members" who are being "politically correct," and they are accused of "political endoctrination" of students. Attacks on revisionist scholarship claim that such research is an "unfounded attempt at thought control and denial of the harsh truth about the actions of enemies of the South during Reconstruction."[6] This fixation with Fleming's image of Reconstruction ignores the flood of exciting research that has been published in the last sixty years that revises Fleming's stereotypes.[7] It is difficult to imagine any subject other than Reconstruction about which intelligent people accept a view popular one hundred years ago and absolutely refuse to consider the facts that more recent scholarship has proven.

The aftermath of recent civil wars in Southeast Asia, the Balkans, and Central Asia differ significantly from the course of Reconstruction in the American South. As the communists prevailed in Cambodia in 1975, a bloodbath began. The first victims were former government officials and former officers of the Cambodian army down to the rank of second lieutenant, as well as their wives. At a crowded hospital in Phnom Penh, a doctor was forced at gunpoint to halt an operation on a patient. At another hospital, "amputees were forced into the streets on their crutches, and patients who could not walk were wheeled out in their beds." Two million people were "force-marched into the countryside" from the city, a "reversion to the agrarian society" of a previous century.[8]

Equally grim was the situation in 1992 in Bosnia-Herzegovina. In the Bosnian war both sides practiced "ethnic cleansing"—depopulation and repopulation—in regions where each possessed a majority. Newspapers reported that Serb fighters forced an estimated thirty thousand Muslims from their homes in Banja Luka, the second largest city in Bosnia, because of their ethnic background. Some were "packed in sealed freight cars" that "had no toilets—only holes in the floors" for "sweltering journeys [that] sometimes lasted four days." In areas where Muslims and Croats predominated, Serbs were victims of the same ethnic cleansing by deportation. Both sides accused their opponents of atrocities "since the start of the bloodshed, which began after Muslims and Croats voted . . . to secede from Yugoslavia."[9]

In southern Kyrgyzstan nearly four hundred thousand ethnic Uzbeks fled their homes to escape ethnic violence, and entire Uzbek neighborhoods were "reduced to scorched ruins by rampaging mobs of ethnic Kyrgyz." Refugees crowded into "gray canvas tents on a patch of arid scrub." Uzbeks interviewed by journalists accused Kyrgyz men of assaulting Uzbek women and girls and claimed that Uzbeks had been virtually "purged from some parts of the south." The UN estimated that as many as one million people needed aid owing to shortages of food and water.[10]

Considered against the background of the aftermath of civil wars in Cambodia, Bosnia, and Kyrgyzstan, the clemency of the U.S. government after the American

Civil War is noteworthy. Southerners have chosen to ignore the fact that there was no forced mass eviction of the Southern white population from their homeland, as had befallen the Creeks, Choctaws, and Chickasaws thirty years earlier. Only one war crimes trial was held, resulting in political execution; only one other high-ranking civil or military leader, Jefferson Davis, was arrested, endured a lengthy imprisonment without a trial, and was released while still under indictment for treason. The property of defeated Southerners was not confiscated and redistributed to Northern adventurers or to freed slaves, notwithstanding the talk of "40 acres and a mule," though today Southerners complain that the dramatic increase in property taxes during Reconstruction represented a form of confiscation of property. Although few battles occurred on Alabama's soil, war destroyed the state's thriving prewar economy. Devastation of the countryside was particularly acute in north Alabama counties caught alternately between invading and retreating Confederate and Federal armies. The exhausting disruptions and deprivations of wartime brought agricultural life to a standstill and left both whites and blacks destitute. By 1865, given the effects of a war fought in the South's own backyard and the evaporation of the real property (otherwise known as slaves, valued in 1860 at $200,000,000) on which antebellum taxes largely had relied, what else was left to tax but land?

If the course of events in the aftermath of civil wars in Asia and the Balkans seem too farfetched to have been possible in the postwar American South, consider one proposal sent to Congressman Thaddeus Stevens: "If I had my way, no man that ever took the oath to support the Rebel government that had any position in the Army as high as Captain ever should hold any office—I would likewise let no man hold property over two or three thousand dollars that aided or abetted in the Rebellion—I go for *confiscation*.... for Gods sake give the Rebels no quarter."[11]

If what was *not* done influences our understanding of Reconstruction, what *was* done also needs to be placed in some perspective. Corruption in Alabama's politics was ghastly but not unique to the state during Reconstruction, a period that saw a national decline in public and private morals. Alabama's corruption during Reconstruction pales next to the flamboyant greed of New York's Tammany Hall Democrats or the rapacious avarice of Republican president Ulysses S. Grant's appointees in Washington or the New Orleans customhouse. Alabama's Democrats were no more honest than its Republicans and no more reluctant to use a well-placed bribe to ensure passage of legislation that was financially beneficial to their friends. Alabama's Republicans freely dispensed bribes to obtain state subsidies to support construction of the Republican-financed Alabama Chattanooga Railroad, whose backers were primarily Northerners. When Democrats controlled the executive and legislative branches of the state government from 1870 through 1872, they also freely distributed bribes to obtain state subsidies, this time to support the construction of the Democratic-financed South and North Railroad (later part of the Louisville and Nashville Railroad).[12] One traveler in Alabama in the 1870s observed that the Democratic governor was "little, if at all, more economical than either his Republican predecessor or successor."[13] The conduct of our contemporary governors and legislators reminds us that the Reconstruction era possessed no corner on imaginative corruption or creative bookkeeping. Many critics of Reconstruction consider corruption to be a disease of Alabama's Republicans when in fact it was a national and bipartisan epidemic after the Civil War, not a local disgrace.

The Reconstruction era saw an enormous state debt rapidly accelerate upward, a debt that appears especially large when compared to state debt in 1860 and 1880. Much of Alabama's prewar tax structure had rested on slaves as property, supplemented with only a small land tax and poll tax to fund the few public services offered. Most of the state money that was spent on public education came from income from the sixteenth section of each township. Although prewar Alabama did have a public school system, the small elementary schools offered only the most rudimentary education to white males, and education for slaves was outlawed. After the war, blacks pressed for education, and in 1868 the state created a new public school system, segregated by race and inadequately funded. When Democrats overthrew the Republicans in 1874, the state hovered near bankruptcy; one of the Democrats' primary goals was debt reduction. They accomplished this goal by 1880, primarily by strangling public education.[14]

The second of the programs that incurred mounting state debt during Reconstruction was federal subsidies to encourage the construction of railroads in Alabama. Railroad expansion and industrial development exploded across the nation in the decade after the Civil War, as speculation in railroad construction was viewed as the era's favorite get-rich-quick scheme of the men who became known as the robber barons. Scandal after scandal occurred on the national scene as millions were made and lost in railroad construction. Alabama's prewar transportation system had been a limited one, and now both political parties promoted stimulation of their favorite railroad through the sale of state-backed bonds. Reckless bookkeeping reduced the state to disagreement about what the amount of the state debt actually *was* by 1874; the Democrats repudiated all of it. Neither the Democratic Party nor the Republican Party can be considered without sin as far as responsibility for the accumulation of the debt and the mishandling of state funds.[15] However, the willingness of both political parties to indebt themselves and future generations for what they considered essential projects foreshadowed the priorities of twenty-first-century Alabamians on behalf of public education and highway construction.

Critics of Reconstruction in Alabama see the Republican Party of that era as composed of Yankee adventurers (carpetbaggers), ex-slaves, and prewar free blacks. These three groups did dominate the politics of such states as South Carolina and

Louisiana, but although Alabamians are reluctant to admit it, native white Republicans (scalawags) actually dominated Republican politics in this state. Scalawags included Unionists who had been opposed to secession in 1861, ex-Confederates, Northerners who had resided in Alabama before 1861, and ex-Democrats. The popular image of Republican leaders is that scalawags were so unprepared for leadership that they stood no chance of holding office or of influencing the course of Reconstruction. The facts do not substantiate such a view. Scalawags held most statewide executive and judicial offices to which Republicans were elected and more than one-third of available legislative positions. Both Republican governors during Reconstruction were scalawags. However, carpetbaggers won most available federal positions.[16]

Alabamian scalawags were not all poor, ignorant, small farmers with no political experience who resided in Alabama's white counties. Most scalawag voters did live in the state's northern white counties where, as loyal Unionists, they were constantly assaulted by Confederates. However, scalawag leadership came from black counties as well as white. Many native white Republican leaders were college educated or had read law, and many were members of prominent Alabamian families or were longtime residents of the state. Many were men of wealth. Most important was their extensive political, judicial, and legislative experience; they often had active public careers in a variety of elected and appointed offices. Most of the scalawag leaders in Alabama had supported Douglas or Bell in 1860 and opposed secession in 1861.[17] One scalawag who had left the Democrats to join the Republicans observed with remarkable frankness that having voted against the Republican Party "as long as it was worth while," it was better to come to terms with them, work with them, and acquire their confidence.[18] In plain language: "if you can't beat them, join them." These were men who understood that Alabama had lost a civil war; they accepted Reconstruction and tried to control it. Perhaps they were opportunists with an eye on their own political futures, but they were also pragmatic political realists and paid a dear price in social ostracism thereafter.[19]

Carpetbaggers were Northerners who came to Alabama for political, ideological, or economic reasons and used politics to advance their cause. All types of Northerners appeared in Alabama early in Reconstruction; most had been in the Union army. The plunderers took advantage of the economic opportunities that were available as the South attempted to rebuild after four years of war. Political and judicial offices offered a way for them to enrich themselves, and they had no scruples about using bribery and fraud or about manipulating the black vote to secure positions from which they could advance their financial aims. After a few years in Alabama, many returned north or moved on to seek fresh economic opportunities.[20] Such flamboyant individuals provide the basis for the unflattering stereotype of the carpetbagger.

However, not all Northerners who came to Alabama after the war were plunderers or scoundrels. Those who entered economic life and eschewed politics did not draw the enmity of native Southerners. Many genuinely sought economic opportunities and quickly found these in the state's undeveloped mineral resources, while some engaged in cotton planting. One Ohioan observed that his partner who had been alone on an Alabamian plantation for months had received "only the kindest treatment and the *heartiest encouragement*" from neighbors. He added that a "Northern man, who is not a natural fool, or foolish fanatic, may live pleasantly any where in Alabama, without abating one jot of his self-respect, or independence."[21] A Selma newspaper advised prospective immigrants to be industrious and mind their own business, "letting politics and tangle foot whiskey alone."[22] Many carpetbaggers became permanent residents of Alabama and married into old families whose eligible daughters outnumbered the available Confederate survivors.[23] Still other Northerners came to Alabama with lofty ideals of educating the freedmen and improving their lives in other ways. The ideologist rather than the rogue constituted the greater long-term threat to the Southern social structure. Nevertheless, the stereotype of the scandalous carpetbagger persists, as carpetbaggers have generally had their history written by their enemies.

Reconstruction-era black Republicans have often been dismissed as ignorant ex-slaves easily manipulated by white Republicans. That image is inaccurate. African Americans among the Republican leaders included men who had been free blacks before 1861 as well as those who had been slaves. Many of those who had been free before the war were educated men and successful artisans, tradesmen, or businessmen. The ex-slaves included a remarkable number of men who had learned to read and write despite laws that forbade such instruction. Others acquired a rudimentary education immediately after the war ended. Many had been skilled craftsmen and artisans before the war, while others ran bars or livery stables, and designed buildings including the Alabama capitol in Montgomery. Many became property owners. Although white Republicans were stingy in nominating blacks to state office, many African Americans nonetheless served in the state legislature. Despite their lack of political experience before Reconstruction, black Republican leaders quickly mastered the Byzantine mechanics of political maneuvering and pushed for civil rights legislation, although without success. Unfortunately, economic dependence on white landowners and Ku Klux Klan violence and intimidation prevented African Americans from freely voting in state elections. Nevertheless, the perception that black Republicans were compliant tools of the white members of their party is false.[24]

The three elements of the Republican Party quarreled incessantly over the spoils of office, especially the scalawags and carpetbaggers, who begrudged any office that the other group gained. Factionalism consumed much of the party's attention and energy. One scalawag loudly complained that carpetbaggers had "landed everything that is Republican in Hell. . . . Political offices, the University, Schools, all carpet-bagged."[25] Meanwhile, a carpetbagger U.S. senator, George Spencer, schemed to manipulate the 1870 state elections to defeat his own party's candidates and control federal patronage for the next two years. Then, when he faced reelection in 1872, the legislature reelected him to the U.S. Senate. These incredible maneuvers to sacrifice fellow Republicans to ensure personal victory actually succeeded, and the Democrats won not only the legislature but also the office of governor in 1870.[26] These bitter divisions within the party never healed, and such jealous factionalism undermined the party's success in future elections.

On the race issue, white Republicans hedged. Scalawags, like Democrats, were convinced of the inferiority of blacks, and carpetbaggers and scalawags dragged their feet whenever the issue of extension of civil rights to blacks arose. They solicited black votes but only reluctantly nominated African Americans for office and then only for the less choice positions. Such half-a-loaf gestures satisfied no one. The fatal weakness of the Alabama Republicans was their inability to create a united biracial political party. In 1874, Democrats pounced on white Republican discomfort at sharing the party and offices with African Americans and successfully used the race issue to frighten whites away from the Republican Party.[27] Playing the race card has been a popular ploy of Alabama's politicians ever since. It is important not to judge Reconstruction Republicans by our standards—what is termed "presentism"—but instead to see them in the context of their own time, not ours.[28] If Republicans were not color-blind, they were more enlightened than most Southern whites during Presidential Reconstruction.

Democrats won state elections in a landslide in 1874 and ended Reconstruction in Alabama not only because of their use of the race issue. Whites also flocked to the Democratic Party in their fury at finding themselves now paying taxes on their land. When prewar taxes lay heavily on slaves, few small white farmers shouldered much tax burden.[29] Between the issues of race and taxes, the Democrats possessed two fail-safe inflammatory issues with which to attract white voters in 1874.

Alabama's Reconstruction governments broke with the past traditions—were radical—only in their relaxation of suffrage requirements. The 1868 Alabama constitution enfranchised black males over twenty-one, while disenfranchising many white males.[30] However, the following year the Republican legislature, not a Democratic one, began a gradual relaxation of this proscription of whites so that by 1870 most adult males could vote in Alabama, whether ex-Confederates or former slaves. The result was a Democratic victory in state elections in 1870. Most critics of Reconstruction ignore the fact that for two years in the middle of Reconstruction, Democrats, not Republicans, controlled state executive offices and the legislature in Alabama.[31] It is important to remember that illiterate former slaves differed little from the illiterate frontiersmen enfranchised in the late 1820s or the immigrants unable to communicate in English who were enfranchised in the late nineteenth century. What was more significant than the literacy level of Alabamian voters was that the economic dependence of blacks on white landowners undermined their political independence.

This black dependence on whites for a livelihood, especially in rural areas, permitted employers to manipulate the black vote, and Alabama's Democrats made no effort to disenfranchise blacks after overthrowing the Republicans in 1874. What Democrats did immediately do was gerrymander legislative and congressional districts to ensure the election of Democrats and to alter bond requirements to limit opportunities for blacks to hold office. Alabama's politicians still gerrymander congressional districts to ensure the election of certain groups. Not until blacks demonstrated alarming signs of political independence with the emergence of the Populists in the 1890s did Democrats move to disenfranchise blacks. As long as Alabama's Democrats could control black voters, Democrats had no objection to black suffrage; it was officeholding that Democrats, like Reconstruction Republicans, were unwilling to share.[32]

Although Reconstruction is a subject that Alabamians prefer to ignore, the events of that period have had consequences that are still felt today. In the antebellum period, neither the national government nor the state government provided relief after a natural disaster struck; neighbors did. The Civil War so reduced the male population of the South that neighbors could no longer be depended upon for help in the event of a disaster. The Civil War was the biggest disaster to hit the South. Wartime devastation left Alabamian whites and blacks hungry, homeless, without income or medical care, and in desperate need.[33] What they needed was a Marshall Plan; what they got was the Freedmen's Bureau.

Created in 1865 to aid freedmen and white and black refugees, the Freedmen's Bureau became the most significant agency in the social and economic life of post–Civil War South. Immediately after the war, the bureau organized a massive relief program of food and fuel for freedmen and whites left destitute by the war and by crop failures. Gradually the bureau expanded its role, as additional needs demanded a response of assistance. It found employment for former slaves, supervised labor contracts, established schools, created home colonies where sick, disabled, indigent, or aged freedmen received care (including medical attention), organized courts to protect the civil rights of blacks, established hospitals and dispensaries, and created banks. After Reconstruction, Alabama's impoverished state government had no resources to continue what the bureau had begun. But the germ of the idea had been planted that government should assume responsibilities in the areas of social and economic welfare, areas that pre–Civil War Americans could not have conceived to be the purview of government.[34] Over the course of decades these services gradually grew; today they are considered entitlements in the minds of Alabamians and other Americans. It is from these new assumptions that the numerous, enormous, and expensive federal social and economic programs of the twentieth century originated: disaster relief, labor regulation, old-age pensions, health care, education, transportation, business regulation, and race relations, to name a few. The legacy of Reconstruction is too massive and too enduring to be termed a "splendid failure."[35]

Reconstruction should be understood as a continuation of the Civil War argument about the nature of the Union and the meaning of self-government. It is best understood as a long-term process that began with the outbreak of the Civil War in 1861 and extended beyond 1874 to the movement to disenfranchise blacks in Alabama in 1901. It was an era remarkably like our own, one that saw collisions between state and federal authority, terrifying uncertainty about the economic future, conflicts in restructuring race relations, and frantic efforts to stretch shrinking tax revenues to cover expanding and expensive public services. Although the past does not offer solutions for our present ills, it can provide perspective with which to approach our problems. History is not "comfort food for an anxious present," but it does offer "a way of coming to terms with an anxious present and an unpredictable future."[36] The Reconstruction years remind us that today's issues transcend our own time. Reconstruction may not merit a sesquicentennial celebration of its own, but Alabama in the twenty-first century probably can learn more from the state's struggles during this period than from any other in our state's history.

Notes

1. *New Yorker*, August 10, 17, 2009.

2. For a perceptive commentary on the postwar attitudes of white Southerners, see Anne Sarah Rubin, *A Shattered Nation: The Rise and Fall of the Confederacy, 1861–1868* (Chapel Hill: University of North Carolina Press, 2005).

3. For a discussion of the impact of the war on the Southern psyche, see Gaines M. Foster, *Ghosts of the Confederacy: Defeat, the Lost Cause, and the Emergence of the New South, 1865 to 1913* (New York: Oxford University Press, 1987).

4. Walter Lynwood Fleming, *Civil War and Reconstruction in Alabama* (New York: Columbia University Press, 1905).

5. Ibid., 569, 517, 518, 524.

6. *Alabama Confederate*, January 1992.

7. In the mid-twentieth century, revisionist scholars began studying Reconstruction and correcting earlier stereotypes. Two essays stimulated this scholarship: David Donald, "The Scalawag in Mississippi Reconstruction," *Journal of Southern History* 10 (November 1944): 447–60 and Richard N. Current, "Carpetbaggers Reconsidered," in *A Festschrift for Frederick B. Artz*, ed. David H. Pinkney and Theodore Ropp (Durham: Duke University Press, 1964), 139–57 (a revision of a paper read the Mississippi Valley Historical Association meeting, December 28, 1959). Significant examples of revisionist surveys of Reconstruction are John Hope Franklin, *Reconstruction: After the Civil War* (Chicago: University of Chicago Press, 1961); Kenneth M. Stampp, *The*

Era of Reconstruction, 1865–1877 (New York: Alfred A. Knopf, 1965); and Eric Foner, *Reconstruction: America's Unfinished Revolution, 1863–1877* (New York: Harper and Row, 1988). For surveys of recent scholarship of the Reconstruction era across the South, see Michael W. Fitzgerald, "Reconstruction Politics and the Politics of Reconstruction," in *Reconstructions: New Perspectives on the Postbellum United States*, ed. Thomas J. Brown (New York: Oxford University Press, 2006), 91–116 and Fitzgerald, "Political Reconstruction, 1865–1877," in *A Companion to the American South*, ed. John B. Boles (Malden, MA: Blackwell, 2002), 284–302.

8. *Newsweek*, May 12, 19, 1975.

9. *Tuscaloosa News*, July 27, 1992.

10. Ibid., June 18, 19, 2010.

11. Henry V. McVay to Thaddeus Stevens, March 1, 1867, Thaddeus Stevens Papers, Division of Manuscripts, Library of Congress, Washington, DC.

12. Mark W[ahlgren] Summers, *Railroads, Reconstruction, and the Gospel of Prosperity: Aid under the Radical Republicans, 1865–1877* (Princeton: Princeton University Press, 1984), 213–36; Summers, *The Era of Good Stealings* (New York: Oxford University Press, 1993), 154–55.

13. Charles Nordhoff, *The Cotton States in the Spring and Summer of 1875* (New York: D. Appleton, 1876), 89.

14. J. Mills Thornton III, "Fiscal Policy and the Failure of Radical Reconstruction in the Lower South," in *Region, Race, and Reconstruction: Essays in Honor of C. Vann Woodward*, ed. J. Morgan Kousser and James M. McPherson (New York: Oxford University Press, 1982), 349–94; Summers, *Railroads*, 213–36; Peter Kolchin, *First Freedom: The Responses of Alabama's Blacks to Emancipation and Reconstruction* (Westport, CT: Greenwood, 1972); Robert G. Sherer, *Subordination or Liberation? The Development and Conflicting Theories of Black Education in Nineteenth Century Alabama* (University: University of Alabama Press, 1977); Horace Mann Bond, *Negro Education in Alabama: A Study in Cotton Steel* (Washington, DC: Associated Publishers, 1939); Bond, "Social and Economic Forces in Alabama Reconstruction," *Journal of Negro History* 23 (July 1938): 290–348.

15. Summers, *Railroads*, 213–36; Michael W. Fitzgerald, "Railroad Subsidies and Black Aspirations: The Politics of Economic Development in Mobile, 1865–1879," *Civil War History* 39 (September 1993): 240–56; Fitzgerald, *The Union League Movement in the Deep South: Politics and Agricultural Change during Reconstruction* (Baton Rouge: Louisiana State University Press, 1989), 98; Ethel Armes, *The Story of Coal and Iron in Alabama* (1910; reprint, Birmingham: Beechwood Books, 1987), 195–265; Louis M. Kyriakoudes, "The Rise of Merchants and Market Towns in Reconstruction-Era Alabama," *Alabama Review* 49 (April 1996): 83–107.

16. Sarah Woolfolk Wiggins, *The Scalawag in Alabama Politics, 1865–1881* (University: University of Alabama Press, 1977); Wiggins, "What Is a Scalawag?" *Alabama Review* 25 (January 1972): 56–61; Sarah Van V. Woolfolk, "Five Men Called Scalawags," *Alabama Review* 17 (January 1964): 45–55; Margaret M. Storey, *Loyalty and Loss: Alabama's Unionists in the Civil War and Reconstruction* (Baton Rouge: Louisiana State University Press, 2004); Storey, "Civil War Unionists and the Political Culture of Loyalty in Alabama, 1860–1861," *Journal of Southern History* 69 (February 2003): 71–106; Storey, "The Crucible of Reconstruction: Unionists and the Struggle for Alabama's Postwar Home Front," in *The Great Task Remaining before Us: Reconstruction as America's Continuing Civil War*, ed. Paul A. Cimbala and Randall M. Miller (New York: Fordham University Press, 2010), 69–87; William Warren Rogers Jr., *Black Belt Scalawag: Charles Hays and the Southern Republicans in the Era of Reconstruction* (Athens: University of Georgia Press, 1993); Paul Horton, "Lightning Rod Scalawag: The Unlikely Political Career of Thomas Minott Peters," *Alabama Review* 64 (April 2011): 116–42; Harriet E. Amos, "Trials of a Unionist: Gustavus Horton,

Military Mayor of Mobile during Reconstruction," *Gulf South Historical Review* 4 (Spring 1989): 134–51; James Alex Baggett, *The Scalawags: Southern Dissenters in the Civil War and Reconstruction* (Baton Rouge: Louisiana State University Press, 2003); Robert Arthur Gilmour, "The Other Emancipation: Studies in the Society and Economy of Alabama Whites during Reconstruction" (PhD diss., Johns Hopkins University, 1972); Michael W. Fitzgerald, "Radical Republicanism and the White Yeomanry during Alabama Reconstruction, 1865–1868," *Journal of Southern History* 54 (November 1988): 565–96; Allen W. Trelease, "Who Were the Scalawags?" *Journal of Southern History* 19 (November 1963): 445–68; William McKinley Cash, "Alabama Republicans during Reconstruction: Personal Characteristics, Motivations, and Political Activity of Party Activists, 1867–1880" (PhD diss., University of Alabama, 1973), 240–74.

17. Wiggins, *The Scalawag in Alabama Politics*; Wiggins, "What Is a Scalawag?"; Woolfolk, "Five Men Called Scalawags"; Storey, *Loyalty and Loss*; Storey, "Civil War Unionists and the Political Culture of Loyalty in Alabama"; Storey, "The Crucible of Reconstruction"; Rogers, *Black Belt Scalawag*; Horton, "Lightning Rod Scalawag"; Amos, "Trials of a Unionist"; Baggett, *The Scalawags*; Gilmour, "The Other Emancipation"; Fitzgerald, "Radical Republicanism and the White Yeomanry during Alabama Reconstruction"; Trelease, "Who Were the Scalawags?"; Cash, "Alabama Republicans during Reconstruction."

18. United States Senate *Reports*, No. 22, "Alabama Testimony in Ku Klux Report," 42nd Cong., 2nd Sess., vol. VIII, 95, 99.

19. Sarah Woolfolk Wiggins, "Ostracism of White Republicans in Alabama during Reconstruction," *Alabama Review* 27 (January 1974): 52–64; R. C. Goodrich to Rutherford B. Hayes, August 30, 1876, W. H. Smith to Rutherford B. Hayes, January 8, 1877, both in Rutherford B. Hayes Papers, Rutherford B. Hayes Library, Fremont, Ohio.

20. Richard Nelson Current, *Those Terrible Carpetbaggers* (New York: Oxford University Press, 1988); Sarah Van V. Woolfolk, "George E. Spencer: A Carpetbagger in Alabama," *Alabama Review* 19 (January 1966): 41–52; Woolfolk, "Carpetbaggers in Alabama: Tradition versus Truth," *Alabama Review* 15 (April 1962): 133–44; Sarah Woolfolk Wiggins, "J. DeForest Richards: A Vermont Carpetbagger in Alabama," *Vermont History* 51 (Spring 1983): 98–105; Wiggins, "Ostracism of White Republicans," 52–64; Michael W. Fitzgerald, "Republican Factionalism and Black Empowerment: The Spencer-Warner Controversy and Alabama Reconstruction, 1868–1880," *Journal of Southern History* 64 (August 1998): 473–94; Michael J. Daniel, "Samuel Spring Gardner: A Maine Parson in Alabama," *Maine Historical Society Quarterly* 23 (Spring 1984): 151–76; Lawrence H. Powell, "The Politics of Livelihood: Carpetbaggers in the Deep South," in *Region, Race, and Reconstruction*, 315–47.

21. Willard Warner to John Sherman, April 15, 1866, John Sherman Papers, Division of Manuscripts, Library of Congress, Washington, DC.

22. *(Selma) Morning Times*, June 20, 1866.

23. Cash, "Alabama Republicans," 388.

24. Richard Bailey, *Neither Carpetbaggers nor Scalawags: Black Officeholders during the Reconstruction of Alabama, 1867–1878* (Montgomery: Richard Bailey Publishers, 1991); Loren Schweninger, *James T. Rapier and Reconstruction* (Chicago: University of Chicago Press, 1978); Schweninger, "Alabama Blacks and the Congressional Reconstruction Acts of 1867," *Alabama Review* 31 (July 1978): 182–98; Howard N. Rabinowitz, "Holland Thompson and Black Political Participation in Montgomery, Alabama," in *Southern Black Leaders of the Reconstruction Era*, ed. Howard N. Rabinowitz (Urbana: University of Illinois Press, 1982), 249–80; Allen W. Trelease, *White Terror: The Ku Klux Klan Conspiracy and Southern Reconstruction* (New York: Harper and Row, 1971), 81–89, 246–73, 302–10; Michael W. Fitzgerald, "Extralegal Violence and the Planter Class: The

Ku Klux Klan in the Alabama Black Belt during Reconstruction," in *Local Matters: Race, Crime, and Justice in the Nineteenth-Century South*, ed. Christopher Waldrep and Donald G. Nieman (Athens: University of Georgia, 2001), 155–71; Fitzgerald, *Urban Emancipation: Popular Politics in Reconstruction Mobile, 1860–1890* (Baton Rouge: Louisiana State University Press, 2002); Jonathan M. Wiener, *Social Origins of the New South: Alabama, 1860–1885* (Baton Rouge: Louisiana State University Press, 1978), 35–73.

25. David P. Lewis to William Hugh Smith, August 12, 1868, Governor William Hugh Smith Papers, Alabama Department of Archives and History, Montgomery.

26. John A. Minnis to A. T. Akerman, May 29, 1871, Source Chronological Files, Department of Justice, Ala-Northern, Record Group 60, National Archives, Washington, DC; George E. Spencer to William E. Chandler, July 19, 21, September 8, 1874, William E. Chandler Papers, Division of Manuscripts, Library of Congress, Washington, DC; Wiggins, *Scalawag*, 57–71, 76–78; Powell, "The Politics of Livelihood," 330–37.

27. Sarah Woolfolk Wiggins, "Alabama: Democratic Bulldozing and Republican Folly," in *Reconstruction and Redemption in the South*, ed. Otto H. Olsen (Baton Rouge: Louisiana State University Press, 1980), 47–77; Edward C. Williamson, "The Alabama Election of 1874," *Alabama Review* 17 (July 1964): 210–18; Cash, "Alabama Republicans," 384.

28. Gordon S. Wood, *The Purpose of the Past: Reflections on the Uses of History* (New York: Penguin, 2008), 8–10, 11, 293.

29. Thornton, "Fiscal Policy," 383–94.

30. For details of the 1868 constitutional convention, see Malcolm Cook McMillan, *Constitutional Development in Alabama, 1798–1901: A Study in Politics, the Negro, and Sectionalism* (Chapel Hill: University of North Carolina Press, 1955), 110–74; Richard L. Hume and Jerry B. Gough, *Blacks, Carpetbaggers, and Scalawags: The Constitutional Conventions of Radical Reconstruction* (Baton Rouge: Louisiana State University Press, 2008), 74–83, 95–109, 282–85, 309–13, 362–63, 390–91.

31. Wiggins, *Scalawag*, 67.

32. Wiggins, "Alabama: Democratic Bulldozing," 47–77; Cash, "Alabama Republicans," 384; Allen Johnston Going, *Bourbon Democracy in Alabama, 1874–1890* (University: University of Alabama Press, 1951), 27–60.

33. Robert H. McKenzie, "The Economic Impact of Federal Occupations in Alabama during the Civil War," *Alabama Historical Quarterly* 38 (Spring 1976): 51–68. For a study of an example of the postwar shift from reliance on friends and neighbors to reliance on government for disaster assistance, see Jeffrey W. McClerken, *Take Care of the Living: Reconstructing Confederate Veteran Families in Virginia* (Charlottesville: University of Virginia Press, 2009).

34. Elizabeth Bethel, "The Freedmen's Bureau in Alabama," *Journal of Southern History* 14 (February 1948): 49–92; Kenneth B. White, "Wager Swayne: Racist or Realist?" *Alabama Review* 31 (April 1978): 92–109; White, "Black Lives, Red Tape: The Alabama Freedmen's Bureau," *Alabama Historical Quarterly* 43 (Winter 1981): 241–58; LaWanda Cox, "The Perception of Injustice and Race Policy: James F. McGogy and the Freedmen's Bureau in Alabama," in *Freedom, Racism, and Reconstruction: Collected Writings of LaWanda Cox*, ed. Donald G. Nieman (Athens: University of Georgia Press, 1997), 172–242; Michael W. Fitzgerald, "Emancipation and Military Pacification: The Freedmen's Bureau and Social Control in Alabama," in *The Freedmen's Bureau and Reconstruction: Reconsiderations*, ed. Paul A. Cimbala and Randall M. Miller (New York: Fordham University Press, 1999), 46–66; Fitzgerald, "Wager Swayne, the Freedman's Bureau, and the Politics of Reconstruction in Alabama," *Alabama Review* 48 (July 1995): 188–218; Gail Snowden Hasson, "The Medical Activities of the Freedmen's Bureau in Reconstruction Alabama, 1865–

1868" (PhD diss., University of Alabama, 1982); Hasson, "Health and Welfare of Freedmen in Reconstruction Alabama," *Alabama Review* 35 (April 1982): 94–110; John B. Myers, "The Freedmen and the Law in Post-Bellum Alabama, 1865–1867," *Alabama Review* 23 (January 1970): 56–69; Myers, "Reaction and Readjustment: The Struggle of Alabama Freedmen in Post-Bellum Alabama, 1865–1867," *Alabama Historical Quarterly* 32 (Spring and Summer 1970): 5–22; Myers, "The Alabama Freedmen and Economic Adjustments during Presidential Reconstruction, 1865–1867," *Alabama Review* 26 (October 1973): 252–66; Richard L. Hume, "The Freedmen's Bureau and the Freedmen's Vote in the Reconstruction of Southern Alabama: An Account by Agent Samuel S. Gardner," *Alabama Historical Quarterly* 37 (Fall 1975): 217–24; Daniel, "Samuel Spring Gardner," 151–76; Wiener, *Social Origins*, 47–73.

35. Michael W. Fitzgerald, *Splendid Failure: Postwar Reconstruction in the American South* (Chicago: Ivan R. Dee, 2007).

36. Wood, *Purpose of the Past*, 14.

11

Of Ambition and Enterprise
The Making of Carpetbagger George E. Spencer
Terry L. Seip

In his final speech to the U.S. Senate in March 1871, the defensive Alabamian carpetbagger Willard Warner argued that men like him were "like men everywhere; there are some good and some bad among them." That Warner counted himself and his supporters among the "good" perhaps goes without saying, but he also left no doubt as to who epitomized the "bad"—it was his Senate colleague and fellow carpetbagger George E. Spencer.

Spencer had just completed the first stage of a rather amazing political maneuver in which he turned on Warner and William H. Smith, a onetime friend and scalawag governor who was up for reelection in fall 1870. Public sniping between the Spencer and Warner-Smith factions certainly contributed to the Republican defeat, and Spencer's opponents charged him with helping Alabama elect a Democratic governor and legislature, which in turn selected a Democrat to replace Warner in the Senate. But this was not all. Over the next two years, Spencer, now largely in control of federal patronage in the state, worked systematically to deny Warner the collectorship at Mobile, a prime patronage plum. And then, in an astonishing move, Spencer engineered his own reelection to the Senate in 1872 by shifting alliances and pushing for the election of a Republican governor and legislature. The election results were sharply disputed, but from the political chaos of rival legislatures and Spencer's alleged use of nefarious means throughout the process, he prevailed and would serve until March 1879, nearly five years after Alabama had been redeemed, much to the distress of his detractors, Republican as well as Democratic.[1]

George Spencer's political maneuvering in the early 1870s sealed his historical reputation. His carpetbag, scalawag, and conservative opponents piled on the terms of derision: he was unscrupulous, unprincipled, vulgar, coarse, cunning, and corrupt, a schemer, manipulator, intriguer, plunderer, spoilsman, freebooter, and criminal—ill repute freely echoed among early Reconstruction historians. Even when Reconstruction historiography headed into revisionist stages in the 1960s, Spencer remained outside those who were rehabilitated, a "memorable model for the concept of the corrupt Carpetbagger interested primarily in his own advancement," as Sarah Woolfolk Wiggins put it in 1966. As historical attention has shifted to the experiences of the freedpeople and black participation in Alabama politics, the derisive rhetoric aimed at Spencer has fallen a notch, and there is a leaning toward downplaying his activity and influence and some acknowledgment that his support for the freedpeople remained strong and consistent. Still, his reputation has not greatly changed and remains primarily based on a rather restricted examination of his activity at the state level.[2]

This essay deals not with the rancorous partisanship and factionalism of Alabama politics after Spencer's selection to the Senate in 1868 but his previous thirty-one years, especially his wartime service with northern Alabama Unionists and his postwar reasoning for settling among them. Carpetbaggers have generally proven to be elusive targets for biographers, most often because of a paucity of primary evidence on their pre- and post-Reconstruction years, but the extraordinary movement and activity of Spencer's early years can be pieced together from widely scattered sources and are invaluable for understanding his later behavior. Spencer represents an exaggerated, almost stereotypical case study of the first generation of Republican leadership that emerged along the American frontier during the 1850s, a strikingly ambitious, enterprising, entrepreneurial cohort of young men imbued with the tenets of economic mobility at the heart of the Republican free labor ideology. Most noteworthy is a remarkable consistency in Spencer's consuming economic and political drive across a series of episodes in which Alabama, in some sense, was just another stop.

Born in a crossroads village in upstate New York in 1836, Spencer was the last of four sons of a physician who had settled in the frontier area following service in the War of 1812. George and his brothers were raised during the later stages of frontier settlement, where speculation and opening up the land, loaning and borrowing money, and ambition were valued. The family was certainly enterprising; his hardworking father was intensely dedicated to his profession and steadily accumulated property. While the oldest brother followed his father into a stable medical practice, the next two brothers speculated in land, tanneries, and sawmills, but as their enterprises faltered, they left for the western frontier. The first landed well beyond continental bounds on Maui in the Sandwich Islands in the late 1840s, where sugar cultivation was opening to Americans; the second brother soon joined him. Meanwhile, George, the youngest by a decade, went north to pursue studies at a Montreal college, returning to New York to read law in 1855. But for the young and motivated, the North Country seemed economically stagnant as the 1850s unfolded; thus at age nineteen he headed for Iowa, a magnet for footloose young easterners looking for new beginnings.[3]

From the moment of his arrival in March 1856, notions of a settled career in law faded as Spencer joined a remarkable generation of aggressive young Iowans, most of them adherents to the just emerging Republican Party that celebrated and encoded their ambitions. Spencer was reliably blunt in expressing his opinion; his first letters from Iowa typically jumped from topic to topic, mingling sharp questions and observations. There is little that is inscrutable—he usually made no bones about his own speculative ventures, his strategizing to gain position or influence, and his manipulation of friends and foes. A prototype of the frontier boomer, he could show a smoother, more urbane side as he sidled up to men of power, but he was also quick to denigrate those he found to be weak or fools. One might even argue that his candor and tendency for extreme statement, even vituperation, which make him quite quotable, have not served him well among historians.[4]

Spencer temporarily settled in Newton, a frontier town east of Fort Des Moines and jumping-off point for speculators and pioneer families fanning out to the north and west. With newfound friends he engaged in land speculation and moved with surprising speed into local and state Republican politics, cultivating local politicos along the line running from Iowa City through Newton and Des Moines to Council Bluffs on the Missouri River. Most important to Spencer in the long run was a chance meeting with Grenville Dodge during twenty-four hours atop a crowded stagecoach between Iowa City and Newton in mid-1856. Although Dodge was much better grounded in family and place, a critical consideration in politics, he and Spencer were in many respects two of a kind. In early 1856, Dodge had launched the banking and general business firm of Baldwin, Dodge, and Company in Council Bluffs, specializing in land, railroads, and merchandise. Well aware of the potentially fruitful connections between politics and business, Dodge and his associates, as biographer Stanley Hirshson observed, "had the necessary ingredients for success: a yearning for large rewards, a propensity to seek out and act upon inside information, a desire to bring people of fame, wealth, and influence into their operations, and a willingness to use methods bordering on the immoral and illegal."[5]

These friendships yielded Spencer's first political appointment as assistant secretary then secretary of the state senate beginning in December 1856 at Iowa City. A clerk later remembered Spencer as "a genuine politician, shrewd, talented, and a little sporty" who "kept a bottle of whiskey in his desk, but was a good secretary." Here we have a first taste of the calculating, highly particularistic way Spencer thought about democratic politics. When he learned of his friend Orlando Howe's interest in a local judgeship, Spencer promptly threw himself into the necessary "sharp figuring" to get him elected. After enumerating the strengths of the other four candidates, he began canvassing for support, offering Howe a running analysis and a host of politicians to target. The rhetoric is classic: in one case, Spencer proposed to see his friend Kellogg "and he will straighten things," to do "something with McPherson," a senator from Madison County, and to have Howe write Asa Grow, another politico: "He don't amount to much but he might be appointed a delegate and could help you very much." When another opponent returned to Iowa City, Spencer planned to "make a bargain of some kind with him," he promised to send a friend "to work on" potential Warren County delegates, and after he learned that one politician could not be turned, he pushed Howe to "see some of the politicians and fix things." If given a trip to Des Moines, Spencer predicted that he "could scare the delegation off from bringing forward any man there and get them to support you. I know that they would when they understood things.... Management will do all." Spencer even crossed party lines to work on young Democrats like M. M. Crocker, a self-described "Locofoco, Tro'slavery, Border Ruffian." While he worried about the competition, Spencer nevertheless thought that "if your matters are managed very shrewdly, you can get the nomination." And all of this from a scarcely twenty-year-old who had been in the state less than ten months. In the end Howe lost, but Spencer's enthusiasm and activity are noteworthy—a performance to be repeated time and again for the rest of his life. He relished the detailed scheming and manipulation of politics and became quite skilled at it—"shrewd," as his friends and detractors constantly put it.[6]

While still working legislative politics, in early 1857 Spencer and Howe turned to a time-honored means of escape from a depressed economy: looking farther west, in this case engaging in aggressive town-building on the fringes of northwestern Iowa. After Howe scouted the area on the Minnesota border in late 1856, Howe, Spencer, and three other investors brought in a sawmill to begin building a rudimentary town named after Spirit Lake to the north and nestled between the shoestring Okoboji Lakes. The motive was purely pecuniary: "All of the young men comprising the [Newton] party," a later chronicler noted, "were animated with a high ambition to become rich and famous over night." As Spencer registered their land claims in Sioux City, they had the town declared the Dickinson County seat and began advertising to lure settlers. By 1858, Howe and others had moved their families into the area and Spencer had put up the biggest house in town. Years later one of Howe's daughters wrote that Spencer, whom she identified as a "speculator" not "settler," was "a part of most all that was being done." But even as he was helping develop Spirit Lake, he laid claim to timbered land about twenty miles south along the Little Sioux River in Clay County, brought in a surveyor friend, and tentatively laid out a town he named after himself. By September he had won the right for a post office, in November he went to Washington to secure a land office for the area, and he worked with the legislature to get the still paper town designated as the county seat.[7]

Times remained tough. While Howe and others gutted it out, Spencer was discouraged. Neither the Spirit Lake nor the Spencer town site attracted emigrant interest, the hopes for quick riches vanished, and there were building legal hassles over disputed claims and titles, including some serious friction within the Newton group. It seemed a good time to move on. Sensing another possibility on the western horizon, Spencer sold out most of his holdings, making the final transactions in early July 1859. Less than a month later he led a party of miners over the Continental Divide into Utah Territory west-southwest of Denver.[8]

Spencer's Colorado gold rush experience has to be pieced together from fragmentary evidence. In all likelihood supported by Dodge, in late July 1859 Spencer pulled together a prospecting group in Denver under the name of Spencer, Humphreys, McDougal, and Wagstaff to "prospect the western slopes of the Rocky Mountains." The group of about thirty left Denver on August 2, heading up into South Park and then over the Continental Divide in two spots, reconvening in the Blue River Valley, the first mining party of any significance on the western slope. Some quick panning showed gold and the party enthusiastically turned to building sluices, staking out claims, and organizing mining districts.[9]

Spencer probably had his eye on town-building from the beginning. Working with a Democratic lobbyist for the area in Washington, Spencer decided that the quickest way to get approval for a postal route from Denver to the Blue River Valley would be to name the town in honor of Democrat John C. Breckinridge, the vice president of the United States. The scheme worked, and in early 1860 Spencer headed back into the mountains, bent on establishing the town—he had already arranged to have himself named postmaster. He arrived to find that the land on which he had intended to plant his town had been claimed, so he jumped the town site of a competitor. As the rival later recalled, Spencer moved "to prejudice [my] boys against me. He told them his company was rich and . . . if they would give him the townsite he would survey it and give each one, excepting myself, twelve choice lots. . . . he insisted he must have the townsite and the right of naming it. For two weeks we disputed and argued, and I saw Spencer's influence was working on the boys. Finally I got tired of it and . . . we turned the townsite over to Spencer."[10]

Spencer & Company laid claim to 320 acres but surveyed no more than a Main Street along the river, which immediately filled with tents, shanties, and log cabins. According to newspaper reports, Spencer was developing a successful law practice among the miners, and he and a partner began working a nearby salt deposit to supply the community. He had at least two claims (one gold, one silver), he was the postmaster until he handed it over to a local merchant in March, and he was still the acting agent for the mushrooming village in June but he disappears from the local records by late summer. With close to ten thousand miners in the area by the summer of 1860, perhaps it just got too crowded or maybe the payoff was not big enough. Through an attorney, he sold off one of his mining claims for $70 in November; the other claim apparently lapsed.[11]

Spencer was probably back along the Missouri River by the time of Abraham Lincoln's election, and by late winter he was working for Baldwin & Dodge to establish a branch office in St. Joseph, Missouri. "Excitement is very high," he wrote in April, shortly after the fall of Fort Sumter, and his restlessness was clear: "I am doing nothing & I am d____d tired of it I would like some active service of some kind, and would not object to a guerrilla warfare anything for excitement or that would pay." When Dodge accepted a gubernatorial appointment as colonel of the 4th Iowa Infantry Regiment, Spencer went to help recruit in Council Bluffs. Soon thereafter he caught an opportunity across the river in Omaha where he became personal secretary to a friend from Iowa, Alvin Saunders, whom Lincoln had just appointed territorial governor. A few weeks later, with Nebraskans preparing for war, Saunders selected Spencer as sutler for the 1st Nebraska regiment and he went into Missouri with the unit that summer. A local journalist thought Spencer "worthy and well qualified" for the position, which was something that he could "make pay," and in Dodge's network, he had ample connections to purchase goods for resale to soldiers in the 1st Nebraska.[12]

Nebraskans applauded Spencer's work in supplying their regiment as it moved around Missouri in the summer and fall of 1861 and then in the early 1862 campaigns up the Tennessee and Cumberland Rivers when the regiment was attached to Lew Wallace's division. He was cited for serving as a voluntary aide to John Thayer, the regimental commander, during heavy fighting on the second day at Shiloh. But when the 1st Nebraska moved south to Memphis and then on to Arkansas in July, Spencer stayed in the Memphis-Corinth, Mississippi, area, primarily because his friend Dodge, now a brigadier general, was rebuilding the Mobile and Ohio Railroad from Columbus, Kentucky, to Corinth. By November, Dodge was in command of the Second Division of the Army of the Tennessee at Corinth and charged with watching Ulysses Grant's flank as he moved on Vicksburg. Spencer's other reason for staying flowed from a concern that the new conscription law might "make it necessary for all of us to do military duty," so in early August he appealed to Dodge for a staff position. "I have got over being ambitious," he assured his friend, "and only want to situate myself pleasantly & would serve your interests with fidelity." Dodge responded with an appointment as an assistant adjutant general (AAG) with the rank of captain.[13]

Once in the army, Spencer adapted well and his never-abated ambition, now to win reputation and glory, took over. From November 1862 until the summer of 1864, Dodge and Spencer operated along a highly contested line from Corinth to northwest Georgia, cut through by two highly desirable arteries, the Tennessee River and the Memphis and Charleston Railroad. While Dodge was to provide Grant the best intelligence possible on enemy movement into the Mississippi arena, Confederate forces, primarily the cavalry of Philip Dale Roddey, were especially concerned with protecting northern and central Alabama and keeping communications and avenues of movement open between Braxton Bragg's forces in East

Tennessee and those of Joseph E. Johnston and John Pemberton in Mississippi. Warfare in this borderland was thus more of a guerrilla nature, ranging through the productive plantation country along much of the Tennessee River and its tributaries and into the heavily thicketed, timbered, and mountainous terrain back from the river bottoms. Each side watched the other, sending spies and small cavalry units on quick slash-and-burn incursions back and forth across the Tennessee River, gathering intelligence on troop strength, placement, and movement.

Complicating the situation in the mountainous counties was considerable Unionist sentiment that opposed Confederate conscription, revenue gathering, and confiscation practices. A good many of these so-called Tories fled to Union lines where Dodge quickly saw their potential as spies and as scouts to lead his troops on raids into Confederate territory. As his AAG, Spencer became close to Alabama Unionists such as William Hugh Smith from as far southeast as Randolph County and a host of others, including many future scalawag Republicans, most of whom were from the mountainous northwestern counties. Most of these refugees were leaving an increasingly dangerous terrain that had become a haven for deserters from the Confederate infantry units, some of whom would join cavalry units such as Roddey's. Others turned to guerrilla activity, often operating in small bands, or to simple outlawry, preying on the local citizenry, Unionists and Confederates alike— a mutating culture of bushwhackers and "mounted robbers." Even Confederates decried the "great increase of stragglers, who now infest the mountains of North Alabama, and who are so formidable in numbers and so thoroughly armed and organized as to hold the citizen population in terror of their displeasure. They rob, burn, and murder the unarmed and defenseless population of the country with impunity."[14]

This open, shifting arena suited Spencer, and even before Dodge requested his appointment Spencer was providing information, writing Dodge in mid-September 1862 from Corinth that he had "just returned from a two days cruise through the Country picking up information" and offering the first of many blunt assessments of Union army leadership up and down the line: "Really, our Generals here are small potatoes & do not see a mile into a mill-stone." Before he settled in with Dodge, Spencer went to Washington to get General-in-Chief Henry Halleck's staff to allow his "claims against dead men & discharged soldiers of the Nebraska regt" and to work on a promotion for Dodge: "Halleck runs the machine here now, and has everything his own way." During an evening with him, Spencer took "took special pains to give him [an] extra good opinion of you," confidently assuring Dodge that "he is a peculiar man & I know how to manage him."[15]

In the AAG position by mid-November, Spencer did much routine work in handling divisional communications and learning the parameters of Dodge's growing network of scouts and spies. He spent Christmas in the East, going to Washington to pursue lingering claims and again lobby Halleck for Dodge's promotion. Somewhere in this time frame, he married twenty-two-year-old Bella Zilfa of Philadelphia. Born in England in 1840, she came to the United States as an infant, but nothing is known of her coming-of-age years; she only comes into view in 1863 when she spent part of the winter at Corinth with Spencer, Dodge, and his wife, Anne. Well educated with literary interests, she published poetry, short stories, and novels, drawing on her wartime experience with Spencer, and late in the war she signed on as an editor with the *Saturday Evening Post*. Her correspondence and writings reveal an independent, bold, and ambitious personality; she seems a perfect match for Spencer.[16]

Back in Corinth as 1863 opened, it became apparent that Spencer was not about to settle into a desk job as most AAGs did. From the beginning he pushed to be involved directly in military action, he studied cavalry tactics, and Dodge began to give him increasing responsibility and latitude in the field. Through the late winter and spring of 1863 he quickly won attention for his intelligence-gathering raids into the borderland area where steady pressure on Richmond from north Alabama politicians, planters, and businessmen kept Philip Roddey's cavalry stationed. Roddey's forces usually numbered between 1,200 and 2,000, with a floating headquarters across northern Alabama ranging from Tuscumbia and Florence to Courtland, Moulton, Decatur, and Huntsville, depending on the location of Federal forces at any point. While Dodge and Spencer were always concerned with the whereabouts of Nathan Bedford Forrest's cavalry, Roddey was a constant in their thinking and activity. Dodge had Spencer conduct a prisoner exchange with him on neutral ground in Glendale, Mississippi, in January 1863, the first of several meetings between the two, often under a flag of truce. The relationship, which seems to have taken on a "respected adversary" tone, continued into the immediate postwar period when Roddey apparently assisted Spencer in his cotton-buying operations in Alabama and even extended into Nevada mining operations in the 1880s.[17]

Spencer's initial prisoner exchange with Roddey was only the first of a number of forays Spencer took to the east. Dodge's diary shows the increasing number of missions: "Spencer with 150 men went to Hamburg" (February 22); "Spencer with 150 mounted infantry & Col [James B. Weaver] with 2nd Iowa To attack White Sulphur Springs enemy" (February 25); "Capt Spencer went on scout [with] 150 mounted [and] five days rations" (March 2); "Spencer returns from scout to Bear Creek [and along the way 'broke up a gang of conscripts at Eastport']" (March 6); "Spencer left with 300 Calvary for Bear Creek" (March 19). If he was out for more than a couple of days, he usually sent reports to Dodge. For example, from Red Sulphur Springs in late February he reported finding "no enemy in force here, but the woods and hills are full of them. . . . about 50 in this vicinity," and he spotted "about two hundred mattresses, with pillows and bedding" in storage, which he figured "would be useful in our hospitals." In March from Brownsville he sent in "16 prisoners, with their horses and equipments.... We had a skirmish with Warren's men yesterday morning. They skedaddled, and we captured 8 of their men.... There are 800 men at Oakes', just across Bear Creek. There are 1,000 (regiments and battalions) at Cherokee, 6 miles from Bear Creek, and one regiment of infantry, about 600 men, at Tuscumbia, the whole under the command of Colonel [M. W.] Hannon."[18]

A prime example of the increased latitude given to Spencer is when Dodge sent Spencer under a flag of truce to Roddey's main encampment at Tuscumbia in early April. Spencer and his small force cleverly worked through several Confederate picket lines, claiming that he was on a mission to set up a prisoner exchange, and he came out of it with a note from Roddey indicating that all prisoners of war had been paroled and sent to Federal lines five days earlier—and with a load of intelligence. As Dodge reported to his immediate superior Richard Oglesby, Spencer "succeeded in getting through all the enemy's camps" and brought back the exact number of forces and leadership at eight Confederate cavalry locations and the breakdown for one brigade of infantry, along with an estimation of artillery. Oglesby sent Dodge's message up the line to his superior, Stephen A. Hurlbut in Memphis, who forwarded it to Grant at Milliken's Bend, noting that Spencer "deserves great credit" for his bold move.[19]

Dodge immediately followed up with a large raid into the area to disrupt Confederate control and communications—and to cover a deeper cavalry penetration by Col. Abel Streight of William Rosecrans's command to destroy railroads from central Alabama into Georgia. While Streight's raid fell victim to mismanagement and misfortune, and a persistent and skilled N. B. Forrest, Dodge's operation was a success. He quickly pushed Roddey from the Mississippi state line back through Tuscumbia to Decatur with tremendous damage to crops, livestock, small manufacturing, and river traffic. "It has rendered desolate one of the best granaries of the South," Dodge reported, "preventing them from raising another crop this year and taking away from them some 1500 negroes." But as Dodge withdrew, Roddey moved back into the devastated valley, "his command jaded and much crippled," according to Bragg. From Tuscumbia on May 8 Roddey requested a seventy-prisoner exchange with Dodge and wisely turned back another flag-of-truce intrusion, probably under Spencer, coming up the valley. The equilibrium had been disturbed, but only for a short while.[20]

In July Spencer added to his reputation with another flag-of-truce trip nearly ninety miles south of Corinth to the headquarters of Confederate general Daniel Ruggles near Okolona, Mississippi. He talked his way through all enemy outposts and was finally stopped just a mile from Ruggles's headquarters. "The Southern officers, hearing that Spencer was deep within their lines, were dumbfounded," Hirshson noted. "Spencer enjoyed himself in the Confederate camp, where he and his men stayed up all night debating Negro rights and other subjects with their hosts." Spencer began his return to Corinth the next morning via a different route, which allowed him to gather additional intelligence, and when he was challenged, he "insisted that he was travelling under orders from Ruggles and continued on his way." Again, the intelligence gathered was detailed, and Dodge immediately followed up with another raid.[21]

It was a productive period for Spencer; Dodge clearly liked his boldness and self-confidence, his willingness to go beyond orders when the circumstances seemed to merit, and his ability to talk himself through hot spots. While he could be impulsive and sometimes needed a firm guiding hand, he was not likely to be intimidated in any situation—if not fearless, he seemed to relish the tension and potential danger of going into enemy territory. Years later, after their friendship had faded, Dodge recalled that Spencer was "very efficient"; with the flag of truce he "was ingenious and sharp, and would catch [a] picket officer who was not up on the rules and claim he had a very important communication for the commanding general & had to deliver it in person." Those up the line also noticed: "Does Capt. Spencer still run his flags of truce?" Oglesby wondered in August 1863. "Spencer has a good style. He goes with a truce in one hand and a revolver in the other." To a fellow staff officer who had known Spencer in Colorado as well as Iowa, Spencer was simply "a very shrewd fellow . . . a shrewd politician . . . a shrewd intriguer." When Dodge sent a picture of his staff to his father in August, he noted that they were all "hard working efficient men" selected "for their usefulness and not for show." In the photo Dodge is sitting, legs crossed, on one side of a map-draped table, Spencer, legs crossed the other way, is on the other side, both in armed chairs, trim and in full view, with a dozen other staff officers sitting or standing behind them. Dodge had found his second in command.[22]

In late July, Spencer was promoted to colonel and given command of a unique creation, the 1st Alabama Cavalry, Union. After taking control in fall 1862, Dodge built on the work of his predecessors in Corinth, and with Spencer's help began shaping companies of native Unionists into a cavalry regiment. Since these were no Northern mothers' sons, there was no Northern community and press watching to see how the military was using its boys, so there are some indications that the unit was viewed and handled differently. For example, there seemed to be somewhat less concern with their initial training and equipment, including weaponry and horses. And if they failed, it was easier to blame them more openly or simply write them off—the Union hierarchy did not need to fear the wrath of Northern communities. Their chief value was that they knew the country and the mentalities of the enemy, a good rationale, of course, for using them on the more dangerous incursions into Confederate territory and to put them out front as was later the case with William Tecumseh Sherman's march through Georgia. Although in a sense they were outsiders, they came to be respected and trusted for their loyalty—it took genuine patriotism to join Union forces as it often brought increasing danger for their families behind Confederate lines. But motivation was mixed; at certain times and among certain men, it seems to have been less a patriotic call to duty than a way to strike back against the unwanted Confederacy and the slaveholding classes that supported it. In short, motivations included revenge and sometimes a greater willingness, under the cover of war, to extract more than the usual toll. All of this and more made the 1st Alabama distinctively useful to Dodge and Spencer.

While still partial and quite green, the 1st Alabama had a mixed initial encounter with the enemy in Dodge's raid up the Tuscumbia Valley in April 1863. Dodge's cavalry was then under Florence M. Cornyn, who early on "ordered a charge by the First Alabama Cavalry, which, I am sorry to say, was not obeyed with the alacrity it should have been. After charging to within short musket-range of the enemy, they halted for some cause I cannot account for, and the enemy escaped to the woods" only to turn and pour "a perfect hail of lead into our ranks." Dodge immediately protected the unit by removing it from Cornyn's command the following day and placing it in the 3rd Infantry Brigade of Moses M. Bane, a close friend in Dodge's inner circle. He also defended the regiment in his report to Oglesby: "The charge of the Alabamians with muskets only, and those not loaded is creditable, especially as they are all new recruits and poorly drilled," and, while praising Cornyn overall, Dodge characterized the charge as "injudicious, and against my instructions." Upon returning to Corinth, Dodge soon put the Alabamians back into action, often with Spencer, and diligently reported their successes up the line to Oglesby, Hurlbut, and Grant. Ultimately Dodge reasoned that the regiment should go to a flexible, enterprising type who could use this sort of native force to its greatest advantage. And who better than Spencer?[23]

Following his promotion and during a lull in action, Spencer left the regiment under the command of Maj. Michael F. Fairfield in early August 1863 and began a month-long break with Bella in the Northeast. While he confessed to "enjoying my self more than I expected," he hoped that when he got back "we will make an advance somewhere & accomplish something worthy of note. I have been studying Cavalry tactics very hard since I left & am getting pretty well posted." But Dodge was in St. Louis recuperating from illness, so when Spencer returned to Corinth in early September he had to deal with Dodge's temporary replacement, Eugene H. Carr, who ordered him east to command the post at Glendale. Even as he provided a steady flow of intelligence to Carr and up the line to Hurlbut and worked diligently to staff and build up the 1st Alabama, Spencer chafed under the new command and regularly vented to Dodge. He pressed Carr to allow him to take the unit to the mountain counties to recruit, or maybe even on a great raid, "but I can get no show to do anything for the benefit of the Regt [on account] of Carr," he fumed. "Carr is a d____d fool & idiot instead of being a General," so Spencer went over his head and began pushing Hurlbut to approve a raid.[24]

In early October, Hurlbut caved in and the orders that came to Spencer on October 3 were grandiose, to say the least, and in all likelihood would never have been approved for any regular Union cavalry regiment, but they smacked of Spencer's thinking. The 1st Alabama was to "proceed rapidly through Jasper, Ala., to Montgomery, or to some point east of Montgomery on the West Point railroad," avoiding "all public and known roads before striking this road," and then "proceed[ing] to destroy effectually the Montgomery and West Point Railroad in its rolling-stock, track, and depots, doing the most thorough amount of damage possible." But there was more: "If it be possible, you will strike for the Georgia road, east of Atlanta, and do all damage possible there. . . . The movements of the command, however, must be governed by circumstances, and will be left in the discretion of Colonel Spencer. The line of escape will probably be by Pensacola." Given the sheer distances and no evidence of any thought about the potential of Confederate opposition from any direction, the venture appears foolhardy at best. Fortunately a hold was put on until Dodge returned in mid-October, and he modified the raid to hit the somewhat closer government works at Selma and the Alabama and Tennessee Railroad from Selma to Rome, Georgia. Although this objective was more sensible, it was still a deep raid with relatively few men.[25]

"Spencer has gone on his great raid," Dodge informed his wife on October 20. The expedition started well, but it did not end well. While the widely circulated rumor in the Northern press that Spencer and the 1st Alabama had been captured proved untrue, the venture ended in a rout of the Alabamians near Vincent's Cross-Roads in eastern Mississippi. The most straightforward account is in the daily diary of Sgt. Maj. Francis Wayland Dunn, who recorded that Spencer and about five hundred of the 1st Alabama left on the morning of October 19 on what he described as "a dangerous trip," but after they entered the "stoney and rough country" of the mountains, it began to rain and they had to burn their wagons and pack as much as they could on mules. They got within ten miles of Jasper on October 24, Spencer was sick that evening, and in the morning rain of the next day they turned back, "a disappointment to most of the men." Two days later they started at 6:00 AM and heard "there were plenty of Rebels, 5,000 of them ahead of us at Vinsons [Vincent's] Crossroads," but then they were told it was only a Confederate battery, and at the crossroads they found no tracks. A half-dozen miles farther along they encountered major opposition. They deployed and engaged a Confederate line that was long enough to begin flanking the Alabamians' line. As the companies one by one had to fall back, the situation deteriorated, with the retreating men not sticking to the road as Spencer wanted. Spencer came up and they made a stand with two artillery pieces to little avail; Spencer "drew a pistol and tried to form a line," and Dunn tried to help "but there was no use." While taking fire, the men moved in two streams around Spencer, Dunn joining the one that "went right into the woods away from roads of any kind," and ultimately a local boy guided the 122 men back to the safety of Iuka by 4:00 PM. Spencer got to Glendale the next morning with about the same number, and Lieut. Col. Ozro J. Dodds and others continued to drift in as Spencer came down to Iuka on October 29.[26]

Spencer submitted no report, but the following spring he told a Northern reporter that the Confederate cavalry under Samuel W. Ferguson "was not less than 2,300 in number" and that the fight lasted from 2:00 to 8:00 PM, "when Col. Spencer withdrew his force under cover of night, leaving his surgeon to take care of the wounded." Corinth also heard an estimate of Confederate strength at "2,000 strong," but Ferguson claimed that his "force scarcely equaled that of the enemy" and that he only took about 300 effective men and one squadron into the battle. Still, his men quickly turned it into a rout, "the fleeing enemy were hotly pursued and their retreat converted into a wild panic" over a ten-mile chase, but most of them escaped "by separating into small squads and leaving the road." Although he did not have exact casualty figures, Ferguson thought he had "succeeded in effectually destroying the First Alabama Tory Regiment."[27]

Sherman, nearby at Iuka and operating to the south against Stephen D. Lee, initially speculated that Lee may have "caught this erratic Alabama regiment of ours, which had gone off recruiting or other errand," but he later informed Halleck and Grant that Ferguson had "encountered the First Alabama (Union) Regiment, on its return from a raid, and worsted it." Dodge again promptly put the regiment back in the field, later informing his brother Nathan that "Spencer only lost 40 men" at Vincent's Cross-Roads and that "Spencer's regiment of Alabamians had another fight and cleaned out the rebels and won a good deal of credit."[28]

With Spencer's appetite for independent action perhaps tempered for a while, he became chief of staff when Dodge, rewarded with command of the Left Wing, 16th Army Corps, moved to Pulaski, Tennessee, to rebuild the Nashville and Decatur Railroad. Before he joined Dodge, Spencer finished reorganizing the 1st Alabama for three years through reenlistment and recruitment, and then left Dodds in command at Camp Davies outside Corinth until the unit rejoined Spencer and Dodge in April 1864. From Pulaski, Dodge sent Spencer south to Athens as a satellite commander as they worked to secure the area south to Decatur with Col. Jesse J. Phillips's cavalry. Skirmishes with Roddey's forces continued, Spencer exchanged prisoners with him at the end of January, and under a flag of truce he once stayed overnight with Roddey in Decatur. Throughout the winter and into the spring, first Pulaski, then Athens, Mooresville, and finally Decatur were made safe for Bella Spencer, Anne Dodge, and other family members, all of whom headed for St. Louis when Dodge finished his rebuilding job, and the Left Wing, including Spencer and the 1st Alabama, moved east in late April and early May.[29]

On May 5 Dodge and Spencer joined James B. McPherson, now commanding the Army of the Tennessee, just as Sherman's push toward Atlanta was approaching Dalton. Here Spencer and the Alabamians had their first taste of large army action when Sherman sent Dodge's 16th Corps on a long sweep around Joseph Johnston's heavy fortifications at Dalton to threaten his left flank and rear near Resaca. Dodge moved more quickly than anticipated, catching Resaca only lightly guarded in Johnston's rear. On May 9, Spencer and the 1st Alabama were supposedly ready to charge into Resaca, when McPherson appeared and ordered a halt—saying to take the town was in disobedience to Sherman's orders. As McPherson later admitted, stopping was a mistake; when Sherman attacked Resaca four days later, he found that Johnston had moved his whole army down from Dalton. The fight was prolonged before Johnston began a long and bloody retreat toward Atlanta. As Hirshson notes, Spencer caught the episode with his "usual hindsight" when he later "argued that if he had been allowed to charge 'which Gen'l Dodge was very anxious should be done, we would have captured Resaca that day, destroyed the railroad bridge there and the railroad, and then and there ended the Atlanta campaign.'" Some Spencer hyperbole, to be sure, but one wonders how taking Resaca might have changed the face of the long days to come.[30]

The 1st Alabama and a few other regiments were dispatched to Rome, Georgia, in late June, essentially to protect Sherman's right wing as he moved further southeast toward Atlanta. After an extended bout with dysentery, which he eventually beat down by eating "nothing but boiled milk" and taking "blue moss & opium pills [four every day]," Spencer rejoined his regiment in mid-July. Astride the railroad at Rome, post commanders William Vandever and then John Corse used the 1st Alabama and other units to probe the countryside and gather intelligence, often encountering local guerrilla opposition and sometimes pieces of Confederate cavalry. But Rome seemed too much on the fringes of the Atlanta Campaign for Spencer. "I am totally disgusted here," he wrote in late July, "we are guarding small wagon trains about the country & doing picket duty. *I want to do something* & will if I can get an opportunity." While Vandever was "a granny besides being only half witted," Spencer was careful to "only obey orders" as he was "*waiting, hoping, & praying* for something to turn up. I wish I could get *Carte Blanch* to go where I choose for a couple of months I would get up a breeze sure." His restlessness was palatable; ten days later the message was almost identical: "I have a good Regiment the best I ever saw & if I could get Carte Blanche to go where I [wanted] to for about two months I could make for myself & Regiment a name & reputation."[31]

His venting continued until late October, but after August 19 it became long distance when Dodge suffered a head wound and went north to recuperate—

ultimately never to return. Spencer had lost a friend in Sherman's headquarters who understood him well, but Spencer was enterprising and maintained his connections with the hierarchy of Sherman's army. As one of his men noted, "Spencer seems to be a great favorite at headquarters and gets the news." He fretted that he was not directly involved in the fall of Atlanta, but he continued to do his duty—in September, for example, he went out "with three hundred men & had a running bushwhacking fight for three days lost one killed & one wounded & brought in 18 prisoners." He was also "recruiting very rapidly just now" with the regiment up to 868 men, and he kept Dodge informed of the court intrigue at Sherman's headquarters as Dodge's Left Wing was being broken up.[32]

Much-anticipated change finally came when Corse's command was ordered to join Sherman's march to the sea. "We are all bustle and excitement here just now being on the eve of another campaign," Spencer wrote on November 1. "I think I can make some reputation on this trip. Genl Sherman & Howard & Corse have complimented me for the part I took in the late short campaign when Hood went north & have made some good promises." As they moved from Rome to join O. O. Howard's Corps on November 11, Spencer and the Alabamians led the way to White Hall near Atlanta. Howard commanded the 15th and 17th Corps and the 1st Alabama was assigned to the latter, under Francis Blair Jr. And when Blair's column left White Hall on November 14, "the first Alabama Cavalry, Colonel Spencer commanding," took "the advance at 5:30 A.M." In fact, although scarcely mentioned in the histories of the campaign, Spencer and the 1st Alabama were consistently in the lead of the 17th Corps, occasionally sharing the front action with other units, but rarely in conjunction with Sherman's cavalry leader, Judson J. Kilpatrick, who worked with other columns or directly under Sherman's orders. Time and again, Blair's almost daily orders put "the First Alabama Cavalry . . . moving in advance."[33]

Being in front, of course, meant that Spencer's men were under orders to take control of particular objectives including towns, ferries, bridges, and railroad stations. A company of the 1st Alabama, for example, quick on the heels of a few Union scouts to whom the mayor of Milledgeville surrendered, promptly moved in, "destroyed the depot and some 75 or 100 boxes of ammunition and telegraph office, . . . [and] replenished mules and horses." Fourth Division Commander Giles Smith noted that his command arrived at "Gordon on the 21st ultimo, which was occupied after a short skirmish with the enemy by my advance, the First Alabama Cavalry." A day later, Blair ordered Smith "to proceed with my division and Colonel Spencer's First Alabama Cavalry to the railroad bridge across the Oconee, between [railroad] Stations 14 and 15. The cavalry having the advance." Smith wrote Blair that his advance unit had "driven the rebels out of two stockades. Spencer got the first one before we got up, and we now occupy this side of the river." From there Smith "directed Colonel Spencer to send 150 men from Station 15 to Ball's Ferry. The major in command has just sent a dispatch that he has the ferry—after sharp skirmish." Near Ball's Ferry, Blair ordered Spencer to "immediately upon completion of the bridge cross the river, and, moving to Station No. 14, destroy the remainder of the railroad bridge and trestle-work at and near that point."

And so it went as the 1st Alabama counted down the railroad stations to Savannah with leading action at Stations Nos. 11, 9, 7, 5½, and 3. The regiment's advance work for Blair, Howard, and Sherman was constant for nearly a month, and one wonders if the unit had been of Northern origin if it would have been put so consistently out front or whether it would have received better press and historical coverage. But again, the men of the regiment were Southerners who understood the native population and the lay of the land, and it seemed that they belonged in front. A bit of recognition came when Sherman formally reviewed the troops in Savannah on December 27, and Blair put the Alabamians first in line, a well-earned position of pride.[34]

There were other consequences of being in the lead: the regiment was the first to face whatever resistance cropped up in their path, from Confederate skirmishers to land mines, the first to encounter the civilian population, and the first to forage, to confiscate or destroy property, and, occasionally, to plunder. Only six days into the campaign, Spencer received a sharp rebuke from Blair: "The major-general commanding directs me to say to you that the outrages committed by your command during the march are becoming so common, and are of such an aggravated nature, that they call for some severe and instant mode of correction. Unless the pillaging of houses and wanton destruction of property by your regiment ceases at once, he will place every officer in it under arrest, and recommend them to the department commander for dishonorable dismissal from the service." That was all, and the fact is, Spencer and his men were pretty much doing what Sherman wanted done, he knew Spencer and the Alabamians were capable of doing it, and the regiment remained in the vanguard.[35]

When the campaign reached the sea, Spencer reopened contact with Dodge, now in charge of the Department of Missouri at St. Louis: "We have had a delightful trip & all have enjoyed it." There was no modesty: "I have done all the fighting that was done by our Column (the 17th Corps) & have made a reputation for both myself & Regiment. I lost 48 men Killed & wounded on the trip & led the Corps to the breastworks just three miles from Savannah without their firing a gun or forming a line of battle all the fighting was done by my Regiment." Sherman "traveled for 15 days with Genl Blair & at the rear of my Regiment. He took occasion yesterday to say to me that I had the best Cavalry Regiment he ever saw & has taken his escort from the Regiment." Not certain that his letters were getting through to Dodge, he repeated the exploits in January 1865 and reminded Dodge that he had "made more reputation on the march than any other officers." Ten days later, Spencer was assigned to Judson J. Kilpatrick's Cavalry for the march into the Carolinas and given command of the 3rd Brigade, including his 1st Alabama, the 9th Illinois, 5th Kentucky, 9th Michigan, and 5th Ohio, and a battery of Rodman guns. "I shall endeavor to acquit myself with credit," he said. "I have a good Brigade & am certain that I can manage it."[36]

Seven weeks lapsed before he again wrote Dodge from Fayetteville, North Carolina, as Sherman was ready to feint toward Raleigh and move on Goldsboro. "The army [has] had no fighting thus far but the Cavalry has had a good deal," he wrote, quickly noting that "I have won two brilliant victories with my Brigade." He had, in fact, been sharply tested and performed well in early February near Williston, South Carolina, when his brigade, holding the road to Augusta, Georgia, was attacked by the Alabama Brigade of Joseph Wheeler's cavalry. Spencer's brigade not only held but counterattacked, and "Then commenced one of the most thorough and complete routs I ever witnessed. The ground was completely strewn with guns, haversacks, &c. Five battle-flags were captured, including the brigade and four regimental flags, and a large number of horses and over thirty prisoners." A seven-mile pursuit dispersed the Confederate Alabamians "in every direction through the woods and swamps." Viewing the encounter as a major early victory, Kilpatrick was quick to give him credit: "Colonel Spencer alone conducted the fight, displaying much skill and great gallantry."[37]

After Williston, Kilpatrick often put Spencer's brigade out front, using it to secure crossroads and stream crossings, to find usable roads, and to flank and feint. Engagements with enemy cavalry were relatively few until a sharp skirmish in early March, followed by the notorious Monroe's Cross-Roads encounter, known as Kilpatrick's Shirt-tail Skedaddle in much-repeated Confederate versions. According to Kilpatrick's frank report, he and Spencer had been moving in parallel with Wade Hampton's Confederate cavalry and had a rough encounter on March 9 when Kilpatrick, his staff, and Spencer accidentally rode through one of Hampton's divisions and Kilpatrick lost his escort. In the late evening, Kilpatrick (and a lady friend, not mentioned in his report) settled into a log cabin with Spencer's encampment at Monroe's Cross-Roads. Hampton followed and at daybreak on March 10, three divisions of Confederate cavalry stormed the camp, rousting Kilpatrick, Spencer, and most of the men in some stage of undress, often just shirttails and drawers. According to Kilpatrick, "in less than a minute" the charge "had driven back my people, had taken possession of my headquarters, captured my artillery, and the whole command was flying before the most formidable cavalry charge I have ever witnessed. Colonel Spencer and a large portion of my staff were virtually taken prisoners." Most of the Union soldiers were forced back into a swamp, but when the Confederates faltered and turned to gathering up the scattered plunder, the Union forces "re-established our lines, and for an hour and a half foiled every attempt of the enemy to retake it." Spencer added that when Maj. Frances Cramer was wounded and captured, J. J. Hinds led a 1st Alabama charge, "which drove the enemy into the swamp, resulting in the capture of their horses." It was an embarrassing encounter, and yet as Kilpatrick later noted, "no matter what the facts may be regarding the conduct of my people under the first terrible onset of the foe, they can proudly boast that without assistance they regained their camp, animals, artillery, and transportation, and drove the enemy in confusion from the ground."[38]

It was close to the end of the war when Spencer wrote Dodge from Faison's Depot, North Carolina, on April 4. Though tired, he had not lost his touch in rendering extreme judgment; he noted in particular that Kilpatrick "is the greatest humbug of the age . . . our relations are pleasant enough & I am too sharp to quarrel with him. Still. . . . Kil is the greatest liar that ever lived & would not under any circumstances let an opportunity slip to manufacture any tale that would reflect to his credit at the same time he is no braver than he should be." As for himself, "I have done well my Brigade has done all the fighting that has been done by the command and all the flanking & in all the exposed places I have lost heavily & have each time been successful Kilpatrick places every confidence in me." He assumed that he would soon "be Brevetted all of which does not amount to a row of pins." He was headed to Goldsboro to again see Kilpatrick about a leave of absence, but he was not hopeful. Worn down, he confessed to his friend Dodge that he was "Having the blues dreadfully tonight."[39]

In fact, Sherman approved a thirty-day leave and Spencer was much refreshed as he headed for Watertown, New York, with Bella. Although "perfectly horrified" at the "terrible calamity" of Lincoln's assassination, he did not dwell on it long. He asked Dodge for a letter—Sherman, Howard, Blair, Kilpatrick, Corse, and Vandever, all of whom he had denounced at one point or another to Dodge, had "all have given letters of the most complimentary character. Genl Sherman says 'I consider you the best "Cavalier" I ever met & your services have been of inestimable value to me.'" As for the future, "My army friends advise that I settle in Ala," a move Spencer had been considering since as early as August 1864 when, with a typically jumbled and mixed motivation, he contemplated buying a plantation near Mooresville: "& if I do I shall settle there & live and my connections with this Regiment will do me a great deal of good in after life & will give me a good position in the state & a good deal of capital can be made out of it and I can do the country some good." By May 1865 he was "strongly of the opinion that I shall settle somewhere south as I think the chances for making a fortune there the best." After six days of looking after the interests of Alabama in Washington, he was fully back in the "political figuring" he so loved: "I am urging Wm. H. Smith of Randolph Co for Military Governor. I have received large petitions for him & had three interviews with the President [Andrew Johnson]." He was headed for Huntsville to "hold meetings for Smith

& send forward petitions for him. . . . If we can get Smith we can control the state without trouble." In the meantime, his promotion to brevet brigadier general came through, thanks to "Genl Grants kindness," and he was mustered out on July 5.[40]

But by August, having almost no success with President Johnson in getting his Unionist friends appointed, he had taken a Radical stance: "When you get out of the army I wish you would come south & operate. We are bound to succeed ultimately and if we cant any other way we can by 'Negro Suffrage' I have been figuring with the radicals & think I am in the ring As I am in business with Gov [William] Sprague I can get his & the [Salmon P.] Chase influence & expect when Congress meets to knock this Provisional Governor system higher than a kite. I am in favor of Negro suffrage or reducing all these states to the position of Territories & keeping them so for years to come or until the leaders are all dead or have left the country. This is the only safe course of procedure." At least his economic future had brightened as he headed back to Tuscaloosa: "I have bought a lot of cotton there & now return with money to finish paying for it. I ought to make at least fifty thousand dollars but shall be satisfied with half that amount." He secured capital from several sources including former Rhode Island governor and now senator William Sprague, a wealthy textile manufacturer, and spent the better part of August, September, and October crisscrossing the state purchasing cotton and preparing it for shipment from Mobile to New York. He figured he could land the cotton in New York for 28 cents a pound and sell it for 60 cents. He had a quarter interest in 1,000 bales by mid-October and anticipated more: "I think I shall make a good year's work out of it."[41]

There was one allegation that his cotton-purchasing methods were not always aboveboard. In September, John S. Kennedy of Tuscaloosa charged that Spencer, "the agent for A. & D. Sprague," and/or a partner, "Mr. Mitchell," bought two lots of cotton, one from a Tuscaloosa individual (50 bales at 20 cents per pound) and one from a Tuscaloosa firm (1,500 bales at 22 cents per pound), asserting that both parties "were on the list of those whose property would be libeled for confiscation." Under the fear of confiscation, the two parties sold the cotton at a low price. Kennedy, a partner in the firm who was out of town at the time of the transaction, saw this as a "great fraud and swindle," but he was unable to cancel the contract so he reported it to Provisional Governor Lewis Parsons, admitting that his "knowledge of the facts is not definite, because I was too much incensed to investigate them." Such tactics were probably not out of the reach of Spencer, but he was certainly smart enough to see the negative consequences of such practices in a tight community such as Tuscaloosa. Apparently the allegations never became public or they surely would have resurfaced in politics later.[42]

In the meantime, he put his cotton on the way to New York and came north "like Micawber [to] wait for something to turn up." Politics in Alabama had "played out" with ex-Confederates fully in control: "A Yankee stands no show.... No loyal Union man can hold a position in the South if the Presidents policy is carried out." He hoped Congress would stand up to Johnson, and he tried to help the Radicals by testifying before the Joint Committee on Reconstruction in late January. Saying that he now considered Decatur his residence, he was fairly careful in his wording but often blunt. He estimated that only about 10 percent of white Alabamians were loyal, a majority of whom were concentrated in five mountain counties. Southern public sentiment had changed greatly to hostility, thanks in large part to the policy of the Johnson administration in "appointing secessionists and rebels to office, and in pardoning them." He thought that "the treatment of the negro is terrible in the extreme," but he firmly believed that the freedmen were willing to work for just compensation: "I have always said everywhere that there is more disposition among the negroes to work than among the white people." Finally, he thought that the legislative "arming of the militia is only for the purpose of intimidating the Union men, and enforcing upon the negroes a species of slavery." Spencer knew his audience well, and as he told Dodge two days later, "I think a rupture between the President and party very probable.... The slavery of the negro is more terrible than formerly and the Country has spent millions of both blood and treasurie in an idle and foolish war; although we conquered their armies they are in reality the victors."[43]

In February 1866, his cotton arrived in New York. Just how much he made is unknown, but Bella indicated that he was "well satisfied with his venture." Given the situation in Alabama, he was "at a great loss to know what I shall do; would like to remain South but things look squally. It will be a rough place to take Mrs. Spencer. Money can be made very fast there but it is terrible to live in." So, like several times before, he headed west, and during the last half of 1866 he scouted "for something that would pay" in California. Settling in San Francisco with Bella, he "made about my expenses" by speculating in mining stocks, but generally he thought that "Business in California is badly overdone and there is no inducement for any one to come here to settle." Alabama remained on his mind. "If Congress will impeach 'Moses' [Johnson]," he wrote Dodge, "I would go back to Ala." The rejection of Johnson's policy in the congressional elections of 1866 cheered Spencer, and with the advent of congressional reconstruction, Alabama became more promising. By February 1867, he had decided to return to Decatur, while Bella planned to take a yearlong, round-the-world trip and send back travel pieces to newspapers. He advised Dodge, soon to be seated in the Fortieth Congress, that the best policy would be a radical one: impeach Johnson and reduce the Southern states to territories or place them under military rule.[44]

Things turned Spencer's way. By April he was in Tuscaloosa, and, thanks to the endorsements of Dodge, Sprague, Chase, the Iowans, and numerous military friends, he secured an appointment as register in bankruptcy for Alabama's fourth congressional district and began working to "carry Alabama and secure it permanently to the Republican party." In early July, he urged Dodge to oppose any effort to remove political disabilities from any ex-Confederate, even those "who are now acting temporarily with us," a hint that he was already wary of some moderate scalawags. Bella had put off her trip and joined him in Tuscaloosa in the late spring, but tragically, she caught typhoid fever and she and their unborn child died in August. Her death was a real blow, and he lamented to Dodge in October that he had lost all ambition and had no interest in politics: "I am completely broken down in spirits and care but very little for the future." Still he felt "that my duty is to remain here and help reconstruct this God forsaken and miserable country. It is truly an awful place to live in, but since we have the colored men to help us we can out vote them and I think if it becomes necessary that we can out fight them." He thought that he could be elected to Congress but did not feel like pursuing it: "Six months may change my views. I stand as well as any Union man in the state and do not believe that there is any man in [the] party that wields more influence than I do."[45]

As it always did, his ambition resurfaced, and by the spring of 1868 he had his eye on one of Alabama's two Senate seats. He moved his office from Tuscaloosa to the more friendly environs of Decatur, he asked Dodge to secure letters of endorsement from prominent Northern politicians, and he offered to pay Dodge's expenses to come and aid him: "You could help me a great deal & I think secure my election." He wanted, he explained, "to show the members [of the legislature] that I would have more influence if elected than other candidates." As an additional lure, he offered to show Dodge "some good speculations that will pay you tenfold." There is no indication that Dodge went, but for the moment, the Republican effort was almost completely successful. Republicans dominated the new legislature, and after ratifying the Fourteenth Amendment the legislature turned to the election of senators. Thanks to his efforts, Spencer emerged as a U.S. senator, taking the four-year term while fellow carpetbagger and quite recent arrival Willard Warner took the two-year term.[46]

In some ways Spencer's selection was a remarkable achievement, but during the war years he had carefully laid a base of camaraderie in cause and arms among north Alabama Unionists, he had futilely intervened on their behalf with Andrew Johnson, and he had spent the last half of 1865 traveling around the state. He kept ahead of the pace of congressional sentiment regarding black enfranchisement, and when he returned in 1867 he immediately threw himself into politics, reestablishing connections with his Unionist friends, making new ones among others dedicated to the Republican cause, many of them new arrivals, and befriending an emerging cluster of black leaders. Bella's death set him back for several months, but he emerged to travel the bankruptcy circuit relentlessly and piled up a caseload of four hundred by January 1868 as he reengaged in political figuring with others to set the course for Alabama's readmission to the Union. He worked diligently for legislative and congressional candidates in the elections of February 1868, used his position as register in bankruptcy to aid his friends, and brought in powerful outside endorsements for his Senate candidacy. He took a radical position, already expressing some distrust of moderate scalawags, as he cultivated the support of the freedmen and Unionists in the northern half of the state and fought against conservatives, the most rabid of whom he characterized as *"perfect fiends in human shape."*[47]

Although Spencer was obviously opportunistic, there is good reason to believe that he had become genuinely invested in Alabama. His activity seems well within the legitimate parameters of postbellum political practices and reflected his conviction that army men like himself, the freedmen, and "true" Southern Unionists should control Reconstruction and the process of "regenerating" the South. He was, however, now a Yankee holding a Southern political office—that made him a "carpetbagger," already an opprobrious epithet to an overwhelming majority of white Southerners. He would find that he could do almost nothing over the course of the next eleven years to please this ultimately triumphant portion of the Alabamian electorate.

Notes

1. Warner's speech is in *Congressional Globe*, 41st Cong., 3rd Sess., 576, appendix, 268–77. For Spencer's response to his alleged role in Warner's defeat, see *Alabama Weekly State Journal*, December 16, 1872, and *Daily State Journal*, October 22, 1872. Unfortunately for Spencer, national criticism grew with Horace Greeley's *New York Tribune* leading the way, charging that Spencer had engineered the Republican defeat in the election of 1870; see *New York Tribune*, December 8, 10, 1870.

2. Walter L. Fleming, *Civil War and Reconstruction in Alabama* (New York: Macmillan, 1905), 737; C. Mildred Thompson, "Carpet-baggers in the United States Senate," in *Studies in Southern History and Politics Inscribed to William Archibald Dunning* (New York: Columbia University Press, 1914), 164–65; John W. DuBose, *Alabama's Tragic Decade: Ten Years of Alabama, 1865–1874*, ed. James K. Greer (Birmingham: Webb Book Company, 1940), 100n, 288; Sarah Van V. Woolfolk (Wiggins), "George E. Spencer: A Carpetbagger in Alabama," *Alabama Review* 19 (January 1966): 52; see also Wiggins, *The Scalawag in Alabama Politics, 1865–1881* (University: University of Alabama Press, 1977), especially chaps. 2–5. For a more recent look at the ways in which the Spencer-Warner dispute played itself out in local politics and a more critical look at Warner himself, see Michael W. Fitzgerald, "Republican Factionalism and Black Empowerment: The Spencer-Warner Controversy and Alabama Reconstruction, 1868–1880," *Journal of Southern History* 64 (August 1998): 473–94, and Fitzgerald, *Urban Emancipation: Popular Politics in Reconstruction Mobile, 1860–1890* (Baton Rouge: Louisiana State University Press, 2002), especially chaps. 5–6. Biographies of the more radical Republicans, usually allied with Spencer, have also been more favorable in tone; see, for example, Loren Schweninger, *James T. Rapier and Reconstruction* (Chicago: University of Chicago Press, 1978) and William Warren Rogers Jr., *Black Belt Scalawag:*

The Making of Carpetbagger George E. Spencer / 213

Charles Hays and the Southern Republicans in the Era of Reconstruction (Athens: University of Georgia Press, 1993).

3. Most of what can be discerned about Spencer's New York upbringing and background comes from entries on his father and oldest brother in such sources as R. A. Oakes, comp., *Genealogical and Family History of the County of Jefferson, New York*, 2 vols. (New York: Lewis Publishing Company, 1905); Samuel W. Dupont and Henry B. Pierce, comps., *History of Jefferson County, New York* (Philadelphia: L. H. Everts & Company, 1878); Edgar C. Emerson, ed., *A Descriptive Work on Jefferson County, New York* (Boston: Boston History Company, 1898); along with U.S. Manuscript Census, Population Schedules, 1820–1870, Jefferson County, NY, Champion and other Towns; New York State Manuscript Census, 1825–1865, Jefferson County, Champion and other Towns; Jefferson County, NY, Offices of County Clerk and Surrogate's Court (Watertown), Deeds, Mortgages, Surrogate's Court, Wills/Probate, liber from 1820s through 1860s; and the Jefferson County, Watertown, and Champion Town clipping files in Genealogy Department, Flower Library, Watertown, NY.

4. For this first generation of Republicans, see Eric Foner, *Free Soil, Free Labor, Free Men: The Ideology of the Republican Party before the Civil War* (New York: Oxford University Press, 1970); William E. Gienapp, *The Origins of the Republican Party, 1852–1856* (New York: Oxford University Press, 1987); and Robert J. Cook, *Baptism of Fire: The Republican Party in Iowa, 1838–1878* (Ames: Iowa State University Press, 1994).

5. "Conversation with Ex-Senator George E. Spencer" (unpublished manuscript, ca. 1879) in Grenville M. Dodge Papers, State Historical Society of Iowa, Des Moines (hereafter Dodge Papers), 461–62; Stanley P. Hirshson, *Grenville M. Dodge: Soldier, Politician, Railroad Pioneer* (Bloomington: Indiana University Press, 1967), chaps. 1–2 (quote is from p. 24); Grenville Dodge Diary, January 22, April 7, 1857, Dodge Papers; Grenville Dodge Correspondence, folders 1–2, Dodge Family Papers, Western History Collection, Denver Public Library (hereafter Dodge Family Papers).

6. A. S. Bailey, "First Assembly at Des Moines," *Annals of Iowa* 31 (January 1953): 530; Spencer to Howe, December 14, 26, 1856, M. M. Crocker to Howe, January 11, 1857, Spencer to Howe, January 14, 1857, Howe to Maria Howe, January 10, March 8, 1856, H. S. Winslow to Howe, March 25, 1857, all in Orlando Howe Papers, State Historical Society of Iowa, Des Moines (hereafter Howe Papers).

7. For the Spirit Lake venture, see Spencer to Howe, December 14, 26, 1856, Howe to Maria Howe, correspondence February–April 1857, Spencer to Howe, April 29, May 15, November 16, 1857, January 12, October 30, 1858 (Howe's daughter's quote written in the margin), B. F. Paramenter to Howe, January 12, February 7, 1858, H. Kellogg to Howe, January 22, 1858, A. L. Harvey to Howe, October 17, 1858, all in Howe Papers. For the movement into the Spirit Lake area, see Thomas Teakle, *The Spirit Lake Massacre* (Des Moines: State Historical Society of Iowa, 1918); R. A. Smith, *A History of Dickinson County, Iowa* (Des Moines: Kenyon Printing, 1902); *History of Emmet County and Dickinson County, Iowa*. . . ., 2 vols. (Chicago: Pioneer Publishing Company, 1917), 1:252 ("young men" quote). Spencer's acquisition of Clay County land around the Spencer townsite during 1857–59 and his sale of most of this can be traced through the Grantor and Grantee Deed Records, general index and Book A, 7, 24, 33, 54, Book B, 61–62, 123–24, 127–28, 130–31, 133–34, 134–35, Clay County Recorder's Office, Spencer, IA.

8. H. Kellogg to Howe, January 22, 1858, Howe Papers; on Spencer selling out, see Land Deeds, Grantor, Book 1, Quit Claims, pp. 16, 20, Clerks Office, Dickinson County Court House, Spirit Lake, IA. Spencer netted only about $2,000, not a great amount given his aspirations. A revealing letter from Spencer to Howe in 1861 suggests that he had left the Spirit Lake area under

a cloud in 1859: "Please tell me what the people say of me there, whether it is good or bad." He indicated that he wanted to visit later in the summer but told Howe not to mention his coming to anyone: "When I come up I want to take them by surprise & accomplish some things that I could not were they expecting me, being forewarned would be forearmed." Spencer to Howe, June 6, 1861, Howe Papers. When Spirit Lake was reorganized at the beginning of the 1870s, Spencer bought two full blocks and a large lot in another block for $150, and named the adjacent streets "Alabama" and "Spencer." Town Deeds, Grantee, Warrantee Deed, Book A, 5, Town Plat, p. 630 (July 12, 1871), Clerks Office, Dickinson County.

9. Frank Hall, *History of the State of Colorado*, 4 vols. (Chicago: Blakely Printing Company, 1889–95), 4:325–28. Hall, the standard account, relied heavily on interviews with a couple of miners in the Spencer group. Spencer's mining claims can be partially traced through the record books of the Illinois District, Illinois & Dry Gulches Mining Claims Book, pp. 1, 25, 153, and Quandary Lode, Peruvian District Mining Claims Book, n.p., Office of the County Clerk, Summit County Courthouse, Breckenridge, CO.

10. "Some Interesting Breckenridge History: How the Name Breckenridge Was Given— Notes on the History of Our Town," and Felix Poznansky letter to the *Breckinridge Bulletin*, May 12, 1906, Breckenridge Clipping File, Western History Collection, Denver Public Library; "Early History of Mining on the Blue River and Vicinity," ms in Felix Poznansky Papers, Western History Collection, Denver Public Library. The town's name, of course, soon proved problematic when Breckinridge became the Southern Democratic presidential candidate in the campaign of 1860 and ultimately joined the Confederacy. Although a local historian suggested that "Spencer may have regretted that he had not named the new settlement for himself," he was probably little concerned; by late 1860, he was long gone from the Blue River area as the community quietly changed the spelling of its name to "Breckenridge."

11. Sandra Dallas, *Colorado Ghost Towns and Mining Camps* (Norman: University of Oklahoma Press, 1984), 34–35; Maxine Benson, *1001 Colorado Place Names* (Lawrence: University Press of Kansas, 1994), 24; U.S. Post Office, Post Offices and Postmasters in Colorado Territory, ms, microfilm, Western History Collection, Denver Public Library; Quandary Lode, Peruvian District Mining Claims Book, n.p., Office of the County Clerk, Summit County Courthouse, Breckenridge, CO. The sudden growth of the Blue River mining district is chronicled in the *Rocky Mountain News*, Weekly Edition, October 20, November 17, 1859, March 17, 21, April 18, 25, May 23, 30, June 13, 20, 1860 (the June 13 issue contains the last reference to Spencer).

12. Spencer to Dodge, April 18, May 4, 1861, Dodge Papers; Grenville Dodge Diary, April 25, 1861, Dodge Papers; *St. Joseph Free Democrat*, April 13, 1861; "Conversation with Ex-Senator George E. Spencer," Dodge Papers; *Nebraska Advertiser* (Brownsville), April 4, May 15, June 13, 20, 1861. Sutlers, usually one to a regiment, were essentially officially appointed vendors who offered soldiers certain approved items such as shoes, food, tobacco, books, newspapers, and cooking and dining ware for purchase. In the Spencer quotations in this chapter, the original wording has been left intact and no punctuation has been added.

13. First Regiment, Nebraska Volunteers, Northeast Military Department, RG 018, Subgroup 1, series 2, box 2, header information, Nebraska State Historical Society, Lincoln; *Nebraska Advertiser* (Brownsville), July 11, 17, August 1, 8, 15, 29, September 23, October 2, 1861, January 30, 1862, February 6, 27, March 6, 20, 1862; Regimental and Company Reports, September 1–October 31, 1861, January–October 1862, First Nebraska Regiment, U.S. Office of Adjutant General, RG 535, series 5, roll 46; John Thayer Report on Shiloh, *War of the Rebellion: A Compilation of the Official Records of the Union and Confederate Armies*, 128 vols. (Washington, DC, 1880–1901), ser. I, vol. 10, pt. 1, p. 195 (hereafter *OR*); Hirshson, *Dodge*, 45–66; Spencer to Dodge, August 12,

The Making of Carpetbagger George E. Spencer / 215

1862, Dodge Papers; Grenville Dodge to Nathan P. Dodge, September 28, November 16, 1862, in Dodge Family Papers. Spencer's appointment certainly did not please some—Dodge's brother Nathan, back at Council Bluffs, was blunt: "I don't think much of your contemplated AAG appointment. People here who have had business with him do not think much of him as a man. He left owing a great deal on this side & at Omaha, which he has shown no disposition to pay." Nathan was right—Spencer left some unpaid sutler debts to at least six suppliers, and the creditors came frequently to Dodge, who covered for Spencer and often collected from him over the next two years. See, for example, J. M. Phillips to Dodge, January 1, 1863, Nathan Dodge to Dodge, February 8, April 27, June 18, September 16, 1863, Dodge to Nathan Dodge, June 27, October 26, 1863, Grenville Dodge Diary, July 15, 1864, all in Dodge Papers; Dodge to Nathan P. Dodge, May 27, June 19, 27, 1863, Dodge Family Papers.

14. Dodge to Cole Baldwin, November 10, 1862, Dodge Family Papers; Hirshson, *Dodge*, 65–69, 73–75; George E. Spencer to Capt. Harn (Confederate), February 21, 1863, Dodge Papers; Dodge to August Mersy, July 20, 1863, *OR*, I, 24, pt. 3, p. 538; Dodge to Philip Roddey, January 17, 1863, *OR*, II, 5 (only one pt.), p. 185; R. J. Oglesby to Henry Binmore, May 29, 1863, *OR*, I, 24, pt. 3, p. 364; Gideon J. Pillow to William W. Mackall (with Braxton Bragg endorsement), July 14, 1863, Pillow to General S. Cooper, August 28, 1863, *OR*, IV, 2 (only one pt.), pp. 638–39, 775–76. On wartime north Alabama, see Margaret M. Storey, *Loyalty and Loss: Alabama's Unionists in the Civil War and Reconstruction* (Baton Rouge: Louisiana State University Press, 2004); Joseph W. Danielson, *War's Desolating Scourge: The Union's Occupation of North Alabama* (Lawrence: University Press of Kansas, 2012); Michael Fitzgerald, "'He Was Always Preaching the Union': The Wartime Origins of White Republicanism during Reconstruction" (in this volume); and Daniel E. Sutherland, *A Savage Conflict: The Decisive Role of Guerrillas in the American Civil War* (Chapel Hill: University of North Carolina Press, 2009).

15. Spencer to Dodge, September 18, 21, October 9, 1862, Dodge to Lorenzo Thomas, September 25, 1862, Dodge Papers; Dodge to Nathan P. Dodge, September 28, November 16, 1862, in Dodge Family Papers.

16. Spencer to Dodge, December 21, 1862, Dodge Papers. For Dodge's extensive spy network and use of native scouts, see Hirshson, *Dodge*, 67–69 and William B. Feis, *Grant's Secret Service: The Intelligence War from Belmont to Appomattox* (Lincoln: University of Nebraska Press, 2002), 125–30, 166–70. For Bella, see *National Cyclopedia of American Biography* (New York: J. T. White, 1906), 13:72 and her preface to Bella Z. Spencer, *Tried and True, or Love and Loyalty: A Story of the Great Rebellion* (Springfield, MA: W. J. Holland, 1866).

17. Thomas Jordan to Sterling Price, July 24, 1862, *OR*, I, 17, pt. 2, pp. 657–58, Braxton Bragg, Special Orders, No. 81, *OR*, I, 23, pt. 2, p. 728; Dodge to Philip Roddey, January 17, 1863, *OR*, II, 5 (only one pt.), p. 185; Dodge to Philip Roddey, January 17, 1863, Dodge Papers. For Spencer and Roddey's postwar mining connection, see *White Pine News* (Ely, NV), September 23, 1882, and Effie O. Read, *White Pine Lang Syne: A True History of White Pine County, Nevada* (Denver: Big Mountain Press, 1965), 123, quoting the *Ward (Nevada) Reflex*, September 1882. Although Roddey later spent a brief amount of time in Georgia and elements of his command joined other units from time to time, he was always soon back in north Alabama. For a sampling of later arguments to make sure that Roddey stayed in northern Alabama and defining his command, see Thomas J. Foster et al. to James A. Seddon (secretary of war), January 1864, *OR*, I, 32, pt. 2, pp. 514–15; Charles Pollard et al. to James A. Seddon, January 15, 1864, *OR*, I, 32, pt. 2, p. 561; Jno. D. Rather & J. W. S. Donnell to Robert Jemison Jr., February 7, 1864, James E. Saunders to Jemison, January 30, 1864, and endorsements, *OR*, I, 52, pt. 2, pp. 609–14; and T. H. Watts (Alabama governor) to Leonidas Polk, January 30, 1864, *OR*, I, 26, pt. 2, p. 554.

18. Grenville Dodge Diary, February 22, 25, March 2, 6, 19, 22, 1863, Dodge Papers; C. S. Hamilton to S. A. Hurlbut, March 6, 1863, *OR*, I, 24, pt. 3, 88 (conscripts quote); Dodge to Mother, March 8, 1863, Dodge Family Papers; Spencer to Dodge, February 27, 1863, March 22, 1863, A. B. Stuart to Dodge, March 22, 1863, *OR*, I, 24, pt. 3, pp. 72, 129–30.

19. Grenville Dodge Diary, April 9, 10, 18, 1863, Dodge Papers; P. D. Roddey to Spencer, April 12, 1863, *OR*, II, 5 (only one pt.), p. 924; Dodge to Richard Oglesby, April [13], 1863, *OR*, I, 23, pt. 2, pp. 245–46; Richard Oglesby to S. A. Hurlbut, April 14, 1863, S. A. Hurlbut to Grant, April 15, 1863, *OR*, I, 24, pt. 3, pp. 192, 195–96. Spencer caught a bit of much desired Northern attention for his raid; see *Cincinnati Gazette*, April 13, 1863, Dodge Papers.

20. Dodge to Oglesby, May 2, 5, 1863, *OR*, I, 23, pt. 1, pp. 247–58; W. H. Chamberlin, *History of Eighty First Regiment, Ohio Infantry Volunteers* (Cincinnati: Gazette Steam Printing House, 1865), chap. 5; R. J. Oglesby to Henry Binmore, May 3, 1863, *OR*, I, 28, pt. 1, p. 245; Florence M. Cornyn Report, May 16, 1863, *OR*, I, 28, pt. 1, p. 253; Braxton Bragg to General Joseph E. Johnston, May 20, 1863, *OR*, I, 52, pt. 2, p. 474; Joseph H. Sloss to Dodge, May 8, 1863, *OR*, II, 5 (only one pt.), p. 570; Oglesby to Henry Binmore, May 12, 20, 1863, *OR*, I, 23, pt. 2, p. 343.

21. Hirshson, *Dodge*, 76–77; Dodge to August Mersy, July 21, 1863, *OR*, I, 24, pt. 3, p. 540; Oglesby to Hurlbut, June 22, 1863, *OR*, I, 24, pt. 2, p. 474.

22. Personal Autobiography of Grenville Mellen Dodge, 1831–1870, 4 vols., mss, 1:72, 4:1207, Oglesby to General Dodge, August 10, 1863, Dodge to Anne Dodge, November 14, 1863, Anne Dodge to Dodge, November 15, 1863, all in Dodge Papers; Cyrus Clay Carpenter to Susan C. Burkholder, March 29, 1863, Cyrus Clay Carpenter Papers, University of Iowa, Iowa City; Dodge to Sylvanus Dodge, August 6, 1863, Dodge Family Papers.

23. Florence M. Cornyn to Spencer, May 16, 1863, *OR*, I, 23, pt. 1, p. 253; Dodge to Oglesby, May 5, 1863, *OR*, I, 23, pt. 1, pp. 247, 250, 251, 253, 254, 258; Glenda McWhirter Todd, *First Alabama Cavalry, U.S.A.: Homage to Patriotism* (Bowie, MD: Heritage Books, 1999), 9; Moses M. Bane Report to Spencer, May 19, 1863, *OR*, I, 23, pt. 1, pp. 259–60; F. M. Windes (Confederate) to Dodge, July 16, 1863, *OR*, II, 6 (only one pt.), p. 123; Hirshson, *Dodge*, 76–77; Dodge to August Mersy, July 21, 1863, *OR*, I, 24, pt. 3, p. 540; Dodge to E. M. Stanton, August 13, 1863, Dodge Papers. Some in the unit probably had personal arms; regiment historian Glenda Todd has suggested that in this skirmish, the unit had only "arms unfit for that branch of service" (9). For a brief history of the 1st Alabama, in addition to Todd's, see W. Stanley Hoole, *Alabama Tories: The First Alabama Cavalry, U.S.A., 1862–1865* (Tuscaloosa, AL: Confederate Publishing Company, 1960), and the unit's informative website, http://www.1stalabamacavalryusv.com, managed by Ryan Dupree, Madison, AL (accessed December 10, 2011).

24. Spencer to Dodge, August 9, 15, 26, 1863, Bella Spencer to Anne Dodge, August 17, September 2, 1863, J. W. Barnes to Dodge, August 27, September 6, 1863, Spencer to Dodge, September 7, 19, 30, 1863, all in Dodge Papers. For samples of Spencer's intelligence gathering, see E. A. Carr to Hurlbut, September 12, 15, 24, October 10, 1863, *OR*, I, 30, pt. 3, pp. 560, 642, 811, pt. 4, p. 243.

25. S. A. Hurlbut to John A Rawlins, September 29, 1863, *OR*, I, 30, pt. 3, p. 924; Hurlbut to Col. J. C. Kelton, October 6, 1863, enclosing Hurlbut to Spencer, October 3, 1863, *OR*, I, 30, pt. 4, pp. 118–19; Dodge to Hurlbut, October 18, 1863, *OR*, I, 30, pt. 4, p. 452; Dodge to Hurlbut, October 21, 1863, Hurlbut to Dodge, October 23, 1863, Hurlbut to McPherson, October 23, 1863, *OR*, I, 31, pt. 1, pp. 692, 705, 709.

26. Dodge to Anne Dodge, October 20, 1864, Dodge Papers; Dodge to Nathan P. Dodge, October 21, 1863, Dodge Family Papers; "Civil War Diary of Francis Wayland Dunn," excerpted in Todd, *First Alabama*, 104–7. For reaction to the rumor of capture, see Call Linton to Mrs.

Dodge, October 27, 1863, Julia Dodge to Anne Dodge, October 31, 1863, Nathan P. Dodge to Dodge, November 6, 1863, Bella Spencer to Anne Dodge, November 5, 1863, all in Dodge Papers.

27. Correspondent of the *N.Y. Post*, Pulaski, TN, February 1, 1864, taken from a California newspaper, the *Daily Evening Bulletin*, March 17, 1864, submitted by Marie Young to 1st Alabama, Union, website, http://www.1stalabamacavalryusv.com/ (accessed January 10, 2012); "On Skirmish at Vincent's Cross-Roads, near Bay Springs, Mississippi, October 26, 1863," Barnes Report, October 27, 1863, *OR*, I, 31, pt. 1, p. 37; Samuel W. Ferguson to S. D. Lee, October 31, 1863, *OR*, I, 31, pt. 1, pp. 37–38; Stephen D. Lee to George William Brent, October 30, 1863, Lee to B. S. Ewell, October 31, 1863, *OR*, I, 31, pt. 1, pp. 29–32. For a biting satire on Spencer's actions at Vincent's Cross-Roads, see *Moulton (AL) Advertiser*, September 4, 1868.

28. Sherman to F. P. Blair, October 27, 1863, *OR*, I, 31, pt. 1, pp. 762–63; Sherman to Halleck (same to Grant), Iuka, MS, October 28, 1863, *OR*, I, 31, pt. 1, p. 766; Dodge to Hurlbut, October 23, 1863, *OR*, I, 31, pt. 1, p. 709; Dodge to Nathan P. Dodge, November 24, December 3, 1863, Dodge Family Papers. Glenda Todd counted eight killed with many more missing in the immediate aftermath; see Dunn Diary, in Todd, *First Alabama*, 107.

29. Dodge to Nathan P. Dodge, December 3, 1863, Dodge Family Papers; Dunn Diary, October 30, 1863, April 3–23, 1864, in Todd, *First Alabama*, 107; Dodge to Spencer, Telegram, November 14 [17], 1863, Spencer to Dodge, November 19, 27, December 10, 1863, Grant to Dodge, December 6, 1863, Dodge to Spencer, December 7, 1863, Hurlbut S.O. 313, Memphis, December 9, 1863, Bella Spencer to Anne Dodge, November 27, 1863, Grenville Dodge Diary, January 17, 31, 1864, all in Dodge Papers; Dodge to Sherman, January 12, 1864, *OR*, I, 32, pt. 2, p. 35; Dodge to E. M. Stanton, January 9, 1864, *OR*, III, 4 (only one pt.), p. 16; Dodge to Spencer, January 27, 1864 (five messages), January 31, 1864, *OR*, I, 32, pt. 2, pp. 223, 277; Dodge to Rawlins, February 2, 1864, *OR*, I, 32, pt. 2, p. 313; Dodge to Nathan P. Dodge, January 21, 1864, Julia Dodge Diary, April 15, 16, 17, 1864, both in Dodge Family Papers.

30. Dodge Report, Atlanta Campaign, November 25, 1864, *OR*, I, 38, pt. 3, pp. 374–90; Tichenor's Journal, 16th AC Campaign 1864, Dodge Papers; Hirshson, *Dodge*, 93–95; Steven E. Woodworth, *Nothing but Victory: The Army of the Tennessee, 1861–1865* (New York: Vintage/Random House, 2005), chap. 28. Woodworth does not mention Spencer and the 1st Alabama at the forefront of Resaca, but the Dodge Papers seem reliable and since Spencer and the 1st Alabama were attached to Dodge's headquarters, they were undoubtedly there with John W. Fuller's Brigade, which Woodworth cites as in the lead.

31. Spencer to Dodge, July 22, 25, August 4, 10 (two letters), 1864, Dodge Papers.

32. George Tichenor to Nathan P. Dodge, August 21, 1864, Dodge Family Papers; Dunn Diary, November 3, 1864, in Todd, *First Alabama*, 158; Spencer to Dodge, September 11, 25, 1864, Dodge Papers; Jno. Corse, General Orders No. 7, October 12, 1864, *OR*, I, 39, pt. 3, p. 229; Corse Report, October 27, 1864, *OR*, I, 39, pt. 1, pp. 761, 771.

33. Spencer to Dodge, November 1, 1864, Dodge Papers; Organization of Troops Table, Howard, *OR*, I, 39, pt. 3, p. 563; Sherman to Grant, October 22, 1864, *OR*, I, 39, pt. 2, pp. 394–95; Corse order of movement, November 10, 1864, *OR*, I, 39, pt. 3, p. 729; O. O. Howard Special Orders 167, November 14, 1864, *OR*, I, 44 (only one pt.), p. 453.

34. Howard Special Field Orders 172, November 19, 1864, *OR*, I, 44, p. 493; Howard to Sherman, November 21, 1864, *OR*, I, 44, p. 509; Giles A. Smith Report, Savannah Campaign, *OR*, I, 44, pp. 154–55; Giles A Smith to F. P. Blair, November 23, 1864, *OR*, I, 44, pp. 531–32; Blair, Special Orders No. 290, near Ball's Ferry, November 26, 1864, *OR*, I, 44, p. 550; Spencer to Blair, November 28, 1864, *OR*, I, 44, p. 566; C. Cadle Jr. to Spencer, December 1, 1864, *OR*, I, 44, p. 596; Blair, Special Orders No. 297, December 3, 1864, Blair, Special Orders No. 298, December 4,

1864, Blair, Special Orders No. 308, December 16, 1864, Blair, Special Orders No. 317, December 26, 1864, Blair, Special Orders No. 318, December 27, 1864, *OR*, I, 44, pp. 614–15, 623, 732, 815, 822.

35. C. Cadle Jr. to Spencer, November 20, 1864, *OR*, I, 44, pp. 504–5.

36. Spencer to Dodge, December 16, 1864, January 5, 15, 18, 22, 1865, Dodge Papers; Sherman, Special Field Orders No. 7, January 9, 1865; *OR*, I, 47, pt. 2, pp. 29, 30.

37. Spencer to Dodge, March 14, 1865, Dodge Papers; Judson J. Kilpatrick to L. M. Dayton, February 8, 1865, *OR*, I, 47, pt. 2, pp. 351–52; Spencer Report of Operations, January 28–March 24, 1865, March 30, 1865, *OR*, I, 47, pt. 1, pp. 891–95; Kilpatrick Report No. 212 of Operations, January 28–March 24, April 5, 1865, *OR*, I, 47, pt. 1, pp. 857–64.

38. Kilpatrick Special Field Orders No. 28, February 27, 1865, Kilpatrick Special Field Orders No. 29, March 1, 1865, *OR*, I, 47, pt. 2, pp. 603–4, 635; Kilpatrick to L. M. Dayton, March 3, 11, 1865, *OR*, I, 47, pt. 2, pp. 671, 786–87; Report of Major Christopher T. Cheek of Operations, January 28–March 24, March 28, 1865, *OR*, I, 47, pt. 1, pp. 898–900; Sherman Report to Halleck, April 4, 1865, *OR*, I, 47, pt. 1, p. 23; Spencer Report of Operations, January 28–March 24, 1865, March 30, 1865, *OR*, I, 47, pt. 1, pp. 891–95; Kilpatrick Report No. 212 of Operations, January 28–March 24, April 5, 1865, *OR*, I, 47, pt. 1, pp. 857–64. Also see Eric J. Wittenberg, *The Battle of Monroe's Crossroads and the Civil War's Final Campaign* (New York: Savas Beatie LLC, 2006); Samuel J. Martin, *"Kill-Cavalry," Sherman's Merchant of Terror: The Life of Union General Hugh Judson Kilpatrick* (Teaneck, NJ: Fairleigh Dickinson University Press, 1996), 219–23; and Rod Andrew Jr., *Wade Hampton: Confederate Warrior to Southern Redeemer* (Chapel Hill: University of North Carolina Press, 2008), 271–78.

39. Spencer to Dodge, April 4, 1865, Dodge Papers; Spencer Report of Operations, January 28–March 24, 1865, March 30, 1865, *OR*, I, 47, pt. 1, p. 895.

40. Kilpatrick to Sherman and Sherman reply, April 8, 1865, *OR*, I, 47, pt. 3, p. 133; Spencer to Dodge, April 16, 1865, August 4, 1864, May 1, 20, 1865, Dodge Papers; Spencer to Andrew Johnson, May 17, June 2, 1865, Andrew Johnson Papers, Manuscript Division, Library of Congress; Todd, *First Alabama*, 355.

41. Spencer to Dodge, August 1, October 14, 1865, Dodge Papers.

42. Jno. S. Kennedy to Lewis Parsons, September 23, 1865, Miscellaneous Correspondence, Governor Lewis Parsons Papers, Alabama Department of Archives and History (hereafter ADAH). Kennedy may have meant "A. & W." rather than "A. & D." Sprague—the former was the name of the family's large textile manufacturing firm in Rhode Island. My thanks to Michael Fitzgerald for alerting me to the Kennedy letter.

43. Spencer to Dodge, October 14, 1865, January 28, 1866, Dodge Papers; George E. Spencer Testimony, January 26, 1866, *Report of the Joint Committee on Reconstruction*, 39th Cong., 1st Sess., pt. III, 8–10.

44. Bella Spencer to Anne Dodge, January 17, 1866, Spencer to Dodge, January 28, October 4, 1866, February 9, 1867, all in Dodge Papers.

45. Spencer to Dodge, July 1, 2, October 22, 1867, George C. Tichenor to Dodge, August 28, 1867, all in Dodge Papers; Spencer to J. C. Keffer, July 12, 31, 1867, Wager Swayne Papers, ADAH. For the workings of the bankruptcy law, see *(Montgomery) Weekly Advertiser*, June 25, 1867.

46. Spencer to Dodge, June 15, July 2, 1868, Dodge Papers. For Alabama politics through this period, see Wiggins, *Scalawag*, 5–55; Peter Kolchin, *First Freedom: The Response of Alabama's Blacks to Emancipation and Reconstruction* (Westport, CT: Greenwood Press, 1972); Michael W. Fitzgerald, *The Union League Movement in the Deep South: Politics and Agricultural Change during Reconstruction* (Baton Rouge: Louisiana State University Press, 1989); Storey, *Loyalty and Loss*,

chaps. 5–6; and Storey, "The Crucible of Reconstruction: Unionists and the Struggle for Alabama's Postwar Homefront," in *The Great Task Remaining before Us: Reconstruction as America's Continuing Civil War*, ed. Paul A. Cimbala and Randall M. Miller (New York: Fordham University Press, 2010), 69–87. Fleming, *Civil War and Reconstruction in Alabama*, 473–552, can still be read with profit for its reflection of conservative perceptions.

47. Spencer to Dodge, May 3, 1868, Dodge Papers. For a sampling of Spencer's most vehement opposition, see Rylan Randolph's *Tuskaloosa Independent Monitor*, May 15, 1867, February 2, March 25, April 1, 7, May 26, June 6, 1868; for the origins and power of the terms of derision applied to Republicans, see Ted Tunnell, "Creating 'the Propaganda of History': Southern Editors and the Origins of *Carpetbagger* and *Scalawag*," *Journal of Southern History* 72 (November 2006): 789–822 and K. Stephen Prince, "Legitimacy and Interventionism: Northern Republicans, the 'Terrible Carpetbagger,' and the Retreat from Reconstruction," *Journal of the Civil War Era* 2 (December 2012): 538–63. Unfortunately Spencer is little represented in Alabama manuscript collections in the period from his return to Alabama in spring 1867 to his selection to the Senate in mid-1868. One exception is a handful of Spencer letters in the Wager Swayne Papers, several of them to other Republicans. See, for example, Spencer to William H. Smith, June 26, July 7, October 13, 1867, Spencer to Wager Swayne, July 13, 1867, and Spencer to J. C. Keffer, July 12, 30, 1867, ADAH.

12

"He Was Always Preaching the Union"

The Wartime Origins of White Republicanism during Reconstruction

Michael W. Fitzgerald

Historians have long been perplexed by the native white Republicans of the Reconstruction era, or "scalawags," as the contemporary slur described them. At the turn of the twentieth century, the Dunning school demonized them as apostates. Postwar loyalists were "an unpleasant and violent part of the population," as Walter Lynwood Fleming wrote.[1] Since the 1950s, the revisionist rehabilitation of Reconstruction has improved their reputation, but the centrality of race in this literature leaves their intent somewhat indistinct. By all accounts, the mass of white Republicans were not enticed by the prospect of social equality. Wartime Unionism instead inspired them, but understanding Republicans' motivation is difficult, in part because scalawag scholarship has been characterized by excess attention to low-hanging fruit.[2]

Historians gravitate too readily toward the stories of the most articulate scalawags. Prominent leaders have full individual studies, and collective biographies compare Republican leaders and officeholders to their Democratic opponents. The modern literature tends to emphasize their normality, their rootedness in antebellum political life. But politicians respond to individual motives of patronage and self-interest, so scholars should also seek the voices of more typical white Reconstruction supporters. Fortunately the records of the Southern Claims Commission allow less-prominent Republicans to enter the historical record because agents transcribed or paraphrased the statements of witnesses with limited literacy. This source has its biases: claimants sought Federal recompense for damage by Union troops on the basis of demonstrable loyalty and residence in a war-torn locale.[3] One cannot rely too confidently on these data as a sample, but there are too few sources containing life histories of scalawags to disregard this evidence. Officials evaluated their claims, providing independent verification, and historians have used these statements to hear unlettered rural voices in other contexts. Dylan Penningroth, for example, explored the informal property holding of former slaves.[4] More recently, Margaret Storey used these materials to illuminate the Unionist subculture.[5] But with the exception of Storey's work, scholars have been slow to pan the postwar Reconstruction stories from this river of wartime evidence.

Republican voters spoke volubly about where their dissident politics fit in with the trajectory of their lives. The focus here will be on Alabama, a state where a large Unionist presence generated substantial evidence—thirty-six reels of microfilm in the accepted claims alone.[6] Many additional claimants likely supported Reconstruction, voted "Union" as the common phrase went, but that terminology is ambiguous chronologically and otherwise.[7] Here we consider only individuals characterized by terms like "Republican," "pro-Reconstruction," "Grant voter," or "Ku Klux Klan victim." Being identified so explicitly suggests pronounced Republican beliefs. For example, Henry Stutts, according to one Democrat, would "rather vote for a nigger than one of my sort now."[8] Voters of such conviction describe a wartime experience quite distinct from that of the more familiar Reconstruction spokesmen.

An examination of the higher reaches of the Republican leadership suggests why. A number of studies have concluded that across the South, prominent scalawags tended to be men of political experience, education, and substantial wealth. James Alex Baggett's study concluded that in social background, they resembled their Democratic counterparts except for their politics.[9] Future Republicans were outspoken anti-Confederates, though the specifics differed depending on context. On the whole, they were consistent, and there is no call to minimize their bravery or commitment. But they also had the means and connections to cushion the consequences those less well situated might expect. All Unionists shared the weight of unfavorable public opinion; all perceived themselves as operating under coercion or direct threat; and many were arrested by the Confederate authorities. These experiences fused future Republicans together across class lines. But the specifics of Confederate repression differed drastically, given the socially stratified character of the slaveholder republic. To be direct, prosperous dissidents mostly avoided the more searing forms of wartime trauma.

Charles Hays provides an archetype of the experience of elite dissent, as a rich Black Belt planter who later became a Republican congressman. In 1860, Hays entered political life as a public supporter of Stephen Douglas for president, an urgent anti-secession position that many future Republicans shared. When the war came, he refused to volunteer until the draft forced his hand. In his postwar pardon application, he explained that he had asked friends to find him a staff position that involved no actual fighting. His contacts knew of his ethical misgivings and obliged him; he served for seven months as a "nominal" aide without commission or pay.[10] Future congressman Christopher C. Sheets had a rougher time. Less prosperous and representing highland Unionists, he opposed secession vociferously and was an outspoken anti-Confederate in the legislature. Sheets encouraged draft resistance and helped dissidents pass through the lines. He was jailed as a traitor and threatened with death repeatedly by soldiers. But even he profited from elite connections. Sheets could secure lawyers, visits, and food in jail. Sympathizers even took up a collection for him when he got out.[11]

Narratives of privilege, featuring scruple, favoritism, and considerable shiftiness, prevail among prominent Republican politicos. Congressman R. S. Heflin of Randolph County, a lawyer and legislator, had been repeatedly arrested for his well-known opposition to the war. On one occasion, he was captured and taken to Montgomery, but he won release through the "intercession of several friends in the City, who were men of influence." On another occasion, he was tipped off by a friend that he was to be arrested and would likely "disappear" while in custody.[12] He escaped to sign a Unionist manifesto in the Northern press, though soldiers sacked his home and law office. A Republican leader recalled Heflin and Sheets as the two most endangered Union leaders in Alabama; another termed them the two most persecuted.[13] The point is that leaders whom Confederates viewed as open traitors nonetheless survived. The most prominent Union man in the state, future Republican governor William H. Smith, had a similar experience. Smith found himself embroiled in local draft resistance in Randolph County. Hearing that the cavalry was coming for him, he and several brothers slipped through the lines. The Smiths recruited for the 1st Alabama Union cavalry, and he and Heflin accompanied Sherman's march.[14]

Even Republican leaders of less prominence had similar experiences. The slaveholding South readily deferred to wealthy, educated men; dissenters might be victimized by the undisciplined soldiery or angry citizens, but the legal system was not designed to punish them. J. J. Martin of Macon County was drafted, but a friend found him a position in the quartermaster's department—unpaid, he said, to salve his ethical qualms. He then secured an exemption under the twenty-slave law.[15] According to a Unionist colleague, the rich Montgomery lawyer Adam Felder "dodged service" long enough to gain public odium, though he did eventually volunteer.[16] Jesse W. Mahan of Bibb County was advised to run for office to escape the draft but he failed to get elected. He sought help from a friend, a major, on the plea that it was "none of his fight," and he eventually secured a position in the government niter bureau.[17] Joseph C. Bradley of Huntsville found a position as a taxation official, which he claimed to have taken to shield his substantial network of fellow ex-Union men.[18] Bradley became a nucleus of the burgeoning "Conservative" movement in Montgomery, which sought to push the failing Confederacy toward surrender.

Beyond the ranks of prominent Reconstruction officeholders, dissidents with money commonly fared similarly, as described in the claims records. Middle-aged and older men predominated among those with wealth; they had varied options to evade military service. Samuel M. Wallace escaped as a Confederate tax collector, serving without pay to oblige a friend.[19] Perry Harrison did much the same, protected by "ultra Rebel" in-laws in a hostile neighborhood. Harrison was once arrested, but he volunteered to work in a saltpeter cave until he could reach the Northern troops.[20] Thomas Nation, a future Blount County Republican officeholder, owned twenty-one slaves but "had to play shut mouth."[21] He joined a home guard but never drilled, and the gesture was apparently sufficient for safety. The merchant John Austin also had spoken too freely, but he had friends who prevented a lynching, and his wife persuaded her relations to intervene on his behalf.[22] Austin eventually made it to the North, leaving his wife behind to tend his possessions, as did future Alabama Supreme Court Justice Thomas M. Peters. Peters recalled that because he was a prosperous slaveholder Confederates left his property alone, his emphatic Unionist politics notwithstanding.[23]

Open conflict with Confederate authorities proved more common in some localities than others. Dissidents far behind Confederate lines mostly deferred to overwhelming pro-war sentiment. Especially in the Black Belt, the few future scalawags avoided overt actions certain to bring retaliation. Few were able to entirely evade participation in the Confederate war effort, buying bonds, accepting currency, and the like; they knew the authorities and their neighbors were watching them. Furthermore, as defeat loomed the "Conservatives" in the government sought to open lines of communication northward, which opened possibilities for elites to influence government policy. For example, lawyer and future Republican Milton Saffold accepted a government position from a family friend, former justice John A. Campbell, a well-known Conservative who sought a negotiated peace. Saffold assumed ombudsman duties; he examined political prisoners and arranged their release from jail where possible. Saffold called himself a working friend of the Union who was denounced as a "traitor, schemer, tory & various other epithets." These elite networks operated within Confederate lines; they excluded the bulk of less circumspect and less prosperous Unionists living in contested areas.[24]

Future Republican spokesmen often made themselves unpopular, but they also had layers of social insulation. Politically connected dissidents might anticipate and evade arrest. While elite Unionists often avoided military service, they could generally do so through craft or flight rather than outright resistance. When apprehended, they could afford lawyers or occasionally bribe their way out of jail. Furthermore, prominent future Republicans often resided in cities, locations that were safe relative to the countryside. Recently scholars have noted the existence of Unionist networks in major cities like Atlanta. In urban Alabama, a diverse population existed of Northern and foreign-born merchants, and business connections often shielded such men. One merchant recalled that Northern-origin colleagues celebrated Union victories in Montgomery.[25] He felt relatively protected meeting in private homes, even though he knew Union men were being killed in the nearby hills. Officials generally tolerated such seditious gatherings as long as they yielded nothing overtly traitorous. Furthermore, middle-aged elite dissidents often had sons and sons-in-law serving as Confederate officers or in the government. Such connections both directly and indirectly protected even those known to be unsympathetic to the Confederacy.

It would not do to overstate this point, for prominence in the Union cause was never safe. The probate judge of Winston County, suspected of sheltering draft evaders, would be tortured to death by a Confederate detachment.[26] All Unionists perceived themselves as victimized by common oppression, which helped bind people across socioeconomic lines. But Unionist/Republican spokesmen had to come to terms with the modest economic means of their popular following, which tended to color perceptions of Union men. Margaret Storey notes that dissident planters in the Tennessee Valley commonly expressed frustrations about the Confederacy. Former slaves sometimes even testified to their ex-masters' opposition, but the point is that for some antiwar planters, loyalty largely found expression in griping to their slaves.[27] Most white Republicans, small farmers in the mountains of northern Alabama and refugees in the Tennessee Valley, had a very different experience of dissent.

Limited means generated wartime trauma. This study uses data pertaining to 111 individuals that appear in the claims testimony as Republican voters without apparent postwar officeholding aspirations.[28] Of that number, only 10, or about 9 percent, can be shown to have come from slaveholding households, far below the proportion in the state as a whole. Of those located in the population schedules of the 1860 census, nearly all came from the Tennessee Valley or the hill country south of it. Almost all appear in the census as farmers rather than planters. Their average household wealth of $2,300 looks modest compared to the estimated Alabama white household average of $8,146.[29] Of the forty-six Republicans listed in the census, five lived in households owning no land, and thirteen reported no more than five hundred dollars' worth of land. That is, about two-fifths were below this modest threshold of landed wealth. In studies like the census, poorer transients tend to drop out of the records. Truly destitute tenants would not likely make postwar property claims, and the process itself incurred substantial fees, all of which underscores the relatively low reported wealth.

Statements highlighting the relative poverty of future Republicans reemphasize the importance of these figures. As J. Mills Thornton argued, class resentment of Whig modernizers was the animating force behind the long Democratic domination of Alabama.[30] It is perhaps not surprising that prewar Democrats are heavily represented among the future Republicans of this study. Of those who reported presidential preference in 1860, a majority voted for Stephen Douglas.[31] The national Democratic candidate received a sliver of the overall Alabamian vote, just 15 percent, so the disproportionate support among these future Republicans suggests a mixture of egalitarian and Unionist views. Though John P. Blackwell's invocation of a "rich man's war, poor man's fight" is only occasionally articulated, anti-elite expressions pervade these claims sources.[32] Philip Harwood feared "an aristocratic government, and oppressive to the poor," predicting that a man who did not own slaves would not be allowed to vote.[33] John V. Gross blamed slaveholders for the war, and he reportedly said, "if the rebels were successful the large slave holders would get possession of all the good land in the South, and push all the small farmers out on poor [hilltop] nobs, and that about the first thing they would do would be to establish a property qualification, before a man was allowed to vote."[34] Though Jacksonian-tinged expressions might seem ill placed among postwar Republicans, the claims bristle with them.

Margaret Storey's pathbreaking work on wartime Alabama emphasizes the diverse character of the wartime loyalist network. In her words, the evidence "challenges the usefulness of a class-based, or narrowly antislaveholder/antislavery, explanation of unionism."[35] If this interpretation is correct, contemporaries viewed the subset that later avowed unequivocal Republican loyalties differently. Descriptions of outright poverty pepper the testimony, even in sympathetic discussions. A supportive neighbor called Jasper Harper in Marshall County a "very poor man," and William Underwood was described similarly.[36] J. R. Jack was likewise "a hard working poor man with a large family of girls" who lost his conscript son at Petersburg.[37] Theoron Underwood of Cherokee County actually had multiple people attest to his poverty.[38] Lack of means seemed connected to other less-approved social attributes. A claims agent described Alex Ellenburg as a poor, sallow, despondent man who cried when Rebel soldiers took his last hog.[39] Henry Stutts appears in the 1860 census without any land, and he signed his forms with an "X." He owned a still, but "his farm is a very poor one, and his house is surrounded by timber, it coming up to the very yard on three sides."[40] That is to say, most of his land was uncultivated forest, a description recurring elsewhere that indicates isolation, perhaps implying sloth as well.

When individual farmers are described as poor, it likely means relative to the immediate neighborhood rather than to the broader region. If perceived poverty also connotes a wider social alienation, these sources certainly are suggestive enough. A neighbor described the sometime tenant farmer John McBride as a poor man, a "common liver," but McBride's marginal status did not silence him.[41] He told slaves they would be free and shielded runaways, and he later had trouble with the Klan. McBride's Tennessee Valley was a diverse region of plantations and smaller farms; being a small farmer here, or a wartime refugee, entailed sharp consciousness of relative deprivation. Even away from the valley, the reputation for poverty applied to whole Unionist enclaves, especially on the highland ridges. According to a hearing officer, Shadrach Bray of De Kalb County "was one of the poorest of the poor, living on Sand Mountain, where all were, and are, very poor."[42] In that vicinity alone, Republicans Shadrach Bray, Philip Harwood, and Washington Crow and his wife all signed statements with an illiterate "X." Such imperfect literacy furthered community isolation and limited the weight of outside opinion.

Edgy self-characterizations recur in the testimony, themselves suggestive of marginal status. Both Taylor York and Reuben Garner of Tuscaloosa County referred to themselves directly as poor, disdaining euphemisms.[43] Hiram Barton reportedly referred to himself as poor in conversation, too.[44] The illiterate William Sanders of Scottsboro had "everything that was calculated to make a poor man content"—that is, until the Union troops arrested him as a thief.[45] Forthright assertions of poverty bolstered the claim of loyalty after a fashion; they excused not volunteering material aid to Union troops or explained why family men felt unable to refugee across the lines. Still, Unionists premised their claims on possessing property to seize, so self-interest might have made people avoid such statements. Whatever the calculation, the emphasis on wartime Unionists' poverty presumably also informed the collective Republican identity after the war. Walter Selby was characterized by even a sympathetic fellow Republican as an ignorant man.[46] There are various indications of Republicans' modest background, limited literacy being the most obvious. Many of the claims were signed in an obviously labored handwriting. Jerry Brannon near Huntsville had been a farm laborer, and he and his relations giving testimony signed statements with an "X."[47]

It is likely true that most of these white Republicans were middling farmers rather than poor, but their association with obviously impoverished allies influenced public perceptions. Men of modest origin articulating transgressive views often expressed themselves vigorously. J. R. Jack was called a noisy Union man, difficult to silence.[48] Even political opponents warned him that he imperiled his life, and such uninhibited verbal behavior reinforced the status of community outsider. Planter dissidents might vent harmlessly in relative isolation, but more modest farmers' insurgent talk yielded different results. Jasper Harper was "a bad one on rebels" and some of them knew it.[49] Absolom Coffey in Jackson County talked Union all the time until he feared being murdered.[50] Amon McMillan was "very bold in talking his Union sentiments to every one," and it nearly got him killed.[51] The elderly and apparently poor Jesse Swindel of Tuscaloosa was threatened with death repeatedly for his Union talk, but he defied the dangers because he had so few years left. If his recollection can be believed, Swindel provocatively called himself "an old republican" daring the Confederates to come slay him.[52]

Such statements made in public would seem to be readily disproved. The testimony given in claims cases frequently revolved around friends and relations who were unable to stop reckless conversation. James Cargile talked Union so much that even Rebel women menaced vengeance when their men got home.[53] Hotheads sometimes went beyond talk, courting retaliation in incontrovertible ways. Ebenezer Leath of Cherokee County, a landless twenty-year-old, was denounced and threatened in church as a Union man. Leath and several friends subsequently set upon the offending preacher, pounding him until he pleaded for mercy. Leath received a draft exemption on specious medical grounds, but he had several run-ins with draft agents, one of whom would later be shot in Klan attire. While in custody, Leath allegedly threatened the agents that if they drafted him, he would track them down. This is believable given his later profile. Nightriders once assembled at his home, but they had second thoughts about risking attack, doubtless intimidated by his record of violence. A hearing commissioner reviewing Leath's case marveled that he had not been killed.[54]

Many observers commented on the need for discretion, but a surprising number of future Republicans could not command it consistently. Many opposed secession so vocally that they found it difficult to restrain themselves even when war began. James Morris recalled, "I came very near getting killed for rejoicing over a Federal victory," this in a neighborhood with few Union men.[55] In some mountain areas, like the well-known stronghold of Winston County, Unionists predominated and they silenced opponents. But future Republicans mostly lived in counties where Confederate supporters were plentiful, and the recent election campaigns made everyone's commitments public. One observer stated that "the political sentiment of both parties and of all persons was as well understood as the general subjects of the day."[56] In some places, Confederate sympathizers shielded their neighbors who held differing views. But their relationships with future Republicans appear different because they often disregarded the danger signs—or they simply defied the emerging consensus. Nicholas Stevens of Marshall County refused to accept Confederate money and "seemed to glory in being looked upon or called a Union man."[57] He begged his sons not to volunteer. Given that most of his neighbors had husbands, sons, or fathers off fighting in the Confederate army, his behavior courted community reprisal.

In sum, it is perhaps not surprising, as John McBride observed, that men like him "were not thought as much of as a Negro."[58] Their often plebeian profile likely contributed to the arbitrary treatment so many claimants reported at the hands of Confederate officials. In a slaveholder republic, socially peripheral and seditious farmers could not expect to be treated well, especially by those enforcing the draft in isolated places. The evidence suggests that the poorer Unionist claimants were more likely to become postwar Republicans. They certainly had much less property on average than most white Alabamians and many fewer slaves.[59] Their marginal status exacerbated the response of a stratified social order, and their statements indicate pervasive repression. Of the 111 Republicans in this study, at least 54 reported being threatened with death or grave injury, and 27 were menaced specifically with hanging. Some threats look like intimidation, vague talk relayed by neighbors with unclear motives. But many men experienced frightening dangers, angry curses, or assaults by guerillas. Some had nooses about their necks and a few escaped attempted murder. Overall, about half of the future Republicans reportedly faced lethal violence.

Even allowing for exaggeration, the testimony looks plausible; episodes generally transpired before witnesses, and the bulk appear in the accepted claims. Twenty-seven of the future Republicans recalled arrest by Confederate authorities. People seldom forget that kind of benchmark experience, and the claims accounts contain specific details. Draft agents arrested many, often for short periods to clarify their status or to pressure them to report to camp. Some were seized by cavalry and guerillas operating in various phases of indiscipline. Some were held for weeks, several reportedly were in immediate peril, and a few risked their lives to escape. Republican outrage at this treatment seldom bespoke complete innocence. Union talk clearly got people into trouble, especially at the hands of guerillas operating behind or near Northern lines, but conscription inspired most of the conflict, and the evidence indicates that opposition to it was pervasive among future Republicans. Thirty-four men either fed draft evaders or their families, lay out themselves, or led men through the lines. Five men deserted, another dozen had sons who did so, and their families almost certainly facilitated their escape. Several men appear in multiple categories, which itself emphasizes the searing nature of their wartime experience.

Until the spring of 1862, dissenters might maintain a sort of hands-off attitude toward the war effort, but conscription forced young men and their families to take a stand. Federal troops suddenly seized control of the Tennessee Valley, and outright resistance to Confederate authority became a realistic possibility. Some 7,400 Alabamians signed oaths of loyalty to the Union in a little over a year.[60] Many concluded the war would soon be over or that Federal troops would occupy the region south of the river. Union men in the hills found themselves on the ragged fringe of Confederate authority, with deliverance in sight. They, or their draft-age sons, could avoid service through lying out in the woods; they could desert; or they might attempt the dangerous escape through the well-patrolled mountains. If patient, they could await arrival of a Northern raid or band together to fight draft agents. Some individuals exhausted all these alternatives, one by one. In isolated mountain areas resisters often predominated. One Republican lived in a section of Tuscaloosa County where conscript officers seldom dared to enter, but only a few Republicans were so lucky.[61] Opposing conscription became the defining experience for this cohort of postwar Republicans, the place where their political beliefs intersected with matters of life and death. While a few escaped harm, draft resistance risked horrific consequences for most individuals and families.

Conscription combined with other factors to sharpen the class dimension of dissent as the conflict proceeded. Many Tennessee Valley planters had opposed immediate secession as rash, and some foresaw Confederate disaster and opposed the war. But the Lincoln administration's movement toward emancipation during 1862 and the occupying army's shift toward a "hard war" policy reconciled many of these slaveholders to the Southern cause. This occurred just as Confederate conscription antagonized legions of small farmers in the hills, reinforcing the damage with its "Twenty Negro Law." Surveying the social scene, Federal officers perceived prospective Alabamian recruits in class terms. Gen. William S. Rosecrans highlighted "the poverty and destitution of the mountaineers" coming into their lines, adding that unless the Union army recruited them quickly they would be "driven by want into brigandage."[62] For the future Republicans in this study, escalation of conflict proceeded inexorably. The poorer one was, the more likely draft evasion required direct violation of Confederate laws, thus encouraging harsh conflict with the conscription agents.

Widening circles of immiseration ensued. At first it was easy enough for military-age men to flee temporarily by heading into the woods because it was difficult for men on horseback to operate on mountainous terrain. David Studdard recalled, "my occupation was to evade the conscript, which I did very well."[63] However, doing so interfered with farmwork, which pushed relatives toward destitution. As draft evaders were forced farther afield for weeks or months, someone needed to feed them, which drew whole neighborhoods into conflict with the authorities. One Unionist recalled that the future Republican Wyatt Simpson fed him for three years, along with "more than one hundred others that shared his bounty more or less, all the time."[64] Dozens of future Republicans reportedly fed draft evaders, though perhaps not on this expansive scale. Given the widespread obstruction to conscription, violence snowballed. Draft enforcement became dangerous, as Confederates were slow to divert able-bodied men from the front; resisters took potshots at individual agents, sometimes raiding Confederate supporters for food. Over time, overwhelmed enforcement agents, and still less-disciplined vigilance committees and "bushwhackers," learned who provisioned these men. Collective punishment of recalcitrant families and neighborhoods became common. Pressure increased on the wives, parents, and extended families of draft evaders; if they were not impoverished before the war, their circumstances deteriorated now.

Prospects for draft evaders grew steadily more grim. Confederate agents avowed their hostile intent because threats were the first resort of frustrated officials. Wyatt Poe of Tuscaloosa was feeding several of his sons who were lying out. Confederates jailed him on suspicion, and while he was incarcerated a captain threatened him with death in a speech.[65] David Collins was arrested for harboring and feeding Union men and spent a week in a Tuscaloosa jail. Confederate soldiers warned him to produce his son, rope in hand.[66] In Marion County, Alfred Southern recalled his children being threatened with hanging if they did not divulge his location.[67] These vivid stories should not be dismissed as exaggerated because they often played out in public view. One Tennessee Valley Confederate recalled, "No man was safe in the neighborhood who would say anything in favor of the Union cause. Well, I had a good many friends who were bad men and I could hear them talk."[68]

Bad men seemed to proliferate in positions of authority. Andrew Kirby recalled that Confederates verbally abused his family whenever they were in the vicinity.[69] William Simons of Lauderdale reportedly faced an undisciplined Rebel band bearing a noose and demanding his money; his daughter helped distract them until he ripped into them with a knife, escaping into the night.[70] Similarly, the Confederates could never catch Amon McMillan, and a neighbor remembered feeding him for years.[71] McMillan recalled Confederates "threatened to shoot me and hang me and to burn everything that I had. . . . [T]hey came to my wife, and threatened to throw her out doors and burn down the house." She defied the threats. Conscript agents likewise visited the home of Washington Crow dozens of times. They threw his wife's clothing on the floor and "tromped it down," finally ordering her to leave late in the war.[72] Victorian gender conventions often shielded elite women from the consequences of their menfolk's behavior, but as one moved down the social scale, the restraints on abuse of women loosened.

As trauma deepened in the hill country, collective resistance intensified. A shift toward aggressive conscription enforcement under Gen. Gideon Pillow yielded widespread criticism. The August 1863 state elections repudiated original secessionists, and antiwar men influenced the legislature thereafter, which bolstered popular resistance. A shadowy peace society attracted the attention of Confederate intelligence agents in eastern Alabama; it featured in a mutiny in Clanton's conscript command. In Randolph County, future congressman R. S. Heflin claimed he led 127 Union recruits through the lines at one time.[73] Conscription officers estimated in November 1864 that eight thousand Alabamian soldiers had deserted since April, with six thousand still at large.[74] Waves of deserters joined draft evaders, giving them the numbers to defy conscript officers. Several future Republicans joined self-defense groups, becoming lawless "tories" in the estimate of Confederates, and there are numerous reports of more prosperous Confederate sympathizers being raided for food. Wiley Manasco led a Union League in Winston County and was arrested for it in 1864.[75] In Marion County, the future Republican Green M. Haley gathered over two dozen men to waylay draft officials, though the attempt miscarried.[76] Many future Republicans participated in such groupings, and they inspired enduring hatred. After the turn of the twentieth century, Walter Lynwood Fleming himself observed the "feeling of social contempt" for the tory element, which extended even "to their children's children."[77]

The ultimate recourse for draft evaders was joining the Federal army. When conscription agents gave James Dawson ten days to wrap up his affairs, he volunteered for the Federals as they marched back through Limestone County.[78] Approximately three thousand whites joined the 1st Alabama Cavalry or other Union regiments.[79] Of the future Republicans, three joined the Union army and another dozen had sons join, generally with their aid; still others served as Union auxiliaries, scouts, and the like. Sending family members into the Union army crossed the bright red line of treason to the Confederacy. Relations felt the consequences, if only losing the food supplies issued by local officials for soldiers' dependents. More severe consequences ensued: a Winston County wartime Unionist claimed he had led sixty women and children through the lines. Their farms had been broken up by Confederates, presumably to punish husbands off fighting for the Federals.[80]

Geography determined patterns of resistance. Acts of repression toward families were most intense in the mountains or in the marginally held areas south of the Tennessee River. Under Union control, the situation was often different, especially the areas occupied for most of the war. As Steven V. Ash argued, life in garrison towns like Huntsville could be relatively normal for Union sympathizers under benign army oversight.[81] Confederate partisans, or bushwhackers, operated freely north of the river, but they tended to be concentrated in sympathetic pockets. Republican James Cloud felt safe enough in Jackson County, despite earlier threats, because "after the war commenced in earnest, the secesh pretty much all went out of my neighborhood and I did not have any further intercourse with them."[82] Draft evaders and Union sympathizers gravitated toward secure areas. Twenty-three future Republicans out of the 111 said they had crossed the lines at some point, part of a larger migration northward. Between 1860 and 1866, the mountain region lost 10.2 percent of its white population, while the Tennessee Valley gained 8.4 percent.[83] As Confederates punished noncombatants, the obvious response was to evacuate whole families. This meant abandoning property and a dangerous removal through patrolled lines, with potential capture by minimally disciplined cavalry and bushwhackers. In the longer run, departure permanently marked impoverished refugees as thoroughly Union and uprooted families from their neighborhoods in ways that were difficult to overlook later.

Behind Union lines things often improved dramatically. The army protected and fed Walter Selby and perhaps saved his life; they had done him a "heap of good."[84] Another observer noted of the impoverished Shadrach Bray, "The Government was issuing rations to all in his condition who came in there."[85] That is to say, the more destitute one's family, the more certain the army would provide help. One Union officer stated that in 1864, four thousand rations were handed out per day in Bridgeport. The chaotic circumstances scrambled existing hierarchies; this officer wrote that formerly wealthy women were begging and even prostituting themselves for supplies.[86] In a desperate situation, northern Protestant denominations were providing aid to refugees through groups like the U.S. Christian Commission. Numerous Unionists eventually joined the national Methodist Church, as distinct from secession-tinged denominations. The minister-beating Ebenezer Leath, no less, found himself in the new church. Four other future Republicans joined him in Unionist churches. Religious rivalry reinforced the distinctive status of the Unionist following, a pattern accentuated by aggressive Northern Methodist evangelizing after the war.

Refugee camps and food relief were only short-term options. Though some arrivals joined the Union army, that choice was not always attractive to those who risked death if captured by guerillas. For family men, other options were more appealing than leaving refugee dependents unprotected, and many sought civilian employment. Federal control opened economic opportunities in the Tennessee Valley, and there was a lively commerce in cotton northward. For those situated to take advantage of the trade, it proved lucrative. Government employment also looked reasonably profitable by prevailing standards. One ex-slave recalled that "money was plenty in them times," an appraisal that would have applied to needy white refugees, too.[87] The Memphis and Charleston Railroad running through the valley absorbed much firewood, and it was raided so often that it needed constant repair. Trains and steamboats needed unloading, too. Thus working for contractors or the government figures prominently in Republican narratives. Henry Heald of St. Clair County had been arrested on one occasion and held in conscript camp on another. After his "wild" son deserted, he experienced death threats. Heald fled leaving his family behind, working for fifteen months with the quartermaster corps. He followed Sherman's legions eastward.[88]

Even outside Union lines, residents anywhere nearby found it difficult to live without cooperating with Federal forces. The Union occupation did not much respect civilian property, as the mass of claims demonstrates, and those suspected of disloyal sentiments fared worst. Gen. W. T. Sherman himself warned one Alabamian neighborhood that tolerating guerillas would "bring ruin on them all."[89] Gaylesville ceased to exist within days, in Sherman's estimate, after his army descended on the area long enough to absorb the food supply.[90] Col. George E. Spencer recalled a similar policy of starving out Confederate cavalry south of Tuscumbia. "We laid the country waste," the future Republican senator from Alabama recalled, adding that he sought to spare a Union sympathizer.[91] A Confederate officer returned to the vicinity late in 1864. Nothing much was in cultivation: he found "very few people living between here & Decatur & what few that are here don't rejoice much at our coming."[92] The suggestion is that only those hostile to the Confederacy could persist. In the Tennessee Valley, agriculture was potentially counterproductive because it drew the attention of contending troops disinclined to leave supplies to the enemy. As James Cargile recalled, after his fences were destroyed he did nothing around the farm.[93] This redoubled the need for paid employment, and loyalty would enhance job opportunities. The short-term incentives were overwhelming for destitute refugees, but they were strong enough for residents in general. Much of the white population near the army facilitated the occupation in visible ways, behavior that would long be remembered by neighbors with men still in the Confederate army.

Residents fared ill at Federal hands if perceived as potential guerillas. One way to win army goodwill was to offer information about Confederate movements, to pass on the latest rumor. One Union officer thus had "a number of first-class scouts and spies" operating south of the river.[94] Confederate guerillas knew this, and their relationship with potential Union collaborators was knife-edged. William McGuire, for example, recalled that he had been threatened by bushwhackers for bearing tales, but he turned them in with executions resulting.[95] McGuire also served as a guide for Union raids into the hills. At least seven of the future Republicans similarly served in such auxiliary roles. Federal forces in troubled areas developed a strategy of arming "home guards" in self-defense, and bands of scouts fringed the Union lines.[96] The mixture of self-interest and political commitment as motives for participation is difficult to assess. For example, Hawkins's vedette cavalry reportedly never did any actual service, and the government dissolved it after five months. Rumor had it this home defense battalion formed to gain access to Union rations.[97] Other such units had better military reputations, some serving without pay. The policy's wider tendency was to bring civilians into active conflict with Confederate partisans.

Federal actions thus furthered the polarization in the countryside. One indication is the skittish response of many civilians to threatened Confederate raids. A surprising military turnabout in late 1864 prompted a wave of departure. While General Sherman marched unopposed from Atlanta to the sea, Gen. John Bell Hood took a large and ill-supplied Confederate army through the Tennessee Valley. As the outnumbered Union garrisons fled eastward, "a huge concourse of refugees and contrabands" followed them.[98] And after Hood's catastrophic defeat at Nashville, his command retreated in disorder once more through the region. Hood's soldiers captured and enlisted those who had escaped the Confederate draft, so flight was a discreet response, and standing Union policies encouraged departure anyway.[99] Over the course of the war, at least fourteen of the future Republicans left the state, mostly for Tennessee but often further for extended periods. Jacob Stewart, for example, "was in five Northern States," and because of his Union politics, he was "treated with a great deal of kindness and respect" wherever he went.[100] Favorable treatment shaped his loyalties and presumably those of others who shared his experience.

Confederate holdouts viewed such men as collaborators and traitors; to the rest of the white population, they were marked as pronounced Union sympathizers. The approach of victory did nothing to diminish the profile of these gleeful supporters. After the Nashville defeat, Confederate armies in the west melted away. Desertion became a mass movement in early 1865, and longtime Union men felt buoyed by public support. But when the conflict ended, these allies of circumstance could and often did reconcile with their ex-Confederate neighbors. Unconditional Union men were different; they were marked by the experience in ways that were difficult to walk away from later. William Smith ran four deserter sons through the lines to Tennessee, staying there long enough enroll them in the army. He voted for Lincoln's reelection and found it unsafe to return to DeKalb County for a long time after the war.[101] The claims sources are profuse precisely because Unionists wanted to testify; they had no intention of forgetting anything.

Victory had ironic implications for these future Republicans; it meant that the cocoon of thousands of Union troops would all but disappear. As one Reconstruction supporter observed of the area around Tuscumbia, "This has been a very wealthy portion of the state and the loyal element in it is very small, being chiefly freedmen and the poorer class of whites with an occasional Northern man." In the Tennessee Valley, the implications were particularly threatening; Union leaders soon were demanding black troops, in preference to no protection at all. Even farther south, the return of embittered Confederate veterans changed the social composition of the hill country. Ex-Confederate majorities suddenly transformed localities that had been dominated by draft resisters. Many refugees and Union veterans concluded it was unsafe to return to their former homes. Others were actually driven out after the war concluded. For example, Andrew Kirby of Scottsboro had served as a Federal spy and scout. Before the war ended, he gave a speech endorsing reconstructing under military auspices. According to one source, the public response was so hostile that he did not regard himself as safe thereafter. His family spent the next six years in Indiana. For such future Republicans, their war had just entered a new phase.[102]

Unconditional Unionists had assumed that military success would bring them protection, perhaps some compensation for their suffering, but surely political supremacy under President Andrew Johnson. Presidential Reconstruction shocked them by handing most local positions back to former Confederate officials. In most places, law enforcement and juries would remain in unfriendly hands. Ex-Confederate juries frequently indicted Unionists for wartime conduct, especially members of "tory" bands. The rapid ascension of ex-secessionists to elected office antagonized Union men. Original anti-secessionists who then backed the rebellion and the draft seemed little better, and their rebranding as expedient "Union" men infuriated those with better claim. Unconditional Unionists felt increasingly imperiled, and in several upland areas guerrilla conflict broke out anew in 1866. In St. Clair County, for example, shootings and arson erupted, with Union men resisting taxation and debt collection by civil authorities. After one vengeance killing, outraged Unionists allegedly threatened that if resisted, "they would have 200 Negroes in arms in two hours to destroy & ruin the county."[103] This confrontation continued years of political violence, culminating in a major Klan-related series of firefights in 1870.

Outspoken Union men could hardly accept the situation, and they soon looked to the Republican majority in Congress for a drastic change. Small wonder that when Congressional Reconstruction began, upcountry Unionists expected to be the primary beneficiaries. At the 1867 constitutional convention, Radical scalawags pressed for proscription from office of former Confederates; in most upland areas, black suffrage still left them in the minority, and so they looked for widespread disenfranchisement. They, and not the newly enfranchised freedmen, were seen as the Radical firebrands. The February 1868 election returns on the Republican constitution, polled by race, demonstrate the continuing hold of wartime loyalties. About seventy-five hundred whites, little more than 10 percent of the registered electorate, braved a boycott and voted to ratify the constitution. Only in the mountains, in the poorer Unionist strongholds, did a substantial minority of white voters back ratification.[104]

This brand of Radicalism did not indicate any particular enlightenment about race. Seldom did claims testimony suggest any distaste for slavery before the war. Nor did testimony dwell upon its abstract evils afterward. If these Republicans defended abolition, it was as just desserts for traitors who started the war to protect slave property. Nor did they demonstrate enthusiasm for the Whiggish, corporate ethos of the national Republican Party; the vogue of railroads and economic development passed them by. No matter—their unconditional Unionist identity, their outsider status, had been so forged in the war that not even membership in a Northern-identified, black-majority Southern Republican Party could faze them. The dispiriting reality for the prospects of Reconstruction is that it took so much persecution, turmoil, and violence to get any substantial number of white Alabamians to that point.

Notes

1. Walter Lynwood Fleming, *Civil War and Reconstruction in Alabama* (New York: Columbia University Press, 1905), 316.

2. For a discussion of the literature at greater length, see Michael W. Fitzgerald, "Political Reconstruction, 1865–1877," in *A Companion to the American South*, ed. John B. Boles (Malden, MA: Blackwell, 2002), 84–102, and Fitzgerald, "Reconstruction Politics and the Politics of Reconstruction," in *Reconstructions: New Perspectives on the Postbellum United States*, ed. Thomas L. Brown (New York: Oxford University Press, 2006), 91–116.

3. Emphatic Unionists would be overrepresented in this evidence, which mostly dates from the early to mid-1870s, substantially after the war. No claims came from areas that escaped Union

occupation or raids. Obviously one would be skeptical of using these materials as a scientific sample of Unionist or Republican sentiment.

4. Dylan C. Penningroth, *The Claims of Kinfolk: African American Property and Community in the Nineteenth-Century South* (Chapel Hill: University of North Carolina Press, 2003).

5. Margaret M. Storey, *Loyalty and Loss: Alabama's Unionists in the Civil War and Reconstruction* (Baton Rouge: Louisiana State University Press, 2004); Storey, "The Crucible of Reconstruction: Unionists and the Struggle for Alabama's Home Front," in *The Great Task Remaining before Us: Reconstruction as America's Civil War*, ed. Paul A. Cimbala and Randall M. Miller (New York: Fordham University Press, 2010), 69–87.

6. Southern Claims Commission Approved Claims, 1871–1880: Alabama, National Archives and Records Administration (NARA), Record Number M2062, National Archives (hereafter Accepted Claims, SCC); Barred and Disallowed Case Files of the Southern Claims Commission, 1871–1880, NARA Microfiche M1407, National Archives (hereafter Disallowed Claims, SCC). Using accepted claims sources, Margaret M. Storey recently has presented a somewhat different interpretation; see Storey, "The Crucible of Reconstruction."

7. In her article on accepted Alabamian claimants after the war, Storey contends that Unionists "gave almost overwhelming allegiance to the Republican party from the first." Most likely did, especially those who said that they still voted Union. However, one cannot know with certainty, which provides the rationale for employing a more narrow definition here (Storey, "The Crucible of Reconstruction," 76).

8. Claim of Henry Stutts, Lauderdale County, reel 19, Accepted Claims, SCC. All the individuals identified in the text, utilizing the Southern Claims Commission records, were identified as Republicans unless otherwise indicated.

9. James Alex Baggett, *The Scalawags: Southern Dissenters in the Civil War and Reconstruction* (Baton Rouge: Louisiana State University Press, 2004). On Alabama specifically, see Sarah Woolfolk Wiggins, *The Scalawag in Alabama Reconstruction, 1865–1881* (Tuscaloosa: University of Alabama Press, 1977).

10. Application of Major Charles Hays of Greene, Case Files of Applications from Former Confederates for Presidential Pardons ("Amnesty Papers"), 1865–1867, reel 5, M1003, NARA.

11. Claim of W. J. Mahan, Montgomery County, reel 29, Accepted Claims, SCC.

12. Claim of Joseph H. Davis, Randolph County, reel 30, Accepted Claims, SCC.

13. Ibid.

14. U.S. Congress, "Report of the Joint Committee on Reconstruction," 39th Cong., 1st Sess., part 3, p. 11; Gov. J. G. Shorter to J. A. Seddon, December 23, 1862, *U.S. Congress, the War of the Rebellion: A Compilation of the Official Records of the Union and Confederate Armies* (Washington, DC: GPO, 1880–), (hereafter *OR*), series 4, vol. II, p. 258.

15. Claim of J. J. Martin, Macon County, reel 24, Accepted Claims, SCC.

16. Claim of W. J. Mahan, Montgomery County, reel 29, Accepted Claims, SCC.

17. Claim of Jesse Mahan, Bibb County, Disallowed Claims, SCC.

18. Application of Joseph C. Bradley of Huntsville, "Amnesty Papers," 1865–1867, reel 1, M1003, NARA.

19. Claim of Samuel M. Wallace, Lawrence County, reel 20, Accepted Claims, SCC.

20. Claim of Perry Harrison, Madison County, reel 24, Accepted Claims, SCC.

21. Claim of Thomas Nation, Blount County, reel 1, Accepted Claims, SCC.

22. Claim of John H. Austin, Morgan County, reel 30, Accepted Claims, SCC.

23. Claim of Naomi Peters, Lawrence County, Disallowed Claims, RG 233.

Wartime Origins of White Republicanism / 237

24. Application of Milton Saffold of Montgomery, "Amnesty Papers," 1865–1867, reel 10, M1003, NARA.

25. William Warren Rogers Jr., *Confederate Home Front: Montgomery during the Civil War* (Tuscaloosa: University of Alabama Press, 1999), 104–15; Claim of William J. Bibb, Montgomery County, reel 29, Accepted Claims, SCC.

26. Wesley S. Thompson, *The Free State of Winston: A History of Winston County Alabama* (Winfield, AL: Pareil Press, 1968), 60, 81–85, 92.

27. Storey, *Alabama's Unionists in the Civil War and Reconstruction*, 51–53, 149–51.

28. Focusing on this group eliminates the overrepresentation of the politically prominent; these men should be more representative of the experience of white Republican voters.

29. Estimates prepared from Steven Ruggles, J. Trent Alexander, Katie Genadek, Ronald Goeken, Matthew B. Schroeder, and Matthew Sobek, Integrated Public Use Microdata Series: Version 5.0 [Machine-readable database] (Minneapolis: University of Minnesota, 2010). The estimate is from a weighted sample of 1 percent of the white population of Alabama, prepared with the assistance of Brandon Trampe of the Minnesota Population Center at the University of Minnesota. The future Republicans' median wealth of $1,152 seems still less prepossessing, given the tendency for less prosperous people to disappear from such studies. In his study of Arkansas, Carl Moneyhon uses $1,000 to demarcate the bottom limit of a lower-middle-class household, a figure not much below the median for this group. Carl H. Moneyhon, *The Impact of the Civil War and Reconstruction on Arkansas: Persistence in the Midst of Ruin* (Baton Rouge: Louisiana State University Press, 1994), 42.

30. J. Mills Thornton, *Politics and Power in a Slave Society: Alabama, 1800–1860* (Baton Rouge: Louisiana State University Press, 1978).

31. Among the future Republicans under study, Douglas reportedly received twenty-one votes, the ex-Whig candidate John Bell received sixteen, and only two admitted voting for the states' rights Democrat John Breckinridge. One stated explicitly that he did not vote, another that he did not vote for Breckinridge. Abraham Lincoln was not on the ballot, though one man claimed he would have voted for him if he had been. Voting was a public act during this era, so false statements could be readily disproved. If claimants omitted mentioning Breckinridge votes, as seems more likely, this would only increase the Democratic predominance overall.

32. Claim of John P. Blackwell, Walker County, Disallowed Claims, RG 233, SCC.

33. Claim of Philip Harwood, DeKalb County, reel 7, Accepted Claims, SCC.

34. Claim of John V. Gross, Jackson County, reel 12, Accepted Claims, SCC.

35. Storey, *Loyalty and Loss*, 7, 12–13.

36. Claim of Jasper Harper, Marshall County, reel 28, Accepted Claims, SCC; Claim of William Underwood, Walker County, reel 36, Accepted Claims, SCC.

37. Claim of J. R. Jack, Cherokee County, reel 3, Accepted Claims, SCC.

38. Claim of Theoron Underwood, Cherokee County, reel 4, Accepted Claims, SCC.

39. Claim of Alex E. Ellenburg, Cherokee County, reel 2, Accepted Claims, SCC.

40. Claim of Henry Stutts, Lauderdale County, reel 19, Accepted Claims, SCC.

41. Claim of John McBride, Limestone County, reel 23, Accepted Claims, SCC.

42. Claim of Shadrach Bray, DeKalb County, reel 7, Accepted Claims, SCC.

43. Claim of Taylor York, Tuscaloosa County, reel 31, Accepted Claims, SCC.

44. Claim of Hiram Barton, Walker County, Disallowed Claims, SCC.

45. Claim of William Sanders, Jackson County, reel 14, Accepted Claims, SCC.

46. Claim of Walter Selby, Jackson County, reel 14, Accepted Claims, SCC.

238 / Fitzgerald

47. Claim of Jerry Brannon, Limestone County, reel 21, Accepted Claims, SCC.
48. Claim of J. R. Jack, Cherokee County, reel 3, Accepted Claims, SCC.
49. Claim of Jasper Harper, Marshall County, reel 28, Accepted Claims, SCC.
50. Claim of Absolom Coffey, Jackson County, reel 11, Accepted Claims, SCC.
51. Claim of Amon McMillan, Tuscaloosa County, reel 31, Accepted Claims, SCC.
52. Claim of Jesse Swindel, Tuscaloosa County, reel 31, Accepted Claims, SCC.
53. Claim of James Cargile, Jackson County, reel 11, Accepted Claims, SCC.
54. Claim of Ebenezer Leath, Cherokee County, reel 3, Accepted Claims, SCC.
55. Claim of James Henry Morris, Marshall County, reel 28, Accepted Claims, SCC.
56. Claim of Jesse Mahan, Bibb County, Disallowed Claims, SCC.
57. Claim of Nicholas Stevens, Jackson County, reel 14, Accepted Claims, SCC.
58. Claim of John McBride, Limestone County, reel 23, Accepted Claims, SCC.

59. Storey, *Loyalty and Loss*, 256, provides the decile breakdowns by wealth of the wider group of 264 claimants she located in the 1860 census for her study of Unionists as a whole. The figures for accepted claimants are not directly comparable to the smaller group of individuals that are identified as Republicans in the claims records, and her evidence relies more on individual than household numbers, which would depress her figures relative to these postwar Republicans. Even so, her numbers suggest the possibility that the Republicans in the sample of 111 had substantially lower median wealth than the wider population of successful claimants did. Her findings indicate a median wealth between $1,230 and $1,700 for Unionists as a whole, above the $1,152 median household wealth for the identified Republicans in this study.

60. Mark A. Weitz, *More Damning than Slaughter: Desertion in the Confederate Army* (Lincoln: University of Nebraska Press, 2005), 128.
61. Claim of James Baker, Tuscaloosa County, reel 31, Accepted Claims, SCC.
62. W. S. Rosecrans to Major Rawlins, August 29, 1862, *OR*, vol. 27, p. 191.
63. Claim of David Studdard, Fayette County, reel 10, Accepted Claims, SCC.
64. Claim of Wyatt Simpson, Tuscaloosa County, reel 31, Accepted Claims, SCC.
65. Claim of Wyatt Poe, Tuscaloosa County, reel 31, Accepted Claims, SCC.
66. Claim of David A. Collins, Tuscaloosa County, reel 31, Accepted Claims, SCC.
67. Claim of Alfred B. Southern, Marion County, reel 27, Accepted Claims, SCC.
68. Claim of Moses Maples, Jackson County, reel 13, Accepted Claims, SCC.
69. Claim of Andrew Kirby, Lauderdale County, reel 18, Accepted Claims, SCC.
70. Claim of William Simons, Lauderdale County, reel 19, Accepted Claims, SCC.
71. Claim of Amon McMillan, Tuscaloosa County, reel 31, Accepted Claims, SCC.
72. Claim of Washington Crow, DeKalb County, reel 7, Accepted Claims, SCC.
73. Claim of Joseph H. Davis Jr., Randolph County, reel 30, Accepted Claims, SCC.
74. Weitz, *More Damning than Slaughter*, 266.
75. Claim of Wiley B. Manasco, Winston County, reel 36, Accepted Claims, SCC.
76. Claim of Jesse V. Tiara, Fayette County, reel 10, Accepted Claims, SCC.
77. Fleming, *Civil War and Reconstruction in Alabama*, 321.
78. Claims of James Dawson, Limestone County, reel 21, Accepted Claims, SCC.
79. Richard Nelson Current, *Lincoln's Loyalists: Union Soldiers from the Confederacy* (Boston: Northeastern University Press, 1992), 217.
80. Claim of Thomas Carroll, Winston County, reel 36, Accepted Claims, SCC. Carroll is not identified in the claim as a Republican, though given the locality and his Union League wartime membership he likely was.

81. Stephen V. Ash, *When the Yankees Came: Conflict and Chaos in the Occupied South, 1861–1865* (Chapel Hill: University of North Carolina Press, 1995).

82. Claim of James Cloud, Jackson County, reel 11, Accepted Claims, SCC.

83. Robert Arthur Gilmer, "The Other Emancipation: Studies in the Society and Economy of Alabama Whites during Reconstruction" (PhD diss., Johns Hopkins University, 1972), 74–75.

84. Claim of Walter Selby, Jackson County, reel 14, Accepted Claims, SCC.

85. Ibid.

86. Captain August Horstmann to Parents, April 27, 1864, in *Germans in the Civil War: The Letters They Wrote Home*, ed. Walter D. Kamphoefner and Wolfgang Helbich, trans. Susan Carter Vogel (Chapel Hill: University of North Carolina Press, 2006), 127.

87. Claim of Thomas Thatch, Limestone County, reel 23, Accepted Claims, SCC.

88. Claim of Henry Heald, St. Clair County, reel 30, Accepted Claims, SCC.

89. W. T. Sherman to George Thomas, October 24, 1864, in *OR*, series 1, vol. 39, pt. 3, p. 377.

90. W. T. Sherman to Ellen Sherman, October 27, 1864, in *Sherman's Civil War: Selected Correspondence of William T. Sherman*, ed. Brooks D. Simpson and Jean V. Berlin (Chapel Hill: University of North Carolina Press, 1999), 744.

91. Claim of John C. Goodloe, Colbert County, reel 30, Accepted Claims, SCC.

92. Mark K. Christ, *Getting Used to Being Shot At: The Spence Family Civil War Letters* (Fayetteville: University of Arkansas Press, 2002), 107–10.

93. Claim of James Cargile, Jackson County, reel 11, Accepted Claims, SCC.

94. William Penn Lyon, *Reminiscences of the Civil War* (San Jose, CA: Muerson and Wright, 1907), 107.

95. Claim of William McGuire, Limestone County, reel 23, Accepted Claims, SCC.

96. Daniel E. Sutherland, *A Savage Conflict: The Decisive Role of Guerrillas in the American Civil War* (Chapel Hill: University of North Carolina Press, 2009), 157–61, 258–60.

97. Claim of James Henry Morris, Marshall County, reel 28, Accepted Claims, SCC.

98. R. S. Granger to George Thomas, December 5, 1864, in *OR*, series 1, vol. 45, p. 65.

99. Lyon, *Reminiscences of the Civil War*, 157.

100. Claim of Jacob L. Stewart, Walker County, Disallowed Claims, RG 233, National Archives.

101. Claim of William Smith, DeKalb County, reel 8, Accepted Claims, SCC.

102. Henry H. Russell to John Pope, April 12, 1867, in Wager Swayne collection, Governor's Papers, Alabama Department of Archives and History, Montgomery; Claim of Andrew Kirby, Lauderdale County, reel 18, Accepted Claims, SCC.

103. Anonymous to Patton, July 21, 1866; see also Anonymous to Patton, July 31, 1866; M. H. Cruikshank to Patton, July 29, 1866, all in Governor R. S. Patton Papers, Alabama Department of Archives and History, Montgomery.

104. Michael W. Fitzgerald, "Radical Republicanism and the White Yeomanry during Alabama Reconstruction," *Journal of Southern History* 54, no. 4 (November 1988): 591–95. Here, too, I would commend the treatment of postwar Unionists' motivation in Storey, "The Crucible of Reconstruction."

13
Labor, Law, and the Freedmen's Bureau in Alabama, 1865–1867

Jason J. Battles

The Bureau of Refugees, Freedmen, and Abandoned Lands was established by an act of Congress in March 1865 and was vested with broad powers to assist three million blacks in the transition from slaves to citizens. More commonly known as the Freedmen's Bureau, this division of the War Department operated in all of the states of the former Confederacy during the Reconstruction era. The bureau issued rations to the destitute of both races, constructed hospitals and schools, oversaw labor contracts between freedmen and their employers, and protected blacks' legal, civil, and political rights. The bureau's charge represented a historic effort by the federal government to provide aid and support for those in need. The unprecedented breadth of the bureau's activities has led some scholars to consider it the first social welfare organization in American history.[1]

The Freedmen's Bureau was led by Maj. Gen. Oliver Otis Howard. Appointed by President Andrew Johnson in May 1865, General Howard served as commissioner until the bureau was dismantled in 1872. Since the bureau operated within the War Department, it was administered almost solely by active or former military officers. General Howard was a veteran of Gettysburg and served under Gen. William Tecumseh Sherman during the campaign for Atlanta and the March to the Sea. Often referred to as the "Christian General," Howard was a strong advocate for black rights before and after his time as bureau commissioner. He viewed his appointment to head the bureau as a "great opportunity for Christian service."[2] In filling the bureau posts under his command, he looked for officers that shared his faith and were "sympathetic in their attitude" toward the freedmen.[3]

General Howard selected a fellow Christian and comrade from the Army of the Tennessee, Brig. Gen. Wager T. Swayne, to lead the bureau's efforts in Alabama. Swayne served as assistant commissioner from July 1865 to January 1868. His tenure was the longest of any state commissioner within the bureau and provided a level of stability and consistency in its activities and policies that was unmatched elsewhere in the South. Swayne was a Yale-educated Ohioan and son of U.S. Supreme Court Justice Noah Swayne. When the war began, he was working as an attorney. Swayne worked his way up the officer ranks in the Union army. Like General Howard, he served in Sherman's Army of the Tennessee, where he lost his right leg during action in South Carolina in February 1865.

Historians have long maligned Swayne's leadership of the Alabama Freedmen's Bureau for favoring the planter class over the freedmen and taking a paternalistic attitude toward the population that he was appointed to aid.[4] He is cited as an example of a bureau commissioner relying too much on "prominent whites" and leaving blacks and their newly gained rights "unprotected."[5] Kenneth B. White asserts that Swayne's affluent upbringing also hindered his ability to deal with the racial issues facing him as commissioner.[6] Recent scholarship has recognized Swayne as more than the "pragmatic racist" described by White.[7] Michael W. Fitzgerald applauds Swayne's "zeal on the freedpeople's behalf," but he remains critical of Swayne's early efforts to resolve freedmen labor issues.[8] A fresh examination of Swayne's actions, however, that considers the exceptional circumstances of his office and the conditions of postwar Alabama demonstrates instead his consistent commitment to protecting the rights of the freedmen.

In the summer of 1865, many Alabamians were suffering, but the recently emancipated blacks in the state were particularly hard-hit. Newspapers reported the harsh conditions facing the freedmen throughout the Black Belt region of the state. The *Selma Daily Messenger*, for example, reported that the "mortality of the city is considerable amongst the negroes," with many blacks recently consigned to their "last resting place."[9] In a May 31, 1865, communication from Union Springs, Col. J. Strickton wrote, "What am I to do with the negroes that are driven off the plantations by their former owners on the plea of their inability to support them, many such are accumulating here and I do not wish to forward them to Montgomery." Strickton was not alone in his concern about how planters were dealing with changes to the labor system.[10] Similar letters from Mobile indicated that some planters were forcing out all of their workers, but in other cases just the women and children were evicted while the "able bodied working hands" were retained. This created a problem because the former slaves were now without food, shelter, or money to support themselves. The turning out of the freedmen was attributed in part to the general economic condition of the state in the summer of 1865. As one writer pointed out, "few, if any, planters are in a condition to employ any of these even for their food and clothing."[11]

Some members of the planter class recognized the potential economic catastrophe and pleaded with their fellow landholders to contract with the freedmen. The author of a lengthy article that appeared in the *Montgomery Daily Advertiser* asked planters to accept the new conditions and work within the new labor system. If they did not, the author asserted, the result would "prove fatal to both races—nay, to our country itself." Reminding planters that they owned the land and capital, the article also emphasized that planters "owe it to society, to yourselves—yea, to the ignorant black man, to make every exertion, and every reasonable sacrifice, to save your beautiful and fertile country from desolation, and its inhabitants from want and starvation."[12]

Aside from upheaval in the labor system and the threat of widespread destitution, the state was rife with criminal activity in the summer of 1865. The problem centered on pervasive cotton and horse theft by large bands of armed and disguised men who struck during the night. These crimes led the victims to seek "personal redress of injuries," taking the law in their own hands, thus creating a cycle of reciprocity that was too often violent. In August, Provisional Governor Lewis Eliphalet Parsons finally issued a proclamation seeking to stem the lawlessness and chaos it was causing. He pleaded with the citizenry to stop this activity and report any perpetrators, but he also threatened, "if we cannot do it ourselves, or if you will not aid in doing so through the civil tribunals of the country, there is military force at hand to aid all loyal citizens, that is abundantly able to do it." Even before his proclamation, Parsons had already called on Gen. C. R. Woods to send military force to one county.[13]

Widespread destitution, labor turmoil, and rampant crime defined Alabama in the months after Appomattox. In the intervening period before Swayne's arrival in July 1865, Union forces along the Gulf Coast made an effort to provide temporary assistance to the freedmen. Gen. Edward R. S. Canby appointed Thomas W. Conway to assist in the state until the permanent Freedmen's Bureau commissioner arrived.[14] Conway sought to establish the bureau framework by appointing Chaplain Charles W. Buckley as Assistant Superintendent of Freedmen for Montgomery. Buckley's first responsibilities included disseminating information to the freedmen about the new labor regulations and doing his best to enforce them. He was also instrumental in the bureau's efforts to begin recording property transactions and labor contracts. To carry out his duties, Buckley was instructed to "procure either by details from the army or by hiring at as reasonable rates as possible" any assistance needed. The tumultuous labor situation and limited Union forces in the state made help difficult to secure, but Buckley was successful in spite of the situation. He even managed to establish a "home colony" to aid indigent freedmen and thus reduced the number who flocked to Montgomery seeking relief. In their correspondence, Conway emphasized Buckley's duty to "maintain with unswerving firmness, the freedom, and the rights of the Freedmen."[15] This sentiment was subsequently echoed in many communications among bureau officials. After all, dedication to the freedmen was one of the qualities General Howard sought in selecting his appointees.

When Swayne reached Montgomery in the last half of July 1865, he immediately recognized the problems that would plague his early efforts and affect the course of action he chose to take on labor issues and freedmen rights. He lacked personnel and resources. Throughout the state the bureau had only "four feeble agencies for a negro population of 450,000."[16] The 1865 Freedmen's Bureau Bill did not provide funds for bureau operations. Instead, Swayne and his fellow bureau agents throughout the South relied upon the War Department. He had to get the new labor contract system working, or the need for food and clothing among the destitute would overwhelm the capacity of both the bureau and military to address the problem. Buckley's earlier efforts, particularly with regard to establishing regulations for recording labor contracts, did give Swayne a framework upon which to build. Despite the severity of the economic challenges at the time, Swayne was committed to protecting the freedmen in these new contracts and assuring their legal rights. However, the end of slavery did not mean that native whites viewed blacks any differently in July 1865 than they had in January 1865. Though these entrenched attitudes were muted in the early part of Reconstruction, they later proved to be an obstacle to bureau efforts as conservative elements of the native white population regained power.

The lack of bureau personnel was one of Swayne's greatest problems. In his first weekly report to General Howard, Swayne wrote, "I am practically alone owing to the muster-out which cut off the list I had submitted to you for detail. This will soon be remedied I hope."[17] Considering his lack of resources and staff, Swayne launched his own recruitment effort to encourage members of the recently demobilized Union army to move to Alabama in order to assist in "settling the labor question." One of Swayne's "recruitment" letters to a military friend appeared in a Northern paper. In it, Swayne asserted that the freedmen in Alabama would receive Northerners favorably because they had "more confidence in a 'Yankee,' particularly one who wears a blue coat, than in a native." He also noted the economic opportunities, writing that "[p]lenty of cotton land can be bought here for eight and ten dollars per acre. . . . The negroes are generally ready enough to work."[18] How successful this effort was is unclear, but Swayne struggled with staffing throughout much of his tenure.

In the provisional state government, Swayne found a much-needed partner to support the bureau's work. Governor Parsons worked closely and collaboratively with Swayne until his term ended in December 1865. Parsons was almost as new to his post as was Swayne to his and he had to govern the state under the same conditions the fledgling bureau faced. Upon his appointment Parsons moved quickly to get the apparatus of civil government functioning. He was forthright about the situation in his early proclamation to the people of Alabama that detailed the conditions in the state and the hardships ahead and that outlined the occupancy of all major civil positions. Swayne praised Parsons for his effort to carefully select appointees for these positions.[19] Everyone from sheriff to judge was required to swear an amnesty oath prescribed by President Andrew Johnson. The proclamation outlined the steps to secure civil government and to begin the reconstruction of the state, but it also acknowledged the obvious change in the status of black Alabamians. Parsons emphasized that "[t]hey who once were slaves are now free, and must be governed by the laws of Alabama as free men."[20]

From his office in Montgomery, Swayne received daily reminders of the plight of the state. Despite earlier efforts, the destitute crowded the city and the resulting conditions exacerbated racial tensions. Native whites blamed the chaos on "freedmen-thieves" with a "propensity to steal" but acknowledged that so many freedmen were in the city that "they can't all get work, and they must steal or starve." These white citizens implored the bureau to "adopt some plan, by which the negro shall be made to work." Otherwise, the bureau "had better get Congress to pass a large coffin appropriation bill, for the coming winter will witness starvation, freezing, and death on a scale of such magnitude as to satisfy death itself—then thousands of these freedmen will be permanent land-holders, or the land will hold them permanently enough."[21]

While native whites wanted the bureau to act to relieve the situation, their entrenched bias against the freedmen revealed the divide between what Swayne sought to accomplish in protecting freedmen rights and what the native whites would accept. One writer to the *Montgomery Daily Advertiser* cautioned the bureau against creating a system that made "the negro believe in his equality" or create "a prejudice in his mind against his former owner," threatening that if they did so, "the 'irrepressible conflict' will have just begun." On the one hand, native whites such as the author pleaded with the bureau for "equality in the administration of their office" toward themselves. On the other hand, they asserted that "equality, North or South, can never be; and all ideas of that description thrown out to the negro, must end in discontentment and strife."[22]

The war left many Alabamians completely impoverished. The bureau labored to prevent this problem from becoming more severe by trying to define labor regulations and prod all parties to begin entering into contracts. More immediately, the bureau provided a considerable amount of food and clothing to blacks and whites in need. This assistance continued for many months and was essential in averting starvation for countless residents. Freedmen "home colonies" were established to provide assistance with rations and labor. Huntsville bureau agent A. H. Bynam emphasized the need to "provide suitable places of refuge, where the destitute can be cared for in a proper way" not only to prevent starvation but also because he felt the planters were "waiting until about the time when the negroes will have to either make contracts or leave their old homes, thinking they can dictate their own terms to the negro & will accept any terms rather than be turned out of doors without food or the proper clothing to keep them comfortable."[23] Bynam saw the danger of this tactic. He warned that without a solution, the desperate situation could become violent.

Swayne's efforts to get blacks back to work have been interpreted as examples of his favoritism toward white planters. However, the numerous instances of planters initially driving their former slaves from plantations and the documented planter reluctance to contract with former slaves demonstrate that the landowners were quite culpable in the labor crisis. Swayne wanted the labor system to work to reduce additional economic upheaval in an already difficult situation and prevent starvation among the population. Thus he worked as much toward getting planters to offer contracts rather than turning out their former slaves as he did toward encouraging freedmen to sign them. When viewing his orders in detail and the reaction they received, it is clear that substantial requirements were placed on the planters. Considering the bureau's recording and enforcement of the contracts, Swayne clearly was working to protect freedmen rights.

Swayne's first mark on the labor system came on August 30, 1865, with the issuance of General Orders No. 12, requiring that "all contracts with freedmen, for labor, for the period of one month, and over, must be reduced to writing, approved by an agent of this bureau, and one copy deposited with him." Swayne also outlined regulations for plantation labor. Contracts were to be made with the heads of families and include all the members of the family able to work. Swayne required plantation owners to "provide good and sufficient food, quarters and medical attendance for the entire family." Plantation labor contracts were to be a "lien upon the crop, of which not more than one-half will be removed until full payment is made, and the contract released by an agent of the Bureau, or a Justice of the Peace."[24] Considering the aforementioned turning out of freedmen and/or their families, this order appears aimed to protect them.

Swayne's orders stressed the importance of the freedmen signing and honoring contracts. He asserted that "many persons have not yet learned the binding force of a contract, and that freedom does not mean living without labor." Swayne also warned that any employee absent from labor "without good cause" for more than one day, or more than three days in one month, would be considered a vagrant. Freedmen committed as vagrants "may be set to work on roads, or as other labor, by the county or municipal authorities which provide their support, or they may be turned over to an agent of this Bureau."[25] The vagrancy portion and General Orders No. 12 as a whole remained in line with the societal expectation that work was a necessary part of life for everyone. It is worth noting that the vagrancy provision differed significantly from the harsh and racially biased state vagrancy law enacted in early 1866 that Swayne vehemently opposed.

Swayne was implementing and stabilizing a new labor system that was foreign to a populous whose primary experience was with a slave-based economy. This new system's success required the cooperation of the freedmen. To Swayne, the vagrancy section of General Orders No. 12 was a necessity. He did get some support from the editor of the *Montgomery Advertiser*, who wrote, "The General certainly seems disposed to deal justly by all parties and will not if he can prevent it, allow idle negroes to be roaming through the city."[26] While still placing the blame on blacks, the *Advertiser*, like most state newspapers, rarely mentioned the planters' resistance to contracting with freedmen.

Two days after Swayne issued General Orders No. 12, Governor Parsons issued a statement concurring with the bureau's directive. These orders would be followed for the next few years with bureau agents making it clear that the employers had to demonstrate to an agent at the end of a labor contract that a fair settlement was made. Also, the freedmen were encouraged to "commence suits against all employers who fail to show their proper settlement with their freedmen." Employers had to follow the regulations outlined in General Orders No. 12, otherwise bureau agents would not help them enforce the contracts.[27] The rigidity of the guidelines makes it difficult to argue that the bureau labor regulations were designed to exclusively favor the planter class over the freedmen, as this directive places considerable responsibility on the landowner.

While such plantation labor contracts dominated the Alabama Black Belt, the bureau recorded a great variety of employment arrangements and compensation agreements in other areas of the state. This variety is seen in contracts registered in Huntsville in 1865 and early 1866. Skilled laborers such as blacksmiths could get $15 per month, while a farmer received a 400-pound bale of cotton as payment.[28] Some contracts included the rental of homes and land.[29] Many farm-related labor contracts included rental of acreage in return for a share, often one-third in this region, of the crops' yield.[30] As with large plantation contracts, food and/or housing for the wife and children of the freedmen was provided in exchange for the entire family's labor.[31]

Even with contracts in place, violations on both sides and general mistreatment of blacks occurred. In Huntsville, Chaplain T. M. Goodfellow wrote in December 1865, "I am informed by Frank Johnson (Freedmen) that he has a written contract with you, for a house & thirty acres of land, which he says you have refused to comply with. As we look at each of the contracting parties for faithful performance of their obligations, we should like to be advised why this refusal has been made."[32] Goodfellow sought to resolve the issue by summoning both parties to his office with contract in hand to explain why it should not be upheld. Assigned to a rich farming region such as Huntsville, Goodfellow dealt with many similar disputes. His bureau colleagues in the Black Belt also faced numerous contract cases. In an incident in Selma in June 1866, bureau superintendent S. S. Gardner worked to resolve an issue in which an employer had repeatedly delayed completing a written contract.

The freedman bringing the case had a verbal agreement to receive one-fifth of the crop raised during the year. Gardner responded, "From his statement I think he only wishes to have a contract in order that he may have something to show for his labor (and he has a perfect right to demand this) and with it he is ready and willing to go back and finish working the crop."[33] These particular cases demonstrate why Swayne and the bureau required and recorded written contracts. Many of the letters from Selma during this period also were written to planters or employers accused of not fulfilling contracts, mistreating freedmen, or releasing them from employment.

With great frequency, white employers also dismissed freedmen without cause in order to avoid paying them. Charles W. Pierce wrote Swayne in September 1866 about one such problem that involved freedmen working on a plantation leased by the owner to another white man. The crop had failed for several reasons, including mismanagement. The plantation owner had paid the lessee $100 to leave the land but had no money to pay the freedmen hired by the lessee. Pierce told Swayne that there were several similar cases in the area. He reported other cases of freedmen being "discharged on the slightest pretext, without payment of wages;—violation of contract—& consequent forfeiture of wages is pleaded. The violation of contract is not difficult to prove, yet such course has the tendency to fill the county with vagrants."[34]

Pierce wrote to Swayne again in December 1866 about an unreasonable contract that was brought to him by freedmen from Greene County. Pierce had not seen the contract prior to the freedmen's complaint as it had never been approved by a bureau agent. Pierce continued, "You will observe that it provides that the employer receive two thousand pounds of lint cotton from each hand, before they get anything. This amount per hand is about double the quantity made, so the freedmen get nothing."[35] Pierce suggested that the freedmen sue the landowner for wages earned at $10 per month. Freedmen Courts were in place at this time, so Pierce believed the judge would rule in the employees' favor.[36]

In early 1867 the bureau stopped charging for contracts. To many, this change gave the appearance that contracts were no longer necessary. That was not the case. In early March that year the registration of contracts in the Huntsville bureau office had declined to the point that only one clerk was needed. Observers attributed this decline to General Howard's orders to charge nothing for making and recording contracts. As John Callis reported to Swayne, the impact of the change was compounded because now "the citizens seem to entertain the opinion that the necessity for contracts has passed, the idea however is not prevalent among the Freedmen. But the planters have said so much about the order, and exalted over it to such an extent that it has frightened the Freedmen thereby almost paralyzing the labor of this section."[37] The bureau did not change the requirement of recording contracts, but the confusion caused by General Howard's orders resulted in fewer written contracts, which permanently hamstrung the bureau's efforts to protect black labor rights. Blacks retained the option to pursue a solution to labor disputes through legal means, but without written contracts their chance of successful litigation was severely impaired. Like many of the issues facing blacks in Reconstruction Alabama, labor and legal rights were closely tied together. As with their efforts to protect freedmen labor, Swayne and the bureau set out immediately in July 1865 to ensure basic legal rights for the freedmen.

The acceptance of black testimony in court cases became the first significant issue of freedmen's legal rights in the months after the Civil War's conclusion. The bureau sought to ensure this right for the freedmen. The first bureau representatives began receiving complaints almost immediately that "the testimony of colored people is not received against whites by the Civil Authorities." This particular complainant asked that the trials of freedmen or whites accused by freedmen "be referred to the Provost Marshall or some other designated authority that will give the colored people, free and equal privileges in law."[38] While Swayne initially chose not to create separate Freedmen's Courts, he did move at once to ensure that state courts accepted black testimony.

The situation in Mobile in the summer of 1865 not only testified to Swayne's commitment to ensuring the acceptance of black testimony but also demonstrated the power of the bureau itself in the early months of Reconstruction. Dealing with resistance to bureau authority in Mobile was the first real test of Swayne's tenure. Having traveled through Mobile on his way to assume his post as assistant commissioner in Montgomery, Swayne was aware of the problems in the port city. In his July 21 report to General Howard, Swayne praised the freedmen in Mobile, trumpeting their "zealous support" of schools and churches and their "association to provide work for the unemployed." However, he harshly criticized the "most shameful extortion and outrage" that still was practiced upon them by wartime mayor R. H. Slough.[39] Swayne then consulted with Governor Parsons about the Mobile situation. Parsons was already aware of the problem, having received a communication from Mayor Slough that claimed unjustified and unsubstantiated grievances against the freedmen. Aware of the conditions in Mobile, Parsons dismissed Slough's complaints in his communication with Swayne saying the freedmen's "bill of wrongs against him [Slough] is at least as full and better supported, and that I have transmitted to Washington some account of the same."[40]

While Swayne worked with Governor Parsons, the newspapers in the state joined in on the issue. On August 6, 1865, the *Montgomery Advertiser* cautiously reported, "A most important order appears this morning from Brig. Gen. Swayne of the Freedmen's Bureau, in regard to the admission of negro testimony into our courts. It is a very grave and delicate question." The *Advertiser* commended "the excellent spirit of Gen. Swayne" and asked that "the great practical bearings of his order be most respectfully cogitated by the State courts."[41] The *Mobile Register*, meanwhile, addressed Mayor Slough's misstep of rejecting black testimony as "altogether premature, and not in accordance with existing facts and circumstances."[42] Swayne would not tolerate Mayor Slough's position on the issue. He also wanted to strengthen support for Governor Parsons, so Swayne wrote the governor on August 11:

> Some days since I had the honor to call your attention to the published instructions of the Mayor of Mobile to his Chief of Police denying to the free colored people of that City the right to peaceable assembly and of choosing a plan of habitation and industry. Since that time the course of that officer has been in progressive violation of the policy and orders of the President of the United States. In a formal decision he has announced that the negro cannot sue though he can be sued, cannot testify though he can be testified against and that he has no greater civil rights than under the Slave Code. This policy has its natural fruits. The City of Mobile is in a state of quasi riot. A church and schoolhouse and an entire square of colored people have been destroyed by incendiaries. Colored people are arrested who are out after ten P.M. Steamboat hands are daily at the end of a shift driven off without pay, and in no instance has the Mayor afforded relief but left them to steal that they may live.[43]

Swayne gave Mayor Slough an opportunity to accept bureau authority and correct his actions. He expected and quickly received the mayor's rejection. Immediately responding, Swayne informed Slough that any further exercise of jurisdiction in freedmen cases "would be at his peril as in violation of the order of the President." Swayne then went to Mobile himself with Governor Parsons's adjutant general carrying two commissions for a new mayor. The second commission was drafted in case the first man approached did not accept the post. Fortunately, the preferred candidate, John Forsyth, accepted the commission and became the new mayor of Mobile. Forsyth had edited the *Mobile Register*, served as minister to Mexico, and was a former Democratic mayor of the city. Swayne told O. O. Howard that Forsyth was "more beloved by the colored people of Mobile, than any man in the City."[44] As part of his commission, Forsyth accepted a bureau agency in Mobile under Swayne's order.

The August 18, 1865, issue of the *Montgomery Daily Advertiser* reported Forsyth's appointment as mayor of Mobile. While acknowledging the role of black testimony in the replacement of Slough, the *Advertiser*, perhaps understating circumstances, asserted that Forsyth would "take a more practical view of the question of admitting negro testimony against the whites than his predecessor." The paper recognized that it seemed "wiser to admit negro testimony before our courts for what it is worth, than to have our people dragged before prejudiced tribunals appointed by the Freedmen's Bureau."[45]

While events in Mobile provide the most detailed example of the issue of black testimony, bureau power, and even the relationship between Governor Parsons and Swayne, the subject of black testimony was not wholly settled. Governor Parsons continued receiving advice on the matter from judges throughout the state even after Slough's removal.[46] Swayne initially hoped that protecting black testimony and black rights in general could be handled without the creation of a separate Freedmen's Court system. Swayne believed that the condition of the bureau's offices in Alabama when he arrived prevented him from realistically forming a separate court system. The lack of bureau funding, only four "feeble agencies," and Union troops concentrated in only a few areas of the state prevented any practical extension of bureau power. His limited resources and confidence in Parsons led Swayne to believe that he "could not establish military tribunals on a sufficient scale and of fit character."[47]

His work with and faith in Governor Parsons initially convinced him to try to work through the existing system to secure black legal rights. Parsons had proven an ally in handling the problem with Mayor Slough in Mobile. Swayne communicated to Howard in August that Parsons was "honestly endeavoring to carry out the views of the President." Finally, Swayne told Howard that if he did establish Freedmen's Courts, it would "unite public sentiment against the charge of law," and the courts' verdicts "would be misrepresented and every where trumpeted as outrageous."[48]

Swayne thus believed for the moment that it was possible to promote the rights of freedmen through the civil courts that Governor Parsons was restoring. He emphasized that reliance on the civil courts would give the bureau use of this "vast judicial machinery" and the power to remove officials whenever their actions were "found not to work well." Using the civil courts would not provoke native white Alabamians since they were part of the existing state legal apparatus. Swayne also realized that the bureau would not last forever and that Freedmen's Courts therefore would not be available to protect blacks. If working within the existing civil court system to establish black legal rights succeeded, the system would continue to serve the freedmen long after the bureau left.[49] When Swayne proceeded to make all civil court officials officers of the Freedmen's Bureau, he required that they all accept black testimony as part of their duty as de facto bureau agents.[50]

Despite Swayne's best intentions, the issue lingered. Reinforcing the obligation that judges had to accept black testimony required a constant vigil. Judges were reported and cases removed if they refused after details of violations were reported to the bureau offices.[51] At the same time confusion remained late into the fall of 1865 when some local civilian officials were still unaware that black testimony was admissible while others ignored any bureau authority in civil court. In one Huntsville case the request for aid was sent to a bureau agent about a crime in which a white man had robbed a freedman. The reporting official asked for instruction since "blacks cannot testify in court."[52] In Athens, bureau agents themselves were reprimanded regarding their failure to protect the rights of blacks as well as whites. As Huntsville bureau agent Goodfellow wrote, "The Bureau still lives & will for at least a year, and the law or orders of the Bureau as issued by Genl. Howard making men white & colored, equal before the law of Alabama by the action of the convention until adjournment of the legislature."[53]

Ensuring the acceptance of black testimony was something that Swayne wanted the state legislature to codify. The *Selma Daily Messenger* reported on March 3, 1866, that Swayne was "anxious to witness passage of a bill giving freedmen, the right to testify in courts—to testify in all cases." In the spring of 1866 the state legislature was finally ready to legalize black testimony. The fact that the bureau had established and protected this right for almost a year was not lost on Swayne. The *Messenger* continued with a clear undertone, "Let them testify, and take their testimony for what it is worth. On this principle everyone has always been taking negro testimony."[54] As this statement indicates, black testimony would not necessarily be taken seriously even if it was legally allowed. Months prior to the legislature's final passage of the bill accepting black testimony, Swayne had already concluded that to protect the rights of freedmen the bureau must create separate Freedmen's Courts after all.

By the end of 1865 the environment had shifted. The provisional government of Parsons ended when the former Douglas Democrat Robert M. Patton of Florence took office as governor in December 1865. A newly elected state legislature took office a few days before Patton's inauguration. The state legislators immediately ratified the Thirteenth Amendment to the U.S. Constitution, but the subsequent legislation passed in late 1865 and early 1866 undermined freedmen rights the bureau had worked to guarantee. Patton initially proved as good an ally to Swayne as Governor Parsons, but the legislature was not inclined to aid either the bureau or the freedmen the organization sought to protect. Dominated by many of the same men who had controlled state politics prior to the war, the body moved quickly to pass a series of laws to limit black rights and control their labor.[55] Collectively known as the Black Code, one of the pieces of this legislation sought to regulate freedmen's contracts by effectively locking down their employment. Governor Patton's veto of this new legislation was sustained by the legislature.

Swayne lauded the stand taken by Patton, but he recognized that the veto did not "set to rest" the desire among state representatives for "unchecked control of labor."[56] Two state laws were passed and enacted that Swayne cited as evidence. He pointedly referred to them in his 1866 annual report to General Howard. The first was a stringent vagrancy law that fined offenders an "unusually large" fifty dollars. Those unable to pay were jailed or hired out for six months.[57] The Alabama Stay Law enacted in February 1866 was written, in Swayne's opinion, so that employers could indefinitely postpone paying their workers the wages they were entitled to. While neither law specifically referred to color, Swayne did not doubt that they were intended for the freedmen alone.[58] This legislation played a significant part in Swayne's decision to create the Freedmen's Courts. Clearly the state's legal apparatus would offer blacks few legal rights.

Swayne now believed that separate courts were necessary. He thus began to organize Freedmen's Courts throughout the state. Bureau agents, usually active or former Union officers, served as judges. The *Selma Daily Messenger* of February 21, 1866, reported the formation of one of the first Freedmen's Courts in Mobile "much to the surprise of the *Advertiser & Register*." The editor questioned whether General Swayne sanctioned the formation of the court, citing Swayne's orders from the summer of 1865 that called for turning over the trial of cases in which freedmen were interested parties to various state courts on the condition that black testimony was allowed. At that time all the judicial officers of the state had accepted Swayne's appointment of them as agents of the Freedmen's Bureau, and the state constitutional convention had adopted an ordinance "requiring them to continue to act in that capacity."[59] Swayne was content to rely upon these officials and the state courts over which they presided as long as they adequately handled freedmen rights. That was no longer the case, so Swayne saw the separate Freedman's Courts as the only way to provide basic legal rights to Alabamian freedmen. Nonetheless, this policy shift was clearly unexpected by many.

The Mobile paper was not pleased with the formation of the Freedmen's Court. The *Advertiser & Register* stated, "If we are not greatly mistaken the creation of this tribunal alien to the laws of the State, involves a breach of faith, which Gen. Swayne cannot countenance."[60] According to the editorial, the people of Mobile had an understanding with Swayne, and the formation of the Freedmen's Courts clearly violated that agreement. The fears that Swayne had conveyed to General Howard in August 1865 regarding the creation of Freedmen's Courts proved valid.

The Selma paper had reported the formation of the Mobile Freedmen's Court in February 1866, but less than a month later Swayne formed a similar court there. Special Orders No. 48 of March 15, 1866, established a court to preside over cases in which freedmen were "interested parties." Its jurisdiction extended over the District of Selma. Union Major S. S. Hoge of the 7th Reserve Corps was assigned to duty as judge of the court. He took notice of all cases referred to him by Chaplain S. S. Gardner, Superintendent of the Bureau for the District of Selma. The special orders required the recording of court proceedings and provided that all fines collected would be paid to the superintendent.[61]

The majority of the court cases pertained to labor contract disputes, but a significant minority concerned assault and battery. Many of those cases, however, also arose from labor disputes. Often they involved the flogging of the freedmen and sometimes their families as well.[62] One such case was brought against Richard Pierce in early April 1866. Robert Lile, a freedman, made the complaint against Pierce, alleging that he had been assaulted on March 27 while working at Pierce's Foundry. Pierce pled not guilty, but the court did not agree. He was forced to pay a fine of ten dollars. On the same day Pierce appeared again to face assault and battery charges brought by Louisa Huntington after an incident at Pierce's Foundry on March 10, 1866. He pled guilty and was fined twenty dollars.[63] It is unknown whether the penalty was increased because there were multiple offenses or because of the victim's sex. Few scholars have studied the activities of the Freedmen's Courts in Alabama, but this case provides a brief glimpse of the court's activities.

The white population viewed the Freedmen's Courts as a breach of trust, and subsequent political activities of Swayne and other bureau agents would further outrage them. By the fall of 1866 criticism of the bureau appeared frequently in almost every state newspaper. The *Union Springs Times*, for example, commended the progress of the freedmen despite the "ignorant intermeddling of the Bureau, and the worse influence of an idle soldiery."[64] By the end of Swayne's tenure as assistant commissioner, the press and public referred to him as a "tyrant" and "merciless martinet, who basks only in the smiles of deluded negroes and depraved whites."[65]

Ultimately Swayne's increasingly open political activities on behalf of Republican candidates in 1867 led the president to remove him as assistant commissioner at the beginning of the new year. He initially returned to the army but soon resigned to return to Ohio to practice law. The extent to which his partisan activities undermined the bureau itself is more difficult to determine. By the time Swayne left Alabama the bureau had already lost considerable ground in protecting freedmen rights. The black codes, particularly the vagrancy and "stay" laws, passed by the Alabama legislature hurt bureau efforts in labor and legal matters. The Freedmen's Courts brought more criticism to the bureau while only temporarily offering blacks some judicial reprieve. As Swayne himself had recognized in 1865, they could provide no assistance beyond the duration of the bureau itself. Swayne's departure was not the formal end of the bureau in Alabama, but whatever remnants of effectiveness left in the organization soon vanished after his departure.

The Freedmen's Bureau represented an ambitious endeavor that lacked the governmental commitment necessary for it to achieve success. The Freedmen's Bureau Bill of 1865 signified a change in the status of government relative to the individual citizen that did not go unnoticed. In his veto of the 1866 bill to renew and fund the Freedmen's Bureau, President Johnson criticized the expansion of the federal government, stating, "The system for the support of individual persons in the United States was never contemplated by the Constitution."[66] With overwhelming congressional support for the bill, Johnson's veto raised the ire of Republicans. Compounding the political damage, Johnson's veto was overridden, and the Freedmen's Bureau was renewed by legislation in July 1866 and again in July 1868.[67] While Johnson's resistance to continuing the bureau may have helped accelerate his political demise, most Republicans were themselves hesitant to see the bureau continue for very much longer.

With the exception of education and claims divisions, the activities of the Freedmen's Bureau finally were discontinued by order of Congress on July 25, 1868.[68] The bureau itself was completely dismantled on June 30, 1872.[69] Historians have generally seen the bureau as a failure in light of the treatment of blacks in the South throughout the remainder of the nineteenth century and well into the twentieth. That is a harsh assessment considering the circumstances and environment in which the bureau operated. Emerging in the months following a conflict like none other in American history and tasked with the job of protecting the rights of a people that knew only slavery and a white population that knew them only as slaves, the bureau was faced with a monumental task. As a unique federal organization created for the purpose of social welfare whose existence depended on a president and even a Republican Congress unwilling to see it last but for a short time, the ability of the bureau to affect long-term change in the South was doomed from the start.

In Alabama, the bureau prevented a desperate situation in the months and years after the Civil War from turning into tragedy. Large-scale starvation was averted. A completely devastated economy was reborn through a contract system that during the bureau's existence helped both blacks and whites but in its absence clearly benefited the latter at the expense of the former. Swayne's leadership helped protect blacks by providing food and clothing for the destitute, establishing schools, supervising and mediating their labor contracts, and demanding acceptance of blacks' testimony in court.

At the conclusion of the war the white population of the state was tolerant of the bureau and Northern oversight. As time passed, they regained their voice, and the bureau's actions grew increasingly unpopular. Radical Reconstruction accelerated their desire to return to unfettered self-rule. At the same time the bureau's support waned nationwide. Without a sustained commitment to the bureau as protector of black rights, the return of blacks to a different, though still subservient, role in Alabama and throughout the South was not surprising.

With the abrupt end of the slave-based plantation system at the heart of Alabama's agrarian economy, the bureau provided critical leadership and oversight to

Labor, Law, and the Freedmen's Bureau / 255

keep farms operating and prevent economic collapse and starvation. At the same time Swayne made decisive moves to protect the freedmen's newly gained rights in both labor and legal matters, working with the limited resources available to him. He made alliances when needed but forcefully responded to challenges when required to meet his commitment to the freedmen.

Notes

1. 13 Stat. 507; June Axinn and Mark J. Stern, *Social Welfare: A History of the American Response to Need* (Boston: Allyn and Bacon, 2005), 97.

2. William S. McFeely, *Yankee Stepfather: General O. O. Howard and the Freedmen* (New Haven: Yale University Press, 1968), 6.

3. Ibid., 66; LaWanda Cox, "General O. O. Howard and the 'Misrepresented Bureau,'" in *Freedom, Racism, and Reconstruction: Collected Writings of LaWanda Cox*, ed. Donald G. Nieman (Athens: University of Georgia Press, 1997), 151.

4. Eric Foner, *Reconstruction: America's Unfinished Revolution, 1863–1877* (New York: Harper and Row, 1988), 149; Kenneth B. White, "Wager Swayne: Racist or Realist?" *Alabama Review* 31 (April 1978): 107; Jonathan M. Wiener, *Social Origins of the New South: Alabama, 1860–1885* (Baton Rouge: Louisiana State University Press, 1978), 51; McFeely, *Yankee Stepfather*, 77–78.

5. Foner, *Reconstruction*, 149.

6. White, "Wager Swayne," 95.

7. Ibid., 107.

8. Michael W. Fitzgerald, "Wager Swayne, the Freedmen's Bureau, and the Politics of Reconstruction in Alabama," *Alabama Review* 48 (July 1995): 190–91.

9. *Montgomery Daily Advertiser*, August 25, 1865, p. 2.

10. St. Col. J. Strickton to Col. Hough from Union Springs, May 31, 1865, RG 105, box 33, Montgomery, Sub Assistant Letters Received, 1865–1866, National Archives, Washington, DC.

11. George Harmount to Theodore W. Conway, [June 1865], Letter Number 31, RG 105, E. 142, vol. 108, Sub Asst Com Mobile, Letters Sent, April 1865–April 1868, National Archives, Washington, DC.

12. *Montgomery Daily Advertiser*, October 20, 1865, p. 2.

13. "Proclamation to the People of Alabama from Governor Parsons," issued August 19, 1865, and reprinted in the *Montgomery Daily Advertiser*, August 22, 1865, p. 2.

14. Michael W. Fitzgerald, "Emancipation and Military Pacification: The Freedmen's Bureau and Social Control in Alabama," in *The Freedmen's Bureau and Reconstruction: Reconsiderations*, ed. Paul A. Cimbala and Randall M. Miller (New York: Fordham University Press, 1999), 54.

15. Thomas W. Conway to Chaplain Chas W. Buckley, May 26, 1865, RG 105, box 33, Montgomery, Sub Assistant Letters Received, 1865–1866, National Archives, Washington, DC.

16. Swayne to O. O. Howard, August 21, 1865, M809, reel 2, National Archives, Washington, DC.

17. Swayne to O. O. Howard, July 21, 1865, M809, reel 1.

18. *Montgomery Daily Advertiser*, September 5, 1865, p. 2.

19. Swayne to O. O. Howard, August 21, 1865, M809, reel 2.

20. *Montgomery Daily Advertiser*, July 22, 1865, p. 2.

21. *Montgomery Daily Advertiser*, August 5, 1865, p. 2 (letter to the editor from man named "Proxter"; no first name given).

22. Ibid.

23. A. H. Bynam, Bureau Agent, to Goodfellow, November 23, 1865, RG 105, E. III, No. 57, Huntsville, Letters Received, July 1865–March 1866, National Archives, Washington, DC.

24. General Orders No. 12 issued by Swayne on August 30, 1865, reprinted in the *Montgomery Daily Advertiser*, September 9, 1865, p. 2.

25. Ibid.

26. *Montgomery Daily Advertiser*, September 7, 1865, p. 2.

27. Advertisement from [Charles W.] Pierce, [n.d.], RG 105, E. 78, No. 139, p. 18, Demopolis, Letters Sent, January–June 1867, National Archives, Washington, DC.

28. Contract between Jack James and J. Murphy, September 27, 1865, and contract between Martin McCally and Robert Freeman, September 27, 1865, both in RG 105, E. 116, vol. 81, Huntsville, Contracts 1865 part of 1866, National Archives, Washington, DC.

29. Contract involving Augustus Pryor, October 20, 1865, RG 105, E. 116, vol. 81, Huntsville, Contracts 1865 part of 1866, National Archives, Washington, DC.

30. Contract between H. B. Turner and Westley Evers, October 24, 1865, and contract involving E. W. Eastman, October 30, 1865, both in RG 105, E. 116, Vol. 81, Huntsville, Contracts 1865 part of 1866, National Archives, Washington, DC.

31. Contract between William R. Stewart and Manuel (colored), wife, and five children, November 1, 1865, RG 105, E. 116, vol. 81, Huntsville, Contracts 1865 part of 1866, National Archives, Washington, DC.

32. Chaplain T. M. Goodfellow to John Tanner, Madison Station, November 27, 1865, RG 105, E. 109, No. 62, Huntsville, Letters Sent, August 1865–April 1866, National Archives, Washington, DC.

33. S. S. Gardner to Mr. Bolan[?], J.P., June 6, 1866, RG 105, E. 184, No. 175, Selma, Letters Sent, 1866–1867, National Archives, Washington, DC.

34. Pierce to Swayne, September 17, 1866, RG 105, E. 78, No. 138, p. 33, Demopolis, Letters Sent, January–December 1866, National Archives, Washington, DC.

35. Pierce to Swayne, December 6, 1866, RG 105, E. 78, No. 138, p. 71, Demopolis, Letters Sent, January–December 1866, National Archives, Washington, DC.

36. Pierce to Thomas Beville, January 15, 1867, RG 105, E. 78, No. 139, p. 14, Demopolis, Letters Sent, January–June 1867, National Archives, Washington, DC.

37. John Callis to Wager Swayne, [March 1867], RG 105, E. 109, No. 63, p. 351, Huntsville, Letters Sent, April 1866–May 1867, National Archives, Washington, DC.

38. George Harmount to Byran Porter, [June 1865], RG 105, E. 142, vol. 108, Sub Asst Com Mobile, Letters Sent, April 1865–April 1868, National Archives, Washington, DC.

39. Swayne to O. O. Howard, July 21, 1865, M809, reel 2.

40. Lewis E. Parsons to Swayne, July 31, 1865, M809, reel 1.

41. *Montgomery Advertiser*, August 6, 1865, p. 2.

42. *Mobile Register*, August 9, 1865.

43. Swayne to Lewis E. Parsons, August 11, 1865, M 809, reel 1.

44. Swayne to O. O. Howard, August 21, 1865, M809, reel 2, Swayne's Weekly Reports.

45. *Montgomery Daily Advertiser*, August 18, 1865, p. 2.

46. Secretary of State to Governor Parsons, August 11, 1865, Gubernatorial Records of Parsons, RC2:G6, Alabama Department of Archives and History, Montgomery (hereafter ADAH).

47. Swayne to O. O. Howard, August 21, 1865, M809, reel 2, Swayne's Weekly Reports.

48. Ibid.

Labor, Law, and the Freedmen's Bureau / 257

49. Ibid.
50. General Order No. 7, August 4, 1865, Swayne, Wager, Letter, SPR256, ADAH.
51. Goodfellow to C. Harrison, [December 1865], RG 105, E. 109, No. 62, p. 149, Huntsville, Letters Sent, August 1865–April 1866, National Archives, Washington, DC.
52. F. P. Stevenson to J. H. Shirratt, [November 20, 1865], RG 105, E. 111, No. 57, Huntsville, Letters Received, July 1865–March 1866, National Archives, Washington, DC.
53. Goodfellow to Agent of Bureau at Athens, Alabama, January 10, 1866, RG 105, E. 109, No. 62, p. 215, Huntsville, Letters Sent, August 1865–April 1866, National Archives, Washington, DC.
54. *Selma Daily Messenger*, March 3, 1866, Micro #449, ADAH.
55. William Warren Rogers et al., *Alabama: The History of a Deep South State* (Tuscaloosa: University of Alabama Press, 1994), 238–39.
56. Wager Swayne, "Annual Report," October 31, 1866, United States Senate, Executive Documents, No. 6, 39th Cong., 1st sess., 12.
57. Rogers et al., *Alabama*, 238.
58. Wager Swayne, "Annual Report," October 31, 1866, 12.
59. *Selma Daily Messenger*, February 21, 1866, Micro #449, ADAH.
60. Ibid.
61. C. Cadle Jr., by order of Wager Swayne, Special Orders No. 48, March 15, 1866, RG105, vol. 175, E. 184, Selma, Letters Sent, 1866–1867, National Archives, Washington, DC.
62. *State of Alabama v. John F. Burns*, Freedmen's Court, Selma, April 10, 1866, and *Mat Hunter v. David Weener*, Freedmen's Court, Selma, April 17, 1866, both in RG 105, vol. 175, E. 184, Selma, Letters Sent, 1866–1867, National Archives, Washington, DC. Roughly 80 percent of the cases of the Selma Freedmen's Court involved labor or contract disputes whereas about 20 percent involved assault and battery.
63. *State of Alabama v. Richard Pierce*, involving Louisa Huntington, Freedmen's Court, Selma, April 4, 1866, RG105, vol. 175, E. 184, Selma, Letters Sent 1866–1867, National Archives, Washington, DC.
64. *Union Springs Times*, October 31, 1866.
65. *Montgomery Advertiser*, January 7, 1868, p. 3.
66. Andrew Johnson, "Veto of Freedmen's Bureau Bill," *Veto of Freedmen's Bureau Bill* (2009), 3596, *Academic Search Premier*, EBSCO, Web. 6, September 2010.
67. Congressional Acts of July 16, 1866 (14 Stat. 173) and July 6, 1868 (15 Stat 83).
68. 15 Stat. 193.
69. Act of Congress approved on June 10, 1872 (17 Stat. 366) took effect on June 30, 1872.

14
Freedom's Church
Sociocultural Construction, Reconstruction, and Post-Reconstruction in Perry County, Alabama's African American Churches

Bertis English

In "Reconstruction and Its Benefits," a paper presented at the 1909 meeting of the American Historical Association, noted black scholar W. E. B. Du Bois recalled how necessity often drew enslaved blacks and free whites to the same churches before the Civil War. Following the war, white churchgoers quickly removed blacks, asserted Du Bois. When blacks were allowed to remain in predominantly white churches, added historian Eric Foner in his 1988 tome *Reconstruction: America's Unfinished Revolution, 1863–1877*, most white church leaders insisted on segregated pews and monopolized governance. Historian Sylvia Krebs, in contrast, had argued previously that antebellum whites were receptive to the idea of having blacks attend their services. Consequently, the two groups dealt amicably with each other once freedpeople began to create their own churches during Reconstruction.[1]

The Alabama Black Belt offers an excellent opportunity to test the theses of Du Bois, Foner, Krebs, and other scholars regarding religious and social reconstruction. Populated overwhelmingly by African Americans, the subregion was home to some of the oldest and most influential white and black churches in the state. This chapter examines church development in Perry County, one of the Black Belt's most progressive localities.[2] Though religion is the primary focus here, attention is also given to the educational and political importance of black and white church builders. In line with previous studies, including Adam Fairclough's *A Class of Their Own* and Wilson Fallin Jr.'s *Uplifting the People*, two books published in 2007, this chapter maintains that schooling and political activism were natural by-products of religious activity because a large number of literate blacks were pastors or devout followers.[3] The county's largest denominations—Baptists, Methodists, Congregationalists, and Presbyterians—further facilitated the education of thousands of black ministers, teachers, and politicians. Churchgoing blacks and egalitarian whites likewise prepared the black electorate exceptionally well, considering the turbulent atmosphere of the 1860s. By doing so, Perry County's black elites and their white associates provided the 18,000 or so common blacks in the county academic, economic, and political opportunities that in time produced some of the country's leading African American organizations and professionals.[4]

Unfortunately, few scholars have written about Perry County blacks and their offspring. Horace Mann Bond, one of the twentieth century's most distinguished black historians, was a notable exception. Writing in 1972, Bond pointed out that the county's post–Civil War blacks were some of the most privileged freedpeople in the state.[5] Besides being relatively secure financially, they were academically grounded, hardworking, and politically aware. They also were extremely religious. Before 1865, scores of them had attended church, camp meetings, and revivals with their white masters, overseers, and neighbors. Other blacks and whites had worshiped together in private, as was the case in 1844 when two white evangelicals preached to a group of slaves in a grove outside the Hebron Baptist Church in Marion, Perry County's largest town and county seat as well as the Baptist capital of Alabama. Inside the church, meanwhile, white members of the Baptist Bethel Association had discussed foot washing, priestly duties, Sunday schools, and temperance. A similar incident took place in 1847. As members of the Cahaba Baptist Association met in the Hopewell Baptist Church in Marion, the Rev. B. H. Matthews ministered to slaves in a nearby grove. Fellow white clergyman William A. Stickney, founder of St. Wilfrid's Episcopal Church in Marion, preached regularly to slaves who lived in less populated and more rural parts of the county.[6]

While black church attendance was common in Perry County before Reconstruction, it should not be exaggerated. Each week, thousands of slaves were unable to attend church because they had to work when services were held, Sundays included. In 1861, Hugh Davis Sr., a wealthy and somewhat liberal Marion planter, prohibited his bondservants from observing the Sabbath because crop production was behind schedule. Moreover, the cotton they had picked during the weekdays contained too much grass to earn a good profit. Not only did he deny his servants worship, they also did not receive the small pay they normally received for their labor.[7] The Rev. J. F. Smith, a Methodist Episcopalian in Lowndesboro, two counties northeast of Perry in the Black Belt, described another instance of Sunday work in a December 1863 letter to his nephew Thomas, a Confederate soldier from Autauga. "While the white folks were at church professing to be fasting and praying," wrote Smith, "the negroes are in the fields hard at work. What a shame! No wonder our prayers are not heard," he concluded.[8]

One could only imagine what Reverend Smith prayed for in the midst of war, but most African Americans in the area prayed for religious autonomy, academic education, personal property, respect—in a word, freedom. Alexander Goldsby was an enslaved blacksmith and Baptist deacon in a predominately white church outside of Selma in Dallas County, Perry County's southern neighbor. Following the issuance of the Emancipation Proclamation, he assembled slaves each Friday night. Together they begged God to grant them the emancipation that Abraham Lincoln's recent proclamation had not brought.[9] In Marion, meanwhile, blacks held formal prayer meetings each Sunday afternoon and night, and gathered at additional times during the week. Bishop Cobbs, an elderly black Baptist, led many of the services. From time to time, a white person would attend and encourage the slaves to sing European-style hymns; however, they preferred traditional African melodies that had been passed down orally for generations or tunes they themselves had composed. Such jubilee songs, they said, were more spiritual than the pieces of music found in white hymnals.[10]

John W. Blassingame, W. E. B. Du Bois, John Hope Franklin, E. Franklin Frazier, Evelyn Brooks Higginbotham, Thomas Wentworth Higginson, C. Eric Lincoln, Lawrence M. Mamiya, Albert J. Raboteau, Gayraud S. Wilmore, and Carter G. Woodson, among other scholars, have amply shown that religion was one of the strongest forces that slaves had at their disposal to combat the barbarity of the peculiar institution.[11] Religion furthermore provided them a way to preserve African customs, as evidenced by the aforementioned thwarting of European hymns. As important to slaves was singing "Hail Mary," "Roll, Jordan, Roll," "Steal Away to Jesus," and innumerable other spirituals in a manner Du Bois described in his 1903 literary masterpiece *The Souls of Black Folk* as distinctly African. Slaves' characteristic improvisation and emotionalism, he maintained, expressed a combination of deep despair, hope, and sorrow.[12] Slaves on the Storrs plantation in Perry County were particularly fond of "My Jesus Acomin":

My Jesus acomin!
    He's acoming inde mawning,
My Jesus acomin!
    He's coming in his charot,
My Jesus acoming!
    Crac you whip Liga,
My Jesus acomin!
    Open de gate Marthy,
My Jesus acomin!
    Run to meet 'im Mary,
My Jesus acomin!
    His eyes like fire,
My Jesus acomin!
    His legs lik a pilgrems,
My Jesus acomin![13]

According to Ella Storrs, who spent much of her childhood socializing with slaves, they sang the song indefinitely, improvising as they went along. The chorus never changed, but each participant would insert a verse indicating what he or she thought was going to happen when Jesus finally came. Eventually someone would become "happy," a common sign of a pious realization, or epiphany, and worshipers would clasp hands, form a circle, and jump up and down in time with the music.[14] As the singing grew louder and the words blurred, someone would scream, throw up his or her hands as if cataleptic, fall down, and have to be carried away.[15] Unbeknownst to Storrs, she was witnessing a variation of the ring shout, a scheme slaves developed to perpetuate conventional African worship. Incorporating continual movement, vibrant polyrhythmic beats, and constant singing, ring shouting usually was undertaken when a white master or overseer's religious norms, fear of rebellion, or ignorance forbade slaves from openly enjoying religious customs that required a great deal of drumming, arm, leg, or foot crossing, touching others, call and response, and so forth.[16]

That the vast majority of involuntary servants in Alabama's Black Belt had to contrive ways to express their humanity and generate some semblance of freedom before the U.S. Congress ratified the Thirteenth Amendment in 1865, prohibiting racial slavery in the country, is unmistakable. In antebellum and wartime Perry County, however, tens of thousands of slaves got an opportunity to "taste" freedom through clandestine praise meetings.[17] Moreover, a few others already had fellowshiped publicly alongside their white brothers and sisters in Christ. At the historic Siloam Baptist Church, black and white parishioners began to pray, tithe, and be baptized together shortly after its June 1822 founding. In coming years, white officials were surprised to find out that black members were as receptive to biblical study as whites. In some cases, they concluded, blacks were more receptive.[18]

When Siloam was established, Marion was notorious for the iniquity that often accompanied a newly settled town or village. Siloam's first pastor and future president of the Alabama Baptist State Convention, slaveholder Charles Crow, reportedly held services once per month because Marion whites were more interested in the devilment the town offered than in attending church. William Calloway, Crow's successor and fellow slaveholder, encountered similar apathy. Only one person was baptized during Calloway's pastorate from 1830 through 1833; the church claimed merely thirty-five members when he left.[19] James Veasy, Siloam's next pastor, was more successful than his predecessors, however. "The secret of the success of his preaching lay in his dwelling much upon the passion and love of the Redeemer," declared one individual. "These themes animated his soul, and their power was acknowledged by his congregation," blacks included.[20] When Veasy stepped down in December 1834, his biracial membership had risen to 103, 51 of whom had been baptized.[21]

Siloam continued to grow over the next twenty years. The Rev. Peter Crawford, Veasy's replacement and cofounder of the denominational Judson Female Seminary in Marion, was an important part of that phenomenon. Before leaving in 1837 to teach at the Central Female College in Mississippi, he oversaw the construction of an elegant $7,000 parsonage. Siloam's next pastor, James H. DeVotie, purchased a lot at the corner of Washington and Early Streets. Under his supervision, black members built Marion's first brick church, a symbol of prestige in Alabama's rural Black Belt. When the Rev. William H. McIntosh replaced DeVotie in 1855, Siloam had more than 650 members, the majority of whom were enslaved.[22]

A number of Perry County's most enlightened slave masters attended Siloam. In 1850, member Hugh Davis allowed eight of his male bondservants to share in that year's cotton yield. Each servant was paid two cents for every pound of cotton that was picked. Altogether they received almost $70 for their efforts. Even greater dispensations came later. In 1857, Davis gave communal property to several respected slaves. Profits were divided according to each servant's behavior, work ethic, and marital status. Davis did not allow the slaves to work their land on his time, but he did allow them a partial holiday on days when they were exceptionally productive in his fields. The following year, he started sharing peanuts, peas, and cotton with slaves. A small number of them were permitted to transport and sell the items in Perry and Dallas Counties for their own benefit. Davis likewise built above-average slave quarters for the Black Belt, furnished suitable clothing, and held annual summer celebrations that mirrored the Ebony Festivals enjoyed by free blacks in Norfolk, Virginia.[23]

Reverend McIntosh himself was another progressive Siloam member. Besides allowing slaves to sit in the gallery and lower sanctuary during Sunday services, he permitted James Childs, a crippled mulatto leather worker and shoemaker, to hold his own meetings in the basement. That allowance was rare in antebellum Alabama. By the outbreak of war, McIntosh had ordained the literate Childs, whose son Stephen later served as Confederate general George D. Johnston's body servant at the Battle of Chickamauga. The Childses' standing rose during Reconstruction. In 1867, the Reverend Childs and eight additional former slaves helped found Lincoln, a black primary school in Marion. After finishing Lincoln, Stephen went on to become a prominent businessman, church official, politician, and school administrator. Others in the extremely light-skinned Childs family passed as whites. Two male members even married white women. More important than breaking one of the nineteenth century's most prevalent social taboos, the Childses represented the black personal and collective achievement for which postbellum Perry County *should be* better known.[24]

Ocmulgee Baptist Church, out of which Siloam grew, also welcomed blacks during the antebellum years. One of Alabama's first Baptist churches, Ocmulgee had twelve members when William Calloway, Charles Crow, William Harrod, Isaac Suttle, and John Tubb founded it in June 1820. The same year, Pastor Crow received black bondservants Bob and Dafney by letter. Neither was a member for long: Bob died in August 1821, and Dafney was dismissed the following month. Extant church records do not indicate the reason for the dismissal, but they do indicate that he or another bondservant named Dafney was a member in March 1828.[25]

Thanks to competent leaders and a growing membership that included more than one hundred slaves, Ocmulgee continued to flourish without any significant interruption through the Civil War. In the aftermath of war, it and other predominately white churches faced substantial change, especially with regard to black members. Although white religious associations like the Alabama Baptist State Convention did not think former slaves' altered political and legal statuses necessitated any modification to their social or religious condition, numerous black churchmen thought differently.[26]

During Reconstruction, one way Perry County's black citizens expressed their new station in life and understanding of what modern scholars call liberation theology was by "hunting for Jesus" in their own houses of worship. In certain communities, such as Marion and Uniontown, the process actually commenced during the war.[27] As soon as James Childs, Wilson Freeman, Henry King, Orum Parish, and other leading blacks at Siloam heard about Abraham Lincoln's Emancipation Proclamation, designed to end slavery in the Confederacy beginning on January 1, 1863, Childs and his associates began to discuss erecting a church that they themselves controlled. Insofar as slaves had made the brick, mixed the mortar, and performed most of the manual labor to build Siloam, the men were not worried about the physical construction of a new praise house. Their primary concern was raising enough money to purchase the materials needed to build an adequate structure in such an uncertain time. Finding a white person willing to part with land during the war was equally vexing.[28]

Exactly how, when, and from whom the resources needed to build the First Colored Baptist Church of Marion were acquired is unknown, but its wartime existence is certain. Reverend Childs was pastor and remained in the position through much of Reconstruction. In 1871, he and his followers bought a small plot of land at the corner of Washington and DeKalb Streets, about two squares south of Siloam, for their sole use. In 1873, while W. T. Coleman was pastor, First Colored Baptist was renamed the Second Colored Baptist Church. Eventually it also became Berean. Some of the county's most influential blacks were members, including the Billingsley, Childs, Curtis, Freeman, Parish, and Webb families.[29]

Alexander H. Curtis Sr., a former slave from Raleigh, North Carolina, was the church's most influential parishioner. He had come to Marion in 1848 with the family of E. Haywood. Soon thereafter, Curtis became the body servant of John R. Goree, a successful planter and merchant in Dallas County and son-in-law of the immensely wealthy Edwin W. King. Like James and Stephen Childs, Curtis enjoyed a comparatively privileged slave life. Goree allowed him to operate a barbershop whose profits the two men shared. In addition to barbering, Curtis farmed and perhaps undertook clandestine academic study, although he was already literate when the Haywoods brought him to Alabama.[30] In 1851, he married Princess Webb Freeman, a fourth-generation descendent of a legendary Malagasy princess whose offspring also included James Childs's wife, Martha. In 1859, Curtis purchased his freedom and moved to New York. Following the war, he returned to Marion permanently and resumed his barbering and mercantile practices. Together with Pat Billingsley, he operated a small store that offered tobacco and other goods underneath the King House, Marion's first hotel. Besides co-owning a store, Curtis farmed, became a building contractor, delved into education, and entered politics. Not only was he the only black man to preside over the Alabama Senate during the nineteenth century, he also was the only black state legislator to have used personal savings to obtain freedom.[31]

Black Uniontown congregants were as independent minded as their Marion counterparts during the 1860s. In 1866, John C. Dozier, a principled physician and educator from Virginia, was among six African Americans who petitioned the white leadership of the predominantly black Uniontown Baptist Church to form a separate place of worship. In the petition, Dozier and his associates stressed that they had never been accused of disorderly conduct inside or outside church. As a show of goodwill, they asked for help constituting a new church, which they planned to call Uniontown African Baptist. White officials accepted the petition, and the First Colored Missionary Baptist Church was begun.[32]

From 1866 through 1867, First Colored Missionary existed in name only. Members continued to meet in Uniontown Baptist, which nonetheless suffered a tremendous financial hardship when they formally left. Because white church officials were unable to pay for a full-time minister, cadets from the denominational Howard College in Marion often gave sermons. To generate additional revenue, Uniontown Baptist doubled as a school and a courtroom. In the meantime, Dozier and his black colleagues continued to plan for their own church. Why its proposed name was not adopted when it was completed remains unclear, but a compromise might have been engineered. African Baptist perhaps was too radical a name for the first pastor, white minister Lilburn Fox, so it was dropped. Dozier followed as the church's second pastor.[33]

Elsewhere in the state and the nation, former slaves did not have the money and attendant resources to build their own sanctuaries, so whites donated vacant buildings. Dozier and his followers' efforts help demonstrate that Perry County's blacks rarely needed that type assistance, though it was appreciated. Their somewhat privileged prewar circumstance allowed them to be real agents of self-help whom freedpeople in adjacent counties sought to emulate. It also enabled them to give generously to religious institutions and activities as well as manage their own spiritual affairs.[34]

Irrespective of Perry County's blacks' notable degree of self-sufficiency, they were careful not to completely sever the religious and economic ties that had been formed with white community leaders. Their cooperation in these areas suggests that the racial divides for which the Black Belt was known during the antebellum, Civil War, and Reconstruction periods did exist in Perry County, but the divides were not as rigid there as they were in neighboring counties. Existing crime data help corroborate the claim. Whereas hundreds of confirmed cases of racially and politically motivated acts of violence occurred in and around the Black Belt during the 1860s and 1870s, court records, Freedmen's Bureau reports, and other reliable sources show that Perry County was relatively peaceful during those years.[35]

White Perry County churchgoers' prewar courting of blacks adds force to the previous contentions. The competition among white Methodists and Baptists was particularly intense. Legend has it that Methodist elders passed an ordinance mandating the expulsion of any black member found guilty of immorality, intemperance, being unclean, lying, stealing, or attending a Baptist church. As long as black Methodists did not commit one of these *ungodly* acts, they could continue to sit beside, commune with, and drink from the same cup as white Methodists.[36]

An early postbellum religious conversion shores up the notion that Perry County parishioners were not as racially divided as other Black Belt congregants. At a December 1866 through January 1867 revival preached by Jabez L. M. Curry, a former slaveholding Confederate official and president of Howard College, the son of a wealthy antebellum planter was converted. As soon as the young man was baptized, two elderly men who had belonged to the convert's father walked up and extended "the right hand of fellowship," reported the Atlanta, Georgia, *Christian Index and South-western Baptist*.[37] Afterward, the virtuous blacks thanked God in plain but touching words for making the white youth a Christian.[38]

For various reasons, the year 1873 proved an excellent one for black church building in Perry County. Throughout the South, black and white Baptists undertook a campaign to bolster religious activity. A severe financial depression caused many church officials to believe that morality would lapse as people used alcohol, promiscuity, theft, and other potentially debilitating vices to deal with financial and related woes. To prevent a complete moral breakdown, a number of influential black Alabama Baptists worked hard to develop biracial denominational and sometimes interdenominational unions.[39]

Organizers hoped that strengthened relations among black and white churchgoers would produce a spiritual rebirth in the state. As citizens worked together to better their collective plight, Alabama's tense social, political, and economic climate might be eased. Church leaders' labor bore ripe fruit in Perry County. Several churches were constructed during the first half of 1873, and more were scheduled to be completed before year's end. Demand for theological study increased as well. In each endeavor, white Baptists, Congregationalists, Methodists, and Presbyterians helped. Additional assistance was provided by the biracial Young Men's Christian Association and the Perry County Bible Society. Their cooperation strengthens the argument that many Perry County citizens were able to overcome the misunderstandings, stereotypes, and irreverent secular and religious divisions that the Civil War and Reconstruction produced. Rather than accepting complete racial segregation as a fait accompli during those chaotic times, many of the county's residents met "in common purpose and mutual affection."[40]

Creating black Sunday schools, emphasizing the importance of temperance, and developing a seminary to educate black youth were central aims of Perry County church builders. On Sunday, June 15, 1873, members of a countywide Sunday school union assembled in the Congregational Church of Marion to hold the group's first conference. Approximately four hundred individuals attended the meeting, at which some of the Black Belt's most influential white and black citizens delivered addresses. White New Yorker George Card, principal of the state-sponsored Lincoln Normal School in Marion, was a featured speaker. Nathan Willis, an American Missionary Association agent and Lincoln instructor from Massachusetts, joined him on the dais. Union president Alexander Curtis, a Lincoln trustee and devoted black Baptist, gave closing remarks.[41]

In the wake of the June 1873 conference, numerous people claimed that Perry County was leading the Sunday school movement in Alabama. African Americans played key roles.[42] In addition to Curtis, the Reverends Charles O. Boothe, Dozier, and William H. McAlpine were energetic members of the movement. Boothe worked in northern Alabama with William H. Councill, founder of the Lincoln Normal School in Huntsville and the Alabama Agricultural and Mechanical University in Normal before moving to the Black Belt during the 1870s. In Selma, Boothe pastored the St. Phillip Street Church. Elsewhere in the subregion, including Perry County, he taught theology and performed missionary work. In 1877, he helped found the Second Colored Baptist Church in Montgomery, forerunner to Dexter Avenue Baptist. In addition, Boothe was a key proponent of Selma University, a theological school established in 1878 by the Alabama Colored Baptist State Convention, a ministerial alliance organized ten years earlier. A gifted author, his 1895 *Cyclopedia of Colored Baptists of Alabama* remains one of the most comprehensive state studies about black Southern Baptists ever written.[43]

Though Dozier is less familiar than Boothe, his importance to Alabama history is undeniable. One of Reconstruction's most learned black men, Dozier was an accomplished church builder, multilingual educator, and landholding politician. In 1870, he was one among twenty black state officials with real estate valued at $1,000 or more. Of equal significance, his sterling character and political savvy caused his white colleagues in the state legislature to respect him as much as they did Curtis.[44]

McAlpine, another esteemed educator and pastor of Dexter Avenue, issued the 1873 resolution that helped give birth to Selma University. In 1880, he was elected the first president of the separatist Baptist Foreign Mission Convention of the United States of America, an organization formed in Montgomery by the heads of several black Southern Baptist churches and civic groups. Independent missionizing in Africa was the convention's primary purpose. At an 1889 meeting in the same city, delegates from the convention, the American National Baptist Convention, and the National Baptist Educational Convention agreed to merge and form the National Baptist Convention of the United States of America. Although Boothe, Dozier, and McAlpine played strategic roles in the new convention, organized in 1895, they hitherto had supported biracial initiatives and associations. They also had given cheerfully to black and white denominations, especially Baptists.[45]

An examination of the proceedings of the sixteenth annual session of the Alabama Colored Baptist State Convention elucidates how prosperous and giving Boothe, Dozier, and company were. At the 1883 meeting, Perry County was represented by Boothe; McAlpine, the program chair and a member to the convention's mission board; G. J. Brooks of the Hopewell Baptist Church; Jane, John C., J. W., and Leonard Dozier as well as R. Grant and S. Johnson of the First Baptist Church in Uniontown; D. O. Gulley of the Union Baptist Church; W. D. Myree and John W. Harris of the Perryville Baptist Church; and a host of other individuals. Alexander Curtis undoubtedly would have attended the 1883 meeting, but he had died five years earlier. His son Thomas, a Lincoln alumnus and aspiring dental surgeon, represented the family.[46]

Curtis and company's financial contributions attested to their commitment to religious service and their generosity. Among the Uniontown delegates, Admore Hendinson gave $10. Leonard Dozier and Andrew Goldin donated another $8. Miss E. Terrell contributed $6.30, while Ephraim Freeman, Anderson Pitts, and S. Johnson offered $5 apiece. Lucinda Gilbert provided $2 and Jane Dozier $1. Marion delegates also gave bountifully. Curtis donated $3. W. W. Freeman gave $2.75. Mrs. H. M. Hightower and William F. Davis offered $2 each, and M. L. Fowlkes contributed fifty cents.[47]

The Alabama Colored Baptist State Convention generated additional revenue through stock purchases, perhaps in a lumber company owned by blacks William J. Stevens of Selma and Charles Hendley Jr. of Huntsville. The Uniontown Association bought $150 in stock. John C. and J. W. Dozier paid $25 and $5 for stock, respectively. Members of the Hopewell Baptist Church purchased $15 worth of stock. Socially moderate whites John Moore and William Paterson bought stock totaling $10. Moore was an influential Perry County Democrat, physician, and trustee of the quasi-publicly funded Lincoln Normal School and University in Marion. Paterson, the university's president, was a politically independent Presbyterian from

Scotland. Before the convention adjourned, Uniontown delegates gave another $23.80, but the largest single contribution (excluding stock purchases) came from the Second Baptist Church of Marion. Its delegates gave $51.10.[48]

Perry County's blacks' religious commitments and convictions helped propel their upward mobility during and following slavery. While religion provided enslaved blacks a spiritual and psychological refuge, the religious institutions they developed once free afforded them tangible means to make lasting contributions to those who sought personal salvation as well as professional careers in education, business, or politics. The development of the Lincoln School in Marion illustrates this point. In January 1867, Thomas Steward, a white Congregationalist minister and American Missionary Association agent from New York, began teaching freedpeople at a small Methodist church in Marion. Within months, Steward and his pupils had outgrown the facility. With the help of black community leaders and a handful of equalitarian whites, Steward built the Lincoln School. James Childs, Alexander Curtis, John Freeman, Ivey Parish, and five other former slaves incorporated the school in July 1867. Steward was principal. The Marion Nine, as Childs as his fellow incorporators are now known, were trustees.[49]

For its first three years, Lincoln existed largely because of the efforts of local blacks and charitable whites, the American Missionary Association, and the Freedmen's Bureau. In 1870, Steward and his cohorts in the Alabama legislature made Lincoln a state-supported normal school, meaning that its central role was to educate aspiring teachers. In 1874, the year Reconstruction ended in Alabama, Lincoln became a university.[50] Though small and without many of the amenities available at the all-white university in Tuscaloosa, Lincoln prepared its students exceptionally well. Beyond academic excellence, social responsibility and high ethical standards were emphasized continually. The vast majority of students met expectations, although some deserved special recognition. Stephen Childs and Thomas Curtis were two of them. The Rev. William R. Pettiford, a young man with character "as clean as a hound's tooth," was another one.[51] During the early 1870s, he taught and studied concurrently at Lincoln. After a short stint as principal of a black school in Uniontown, he was hired as an assistant teacher at Selma University. In February 1883, following successful tenures as a teacher, school administrator, pastor, politician, and union leader in Perry, Dallas, and Bullock Counties, Pettiford moved to Jefferson County to head the First Colored Baptist Church in Birmingham.[52]

First Colored Baptist had hardly any members and sizable debts when Pettiford accepted the pastorate. His leadership helped transform the church. By August 1884, it had been renamed Sixteenth Street Baptist, it was financially solvent, and a new building was under construction. Having learned the importance of putting one's money where one's mouth was from his parents and black Alabamians like Curtis, Dozier, and Booker T. Washington, principal of the Tuskegee Institute in Macon County, Pettiford donated a substantial amount of the $14,000 that was raised for Sixteenth Street's makeover from his own savings. In 1890, 425 people went there, and Pettiford's reputation as a color-blind community builder was growing. Assisted financially by a small number of wealthy white egalitarians, he cofounded the all-black Industrial (later Parker) High School in Birmingham, the first institution of its type in the city. He also owned a publishing house that produced a periodical called the *Negro American Journal* and was cofounder and president of the Alabama Penny Savings Bank and Loan Company of Birmingham, the state's first black-owned bank.[53]

Pettiford's business acumen was as praiseworthy as his ministerial leadership. In 1893, a nationwide financial depression caused many banking institutions to close their doors, but the Alabama Penny Savings Bank and Loan Company remained open. Two years later, during one of the most intense sociopolitical periods in Alabama and the country's history, white state legislators incorporated the bank with $25,000 in capital stock. With Pettiford at the helm making sound investments, the Alabama Penny Savings Bank and Loan Company became one of America's premier black commercial enterprises. Sixteenth Street grew in similar fashion. In 1900, its membership stood at approximately one thousand. Many were affluent citizens whose socioeconomic status popularized Sixteenth Street as a "class" church similar to Dexter Avenue, but their prosperity did not cause them to neglect the masses.[54] In January 1899, for instance, Booker T. Washington assembled a group of influential black businessmen, educators, ministers, and politicians to discuss conservative and wealthy white lawmakers' call for a state constitutional convention. Washington was certain the lawmakers wanted to completely disenfranchise blacks and financially poor whites. One of his first meetings was held at Sixteenth Street.[55] As for Dexter, some of Montgomery's most educated, socially conscious, and politically active African Americans attended the church. In coming decades it became a de facto headquarters of the freedom rights struggle.[56]

The fact that six of Alabama's most influential postbellum blacks—Boothe, Childs, Curtis, Dozier, McAlpine, and Pettiford—resided or toiled in a single county, Perry, is remarkable. But the significance of their relationship extends beyond that. As first-generation freedom activists and organizers, they faced greater challenges than any successive group of blacks, including those who participated in the modern civil rights movement, which historian C. Vann Woodward termed Second Reconstruction.[57] Not only did Boothe and his colleagues have to deal with the overt racism and constant possibility of violence that their twentieth-century heirs inherited, they also had to shoulder the responsibility of empowering an entire black community that had known little except slavery. As historian Michael Fitzgerald has posited, the "polemical needs of the second Reconstruction [have] obscured certain aspects of the African-American political behavior in the first," but this should not be the case.[58] As much, if not more, emphasis should be placed on first Reconstruction black leaders. Had they not risked their and their loved ones' lives and livelihoods pressing for religious freedom, academic education, equal wages, landownership, voting privileges, and related human and civil rights, there might not have been a second Reconstruction—at least, not in Alabama.[59]

As disputable as the last statement might seem, there is ample support for it. In 1886, for example, a scuffle between Howard College cadets and Lincoln State Normal School and University students caused much uneasiness among Perry County's white and black residents. Tension heightened over the following months. Early in 1887, a group of white cadets attacked some black students. Afterward, the latter individuals sought refuge in the home of Mrs. Henrietta Curtis. She was a kind, intelligent, and virtuous woman who usually followed the Golden Rule, but the cadets' behavior prompted a different impulse. Rather than forgiving and forgetting, she threatened to shoot them. When news of the incident spread through the county, conservative whites acted immediately. A few tried to terrorize Curtis, others attempted to close Lincoln. In response, some blacks armed themselves with weapons, but most prayed for peace and boycotted white businesses. Their campaign was so successful that several white merchants had to declare bankruptcy.[60]

With the county's usually amicable citizens at odds and the survival of its black university in jeopardy, two events guaranteed the university's Marion death. In 1887, Alabama legislators agreed to sponsor a black university anywhere in the state except Marion. The same year, a suspicious fire destroyed the building that housed the university's primary, or elementary, department. After much and sometimes acerbic debate and politicking, the university, or collegiate, department was relocated to Montgomery, over Booker Washington's objections, and named the Normal School for Colored Students. Its first registration session was held in Dexter Avenue's basement. Lincoln's rebuilt primary and undamaged intermediate and high school departments remained in Marion.[61] It was there that Coretta Scott, future wife of Martin Luther King Jr., became valedictorian of the 1945 senior class. Jean Childs, a 1950 Lincoln graduate, married the Reverend Andrew Young, another prominent humanitarian and civil rights activist, in 1954. Jimmy Lee Jackson, who finished Lincoln in 1959, died in February 1965 at the hands of white state trooper James B. Fowler, motivating King, Young, and other freedom fighters to march from Selma to Montgomery to confront Governor George Wallace, a staunch segregationist. What followed is etched in the American memory as Bloody Sunday.[62]

Perry County's connection to the modern freedom struggle is not limited to the second Reconstruction. The Rev. James and Martha Childs had eight children, each one of whom attended the Lincoln School in Marion. One child, Roberta, married a black Mobile native by the name of William Henry Hastie. Their son, William Jr., was born in Tennessee but attended the academically challenging and totally black Dunbar High School in Washington, D.C. From there he went on to Amherst College, where he excelled in mathematics, physics, poetry, and athletics. One of only nine black students admitted to the Harvard Law School during the 1920s, Hastie became the second African American member elected to the celebrated *Harvard Law Review*. His cousin, Charles Hamilton Houston, was first.[63]

After joining the law firm Houston and Houston, a private practice in Washington, D.C., Hastie served on the faculty of the Howard University Law School. He then advised President Franklin Delano Roosevelt on race relations. In 1933, at the height of the Great Depression, Hastie became assistant solicitor in the Department of the Interior. Four years later, he was appointed judge of the federal district court in the Virgin Islands. By accepting the position, he became the second black federal magistrate in American history.[64]

Hastie's prominence increased over the next decade. In 1939, he returned to Howard as dean of the law school. Two years later, he was employed as a civilian aide to Secretary of War Henry L. Stimson but resigned in 1943 to protest discrimination in the nation's militaries.[65] Because of his activism, Hastie received the National Association for the Advancement of Colored People's coveted Spingarn Medal. In 1944, he joined a campaign to end poll taxes and in 1946 became the first black governor of the Virgin Islands. His daughter Karen, an alumna of Bates College and the Catholic University School of Law, clerked for Supreme Court Justice Thurgood Marshall. She later served as general counsel to the Senate Committee on the Budget and, among other notable duties, sat on the trustee boards of the National Association for the Advancement of Colored People, Amherst College, and the National Cathedral School. A retired partner at the Washington, D.C., law firm Crowell Moring, her devotion to family, community, and God are as unyielding as the commitments of the enslaved and emancipated Childs and Curtis families from whom she and her father descend.[66]

In *Black American Scholars*, Horace Bond declared that James Childs, Alexander Curtis, and the ethical, forward-looking, and resourceful blacks and whites with whom Childs and Curtis worked to create and sustain the Lincoln School in Marion developed a "complete social and moral as well as educational community." Historian Andrew Billingsley and sociologist John Brown Childs, whose ancestors resided in Perry County, have confirmed Bonds's assessment. Billingsley and Childs have explained how Lincoln provided a foundation for black achievement and consciousness that extended well beyond the county. Successors Lincoln State Normal School and University and Alabama State College, for instance, prepared some of the most renowned black leaders in modern American history.[67]

From Reverend Pettiford to attorney Fred Gray, a principal legal strategist during the 1955–56 Montgomery bus boycott and lawyer for Martin Luther King Jr., Rosa Parks, and other notable second Reconstruction personalities, Lincoln and its institutional heirs built on the solid foundation of black uplift that the Marion Nine, John Dozier, and their coterie laid during the late antebellum through first Reconstruction periods.[68] Today their legacy continues to expand not only through the accomplished black educators, lawyers, ministers, physicians, and other professionals who descend from them but also through Alabama State University, one of the most recognized historically black colleges or universities in the nation. The university's success fulfills the prophecy of a nameless white man from the North who visited Marion in 1869. "Beyond a doubt," he proclaimed, "the prosperity of the colored people lies in the future, and it is to be attained through the education of the youth. In bringing to a speedy experience this prosperity and happiness under providence, Lincoln School will bear a prominent part. The quickness and eagerness in learning, which the majority of the children evince, furnishes a glorious earnest of the 'good time coming.'"[69] The prophetic Northerner had no idea how correct he was.

Notes

1. W. E. B. Du Bois, "Reconstruction and Its Benefits" (paper presented at the annual meeting of the American Historical Association, New York, December 1909, reprinted in *American Historical Review* 15 [July 1910]: 781–99); Eric Foner, *Reconstruction: America's Unfinished Revolution, 1863–1877* (New York: Harper and Row, 1988); Sylvia Krebs, "Funeral Meats and Second Marriages: Alabama Churches in the Presidential Reconstruction Period," *Alabama Historical Quarterly* 37 (Fall 1975): 206–16.

2. See Bertis English, "A Black Belt Anomaly: Biracial Cooperation in Reconstruction-Era Perry County, 1865–1874," *Alabama Review* 62 (January 2009): 3–36 and English, "Civil Wars and Civil Beings: Violence, Religion, Race, Politics, Education, Culture, and Agrarianism in Perry County, Alabama, 1860–1875" (PhD diss., Auburn University, 2006).

3. Adam Fairclough, *A Class of Their Own: Black Teachers in the Segregated South* (Cambridge, MA: Harvard University Press, 2007); Wilson Fallin Jr., *Uplifting the People: Three Centuries of Black Baptists in Alabama* (Tuscaloosa: University of Alabama Press, 2007).

4. See *Population of the United States in 1860; Compiled from the Original Returns of the Eighth Census*... (Washington, DC: GPO, 1864), 9 and Glenn N. Sisk, "Churches in the Alabama Black Belt, 1875–1917," *Church History* 23 (June 1954): 153–54.

5. Horace Mann Bond, *Black American Scholars: A Study of Their Beginnings* (Detroit: Balamp Printing, 1972).

6. See Mary Ellen Curtin, *Black Prisoners and Their World, 1865–1900* (Charlottesville: University of Virginia Press, 2000), 185; Wayne Flynt, *Alabama Baptists: Southern Baptists in the Heart of Dixie* (Tuscaloosa: University of Alabama Press, 1998), 62, 67, 99–107; W. Stuart Harris, *Perry County Heritage* (Summerfield, AL: W. Stuart Harris, 1991), 70–71, 72; Albert J. Raboteau, *Slave Religion: The "Invisible Institution" in the Antebellum South*, updated ed. (New York: Oxford University Press, 2004), 132–33, 136, 148, 199–200; Sisk, "Churches in the Alabama Black Belt," 157; and Booker T. Washington, *Negro Education Not a Failure* (Tuskegee, AL: Tuskegee Institute, 1904), 8.

7. See Weymouth T. Jordan, *Hugh Davis and His Alabama Plantation* (Tuscaloosa: Univer-

sity of Alabama Press, 1948), 103 and James B. Sellers, *Slavery in Alabama* (Tuscaloosa: University of Alabama Press, 1950), 299.

8. J. F. Smith to Thomas Whetstone, December 11, 1863, SPR 61, Alabama Department of Archives and History, Montgomery (hereafter ADAH).

9. In *Freedom's Lawmakers: A Directory of Black Officeholders during Reconstruction* (New York: Oxford University Press, 1993), Eric Foner discusses Alexander Goldsby holding religious services in Selma as early as the 1840s (88).

10. See John W. Blassingame, *The Slave Community: Plantation Life in the Antebellum South*, rev. and enlarged ed. (New York: Oxford University Press, 1977), 138; Charles O. Boothe, *The Cyclopedia of Colored Baptists of Alabama: Their Lives and Their Work* (Birmingham: Alabama Publishing, 1895), 107, 146–47; Ella Storrs Christian, "The Days That Are No More or Plantation Life as It Was," *Alabama Historical Quarterly* 14 (1952): 339; Sellers, *Slavery in Alabama*, 300; Jay Winik, *April 1865: The Month That Saved America* (New York: Harper-Perennial, 2001), 53.

11. Blassingame, *The Slave Community*; W. E. B. Du Bois, "Of the Faith of the Fathers," in *The Souls of Black Folk* (New York: Dover Publications, 1994), 115–25; John Hope Franklin and Evelyn Brooks Higginbotham, *From Slavery to Freedom: A History of African Americans*, 9th ed. (New York: McGraw-Hill, 2010); E. Franklin Frazier, *The Negro Church in America*/C. Eric Lincoln, *The Black Church since Frazier* (New York: Schocken Books, 1974); T. W. Higginson, "Negro Spirituals," *Atlantic Monthly* 19 (June 1867): 685–94; C. Eric Lincoln and Lawrence M. Mamiya, *The Black Church in the African American Experience* (Durham: Duke University Press, 1990); Raboteau, *Slave Religion*; Gayraud S. Wilmore, *Black Religion and Black Radicalism: An Interpretation of the Religious History of African Americans*, 3rd ed. (New York: Orbis Books, 1999); Carter G. Woodson, *The History of the Negro Church* (Washington, DC: Associated Publishers, 1921).

12. Du Bois, *The Souls of Black Folk*, 116. In *Roll, Jordan, Roll: The World That Slave Made* (1972; reprint, New York: Vintage Books, 1976) Eugene Genovese explored the Western, or European, Judeo-Christian history of dancing and shouting. He noted correctly that such features, or styles, of worship were prevalent in the West before the Protestant Reformation (p. 234). Thomas Merton made the same point in *Seasons of Celebration: Meditations on the Cycle of Liturgical Feasts* (New York: Farrar, Straus, and Giroux, 1965). Other authors who have reached similar conclusions include John F. Szwed, "Musical Adaptation among Afro-Americans," *Journal of American Folklore* 82 (April–June 1969): 112–14, 116–17 and John W. Work, *American Negro Songs and Spirituals; a Comprehensive Collection of 230 Folk Songs, Religious and Secular . . .* (New York: Crown, 1940).

13. "My Jesus Acomin," as quoted in Christian, "The Days That Are No More," 340.

14. Henry H. Mitchell, *Black Church Beginnings: The Long-Hidden Realities of the First Years* (Grand Rapids, MI: Eerdmans, 2004), 36.

15. See ibid., 4, 9–10, 13–14, 36, 39; Du Bois, *The Souls of Black Folk*, 116–17; Fairclough, *A Class of Their Own*, 75–77, 79, 117; C. Eric Lincoln and Lawrence H. Mamiya, "In the Receding Shadow of the Plantation: A Profile of Rural Churches and Clergy in the Black Belt," *Review of Religious Research* 29 (June 1988): 364; Raboteau, *Slave Religion*; and Willie Lee Rose, *Rehearsal for Reconstruction: The Port Royal Experiment* (1964; reprint, Athens: University of Georgia Press, 1992), 91–94.

16. See Andrew Billingsley, *Mighty Like a River: The Black Church and Social Reform* (New York: Oxford University Press, 2003), xx–xxiii, 7, 175, 178; Blassingame, *The Slave Community*; Du Bois, *The Souls of Black Folk*, 116; Genovese, *Roll, Jordan, Roll*, 232–40; Lincoln and Mamiya, *The Black Church in the African American Experience*, 5, 352–53; and Mitchell, *Black Church Beginnings*, 1–45.

17. Emilye Crosby, *A Little Taste of Freedom: The Black Freedom Struggle in Claiborne, County, Mississippi*, annotated ed. (Chapel Hill: University of North Carolina Press, 2005).

18. See *Baptists in Alabama, 1808–1958* (Birmingham: Alabama Baptist State Convention, 1958); Blassingame, *The Slave Community*; Harris, *Perry County Heritage*, 128; Jordan, *Hugh Davis*, 3; *Marion Standard*, April 2, 1909; and Willie Lee Rose, *Slavery and Freedom*, ed. William W. Freehling (New York: Oxford University Press, 1982).

19. See Thomas Perkins Abernathy, *The Formative Period in Alabama, 1815–1828* (Montgomery, AL: Brown Printing Company, 1922), 57–58; "Historic Sketches of the Siloam Baptist Church, Marion, Ala.," typescript, 1849, Alabama Church Records, Coley 7N, ADAH (hereafter Coley Collection); Jordan, *Hugh Davis*, 3, 4; J. Hugh Le Baron, "Ocmulgee Baptist Church, Slave and Black Freedmen Members, Perry County, Alabama" (private record sent to the author via e-mail on July 6, 2004); *Marion Standard*, March 26, 1909; and Samuel A. Townes, *The History of Marion: Sketches of Life in Perry County, Alabama* (Marion, AL: Dennis Dykous, 1844), reprinted in *Alabama Historical Quarterly* 14 (1952): 171–229.

20. "Historic Sketches of the Siloam Baptist Church, Marion, Ala."

21. Ibid.

22. See Harris, *Perry County Heritage*, 70–75 and Lincoln and Mamiya, "In the Receding Shadow of the Plantation," 357.

23. See Jordan, *Hugh Davis*, 107.

24. See "Berean Baptist Church," in *The Heritage of Perry County, Alabama* (Clanton, AL: Heritage Publishing Consultants, 1999), 38; Tommy Bogger, *Free Blacks in Norfolk, Virginia, 1790–1860: The Darker Side of Freedom* (Charlottesville: University Press of Virginia, 1997), 153–54; Bond, *Black American Scholars*, 34–39, 170–71; Horace Mann Bond, *Negro Education in Alabama: A Study in Cotton and Steel* (1939; reprint, Tuscaloosa: University of Alabama Press, 1994), 19; John Brown Childs, *Transcommunality: From the Politics of Conversion to the Ethics of Respect* (Philadelphia: Temple University Press, 2003), 14; Melvin Patrick Ely, *Israel on the Appomattox: A Southern Experiment in Black Freedom from the 1790s through the Civil War* (New York: Alfred A. Knopf, 2004), 462; W. M. Jackson, "The Great-Great-Grandson of a Madagascar King Becomes a Priest of the American Episcopal Church," *Spirit of Missions* 71 (1906): 946; Jordan, *Hugh Davis*; Robert Moats Miller, "Southern White Protestantism and the Negro, 1865–1965," in *The Negro in the South since 1865: Selected Essays in American Negro History*, ed. Charles E. Wynes (1965; reprint, Tuscaloosa: University of Alabama Press, 1967), 236; and Joe M. Richardson, *Christian Reconstruction: The American Missionary Association and Southern Blacks, 1861–1890* (Athens: University of Georgia Press, 1986), 115.

25. See "Baptist Churches by Name," typescript, April 19, 1860, Coley Collection; "Ocmulgee Church," Coley Collection; Flynt, *Alabama Baptists*, 28, 62; Harris, *Perry County Heritage*, 70, 71–72; and Le Baron, "Ocmulgee Baptist Church."

26. See Patience Essah, *A House Divided: Slavery and Emancipation in Delaware, 1638–1865* (Charlottesville: University Press of Virginia, 1996), 146–47; *Minutes of the Forty-Third Annual Session of the Alabama Baptist State Convention, 1865* (Atlanta: Franklin Steam Printing House, 1866), 10; and George H. Watson and Mildred B. Watson, *History of the Christian Churches in the Alabama Area* (St. Louis: Bethany Press, 1965), 52–53.

27. Bower Stewart, *The Work of the Church in the South during the Period of Reconstruction* (Milwaukee: Young Churchman Company, 1913), 39. See James Cone, *Black Theology and Black Power* (New York: Seabury Press, 1969); Curtin, *Black Prisoners and Their World*, 41; *History and Hope in the Heart of Dixie: Scholarship, Activism, and Wayne Flynt in the Modern South*, ed. Gordon E. Harvey et al. (Tuscaloosa: University of Alabama Press, 2006), 108–9; J. Deotis Roberts Sr.,

"Black Theological Ethics: A Bibliographical Essay," *Journal of Religious Ethics* 3 (Spring 1975): 69–109; and Howard Thurman, *Jesus and the Disinherited* (1976; reprint, Boston: Beacon Press, 1996). In *Religion, Race, and Reconstruction: The Public School in the Politics of the 1870s* (New York: State University of New York Press, 1998), Ward M. McAfee argues that Reconstruction did not pivot on religion until 1870 (pp. 25, 162).

28. See "Berean Baptist Church," in *The Heritage of Perry County, Alabama*, 38.

29. Not all black people in Perry County left predominately white churches during Reconstruction. The Perryville Circuit of the Southern Methodist Episcopal Church, for instance, maintained a sizable black membership. Wilson Fallin discusses this phenomenon among black Baptists elsewhere in the state. See Fallin, "God's Gift of Freedom," in *Uplifting the People*, 29–53; Perryville Circuit, Methodist Episcopal Church, South, Quarterly Conference Record, 1853–1869, Coley Collection.

30. Information about Alexander Curtis's early years is scarce. Most scholars now accept that he was born in 1829, but some maintain that 1826 or 1827 was his birth year. Nor has Curtis's birthplace gone without question. The consensus view is that he was from Wake County, North Carolina, although a few people have claimed that he was born in Orange County. Curtis's actual status when he arrived in Alabama has also been debated. He definitely was a servant and probably a slave, but neither condition is certain. One of the best sources available to modern scholars, Boothe's *Cyclopedia of the Colored Baptists of Alabama* (132), states only that Curtis was "the property (?) of E. Haywood." See Richard Bailey, *Neither Carpetbaggers nor Scalawags: Black Officeholders during the Reconstruction of Alabama, 1867–1878*, 5th ed. (Montgomery, AL: New South Books, 2010), 82–83; Bailey, *They Too Call Alabama Home: African American Profiles* (Montgomery, AL: Pyramid Publishing, 1999), 97–99; Bond, *Black American Scholars*, 34–35, 38, 170–75; Charles A. Brown, "A. H. Curtis: Alabama Legislator," *Negro History Bulletin* 26 (February 1962): 100; Idella J. Childs, "Black Elected and Appointed Officials during the Reconstruction Period," in *Perry County Heritage*, 2:4; English, "A Black Belt Anomaly," 13–14, 16, 31, 34–35; English, "Civil Wars and Civil Beings," 5, 253–58; Fallin, *Uplifting the People*, 45, 47; Foner, *Freedom's Lawmakers*, 56; Jordan, *Hugh Davis*, 136–41.

31. Alexander Curtis served as president pro tempore.

32. "First Colored Missionary Baptist Church," and "Uniontown Baptist Church," in *The Heritage of Perry County, Alabama*, 41, 54; Harris, *Perry County Heritage*, 78–79; Martha Huckabee, *First Baptist Church, Uniontown, Alabama* (n.p., n.d.), 1.

33. See Bailey, *Neither Carpetbaggers nor Scalawags*, xii, 269; Boothe, *The Cyclopedia of Colored Baptists of Alabama*, 138–39; Charles Brown, "John Dozier: A Member of the General Assembly of Alabama, 1872–1873 and 1873–1874," *Negro History Bulletin* 26 (November 1962): 113; and Peter Kolchin, *First Freedom: The Responses of Alabama's Blacks to Emancipation and Reconstruction* (Westport, CT: Greenwood, 1972), 166.

34. See James D. Anderson, *The Education of Blacks in the South, 1860–1935* (Chapel Hill: University of North Carolina Press, 1988), 55; Essah, *A House Divided*, 146–47; Michael W. Fitzgerald, *Urban Emancipation: Popular Politics in Reconstruction Mobile, 1860–1890* (Baton Rouge: Louisiana State University Press, 2002), 59; Fairclough, "Freedom's First Generation," in *A Class of Their Own*, 27–58; James M. McPherson, "White Liberals and Black Power in Negro Education," *American Historical Review* 75 (June 1970): 1380; Raboteau, *Slave Religion*, 178; Robert G. Sherer, *Black Education in Alabama, 1865–1901*, also titled *Subordination or Liberation? The Development and Conflicting Theories of Black Education in Alabama* (Tuscaloosa: University of Alabama Press, 1977); Robert Glenn Sherer Jr., "Let Us Make Man: Negro Education in Nineteenth Century Alabama" (PhD diss., University of North Carolina at Chapel Hill, 1970), 403;

and Edwin T. Winkler, "The Negroes in the Gulf States," *International Review* 1, no. 5 (September 1874): 585.

35. See English, "Civil Wars and Civil Beings."

36. See Harris, *Perry County Heritage*, 70, 80–84; Sellers, *Slavery in Alabama*, 294–331; and Sisk, "Churches in the Alabama Black Belt," 157. W. E. B. Du Bois was one scholar who noted a similar rivalry among postbellum black Baptists and Methodists. Their differences, he once said, "overshadow the differences between heaven and hell." Du Bois, "Atlanta University," in *From Servitude to Service: Being the Old South Lectures on the History and Education of Southern Institutions for the Education of the Negro*, ed. Robert C. Ogden (1905; reprint, New York: Negro University Press, 1969), 181.

37. *Christian Index and South-western Baptist*, January 17, 1867.

38. English, "A Black Belt Anomaly," 21. See *Christian Index and South-western Baptist*, June 6, 1867; Edwin A. Alderman and Armistead C. Gordon, *J. L. M. Curry: A Biography* (New York: McMillan, 1911); Flynt, *Alabama Baptists*, 141, 152; *Montgomery Advertiser*, October 26, 1952; Jessie Pearl Rice, *J. L. M. Curry: Southerner, Statesman and Educator* (New York: King's Crown Press, 1949); William H. Watkins, "J. L. M. Curry," in *The White Architects of Black Education: Ideology and Power in America, 1865–1954* (New York: Teachers College Press, 2001), 161–78; and Walter Bell White, "J. L. M. Curry: Alabamian" (master's thesis, Samford University, 1971), 362.

39. See Edward R. Crowther, "Interracial Cooperative Missions among Blacks by Alabama's Baptists, 1868–1882," *Journal of Negro History* 80 (Summer 1995): 132; Harris, *Perry County Heritage*, 75–76; Fallin, *Uplifting the People*, 42, 47; Kolchin, *First Freedom*, 112, 117; Cal M. Logue, "Racist Reporting during Reconstruction," *Journal of Black Studies* 9 (March 1979): 335–36; *Marion Commonwealth*, March 20, April 10, and May 22, 1873; David M. Reimers, *White Protestantism and the Negro* (New York: Oxford University Press, 1965), 25; Sisk, "Churches in the Alabama Black Belt," 154, 160; and Watson and Watson, *History of the Christian Churches in the Alabama Area*, 52–53.

40. English, "A Black Belt Anomaly," 21–22, quoting Flynt, *Alabama Baptists*, 141.

41. See Bailey, *Neither Carpetbaggers nor Scalawags*; Joseph Daniel Caver, "Marion to Montgomery: A Twenty Year History of Alabama State University, 1867–1887" (master's thesis, Alabama State University, 1982); English, "Civil Wars and Civil Beings"; William Warren Rogers Jr., "'The Prospect before Us': A Massachusetts Congregationalist in Reconstruction Alabama," *Alabama Review* 60 (January 2007): 15, 18; Sherer, *Black Education in Alabama*, 137–38; Sherer, "Let Us Make Man," 52, 268, 279n35, 324–29.

42. See English, "A Black Belt Anomaly," 21–22; Flynt, *Alabama Baptists*, 181; and *Marion Commonwealth*, June 19, 1873.

43. See *Africana: The Encyclopedia of the African and African American Experience*, ed. Kwame Anthony Appiah and Henry Louis Gates Jr. (New York: Basic/Civitas Books, 1999), xiii; Boothe, *The Cyclopedia of Colored Baptists of Alabama*; Edward R. Crowther, "Charles Octavius Boothe: An Alabama Apostle of 'Uplift,'" *Journal of Negro History* 78 (Spring 1993): 110–16; Crowther, "Interracial Cooperative Missions," 132; Bertis English, "Dexter Avenue Baptist Church," in *Encyclopedia of African-American History, 1896–Present: From the Age of Segregation to the Twenty-First Century*, ed. Paul Finkelman (New York: Oxford University Press, 2009), 62; Zelia S. Evans and J. T. Alexander, eds., *The Dexter Avenue Baptist Church, 1877–1977* (Montgomery, AL: Dexter Avenue Baptist Church, 1978); Fairclough, *A Class of Their Own*, 28, 74; Fallin, *Uplifting the People*; Foner, *Freedom's Lawmakers*, 51; and Richard D. Morrison, *History of Alabama A&M University, 1875–1992* (Huntsville, AL: Golden Rule Printers, 1994).

44. See Bailey, *Neither Carpetbaggers nor Scalawags*; Brown, "John Dozier," 113; English, "A

Black Belt Anomaly," 16, 18–21, 32–34; English, "Civil Wars and Civil Beings"; Fallin, *Uplifting the People*, 45, 49, 66, 111–12; and Foner, *Freedom's Lawmakers*, 65.

45. See Bailey, *Neither Carpetbaggers nor Scalawags*; William L. Banks, *The Black Church in the US: Its Origin, Growth, Contribution and Outlook* (Chicago: Moody Bible Institute, 1972), 36; Bond, *Black American Scholars*, 171, 172; Bond, *Negro Education in Alabama*, 16; Boothe, *The Cyclopedia of Colored Baptists of Alabama*; Crowther, "Interracial Cooperative Missions," 133–36; Fairclough, *A Class of Their Own*, 94; Lynne B. Feldman, *A Sense of Place: Birmingham's Black Middle-Class Community, 1890–1930* (Tuscaloosa: University of Alabama Press, 1999); Fallin, *Uplifting the People*; Joseph H. Fichter, "American Religion and the Negro," *Daedalus* 94 (Fall 1965): 1090; Eric Foner, *Forever Free: The Story of Emancipation and Reconstruction* (New York: Alfred A. Knopf, 2006), 128, 134–35; Foner, *Freedom's Lawmakers*, 56; August Meier, *Negro Thought in America, 1880–1915: Racial Ideologies in the Age of Booker T. Washington* (Ann Arbor: University of Michigan Press, 1963), 143; Mitchell, *Black Church Beginnings*, 127; Clement Richardson, ed., *The National Cyclopedia of the Colored Race* (Montgomery, AL: National Publishing Company, 1919), 1:82; Sherer, *Black Education in Alabama*, 98, 178n16, 179n52; Sherer, "Let Us Make Man," 141–83, 417–23, 427–43, 454–55, 465; and Jacqueline Trussell, "The Convention Movement of the Black Baptist Church," http://www.blackandchristian.com/articles/academy/trussell1.shtml (accessed September 11, 2010).

46. See *Minutes of the Sixteenth Annual Session of the Colored Baptist State Convention, Held with St. Phillips Street Baptist Church, Selma, Ala., November 14th, 15th and 16th, 1883* (Selma, AL: Baptist Print, 1884), 2–5, 6, 22–23.

47. Ibid.

48. Ibid. See Leliafred Ballard, "The American Negro as Portrayed in the Huntsville Gazette" (master's thesis, Howard University, 1952), 21–22, 25; Curtin, *Black Prisoners and Their World*, 71, 233n43; Fairclough, *A Class of Their Own*, 217; Norwood Kerr, "Highway Markers in Alabama," *Alabama Review* 52 (January 1999): 51–86; Beth Taylor Muskat, "Mobile's Black Militia: Major R. R. Mims and Gilmer's Rifles," *Alabama Review* 57 (July 2004): 188n20; Judith Hillman Paterson, "To Teach the Negro," *Alabama Heritage* 40 (Spring 1996): 10; Paterson, *Sweet Mystery: A Book of Remembering* (Tuscaloosa: University of Alabama Press, 1996), 16–18, 26; William B. Paterson, *Some Facts Concerning the State Normal School Montgomery, Ala.* (Montgomery, AL: n.p., 1905); Sherer, *Black Education in Alabama*, 80–81, 173n7; Sherer, "Let Us Make Man," 232, 359; and Robert G. Sherer, "William Burns Paterson, the Pioneer as Well as Prophet of Negro Education in Alabama," *Alabama Historical Quarterly* 26 (Summer 1974): 135.

49. See, for example, Bertis English, "Prosperity and Happiness under Providence: Race, Religion, and Education in Postbellum Perry County," chap. 4 in "Civil Wars and Civil Beings," 221–341.

50. Allen J. Going, *Bourbon Democracy in Alabama, 1874–1890* (1951; reprint, Tuscaloosa: University of Alabama Press, 1991) remains the standard study on Alabama Redemption, or Restoration, the period when conservative white Democrats regained control of most statewide offices. Adam Fairclough mentions the general academic and sociocultural importance of university, as opposed to another nomenclatorial label, in *A Class of Their Own*, especially p. 141, while Bertis English discusses whether the Lincoln Normal School and University was a bona fide university in 1874 and thereafter. See English, "Civil Wars and Civil Beings."

51. Nathan B. Young Sr., quoted in Arnett G. Lindsey, "The Negro in Banking," *Journal of Negro History* 14 (April 1929): 171.

52. See Boothe, *The Cyclopedia of the Colored Baptists of Alabama*; English, "A Black Belt Anomaly," 14–16, 33–34; Fallin, *Uplifting the People*; Carol Jenkins and Elizabeth Gardner Hines,

Black Titan: A. G. Gaston and the Making of a Black Millionaire (New York: Ballantine Books, 2004), 88–90; *Greensboro Beacon*, July 22, 1871; John N. Ingham and Lynne B. Feldman, *African-American Business Leaders: A Biographical Dictionary* (Westport, CT: Greenwood, 1994), 547–55; *Marion Commonwealth*, July 13, 1871; William Warren Rogers, *The One-Gallused Rebellion: Agrarianism in Alabama, 1865–1896* (Baton Rouge: Louisiana State University Press, 1970), 12; G. F. Richings, *Evidences of Progress among Colored People* (Philadelphia: George F. Ferguson Company, 1904), 340; William Simmons, *Men of Mark: Eminent, Progressive, and Rising* (Cleveland: George R. Rewell, 1887), 460–65; and Booker T. Washington, *The Negro in Business*, limited ed. (Wichita: DeVore and Sons, 1995), 97–119.

53. See Boothe, *The Cyclopedia of Colored Baptists of Alabama*; Crowther, "Interracial Cooperative Missions," 136–37; Bertis English, "Sixteenth Street Baptist Church," in *African American National Biography*, ed. Henry Louis Gates Jr. and Evelyn Higginbotham (New York: Oxford University Press, 2008), 4:321; Fairclough, *A Class of Their Own*, 267–72; Fallin, *Uplifting the People*; Christopher Hamlin, *Behind the Stained Glass: A History of the Sixteenth Street Baptist Church* (Birmingham, AL: Crane Hill, 1998); Feldman, *A Sense of Place*; and Lindsey, "The Negro in Banking," 170.

54. Wilson Fallin, video interview for *We Shall Not Be Moved: The Untold Chapter in the Struggle for American Civil Rights*, prod. and dir. Bernie Hargis (G T Media, 2001), 90 min., DVD.

55. See English, "Dexter Avenue," 62; English, "Sixteenth Street Baptist Church," 321; Louis Harlan, "Dark Clouds and Silver Linings," in *Booker T. Washington: The Making of a Black Leader, 1865–1901* (New York: Oxford University Press, 1972), 288–303; and "To the Members of the Alabama Constitutional Convention," May 23, 1901, SG17778, ADAH.

56. In *Bloody Lowndes: Civil Rights and Black Power in Alabama's Black Belt* (New York: New York University Press, 2009), Hasan Kwame Jeffries does an excellent job defining and outlining the nineteenth-century freedom struggle in certain parts of Alabama, though Perry County receives scant attention. Pages 7–21 and 256–58 are very informative.

57. C. Vann Woodward, *The Strange Career of Jim Crow*, commemorative ed. (New York: Oxford University Press, 2002).

58. Fitzgerald, *Urban Emancipation*, 266.

59. Broader applications of this idea can be found in Foner, *Forever Free*; Eric Foner, *Politics and Ideology in the Age of the Civil War* (New York: Oxford University Press, 1980); Foner, *Reconstruction*; McAfee, *Religion, Race, and Reconstruction*, 220–22; Mitchell, *Black Church Beginnings*, 162–63; Allan Nevins, *The Emergence of Modern America, 1865–1978* (1927; reprint, Englewood Cliffs, NJ: Prentice Hall, 1972); and Armstead L. Robinson, "Beyond the Realm of Social Consensus: New Meanings of Reconstruction for American History," *Journal of American History* 68 (September 1981): 276n1.

60. See *Montgomery Herald*, January 8, 1887, and *Huntsville Gazette*, March 26, 1887.

61. See Bailey, *Neither Carpetbaggers nor Scalawags*; Bailey, *They Too Call Alabama Home*; Caver, "Marion to Montgomery"; *Montgomery Advertiser*, August 18, 1887; *New York Freedman*, September 3, 1887; Fairclough, *A Class of Their Own*, 153–54; Clifton H. Johnson, "Powerful Little School," *Crisis* 79 (May 1972): 156; "The Normal School Relocates to Montgomery," http://www.ruthk.net/marion/lincoln/directory/relocation.html (accessed September 17, 2010); William B. Paterson, *The State Normal School for Colored Students at Montgomery: Its History for Thirty-Seven Years and Its Needs of Today* (n.p.: Paragon Press, c. 1900); Paterson, *The State Normal School at Montgomery: A Plain Statement of Its Principals* (Montgomery, AL: State Normal School Press, c. 1887); and Sherer, *Black Education in Alabama*, 10–12, 64; Sherer, "Let Us Make Man," 34, 51n22, 57–58, 60–67, 296–98, 511.

62. Recently writers have given Jimmy Lee Jackson's death much attention. They include, but are not limited to, Taylor Branch, *At Canaan's Edge: America in the King Years, 1965–1968* (New York: Simon and Schuster, 2006); J. L. Chestnut Jr. and Julia Cass, *Black in Selma: The Uncommon Life of J. L. Chestnut, Jr.* (New York: Farrar, Straus and Giroux, 1990), 145, 204, 360, 374; Adam Fairclough, *Better Day Coming: Blacks and Equality, 1890–2000* (New York: Penguin, 2002), 291; Frye Gaillard, *Cradle of Freedom: Alabama and the Movement That Changed America* (Tuscaloosa: University of Alabama Press, 2005), 238, 240–41, 261; John Hope Franklin, *Mirror to America: The Autobiography of John Hope Franklin* (New York: Farrar, Straus and Giroux, 2005), 237; Jon Meacham, ed., *Voices in Our Blood: America's Best on the Civil Rights Movement* (New York: Random House, 2003), 313, 430; and J. Mills Thornton III, *Dividing Lines: Municipal Politics and the Struggle for Civil Rights in Alabama* (Tuscaloosa: University of Alabama Press, 2005), 486, 487, 489, 690n150.

63. See Childs, *Transcommunality*, 15; Lee Finkle, "The Conservative Aims of Militant Rhetoric: Black Protest during World War II," *Journal of American History* 60 (December 1973): 702; "The First Black President of the Harvard Law Review," *Journal of Blacks in Higher Education* 30 (Winter 2000): 22–25; "Harvard Law School Celebrates Its Black Alumni," *Journal of Blacks in Higher Education* 31 (Spring 2001): 85–87; Gilbert Ware, *William Hastie: Grace under Pressure* (New York: Oxford University Press, 1984); and Karen Hastie Williams, "William Hastie: Facing Challenges in the Ivory Tower," *Journal of Blacks in Higher Education* 24 (Summer 1999): 122–23.

64. Some people have suggested that William Hastie Jr. was the first black federal magistrate in American history. As his daughter Karen recalls in "William Hastie," President Theodore Roosevelt appointed Robert Terrell, a former slave, to sit on a municipal court in the District of Columbia forty years before Hastie's appointment (123).

65. See Childs, *Transcommunality*, 15–16; Phillip McGuire, "Desegregation of the Armed Forces: Black Leadership, Protest, and World War II," *Journal of Negro History* 68 (Spring 1983): 147–58; McGuire, "Judge Hastie, World War II, and Army Racism," *Journal of Negro History* 62 (October 1977): 351–62; McGuire, "Judge Hastie, World War II, and the Army Air Corps," *Phylon* 42 (second quarter 1981): 157–67; McGuire, "Judge William H. Hastie and Army Recruitment, 1940–1942," *Military Affairs* 42 (April 1978): 75–79.

66. Karen Hastie Williams's biographical information is taken from http://www.sec.gov/spotlight/soxcomp/bios/2006/biokhwilliams.pdf (accessed September 18, 2010).

67. Bond, *Black American Scholars*, 40. See also Andrew Billingsley, *Black Families in White America* (Englewood Cliffs, NJ: Prentice Hall, 1978), 117–19 and Childs, *Transcommunality*, 14.

68. See, for example, Fred Gray, *Bus Ride to Justice: The Life and Works of Fred Gray* (Montgomery, AL: New South Books, 2002).

69. *Marion Commonwealth*, July 29, 1869.

Suggestions for Further Reading

Primary Sources

Battle, Cullen Andrews. *Third Alabama!: The Civil War Memoir of Brigadier General Cullen Andrews Battle, CSA.* Edited by Brandon H. Beck. Tuscaloosa: University of Alabama Press, 2000.

Blomquist, Ann K., and Robert A. Taylor, eds. *This Cruel War: The Civil War Letters of Grant and Malinda Taylor, 1862–1865.* Macon, GA: Mercer University Press, 2000.

Brewer, Willis. *Alabama: Her History, Resources, War Record and Public Men from 1540 to 1872.* Montgomery: Barrett & Brown, 1872.

Cannon, J. P. *Inside of Rebeldom: The Daily Life of a Private in the Confederate Army.* Washington, DC: National Tribune, 1900.

Chappell, Frank Anderson. *Dear Sister: Civil War Letters to a Sister in Alabama.* Huntsville, AL: Branch Springs, 2002.

Clay-Clopton, Virginia. *A Belle of the Fifties: Memoirs of Mrs. Clay of Alabama.* With introduction, annotations, and index to the annotations by Leah Rawls Atkins, Joseph H. Harrison Jr., and Sarah A. Hudson. Tuscaloosa: University of Alabama Press, 1999.

Crow, Mattie Lou Teague, ed. *The Diary of a Confederate Soldier: John Washington Inzer, 1834–1928.* Huntsville, AL: Strode, 1977.

Crowson, Noel, and John V. Brogden, eds. *Bloody Banners and Barefoot Boys: A History of the 27th Regiment Alabama Infantry CSA: The Civil War Memoirs and Diary Entries of J. P. Cannon M.D.* Shippensburg, PA: Burd Street Press, 1997.

Cumming, Kate. *Gleanings from the Southland.* Birmingham: Roberts and Son, 1895.

———. *A Journal of Hospital Life in the Confederate Army of Tennessee from the Battle of Shiloh to the End of the War with Sketches of Life and Character, and Brief Notices of Current Events during That Period.* Louisville: John P. Morton, 1866.

———. *Kate: The Journal of a Confederate Nurse.* Edited by Richard Barksdale Harwell. Baton Rouge: Louisiana State University Press, 1959.

Cutrer, Thomas, ed. *Oh, What a Loansome Time I Had: The Civil War Letters of Major*

William Morel Moxley, Eighteenth Alabama Infantry, and Emily Beck Moxley. Tuscaloosa: University of Alabama Press, 2002.

Evans, Augusta Jane. *Macaria; or, Altars of Sacrifice*. Richmond, VA: West and Johnson, 1864.

———. *Macaria*. Edited by Drew Gilpin Faust. Baton Rouge: Louisiana State University Press, 1992.

Folmar, John Kent, ed. *From That Terrible Field: Civil War Letters of James M. Williams, Twenty-First Alabama Infantry Volunteers*. University: University of Alabama Press, 1981.

Gorgas, Josiah. *The Journals of Josiah Gorgas, 1857–1878*. Edited by Sarah Woolfolk Wiggins. Tuscaloosa: University of Alabama Press, 1995.

Gracie, Burton. *Alabama Volunteers: The History of the Fifty-Ninth Alabama Volunteer Regiment*. Gretna, LA: Pelican, 2003.

Griffith, Lucille, ed. *Yours Till Death: Civil War Letters of John W. Cotton*. University: University of Alabama Press, 1951.

Hoole, William Stanley. *History of the Forty-Sixth Alabama Regiment Volunteer Infantry, 1862–1865*. University, AL: Confederate Publishing, 1985.

Hubbs, G. Ward, ed. *Voices from Company D: Diaries by the Greensboro Guards, Fifth Alabama Infantry Regiment, Army of Northern Virginia*. Athens: University of Georgia Press, 2003.

Laboda, Lawrence. *From Selma to Appomattox: The History of the Jeff Davis Artillery*. Shippensburg, PA: White Mane, 1994.

Oates, William C. *The War between the Union and the Confederacy: A History of the 15th Alabama Regiment*. New York: Neale Publishing, 1905.

Park, Robert Emory Park. *Sketch of the Twelfth Alabama Infantry of Battle's Brigade, Rodes Division, Early's Corps of the Army of Northern Virginia*. Richmond, VA: W. E. Jones, 1906.

Rohr, Nancy M., ed. *Incidents of the War: The Civil War Journal of Mary Jane Chaddick*. Huntsville, AL: Silver Threads Publishing, 2005.

Rourke, Norman E., ed. *I Saw the Elephant: The Civil War Experiences of Bailey George McClelen, Company D, 10th Alabama Infantry Regiment*. Shippensburg, PA: Burd Street Press, 1995.

Semmes, Raphael. *Service Afloat: The Remarkable Career of the Confederate Cruisers Sumter and Alabama*. Baltimore: Baltimore Publishing, 1887.

Sexton, Rebecca Grant, ed. *A Southern Woman of Letters: The Correspondence of Augusta Jane Evans Wilson*. Columbia: University of South Carolina Press, 2002.

"Some Confederate Letters of I. B. Cadenhead, Co. H. 34th Alabama Infantry Regiment." *Alabama Historical Quarterly* 18 (Winter 1956): 564–71.

Stocker, Jeffrey D., ed. *From Huntsville to Appomattox: R. T. Cole's History of the 4th*

Regiment, Alabama Volunteer Infantry, C.S.A. Army of Northern Virginia. Knoxville: University of Tennessee Press, 1996.
Vandiver, Frank E., ed. *The Civil War Diary of General Josiah Gorgas.* University: University of Alabama Press, 1947.
Whetstone, Adam Henry. *History of the Fifty-Third Alabama Volunteer Infantry (Mounted).* Edited by William Stanley Hoole and Martha DuBose Hoole. University, AL: Confederate Publishing, 1985.
Wilson, James Harrison. *Under the Old Flag: Recollections of Military Operations in the War for the Union, the Spanish War, the Boxer Rebellion, etc.* 2 vols. New York: D. Appleton, 1912.
Wood, Wayne, and Mary Virginia Jackson, eds. *Kiss Sweet Little Lillah for Me: Civil War Letters of William Thomas Jackson, Company A, Eighth Alabama Infantry Regiment.* Birmingham: EBSCO Media, 2000.
Wynne, Lewis N., and Robert A. Taylor, eds. *This War So Horrible: The Civil War Diary of Hiram Smith Williams.* Tuscaloosa: University of Alabama Press, 1993.

Secondary Sources

Amos, Harriet E. *Cotton City: Urban Development in Antebellum Mobile.* Tuscaloosa: University of Alabama Press, 1985.
———. "Trials of a Unionist: Gustavus Horton, Military Mayor of Mobile during Reconstruction." *Gulf South Historical Review* 4 (Spring 1989): 134–51.
Bailey, Richard. *Neither Carpetbaggers nor Scalawags: Black Officeholders during the Reconstruction of Alabama, 1867–1878.* Montgomery: Richard Bailey, 1991.
Barney, William L. *The Secessionist Impulse: Alabama and Mississippi in 1860.* Princeton: Princeton University Press, 1974.
Bergeron, Arthur W. *Confederate Mobile.* Jackson: University Press of Mississippi, 1991.
Berry, Stephen. *House of Abraham: Lincoln and the Todds, a Family Divided by War.* New York: Houghton Mifflin, 2007.
Bethel, Elizabeth. "The Freedmen's Bureau in Alabama." *Journal of Southern History* 14 (February 1948): 49–92.
Bleser, Carol, and Frederick Heath. "The Clays of Alabama: The Impact of the Civil War on a Southern Marriage." In *In Joy and in Sorrow: Women, Family, and Marriage in the Victorian South, 1830–1900.* Edited by Carol Bleser. New York: Oxford University Press, 1991.
Bradley, George C., and Richard L. Dahlen. *From Conciliation to Conquest: The Sack of Athens and the Court-Martial of Colonel John B. Turchin.* Tuscaloosa: University of Alabama Press, 2006.

Burnett, Lonnie A. *The Pen Makes a Good Sword: John Forsyth of the Mobile Register*. Tuscaloosa: University of Alabama Press, 2006.

Carter, John C. *Welcome the Hour of Conflict: William Cowan McClellan and the 9th Alabama*. Tuscaloosa: University of Alabama Press, 2007.

Cash, William McKinley. "Alabama Republicans during Reconstruction: Personal Characteristics, Motivations, and Political Activity of Party Activists, 1867–1880." PhD diss., University of Alabama, 1973.

Cook, Robert. "Red Termites and Rebel Yells: The Civil War Centennial in Strife-Torn Alabama, 1961–1965." *Alabama Review* 64 (April 2011): 143–67.

———. *Troubled Commemoration: The American Civil War Centennial, 1961–1965*. Making the Modern South Series. Baton Rouge: Louisiana State University Press, 2007.

Cox, LaWanda. "The Perception of Injustice and Race Policy: James F. McGogy and the Freedmen's Bureau in Alabama." In *Freedom, Racism, and Reconstruction: Collected Writings of LaWanda Cox*. Edited by Donald G. Nieman. Athens: University of Georgia Press, 1997, 172–242.

Danielson, Joseph W. *War's Desolating Scourge: The Union's Occupation of North Alabama*. Lawrence: University Press of Kansas, 2012.

Davis, William C. *"A Government of Our Own": The Making of the Confederacy*. New York: Free Press, 1994.

Denman, Clarence Phillips. *The Secession Movement in Alabama*. Montgomery: Alabama Department of Archives and History, 1933.

Dunnavant, Robert, Jr. *Decatur, Alabama: Yankee Foothold in Dixie, 1861–1865*. Athens, AL: Pea Ridge Press, 1995.

English, Bertis. "'Baptized in Fire': Confederate Diarist James Hudson and the Uniontown Canebreak Rifle Guards." *Alabama Review* 64 (April 2011): 85–115.

———. "A Black Belt Anomaly: Biracial Cooperation in Reconstruction-Era Perry County, 1865–1874." *Alabama Review* 62 (January 2009): 3–36.

———. "Civil Wars and Civil Beings: Violence, Religion, Race, Politics, Education, Culture, and Agrarianism in Perry County, Alabama, 1860–1875." PhD diss., Auburn University, 2006.

Evans, David. *Sherman's Horsemen: Union Cavalry Operations in the Atlanta Campaign*. Bloomington: Indiana University Press, 1996.

Fallin, Wilson, Jr. *Uplifting the People: Three Centuries of Black Baptists in Alabama*. Tuscaloosa: University of Alabama Press, 2007.

Fidler, William Perry. *Augusta Evans Wilson, 1835–1909: A Biography*. Tuscaloosa: University of Alabama Press, 1951.

Fitzgerald, Michael W. "Emancipation and Military Pacification: The Freedmen's Bureau and Social Control in Alabama." In *The Freedmen's Bureau and Reconstruction: Reconsiderations*. Edited by Paul A. Cimbala and Randall M. Miller. New York: Fordham University Press, 1999, 46–66.

———. "Extralegal Violence and the Planter Class: The Ku Klux Klan in the Alabama Black Belt during Reconstruction." In *Local Matters: Race, Crime, and Justice in the Nineteenth-Century South*. Edited by Christopher Waldrep and Donald G. Nieman. Athens: University of Georgia Press, 2001.

———. "Radical Republicanism and the White Yeomanry during Alabama Reconstruction, 1865–1868." *Journal of Southern History* 54 (November 1988): 565–96.

———. "Railroad Subsidies and Black Aspirations: The Politics of Economic Development in Mobile, 1865–1879." *Civil War History* 39 (September 1993): 240–56.

———. "Republican Factionalism and Black Empowerment: The Spencer-Warner Controversy and Alabama Reconstruction, 1868–1880." *Journal of Southern History* 64 (August 1998): 473–94.

———. *The Union League Movement in the Deep South: Politics and Agricultural Change during Reconstruction*. Baton Rouge: Louisiana State University Press, 1989.

———. *Urban Emancipation: Popular Politics in Reconstruction Mobile, 1860–1890*. Baton Rouge: Louisiana State University Press, 2002.

———. "Wager Swayne, the Freedman's Bureau, and the Politics of Reconstruction in Alabama." *Alabama Review* 48 (July 1995): 188–218.

Fleming, Walter Lynwood. *The Civil War and Reconstruction in Alabama*. New York: Columbia University Press, 1905.

Gilmour, Robert Arthur. "The Other Emancipation: Studies in the Society and Economy of Alabama Whites during Reconstruction." PhD diss., Johns Hopkins University Press, 1972.

Going, Allen Johnston. *Bourbon Democracy in Alabama, 1874–1890*. University: University of Alabama Press, 1951.

Green, Linda L. *First for the Duration: The Story of the Eighth Alabama Infantry, C.S.A.* Westminster, MD: Heritage Books, 2008.

Griffin, Ronald G. *The 11th Alabama Volunteer Regiment in the Civil War*. Jefferson, NC: McFarland, 2008.

Hasson, Gail Snowden. "Health and Welfare of Freedmen in Reconstruction Alabama." *Alabama Review* 35 (April 1982): 94–110.

———. "The Medical Activities of the Freedmen's Bureau in Reconstruction Alabama, 1865–1868." PhD diss., University of Alabama, 1982.

Hoole, William Stanley. *Alabama Tories: The First Alabama Cavalry, U.S.A., 1862–1865*. Tuscaloosa: Confederate Publishing, 1960.

Horton, Paul. "Lightning Rod Scalawag: The Unlikely Political Career of Thomas Minott Peters." *Alabama Review* 64 (April 2011): 116–42.

Hubbs, G. Ward. *Guarding Greensboro: A Confederate Company in the Making of a Southern Community*. Athens: University of Georgia Press, 2003.

Hume, Richard L. "The Freedmen's Bureau and the Freedmen's Vote in the Reconstruction of Southern Alabama: An Account by Agent Samuel S. Gardner." *Alabama Historical Quarterly* 37 (Fall 1975): 217–24.

Jones, James Pickett. *Yankee Blitzkrieg: Wilson's Raid through Alabama and Georgia.* Lexington: University Press of Kentucky, 1976.

Kolchin, Peter. *First Freedom: The Responses of Alabama's Blacks to Emancipation and Reconstruction.* Westport, CT: Greenwood, 1972.

Longacre, Edward G. *A Soldier to the Last: Maj. Gen. Joseph Wheeler in Blue and Gray.* Washington, DC: Potomac Books, 2007.

Martin, Bessie. *Desertion of Alabama Troops from the Confederate Army: A Study in Sectionalism.* New York: Columbia University Press, 1932.

McKenzie, Robert H. "The Economic Impact of Federal Occupations in Alabama during the Civil War." *Alabama Historical Quarterly* 38 (Spring 1976): 51–68.

McKiven, Henry M., Jr. "Secession, War, and Reconstruction." In *Mobile: The New History of Alabama's First City.* Edited by Michael V. R. Thomason. Tuscaloosa: University of Alabama Press, 2001.

McMillan, Malcolm C. *The Alabama Confederate Reader.* Tuscaloosa: University of Alabama Press, 1963.

———. *The Disintegration of a Confederate State: Three Governors and Alabama's Wartime Home Front, 1861–1865.* Macon, GA: Mercer University Press, 1986.

Milham, Charles G. *Gallant Pelham: American Extraordinary.* Washington, DC: Public Affairs Press, 1959.

Myers, John B. "The Alabama Freedmen and Economic Adjustments during Presidential Reconstruction, 1865–1867." *Alabama Review* 26 (October 1973): 252–66.

———. "The Freedmen and the Law in Post-Bellum Alabama, 1865–1867." *Alabama Review* 23 (January 1970): 56–69.

———. "Reaction and Readjustment: The Struggle of Alabama Freedmen in Post-Bellum Alabama, 1865–1867." *Alabama Historical Quarterly* 32 (Spring and Summer 1970): 5–22.

Newman, Jennifer Ann. "Writing, Religion, and Women's Identity in Civil War Alabama." PhD diss., Auburn University, 2009.

Noe, Kenneth W. "'Alabama, We Will Fight for Thee': The Initial Motivations of Later-Enlisting Confederates." *Alabama Review* 62 (July 2009): 163–89.

O'Brien, Sean Michael. *Mobile, 1865: Last Stand on the Confederacy.* Westport, CT: Praeger, 2001.

Patterson, Gerard A. *From Blue to Gray: The Life of Confederate General Cadmus M. Wilcox.* Harrisburg, PA: Stackpole Books, 2001.

Rabinowitz, Howard N. "Holland Thompson and Black Political Participation in Montgomery, Alabama." In *Southern Black Leaders of the Reconstruction Era.* Edited by Howard N. Rabinowitz. Urbana: University of Illinois Press, 1982, 249–80.

Riepma, Anne Sophie. *Fire and Fiction: Augusta Jane Evans in Context.* Amsterdam: Rodopi, 2000.

Rogers, William Warren, Jr. *Black Belt Scalawag: Charles Hays and the Southern Republicans in the Era of Reconstruction.* Athens: University of Georgia Press, 1993.

———. *Confederate Home Front: Montgomery during the Civil War.* Tuscaloosa: University of Alabama Press, 1999.

———. "'For the Destruction of Radicalism': A Reconstruction Case Study." *Alabama Review* 62 (July 2009): 190–209.

———. "Safety Lies Only in Silence: Secrecy and Subversion in Montgomery's Unionist Community." In *Enemies of the Country: New Perspectives on Unionists in the Civil War South.* Edited by John C. Inscoe and Robert C. Kenzer. Athens: University of Georgia Press, 2001.

Rogers, William Warren, et al. *Alabama: The History of a Deep South State.* Tuscaloosa: University of Alabama Press, 1994.

Schweninger, Loren. "Alabama Blacks and the Congressional Reconstruction Acts of 1867." *Alabama Review* 31 (July 1978): 182–98.

———. *James T. Rapier and Reconstruction.* Chicago: University of Chicago Press, 1978.

Sellers, James B. *Slavery in Alabama.* Tuscaloosa: University of Alabama Press, 1950.

Spencer, Warren F. *Raphael Semmes: The Philosophical Mariner.* Tuscaloosa: University of Alabama Press, 1997.

Sterxx, H. E. *Partners in Rebellion: Alabama Women in the Civil War.* Rutherford, NJ: Fairleigh Dickinson University Press, 1970.

Storey, Margaret M. "Civil War Unionists and the Political Culture of Loyalty in Alabama, 1860–1861." *Journal of Southern History* 69 (February 2003): 71–106.

———. "The Crucible of Reconstruction: Unionists and the Struggle for Alabama's Postwar Homefront." In *The Great Task Remaining before Us: Reconstruction as America's Continuing Civil War.* Edited by Paul A. Cimbala and Randall M. Miller. New York: Fordham University Press, 2010, 69–87.

———. *Loyalty and Loss: Alabama's Unionists in the Civil War and Reconstruction.* Baton Rouge: Louisiana State University Press, 2004.

Thornton, J. Mills III. *Politics and Power in a Slave Society: Alabama, 1800–1860.* Baton Rouge: Louisiana State University Press, 1978.

Trelease, Allen W. *White Terror: The Ku Klux Klan Conspiracy and Southern Reconstruction.* New York: Harper and Row, 1971.

Vandiver, Frank E. *Ploughshares into Swords: Josiah Gorgas and Confederate Ordinance.* Austin: University of Texas Press, 1952.

Walker, Henry. "Power, Sex, and Gender Roles: The Transformation of an Alabama Planter Family during the Civil War." In *Southern Families at War: Loyalty and Conflict in the Civil War South.* Edited by Catherine Clinton. New York: Oxford University Press, 2000.

Walther, Eric H. *William Lowndes Yancey and the Coming of the Civil War.* Chapel Hill: University of North Carolina Press, 2006.

White, Kenneth B. "Black Lives, Red Tape: The Alabama Freedmen's Bureau." *Alabama Historical Quarterly* 43 (Winter 1981): 241–58.

———. "Wager Swayne: Racist or Realist?" *Alabama Review* 31 (April 1978): 92–109.

Wiener, Jonathan M. *Social Origins of the New South: Alabama, 1860–1885.* Baton Rouge: Louisiana State University Press, 1978.

Wiggins, Sarah Woolfolk. "Alabama: Democratic Bulldozing and Republican Folly." In *Reconstruction and Redemption in the South.* Edited by Otto H. Olsen. Baton Rouge: Louisiana State University Press, 1980, 47–77.

———. "Five Men Called Scalawags." *Alabama Review* 17 (January 1964): 45–55.

———. "J. DeForest Richards: A Vermont Carpetbagger in Alabama." *Vermont History* 51 (Spring 1983): 98–105.

———. "The Marriage of Amelia Gayle and Josiah Gorgas." In *Intimate Strategies of the Civil War: Military Commanders and Their Wives.* Edited by Carol K. Bleser and Lesley J. Gordon. New York: Oxford University Press, 2001.

———. "Ostracism of White Republicans in Alabama during Reconstruction." *Alabama Review* 27 (January 1974): 52–64.

———. *The Scalawag in Alabama Politics, 1865–1881.* University: University of Alabama Press, 1977.

———. "What Is a Scalawag?" *Alabama Review* 25 (January 1972): 56–61.

Williams, David. *Rich Man's War: Class, Caste, and Confederate Defeat in the Lower Chattahoochee Valley.* Athens: University of Georgia Press, 1998.

Wills, Brian Steel. *A Battle from the Start: The Life of Nathan Bedford Forrest.* New York: HarperCollins, 1992.

Woolfolk, Sarah Van V. "Carpetbaggers in Alabama: Tradition versus Truth." *Alabama Review* 15 (April 1962): 133–44.

———. "George E. Spencer: A Carpetbagger in Alabama." *Alabama Review* 19 (January 1966): 41–52.

Contributors

Jason J. Battles is an associate professor and the director of the Office of Library Technology at the University of Alabama Libraries. His historical research has focused on the Reconstruction era in Alabama.

Lonnie A. Burnett is the chair of the Department of Social and Behavioral Sciences and a professor of history at the University of Mobile. He is the author of *Henry Hotze, Confederate Propagandist* and *The Pen Makes a Good Sword: John Forsyth of the Mobile Register*.

Harriet E. Amos Doss is an associate professor of history at the University of Alabama at Birmingham. Her major publication is *Cotton City: Urban Development in Antebellum Mobile*. She is currently researching two projects: one on the home front in Mobile during the Civil War Campaign for Mobile, and the other on free churches and race relations in religion during Reconstruction.

Bertis English is an associate dean of the College of Liberal Arts and Social Sciences and an associate professor of history at Alabama State University. He presently is working on a book that deals with Reconstruction in Perry County, Alabama.

Michael W. Fitzgerald is a professor of history at St. Olaf College in Minnesota. He is most recently the author of *Splendid Failure: Postwar Reconstruction in the American South*. His current project is a full-scale study of Reconstruction in Alabama.

Jennifer Lynn Gross is a professor of history at Jacksonville State University. Her work on Confederate widows and widowhood has appeared in several scholarly essay collections. Dr. Gross is currently finishing a manuscript tentatively titled *Rising from the Ashes: Confederate Widows and an Insecure Southern Patriarchy* and beginning new research on a biography of Mary Anna Jackson, the widow of Confederate general Stonewall Jackson.

Patricia A. Hoskins is a native of Kentucky and is an assistant professor of history and College Historian at Limestone College. Her current research focuses on the Civil War and Reconstruction in the Jackson Purchase region of Kentucky.

Kenneth W. Noe is Alumni Professor and Draughon Professor of History at Auburn University. He is most recently the author of *Reluctant Rebels: The Confederates*

Who Joined the Army after 1861. His current research involves the role of weather in the Civil War.

Victoria E. Ott is an associate professor of history at Birmingham-Southern College. Her most recent book is *Confederate Daughters: Coming of Age during the Civil War*. Her current research is on common whites and family relations in Confederate Alabama.

Terry L. Seip taught history at the University of Southern California from 1974 to 2010. Author of *The South Returns to Congress: Men, Economic Measures, and Intersectional Relationships, 1868–1879*, he has also written on pedagogy and is now completing a biography of Alabama carpetbagger George E. Spencer.

Ben H. Severance is an associate professor of history at Auburn University at Montgomery. He is the author of *Portraits of Conflict: A Photographic History of Alabama in the Civil War*. His current research is on the political significance of the state elections of 1863 in Alabama.

Kristopher A. Teters teaches at the University of Cincinnati and Northern Kentucky University. His current project examines the process of emancipation in the Western Theater during the Civil War.

Jennifer Ann Newman Treviño is an instructor at Troy University, Montgomery. Her most recent publication, "Elizabeth Rhodes: An Alabama Woman in the Civil War," appeared in the *Alabama Review*. Her book, *Alabama Women, Their Religious Beliefs, and Construction of Confederate Identity during the Civil War*, is under review.

Sarah Woolfolk Wiggins is a professor of history emerita at the University of Alabama. She is most recently the author of *Love and Duty: Amelia and Josiah Gorgas and Their Family*. Her current project is *The Journal of Sarah Haynsworth Gayle, 1827–1835: A Substitute for Social Intercourse*.

Brian Steel Wills is a professor of history and director of the Center for the Study of the Civil War Era at Kennesaw State University in Georgia. His biography of Union general George H. Thomas, *George Henry Thomas: As True as Steel*, was published recently. He is currently completing a biography of Confederate general William Dorsey Pender and a study of Nathan Bedford Forrest and the Fort Pillow Massacre.

Index

Aarons, Charlie, 172
abolition and abolitionists, 37, 127, 137, 235; and John Brown, 19, 36; Republicans as abolitionists, 18, 92–93. 112
Abraham, David, 155, 157
Abraham, Isaac, 155–56
Abraham, Joseph, 155, 157
Adams, Daniel, 77, 88n44
Adler family, 151
African Americans, 4, 26, 50n21, 84, 192; and activism, 258; and business, 183, 262; and carpetbaggers, 183; and civil rights, 185, 240, 241, 243, 248–51, 278n56; and courts, 248–51; and destitution after war, 180, 185, 241–44; disenfranchisement of, 186, 235; and education, 181, 183, 258, 262, 264, 268, 270–71, 272; elites, 258, 263–64, 270–71; and end of slavery, 7, 168, 172–73, 176n25, 184–85, 240–55, 275nn30–31 and end of war, 241; enfranchisement of, 192, 211, 235; and flogging, 253; and Freedmen's Bureau, 185, 240–55; and interracial relationships, 262; and labor issues, 241–48, 253; and Lincoln's assassination, 168, 172–74; in Mobile, 248–50; in Montgomery, 50n21; mortality rates, 241; office holders, 211, 264, 279n64; passing as white, 262; pastors, 258; and racial tension, 7, 244, 270; and religion, 258–72, 275n29, 276n36; and Republican Party, 8, 9–10, 15, 18, 20, 137, 147n55, 178, 181, 183–84, 235; role in Reconstruction, 8, 9, 178–79, 181, 183; scalawags, 182, 184; soldiers, 82, 92–93, 234; and suffrage, 8, 209, 211; and vagrancy laws, 245–46, 253; voting manipulation of,
182, 185. *See also* "Black Codes"; slaves and slavery
Alabama (Confederate ship), 2
Alabama Agricultural & Mechanical University, 266
Alabama and Tennessee Railroad, 202
Alabama Baptist State Convention, 261, 263
Alabama Chattanooga Railroad, 180
Alabama Colored Baptist State Convention, 266–67
Alabama Confederate Reader, 3, 10
Alabama Department of Archives and History, 10
Alabama Penny Savings Bank and Loan Company, 269
"Alabama Platform," 15–16, 19–22, 23, 28, 36
Alabama River, 72, 150, 157, 158
Alabama Secession Convention, 3, 165
Alabama State College, 271, 272
Alabama troops (Confederate): Alabama Rebels, 156; Autauga Rifles, 96; Bullock's Guards, 113; Emerald Guard, 162n13; Fireman Guards, 155; Greensboro Guards, 170; Kelley's Rangers, 1; Kelley's Troopers, 1; Mobile Independent Rifles, 153; Montgomery Mounted Rifles, 155; Moore Guards, 159; Southern Rifles, 113; State Reserve Forces, 154; Wheeler's Cavalry Brigade, 207; 1st Cavalry, 91, 155; 2nd Infantry, 162n13; 3rd Infantry, 95, 96, 125, 149, 161n1; 4th Infantry, 91, 95, 155; 5th Infantry, 170; 6th Infantry, 92, 94, 96; 7th Infantry, 92; 8th Infantry, 56, 59, 60, 62, 64, 65, 66, 67, 68, 92, 99, 162n13; 9th Infantry, 55, 56, 58, 60–61, 64, 65, 66,

67, 93, 94; 10th Infantry, 55, 58–59, 60, 61, 62–64, 65, 66, 70n18, 92, 156; 11th Infantry, 58–59, 61, 63, 64, 65, 66, 67, 100; 12th Infantry, 153, 154; 14th Infantry, 58, 60, 63, 65, 66; 15th Alabama, 102; 17th Infantry, 98; 18th Infantry, 113; 19th Infantry, 98, 101; 20th Infantry, 102; 21st Infantry, 92; 23rd Infantry, 98; 27th Infantry, 91; 31st Infantry, 92–93; 32nd Infantry, 159; 33rd Infantry, 101; 34th Infantry, 98, 99; 40th Infantry, 90, 98, 100; 46th Alabama, 156; 60th Infantry, 100; militia, 45, 155, 156, 222–23
Alabama troops (Union), 3, 6, 230–31, 234; Hawkins's scouts, 233; 1st Cavalry (U.S.), 3, 9, 200–209, 216n23, 217n30, 222, 230–31
Alltemont, Simon, 153
American Historical Association, 258
American Missionary Association, 266, 268
American National Baptist Convention, 267
American Revolution, 41–43, 46, 62, 91
Amherst College, 271
Anderson, Robert, 39
Andrews, C. C., 170–71
Anniston, Alabama, 160, 164n34
Antietam, Battle of, 96, 100, 153
Appel, John J., 159
Appomattox, Virginia, 2, 67, 149–50, 242
Arkansas, 23, 150, 196
Armstrong, Frank C., 78
Army of Northern Virginia, 2, 71, 120, 170; at Chancellorsville, 55–56, 66
Army of Tennessee, 73, 78
Army of the Potomac, 55–56, 67
Army of the Tennessee, 196, 204, 240–41
Arnett, Will, 1
Ash, Stephen V., 160, 231
Askew, Gus, 172–73
Athens, Alabama, 151, 203
Athens, Greece, 137
Atlanta Campaign, 76, 102, 155, 240
Atlanta, Georgia, 202; fall of, 96–97, 205; importance, 71; Jewish population, 150; unionism in, 223
Atlanta Intelligencer, 171, 173
Augusta, Georgia, 207
Austin, John, 223
Autauga, Alabama, 259; Autauga Rifles, 96

Badeau, Adam, 73
Baggett, James Alex, 221
Baker, Elisha, 94
Ball's Ferry, Georgia, 205–6
Baltimore, Maryland, 16, 23–25, 28, 29, 30, 37, 138
Bane, Moses M., 201
Banks, John Taylor, 92, 93
Bankston, M. L., 63
Baptist Bethel Association, 259
Baptist Church, 36, 55, 95, 158, 258–60, 261–66
Baptist Foreign Mission Convention, 267
Barbour County, Alabama, 27, 50n18, 52n38
Bartlett, James, 62
Barton, Henry, 226
Bates College, 271
Bates, John, 107
Battle, Cullen, 94
Battles, Jason J., 7, 9, 240–57
Bavaria, 151, 153, 157
Baym, Nina, 132
Bean, James, 102
Bear Creek, Alabama, 198–99
Beauregard, P. G. T., 128, 129, 140, 141, 143n13; disdain for Braxton Bragg, 130; and First Battle of Manassas, 131, 145n28
Beck, Charles Thompson, 118
Becoming Alabama, 10
Bell, John, 25, 37; support for in Alabama, 3, 27, 165, 182, 237n31
Benjamin, Judah P., 149
Benning, Henry, 137
Berean Baptist Church (Marion, Alabama), 263
Beulah (novel), 127, 130, 143n12
Bibb, William, 168
Bibb County, Alabama, 222
Billingsley, Andrew, 271
Billingsley, Pat, 264
Biloxi, Mississippi, 170
Birmingham, Alabama, 4, 150; in Civil Rights Era, 10. *See also* Elyton, Alabama
Black Belt, 5, 150, 155, 221, 223; and freedpeople, 241, 246, 258; and religion, 7, 150, 155, 258–66
"Black Codes," 8, 251–52, 253
black people. *See* African Americans
Black Warrior River, 77
Blackwell, John P., 224

Blair, Francis, Jr., 205, 206, 208
Blakeley, Battle of, 150, 165, 170, 174
Blassingame, John W., 260
Blount County, Alabama, 222–23
Blue and the Gray, The (television program), 177
Blum, Elias, 156
Bob (slave), 262
Bond, Horace Mann, 259, 271
Bonner, D. D., 95
Booth, John Wilkes, 26, 172
Boothe, Charles O., 266, 267, 269
Boston, Massachusetts, 141
Bradley, Joseph C., 222
Bragg, Braxton, 130, 196, 199
Brandon, Francis Lawson, 112
Brandon, Hines, 114, 117
Brandon, James, 114–15, 117
Brandon, Zillah Haynie, 41–42, 49n9, 112, 113–15, 117
Brannon, Jerry, 226
Branscomb, James Zachariah, 96, 97, 113–15, 118–19, 120
Branscomb, John Wesley, 115
Branscomb, Louis, 118–19, 120, 121
Branscomb, Lucinda. *See* Hunter, Lucinda Branscomb
Bray, Henry, 98, 99
Bray, Shadrach, 225, 231
Breckinridge, John C., 25, 37, 195, 214n10; support for in Alabama, 3, 27, 113, 165, 237n31
Bridgeport, Alabama, 231
Brooks, G. J., 267
Brooks, William "Bully," 60, 61–62, 65
Brown, Ann M., 110–11
Brown, Ellen J. Vandasdel, 107, 121
Brown, John, 19, 22, 36, 92, 126
Brown, John W., 107, 121
Brown, Morgan G., 110–11
Brownsville, Alabama, 199
Buchanan, Franklin, 129
Buchanan, James, 16, 17, 18, 31n10, 39
Buckley, Charles, W., 241
Bull Run, Battles of. *See* Manassas, First Battle of
Bullock County, Alabama, 268
Bunker, Gary L., 159
Bureau of Refugees, Freedmen, and Abandoned lands. *See* Freedmen's Bureau
Burleson, Alabama, 173
Burnett, Lonnie A., 3, 15–33
Burns, Ken, 177
Bush, Dick, 101
Bush, J. E., 101
Busteed, Richard, 139
Butler, Benjamin F., 152
Butler County, Alabama, 60
Bynam, A. H., 244–45

Cahaba, Alabama, 84
Cahaba Baptist Association, 259
Cahaba River, 77, 78
California, 16, 30, 210
Callis, John, 247
Calloway, William, 261, 262
Campbell, John A., 223
Canada, 173
Canby, Edward R. S., 4, 76, 242
Cannon, J. P., 91, 94, 95
Card, George, 266
Cargile, James, 226, 232
Carleton, G. W., 143n11, 145n29
carpetbaggers, 9, 178, 181–84; "Carpetbag Rule," 178–79; and George E. Spencer, 191–92;
Carr, Eugene H., 201–2
Catholic University, 271
Central Female College, 261
Centreville, Alabama, 78
Chadick, Mary Jane, 168–69
Chalmers, James, 77, 78, 80
Chamberlain, Henry, 170
Chambersburg, Pa., 94
Chancellor, Melzi, 60
Chancellorsville, Battle of, 2, 55–67, 57, 154; action at Stansbury's Hill, 59; Alabama brigade inactive, 58; Banks's Ford, 56, 67; map, 56; Salem Church, 55, 56–56, 59–66, 61
Chancery Courts, 110
Charleston, South Carolina: and Confederate morale, 97; and 1860 Democratic convention, 20–23, 24, 25, 28–29, 36–37; and Fort Sumter, 38; Jewish population, 150, 152, 156
Charleston Mercury, 21
Charley (friend of James Bean), 102
Chase, Salmon P., 209
Cherokee, Alabama, 199

Cherokee County, Alabama, 112, 113, 225, 226
Chicago, 17, 25, 63n27, 163n25
Chickamauga, Battle of, 100, 101, 262
Chickasaws, 180
Childs, James, 262, 263–64, 268, 269, 270, 271
Childs, Jean, 270
Childs, John Brown, 271
Childs, Martha, 264, 270
Childs, Roberta. *See* Hastie, Roberta Childs
Childs, Stephen, 262, 263, 268
Childs family, 262, 263, 270, 271
Chimborazo Hospital, 162n5
Chisholm, Alex, 64
Choctaws, 180
Christenberry, Daniel, 100
Christian, Ella Storrs. *See* Storrs, Ella
Christian Index and South-Western Baptist, 265
Cincinnati, Ohio, 23; and Democratic Party convention of 1856, 16, 18, 20, 21, 23
Citronelle, Alabama, 4, 171
Civil Rights Act of 1866, 8
Civil Rights Era, 10, 150
Civil War and Reconstruction in Alabama, The, 178–79
Civil War centennial, 3–4, 6, 10, 177
Civil War sesquicentennial, 2, 10–11
Claiborne, Alabama, 150
Clanton, Alabama, 230
Clark, George, 59, 65
Clarke County *Journal* (Alabama), 172
Class of Their Own, A (book), 258
Clay, Clement C., 17, 22, 173–74
Clay County, Iowa, 194
Clayton, Henry D., 2
Clemens, Jere, 15, 18–19
Cleveland, Grover, 68
Cloud, James, 231
Cobbs, Bishop, 260
Coffee County, Alabama, 27, 113, 153
Coffey, Absalom, 226
Cohen, Jacob, 151
Cohn, Jacob, 156
Cold Harbor, Battle of, 149
Cold Mountain (film), 177
Cold War, 10
Coleman, W. T., 263
Colling, William, 156
Collins, David, 229

Columbiana, Alabama, 77
Columbus, Georgia, 85, 125, 163n22
Columbus, Kentucky, 196
Columbus, Mississippi, 98
Compromise of 1850, 16
Congregationalist Church, 258, 266, 268
conscription, 225, 233; and unionism, 197, 221–22, 228–31, 234; and war-weariness, 6
Conservatives (faction), 222, 223
Constitution of 1868, 184
Constitutional Convention of 1865, 8
Constitutional Convention of 1867, 9, 235
Constitutional Union Party, 3, 25, 37, 165
Conway, Thomas W., 241
Cook, Robert 10
Cook, Walter, 64
cooperationists, 3, 20
Coosa County, Alabama, 153
Corinth, Mississippi, 196–99, 200, 201, 203
corn women, 5
Cornyn, Florence M., 201
Corse, John, 204, 205, 208
Cosmopolitan Journal, 127
cotton, 158–59, 210, 259; antebellum trade, 151, 155, 157; theft of, 241; wartime trade, 157–58, 159, 164n28, 198, 209
Cotton, John, 97–98, 99, 101, 102–3
Cotton, Mariah, 97, 102–3
Council Bluffs, Iowa, 193, 196, 215n13
Councill, William H., 266
Courtland, Alabama, 198
Cox, Henry, 63
Cramer, Frances, 208
Crawford, Peter, 261–62
Creek War, 10
Creeks, 180
Crocker, M. M., 194
Crossland, Edward, 77, 78
Crow, Charles, 261, 262
Crow, Washington, 225, 230
Croxton, John T., 4, 77, 78, 84, 167, 174
Crusader, The (magazine), 125
Cumberland River, 196
Cumming, Kate, 5, 42, 47n2
Curry, Jabez L. M., 135, 137, 139, 140, 141, 166; as congressman, 126, 144n17; and education, 144n17; as minister, 129, 265
Curtis, Alexander, 266, 267, 268, 269, 271

Curtis, Alexander H., Sr., 263, 275n30
Curtis, Henrietta, 270
Curtis, Princess Webb Freeman, 264
Curtis, Thomas, 267, 268, 269
Curtis family, 271
Cushing, Caleb, 23, 25
Cyclopedia of Colored Baptists of Alabama (book), 266

Dafney (slave), 262–63
Dallas, Texas, 149
Dallas County, Alabama, 20, 56, 259, 263, 268
Dalton, Georgia, 204
Daniel, J. W. L., 50n18
Daniel, John S. M., 38, 50n18
Dauphin Island, Alabama, 95
Davenport, John, 98, 100, 101, 103
Davis, Elias, 55, 65, 92
Davis, George, 151
Davis, Hugh, 261
Davis, Hugh, Sr., 259
Davis, Jefferson, 3, 101, 156, 158; arrest and imprisonment, 180; captured, 85; critics of, 6, 130; inaugurated, 155; reenactments of inauguration, 10, 38
Davis, Nicholas, 20
Davis, Sarah, 38, 44–45
Davis, William F., 267
Dawson, Elodie Todd, 38–40, 43, 51n23, 53n58
Dawson, James, 230–31
Dawson, Nathaniel Henry Rhodes, 38, 51n23, 91
Decatur, Alabama, 210, 211, 232; and Abraham Lincoln's assassination, 168; and military operations, 4, 198, 199, 203; occupation of, 92, 93
Declaration of Independence, 177
DeKalb County, Alabama, 153, 225, 234
Delaware, 23
Democratic Party, 152, 157; and African Americans, 185, 267; convention of 1856, 16, 18, 20, 21, 23; conventions of 1860, 20, 21–25, 28–30, 36–37; and corruption, 180–81; in 1860, 3, 165; and debt, 181; and disenfranchisement, 185, 186; and election of 1870, 184; and election of 1874, 184; and gerrymandering, 185; moderates, 15, 29–30; opposition to Reconstruction, 9–10; opposition to Republicans, 220–21; and race, 184; State Convention of 1859, 19–21, 28; and Tammany Hall, 180; and taxation, 184; and Whigs, 224
Demopolis, Alabama, 150
Demopolis Herald, 173
Denver, Co. 195
Des Moines, Iowa, 193, 194
DeVotie, James H., 262
Dexter Avenue Baptist Church, 266, 267, 269, 270
Dickinson County, Iowa, 194
Diffley, Kathleen, 134
Dinnerstein, Leonard, 159
disenfranchisement, 185, 186
divorce, 107, 110–11, 121
"Dixie" (song), 3
Dodd, Harriet E. Amos, 6, 165–76
Dodds, Ozro J., 203
Dodge, Anne, 198, 203
Dodge, Grenville, 193, 195, 196–205, 206–8, 210–11
Dodge, Nathan, 203, 215n13
Douglas, Adele, 26
Douglas, Stephen A., 3, 23; on African Americans, 26; debates Abraham Lincoln, 17; and election of 1860, 27–30, 165, 237n31; as enemy of Alabama and the South, 17–20, 23; and Freeport Doctrine, 17; and Lecompton Constitution, 17; on Lincoln, 26; in Mobile, 26–27, 165; in Montgomery, 26; national speaking tour, 25, 26–27; role in breakup of party, 28–30; presidential aspirations, 16, 19, 22, 25; and slavery, 16–17; states' rights, 17; and supporters in Alabama, 15–18, 21, 23–24, 29–30, 182, 221, 224, 237n31, 251
Dozier, J. W., 267
Dozier, Jane, 267
Dozier, John C., 264, 266–69, 267, 272
Dozier, Leonard, 267
Dozier, Woody, 65
Dred Scott decision, 16, 17, 22
Dreyfus, Leopold, 155
Dreyfus, Samuel, 155
Du Bois, W. E. B., 258, 260, 276n36
Dublin, Alabama, 36, 38
Dunbar High School, 271
Dunn, Francis Wayland, 202–3
Dunning School, 220
Durgan, Edmund S., 152
Durr, John Wesley, 158

Early, Jubal, 56, 58–59, 94
Eastport, Alabama, 198
Ebenezer Church, Battle of, 78–79
Ebony Festivals, 262
Edmondson, Belle, 133
elections: of 1859, 18; of 1860, 19, 27, 37, 113, 165, 221, 224, 237n31; of 1863, 230; of 1867, 9; of 1868, 235; of 1870, 191; of 1870, 9, 184; of 1874, 184
Ellenburg, Alex, 225
Elmira Prison, 158
Elmore, Vincent, 91
Elyton, Alabama, 77
Emancipation Proclamation, 5, 176n25, 259, 263
England, 198
English, Bertis, 7, 258–79
Episcopalian Church, 36, 166, 168, 259
Espy, Columbus, 43, 116
Espy, Marcellous, 121
Espy, Sarah Rodgers Rousseau, 36, 43, 45, 112; and secession, 37–38, 40, 112–13, 165; and trials of war; 116–18, 119–21
Espy, Virgil, 119
"ethnic cleansing," 179
Eufaula, Alabama, 34, 172
Evans, Augusta Jane, 5; and anonymous articles, 128; and anti-Catholicism, 142n1; background, 125, 142n1; and P. G. T. Beauregard, 128, 129, 130, 131, 140, 143n13, 145n28; and *Beulah*, 127; compared to characters, 136; and Confederate leaders, 128, 129, 140–41; and critics, 127, 133; and J. L. M. Curry, 126, 129, 135, 137, 139, 140–41, 144n17; and Jefferson Davis, 130; and defeat, 138–39; and desertion, 129; on education for women, 134–35; and family, 125–26; as feminist, 146n32; and gender roles, 126, 128, 136; hatred of Lincoln and Republicans, 125, 127, 136–37, 166; hatred of speculators, 129; and history of Confederacy, 140–41; and home front, 129; and *Inez*, 133, 142n1; and *Macaria*, 5, 127, 130–38, 141–42, 144–45n25, 145n29, 145–46n30, 146n32, 148n76; and marriage, 132–39, 142, 147n55; and monuments, 141, 148n75; and New York, 127; as a nurse, 130–31, 134, 144–45n25, 146n43; and orphans, 146n47; and politics, 126; popularity of, 125, 127, 130, 143n11, 143n12, 145n29; and poverty, 134–35, 142n1; and Reconstruction, 139–40; and religion, 132–33; and *St. Elmo*, 127, 143n11, 143n12; and slavery, 129, 136; on soldiers, 129, 139, 140, 142; and substitution, 129–30, 144n17; and support for Confederacy, 136, 125–26, 128, 130–34, 136–40; and Twenty Negro Law, 130; and Unionism, 125–26, 131; and verbosity, 126, 127; and war work, 130–31, 133–34, 144–45n25, 146n43; and womanhood, 128, 134
Evans, Matthew, 125

Fagan, William, 64
Fairclough, Adam, 258
Fairfield, Michael F., 201
Faison's Depot, North Carolina, 208
Fallin, Wilson, 258
Faust, Drew Gilpin, 47n2, 133
Fayetteville, North Carolina, 207
Featherston, John, 60, 63
Federal Writers' Project, 172
Felder, Adam, 222
Ferguson, Samuel W., 203
Fidler, William, 137
5th Alabama Regimental Band, 177
First Baptist Church (Uniontown, Alabama), 267
First Colored Baptist Church (Birmingham, Alabama), 268
First Colored Baptist Church (Marion, Alabama), 263
First Colored Missionary Baptist Church (Uniontown, Alabama), 264
Fitzgerald, Michael W., 2–3, 4, 6–9, 218n42, 220–39, 241, 269
Fitzpatrick, Benjamin, 18, 19, 25
Fleming, Walter Lynwood, 178–79, 220, 230
Florence, Alabama, 4, 198, 251
Florida, 8, 23, 38
Flynt, J. Wayne, 41
Foner, Eric, 258, 273n9
Forney, William H., 58, 62, 64, 65
Forrest, Nathan Bedford, 86; attacks 4th U. S. Cavalry, 81–83; background, 72, 74; after Battle of Nashville, 74, 75; and Battle of Ebenezer Church, 78–79; and Battle of Selma, 2, 80–81, 88n44; captured orders, 78;

controversy in Selma, 11; delayed response to raid, 77; and Grenville Dodge, 198; escapes, 81; impresses civilians, 79; and David Kelley, 1–2; meets with James Wilson, 84–85; and morale of command, 74; operations before Selma, 77–78; popular views of, 75; preparations to defend Selma, 79–80; and promotion, 75; and retreat to Selma, 79; and Emma Sansom, 5; scouts and spies of, 76; and Abel Streight's raid, 199; and surrender, 85; targeted by Sherman, 76; and Richard Taylor, 74–75
Forsyth, John, 24, 249; at 1859 state Democratic convention, 19–21; as opponent of William L. Yancey, 15, 19, 21; role in breakup of party, 29–30; as supporter of Stephen A. Douglas, 18, 23–24, 26, 27–28, 29–30, 165
Fort Gaines, 95, 151
Fort Morgan, 126, 133, 144n25, 151
Fort Pillow, 82–83
Fort Sumter, 42, 157; as beginning of war, 46, 98, 149, 166, 196
Fortress Monroe, 125
Foster, William, 94, 95
Fourteenth Amendment, 8, 9, 211
Fowler, James B., 270
Fowlkes, M. L., 267
Fox, Lilburn, 264
Frank, Leo, 150
Franklin, Battle of, 71, 72
Franklin, John Hope, 260
Franklin County, Alabama, 173
Frazier, E. Franklin, 260
Fredericksburg, Battle of, 149
Fredericksburg, Virginia, 55, 56, 58, 95
"freedmen," 7, 8, 9, 183, 185, 210, 212, 234, 235, 240–55, 257n62
Freedmen's Bureau, 7, 185, 265, 268; before Wager Swayne, 241; and courts, 248–51, 253, 257n62; and destitution, 243–44, 254; and education, 268; established, 240, 253; and funding, 243; and home colonies, 242, 244; and labor, 241–48, 253, 254; leadership, 240; opposition to, 253; and personnel, 243; reputation of, 254; and scope, 240, 254; as social welfare organization, 240; termination, 254; and War Department, 240, 243

Freeman, Douglas Southall, 67
Freeman, Ephraim, 267
Freeman, John, 268
Freeman, Samuel, 82
Freeman, W. W., 267
Freeman, Wilson, 263
"Freeport Doctrine," 17
French, Virginia, 125–26
Fugitive Slave Law, 16, 17

Gadsden, Alabama, 5
Gaines Mill, Battle of, 153
Gainesville, Alabama, 85, 117
Gainesville Independent, 18
Gardner, S. S., 246–47, 252
Garner, Reuben, 226
Garrett, Angie, 173
Gayle, John, 152
Gaylesville, Alabama, 41, 232
Georgia, 25, 26, 38, 99, 129; and Democratic delegates, 23; Jewish population, 150, 162n5; legislature, 125, 137; and military operation, 4, 71, 196; and Reconstruction, 8
Georgia troops, 62, 63, 65, 66; 50th Infantry, 70n24; Semmes brigade, 62, 66, 70n24; Wofford's brigade, 62
Germany, 155
Gettysburg, Battle of, 2, 95, 100, 149, 154, 240
Gilbert, Lucinda, 267
Gillard, Jim, 173
Gillis, Margaret, 37, 38, 166
Gilpin, E. N., 83–84
Glendale, Alabama, 198, 201, 203
Glory (film), 177
Goldin, Andrew, 267
Goldsboro, North Carolina, 207, 208
Goldsby, Alexander, 259, 273n9
Gone With the Wind (film), 177
Goodfellow, T. M., 246, 251
Gordon, Georgia, 205
Goree, John R., 263
Gorgas, Josiah, 2, 71, 84
Gracie, Archibald, 2
Grandberry, Mary Ella, 173
Granger, R. S., 168–69
Grant, R., 267
Grant, Ulysses S., 71, 158, 201, 203, 209; and

General Orders No. 11, 150, 160; and Robert E. Lee's surrender, 172, 173; as president, 180; supporters of, 221; and George Thomas, 75–76; and Vicksburg campaign, 196, 199; and Wilson's Raid, 72, 73
Gravelly Springs, Alabama, 75
Gray, Fred, 271
Great Depression, 172, 271
Greene County, Alabama, 247
Greensboro, Alabama, 172
Greensboro *Alabama Beacon*, 173
Gross, Jennifer Lynn, 5, 125–48
Gross, John V., 224–25
Grove Hill, Alabama, 172
Grow, Asa, 193
Grubb, E. Burd, 69n16
guerrilla warfare, 197, 228, 229, 231
Gulfport, Mississippi, 152
Gulley, D. O., 267
Gutheim, James K., 156, 163n22

"Hail Mary" (song), 260
Haley, Green M., 230
Halleck, Henry W., 75, 85, 197, 198, 203
Halstead, Murat, 23
Hamburg, Mississippi, 198
Hamilton, Alexander, 126
Hampton, Wade, 207
Hanan, Rubin M., 160
Hannon, M. W., 199
Happel, Ralph, 55
Harper, Jasper, 225, 226
Harpers Ferry Raid, 19, 36, 92
Harper's New Monthly Magazine, 139
Harper's Weekly, 18
Harris, Isham, 85
Harris, John W., 267
Harrison, Perry, 222
Harrod, William, 262
Harvard Law Review, 271
Harvard Law School, 271
Harwood, Phillip, 224, 225
Hastie, Karen, 271
Hastie, Roberta Childs, 270
Hastie, William Henry, 270
Hastie, William Henry, Jr., 270–71, 279n64

Hatcher, Richard W., III, 43
Hawthorne, Nathaniel, 146n34
Hays, Charles, 221
Haywood, E., 263
Heald, Henry, 232
Hebron Baptist Church, 259
Heflin, R. S., 222, 230
Hendinson, Admore, 267
Hendley, Charles, Jr., 267
Henry County, Alabama, 27
Herbert, Hilary, 62, 64, 65, 67, 68
Higginbotham, Evelyn Brooks, 260
Higginson, Thomas Wentworth, 260
Hightower, Mrs. H. M., 267
Hill, Benjamin, 129
Hilliard, Henry W., 19
Hinds, J. J., 208
Hirshson, Stanley, 193, 199–200, 204
H. L. Hunley (submarine), 4
Hobbs, Thomas Hubbard, 94
Hogan, Needham, 61, 63, 67
Hoge, S. S., 252
Homestead, Melissa, 145–46n30
Hood, John Bell, 71–75, 233
Hooker, Joseph, 56, 58, 66
Hopewell Baptist Church, 259, 267
Hopkinsville, Ky., 1
Horner, John W., 169
horse thieves, 241
Hosea, Lewis, 76, 81, 84, 87n26, 88n43
Hoskins, Patricia A., 5, 149–64
Houston, Charles Hamilton, 271
Howard College, 264, 265, 270
Howard University Law School, 271
Howard, Oliver O., 205, 206, 208; as general, 240–42; as head of Freedmen's Bureau, 240–41, 248, 250–51, 252; and religion, 240
Howe, Orlando, 193–94
Hundley, Daniel, 92–93, 97
Hunter, Carrie, 38, 43, 44, 45, 46n1
Hunter, Lucinda Branscomb, 113, 114–16, 118, 120
Huntington, Louisa, 253
Huntsville, Alabama, 1, 15, 36, 160, 165, 208; and assassination of Abraham Lincoln, 168–69, 175n6; and education, 266; and Freedmen's Bureau, 244–45, 246–47, 251; and military

operations, 73, 85, 198; and religion, 267; and unionism, 222, 226, 231
Hurlbut, Stephen A., 199, 201–2

Illinois, 15, 30
Illinois troops: 9th Cavalry, 207
immediatists, in 1860, 3, 37
impressment, 6
Indiana, 30, 234
Industrial High School, 269
Inez (novel), 133, 142n1
Inzer, John Washington, 90, 91, 93, 96–97
Iowa, 192–93
Iowa City, Iowa, 193
Iowa troops: 2nd Cavalry, 198; 4th Infantry, 196; 29th Infantry, 170
Israel, Samuel, 151
Issacs, Myer S., 162n10
Iuka, Mississippi, 203

Jack, J. R., 225, 226
Jackson, Jimmy Lee, 270
Jackson, Thomas Jonathan "Stonewall," 55–56
Jackson, William H. "Red," 77, 78
Jackson, William Thomas, 99, 100, 101
Jackson County, Alabama, 56, 153, 226, 231
Jasper, Alabama, 77, 202
Jefferson, Campbell, 110
Jefferson, Lydia Margaret, 110
Jefferson, Thomas, 126
Jefferson County, Alabama, 268
Jews and Judaism, 149–60, 161n2, 161n4, 162n10, 164n28; anti-Semitism, 150, 153, 159–60, 162n5, 164n33; Ashkenazi Jews, 150, and Code Noir, 151; condemned as speculators, 159–60, 164n28; on eve of war, 150–51; in Mobile, 5, 150–53, 154, 156, 159, 160; in Montgomery, 5, 149, 150–51, 154–60; in New Orleans, 150, 152, 156; origins in South, 150, 151; and slavery, 150, 151, 157, 163n27; in South Carolina, 150, 152; in twentieth century, 150; in wartime, 5, 149–59; and xenophoia, 150, 159
John (Sarah Espy's son-in-law), 120
Johnson, Andrew, 7–8, 139, 208–9, 210, 211, 234; and Freedmen's Bureau, 240, 253–54; and Lincoln's assassination, 168, 173–74; and oaths, 244
Johnson, Frank, 246
Johnson, Herschel V., 25
Johnson, S., 267
Johnson's Island Prison, 90, 96–97
Johnston, George D., 262
Johnston, Joseph E., 172, 197, 204
Joint Committee on Reconstruction, 8
Jones, Ann Goodwyn, 128
Jones, Emilie, 156
Jones, Hannah, 172
Jones, Israel I., 151, 156
Jones, Solomon, 151
Judson Female Seminary, 261

Kahl Montgomery synagogue, 155, 156, 157
Kahn, Solomon, 149, 160–61n1
Kansas, 16, 17
Kansas Conference Bill, 19
Kansas-Nebraska Act, 16, 17
Karcher, Ernest, 153
Kelley, David Campbell, 1–2, 11
Kellogg (friend of George Spencer), 193
Kelly's Ford, Battle of, 154
Kennedy, John S., 209
Kentucky, 38, 72, 150
Kentucky troops (Union): 5th Cavalry, 207
Kerber, Linda, 43
Kershaw, Joseph, 62
Kilpatrick, Judson J., 205, 207–8
King, Coretta Scott, 270
King, Edwin W., 263
King, Henry, 263
King, Horace, 67
King, Martin Luther, Jr., 271
Kirby, Andrew, 230, 234
Knipe, Joseph, 76
Krebs, Sylvia, 258
Krum, John, 24
Ku Klux Klan, 9, 10, 183, 235; members shot, 227; twentieth century Klan, 150; victims of, 221, 225, 235

ladies' aid societies, 35, 45, 46, 53n58, 159
Ladies' Home (magazine), 125

LaGrange, Georgia, 150, 153
Lane, Joseph, 25
Larson, James, 82
Lauderdale County, Alabama, 230
Law, Evander, 2
Lazarus family, 151
Leath, Ebenezer, 226–27, 232
Lecompton Constitution, 17, 18
Lee, Robert E., 71, 120, 149–50, 173; and Chancellorsville campaign, 55–56, 59, 60, 66; Gettysburg campaign, 153; surrender, 165, 172
Lee, Stephen D., 203
Lehman Brothers (company), 157, 159, 163n27
Lehman & Durr (company), 158
Lehman, Emmanuel, 157, 160, 163n27
Lehman, Frances, 163n25
Lehman, Henry, 157, 163n27
Lehman, Mayer, 157–60, 163n27
l'Etondal, Jules, 153, 162n14
Levy, Samuel Yates, 162n9
Lile, Robert, 253
Limestone County, Alabama, 230
Lincoln Normal School (Huntsville, Alabama), 266
Lincoln Normal School and University (Marion, Alabama), 262, 266, 267–68, 270–71
Lincoln, Abraham: assassination, 6–7, 165, 168–74, 208; blamed for secession, 41, 46; and election of 1860, 3, 15, 25, 26, 27, 30, 37, 113, 165, 195, 237n31; and election of 1864, 71, 97, 234; and emancipation, 176n25, 163; and Fort Sumter, 38; hated by Confederates, 92, 93, 126, 127, 165, 168, 172; mourned, 172–73, 174; and Nebraska Territory, 196; nominated for presidency, 25; and sisters-in-law, 37, 38; support in Alabama, 234, 237n31
Lincoln, C. Eric, 260
Lincoln-Douglas debates, 17
Lincoln, Mary Todd, 13n7
Little Sioux River, 194
Liverpool, England 158
Livingston, Alabama, 173
Loeb, John, 163n25
Loftis, Mary, 98
London, England, 151

Long, Eli, 78, 80–81
Longacre, Edward, 72
Longstreet, James, 2
"Lost Cause," 149, 174, 178
Louisiana, 149, 150, 159–60, 182; and 1860 Democratic convention, 23, 24
Louisville and Nashville Railroad, 181
Lowndesboro, Alabama, 259
Luvaas, Jay, 59
lynching, 223, 229, 230
Lyon, Francis S., 19, 20, 23
Lyon, Harlan B., 73
Lyons, Rachel, 125, 126, 127, 136, 144–45n25

Macaria (novel), 5, 127, 130–38, 141–42, 143n12, 144–45n25, 145–46n29–30, 146n32, 148n76
Macon, Georgia, 150
Macon County, Alabama, 58, 153, 222, 269
Madison County, Alabama, 19
Madison County, Iowa, 193
Mahan, Jesse W., 222
Mahone, William, 62
Maine troops, 62; 5th Infantry, 62
Malagasy people, 264
Mallory, James, 172
Malloy (associate of William Moxley), 118
Malvern Hill, Battle of, 149, 153, 161n1
Mamiya, Lawrence M., 260
Manasco, Wiley, 230
Manassas, First Battle of, 131
Mann, Horace, 144n17
March to the Sea, 99, 201, 205, 233, 240
Marion, Alabama, 259, 261, 263–64, 266, 268, 272
Marion County, Alabama, 229
"Marion Nine," 268, 272
Marshall, Thurgood, 271
Marshall County, Alabama, 225, 227
Martha (Lehman slave), 163n27
Martin, J. J., 222
Marx, Isaac, 150
Mary (friend of James Woods), 101–2
Maryland, 40, 170
Mason-Dixon Line, 131, 154
Mason, James, 94
Masonic lodges, 157
Massachusetts, 23, 266

Matthews, B. H., 258
Maury, Dabney, 72
May, M. G., 67
McAlpine, William H., 266, 267, 269
McBride, John, 225, 227
McClelen, Bailey, 59, 61
McClellan, William, 64
McCook, Edward, 73, 78
McCrary, Robert, 59
McCullough, W. H., 102
McGuire, William, 233
McIntosh, William H., 262
McKinney, Francis, 76
McKinnon, Malcolme A., 111
McKinnon, Sarah, 111
McLaws, Lafayette, 60, 61, 69n14
McMillan, Amon, 226, 230
McMillan, Malcolm C., 3, 6, 10, 11
McNeely, John W., 153
McPherson (Friend of George Spenser), 193
McPherson, James B., 103n2, 204
Memphis, Tennessee, 25, 196, 199
Memphis and Charleston Railroad, 196, 232
Menawa, 10
Methodist Church, 1, 36, 95; in Black Belt, 258, 259, 265–66; and unionism, 231–32
Mexican-American War, 15, 16, 58, 155
Mexico, 85, 249
Michelbacher, M. J., 149–50
Michigan, 30
Michigan troops, 9th Cavalry, 207; 18th Infantry, 175n6
Milledgeville, Georgia, 126, 137, 147n55, 205
Miller, George, 94
Milliken's Bend, La., 199
Mills, Thomas, 60, 63, 69n16
Minnesota, 194
Mississippi, 23, 38, 150, 197, 199
Mississippi River, 82, 160
Missouri, 24, 196
Missouri River, 193
Missouri troops (Confederate): Cockrell's brigade, 107
Mitchell (partner of George Spencer), 209
Mobile, Alabama, 4, 5, 19, 42, 56, 99, 150, 154; business and commerce, 151, 158, 171, 209; campaign against city, 76, 170; cosmopolitan nature, 162n13; and Stephen A. Douglas, 26–27, 165; and 1859 state Democratic convention, 19, 20; and Augusta Jane Evans, 125, 126, 141, 142, 148n75; and Freedmen's Bureau, 248; and Jewish population, 150–53, 154, 156, 159, 160; and Abraham Lincoln's assassination, 169–70; politics in, 19, 20, 27, 29; in Reconstruction, 9, 148n75, 171, 191, 241, 248, 252; and secession, 166; soldiers from, 130, 153, 154, 162n5; surrender, 165; women of, 36
Mobile Advertiser and Register, 169, 252
Mobile and Ohio Railroad, 196
Mobile Bay, Battle of, 4, 152
Mobile County, Alabama, 27, 153
Mobile Daily Advertiser, 27
Mobile Daily News, 169, 171
Mobile Register, 15, 23–24, 27, 165, 249
Monroe Cross Roads, Battle of, 207–8
Montevallo, Alabama, 77–78
Montgomery, Alabama, *166*, 202, 222, 241, 266–67; and African American businesses, 183; and bus boycott, 271; business and commerce, 149, 151, 152, 155, 156–58; as Confederate capital, 3, 113, 155; and Democratic Party, 19, 20, 23; and 1859 state Democratic convention, 19, 20; and everyday life during war, 5; and Freedmen's Bureau, 241, 244, 248; and Jewish population, 149, 150–52, 154–60, 163n22; and secession convention, 38; and unionism, 6, 168, 223; welcomes Stephen A. Douglas, 26; and Wilson's Raid, 4, 85, 158, 170–71
Montgomery Advertiser, 18, 23–24, 245, 248–49
Montgomery and West Point Railroad, 4, 202
Montgomery Confederation, 15
Montgomery County, Alabama, 153
Montgomery Daily Advertiser, 241–42, 244, 249
Montgomery Daily Mail, 171
Montgomery Post, 159
Montgomery Weekly Advertiser, 19
Montreal, Canada, 192
Moore, Andrew B., 18, 19
Moore, James, 100
Moore, John, 267
Mooresville, Alabama, 203, 208
Mordecai, Abraham, 154

Mordecai, Solomon, 151
Morgan County, Alabama, 153
Morris, James, 227
Morton, John, 72
Moseley, John, 95
Moses, Alfred, 156, 163n25
Moses, Henry, 156
Moses, Joshua, 150
Moses, Mordecai, 156–57, 160
Moses, Moses, 156
Moulton, Alabama, 198
Moxley, Daniel Newton, 118, 119
Moxley, Emily, 113–21
Moxley family, 121, 123n14
Moxley, William, 113–21
Murfreesboro, Battle of, 155
Murphy, W. C., 60, 63
Musser, Charles, 170
"My Jesus Acomin" (song), 260–61
Myree, W. D., 267

Nashville, Battle of, 71–72, 74-76, 78, 233–34
Nashville, Tennessee, 86
Nashville and Decatur Railroad, 203
Nation, Thomas, 222
National Association for the Advancement of Colored People (NAACP), 271
National Baptist Convention of the United States of America, 267
National Baptist Education Convention, 267
National Cathedral School, 271
National Park Service, 58
Nebraska troops: 1st Infantry, 196, 197
Negro American Journal, 269
Netherlands, 169
Nevins, Allan, 10
New Jersey troops, 62; 1st Infantry, 63; 2nd Infantry, 65; 3rd Infantry, 63; 15th Infantry, 63, 65; 23rd Infantry, 62, 64, 67
New Orleans, 26, 151, 152, 157; and assassination of Abraham Lincoln, 169; business in, 151, 152, 157, 158; and the Civil War, 152, 158; and corruption, 180; fall of, 158; and Jewish community, 150, 151, 152, 156, 159, 163n22; refugees, 159, 163n22
"new social history," 4
New York, 127, 192, 264, 266, 268; and election of 1860, 30; and cotton trade in wartime, 209, 210; and Lehman family, 157, 159
New York Times, 127
New York Tribune, 127
New York troops, 62; 16th Infantry, 65; 121st Infantry, 62–63
New Yorker, 177
Newton (Emily and William Moxley's neighbor), 117
Newton, Iowa, 193
Newton, John, 59
Nichols, Roy Franklin, 30
Noe, Kenneth W., 1–14, 106n36
Norfolk, Virginia, 262
Normal School for Colored Students, 270
Normal, Alabama, 266
North and South (television program), 177
North Carolina, 26
Northern Flicker. *See* Yellowhammer

Oak Grove, Alabama, 172
Oates, William C., 2
Ocmulgee Baptist Church (Marion, Alabama), 262–63
Oconee River, 205
Oden, John, 58, 66
Odom, Alexander, 64, 67
Oglesby, Richard, 199, 200, 201
O'Hara, Theodore, 166
Ohio, 23, 183, 240, 253
Ohio troops: 5th Cavalry, 207; 102nd Infantry, 168
Okolona, Mississippi, 199
Omaha, Nebraska, 196, 215n13
O'Neal, Edward, 154
Opelika Weekly Southern Era (Alabama), 23
Oregon, 24
Orrock, James, 61
Ott, Victoria E., 2, 4, 5, 6, 107–24
Owen, Thomas, 100

Palacios, Joseph de, 151
Panic of 1873, 265
Parish, Ivey, 268
Parish, Orum, 263
Parker High School, 269
Parker's Crossroads, Battle of, 81
Parkes, Wesley, 169

Parkhurst, John G., 76
Parks, Rosa, 10, 271
Parsons, Lewis Eliphalet, 8, 209; and crime, 242; and Wager Swayne, 243–44, 246, 248–51
Parsons, Philip W., 69n8
Paterson, William, 267–68
Patterson, Edmund, 55, 60, 66, 93
Patton, Robert M., 8, 251
Peace Society, 6, 230
Pelham, John, 2
Pember, Phoebe Yates Levy, 162n9
Pemberton, John, 197
Peninsula Campaign, 58
Penningroth, Dylan, 220
Pennsylvania, 154
Pennsylvania troops, 62; 96th Infantry, 62, 65; 102nd Infantry, 67
Pensacola, Fla., 77, 202
Perry County Bible Society, 266
Perry County, Alabama, 7, 107, 258–66, 268–71
Perryville Baptist Church (Perry County, Alabama), 267
Perryville, Battle of, 155
Peters, Thomas M., 223
Petersburg, Siege of, 68, 71, 149, 225
Pettiford, William R., 268–69
Pettus, Edmund, 2
Philadelphia, Pennsylvania, 153, 198
Phillips, Eugenia Levy, 152–53, 162n9–11
Phillips, Jesse J., 203
Phillips, Phillip, 152–53, 162n11
Pickens, Samuel B., 153, 170
Pierce, Charles W., 247
Pierce, Richard, 253
Pike County, Alabama, 153
Pike County, Missouri, 107
Pillow, Gideon, 230
Pinckard, Lucius, 58, 60, 63
Piston, William Garrett, 43
Pitts, Anderson, 267
Pittsburgh Landing, Battle of. *See* Shiloh, Battle of
Poe, Wyatt, 229
Point Lookout Prison, 170
"political correctness," 10, 179
Pope, John, 8
popular sovereignty, 16, 17, 18, 21, 23
Populist movement, 185

Prairieville, Alabama, 172
Presbyterian Church, 258, 266, 268
Pritchett, James, 100
Proskauer, Adolph, 152, 153–54, 159, 162n12
Proskauer, Joseph, 162n12
Proskauer, Julius, 153, 162n12
Pugh, George E., 23
Pulaski, Tennessee, 203

Rable, George, 44, 47n2
Raboteau, Albert J., 260
Rains, John, 63
Raleigh, North Carolina, 207, 263
Randolph, Alabama, 78
Randolph, Ryland, 9
Randolph County, Alabama, 197, 208, 222, 230
Rappahannock River, 56, 66, 67
Reconstruction Acts of 1867, 8
Reconstruction, 3, 6–8, 139, 159, 160; African American office holders, 264; beginnings, 168; and carpetbaggers, 181, 182; centrality of race in scholarship, 220; and Congressional Reconstruction, 8–9, 235, 254; in context of world history, 179–80; and corruption, 180–81; and debt, 181; and education, 181, 262; end of, 268; and Augusta Jane Evans, 139–40; and expansion of government, 185–86; and Walter Lynwood Fleming, 178–79; and Freedmen's Bureau, 185, 240–55; Joint Committee, 210; modern historiography of, 179; and literacy, 184–85; popular image of period, 177–79; and post-war devastation, 180; and Presidential Restoration, 7–8, 234, 243–44; and property confiscation, 180; and railroads, 181; Reconstruction Acts of 1867, 8; and religion, 258–59, 263; and Republican Party, 177; revisionism, 220; as "splendid failure," 186; and suffrage, 184; and taxation, 180–81; unpopularity of era, 177–78; war crimes trial, 180; white resistance to, 243
Reconstruction: America's Unfinished Revolution, 1863–1877 (book), 258
Red Sulphur Springs, Tennessee, 198
Redemption, 10, 277n50
refugee camps, 231–32
religion, 60, 168; and African customs, 260–61; antebellum churches, 258–62; and Baptist

Church, 36, 55, 95, 158, 258–65; and Confederacy, 41; and education, 258, 264, 267–68; and Episcopalian Church, 36, 166, 168, 259; and elites, 258; and Augusta Jane Evans, 132–33; and Fort Sumter, 38; firing on, 35; Judaism, 149–60; and Methodist Church, 1, 36, 95, 231–32, 258, 259, 265; and music, 260–61; and pastors, 258; and political activism, 258; and Presbyterian Church, 258, 266, 268; and Protestants, 35, 36, 45; in Reconstruction, 262; and segregation post-war, 258, 263; and slave holders, 262; as slave resistance, 260, 263; and soldier motivations, 94–95, 97, 99–100; and Sunday School movement, 266; and unionists, 231–32; and women, 34, 36, 38, 39–40, 41–42, 44, 45, 47n2, 114–15, 116–17

Republican Party, 6, 8, 9–10, 15, 20, 26, 39, 45, 137; after war, 180–85, 211, 220–35, 236n3, 236n7–8, 237n28–29, 237n31, 238n59, 238n80; and African Americans, 10, 181, 183–84; as anti-Confederate, 221; "Black Republicans," 15, 18, 20, 37, 41, 91, 98, 137, 147n55; blamed for secession, 41, 112; and carpetbaggers, 181, 182–83; and class, 224–27; composition of party, 181–82, 184; in Congress, 8; and corruption, 180–81; and draft resistance, 228–29; and education, 181; and election of 1860, 3, 19, 22, 27, 30; and election of 1870, 184, 191, 212n1–2; factions, 9–10, 183–84, 192; first generation in 1850s, 192–93; flees Alabama, 233; as Jacksonians, 225; and Andrew Johnson, 254; leadership, 221–23; motivations to support, 220–21; nomination of Abraham Lincoln, 25, 37; and outspokenness, 226–27; problems facing party, 9–10; protected by army, 234; and poverty, 225–27; and race, 183–85; Radicals, 254; and railroads, 181; and scalawags, 182, 183–84, 197, 220–21, 235; as scouts and spies, 233; shared experiences, 221; stereotype during Reconstruction, 177–79, 180, 219n47; and Wager Swayne, 253; and suffrage, 184; and taxation, 181, 184; threatened, 231; in twenty-first century, 178; and victory, 234
Resaca, Battle of, 204, 217n30
Rhett, Robert Barnwell, Jr., 21

Rhode Island, 209
Rhodes, Chauncey, 38
Rhodes, Elizabeth, 34, 37, 38, 41
Richmond, Virginia, 6, 23, 24, 134, 149–50, 153; evacuated, 83; as target of Union army, 56, 71, 198
Riepma, Anne, 142n1
Riser, William, 92
Robertson, James I., 10
Roddey, Philip Dale, 2, 77, 196–98, 199, 203, 215n17
Rodes, Robert, 2, 154
Rogan, Richard, 64
Rogers, William Warren, Jr., 5
"Roll, Jordan, Roll" (song), 260
Rome, Georgia, 71, 202, 204
Roosevelt, Franklin D., 271
Roosevelt, Theodore, 279n64
Rosecrans, William S., 199, 229
Rosenau family, 151
Rousseau, Lovell, 4, *167*
Rowell, John, 73
Royston, Young Lea, 56, 62
Ruggles, Daniel, 199–200
Russell, William Howard, 166

Sacerdote, Jacob, 154
Saffold, Milton, 223
Saks, Joseph, 164n34
Salem, Alabama, 173
Salem Church, Battle of, 55, 59–66; church building, 60, *61*; importance of, 55–56; legacy, 67–68. *See also* Chancellorsville, Battle of
Salisbury, North Carolina, 155
Samford, William J., 18
San Antonio, Texas, 125
San Francisco, California, 210
Sanders, John C. C., 58, 60, 67–68
Sanders, William, 226
Sandwich Islands, 192
Sansom, Emma, 5
Saturday Evening Post, 198
Saunders, Alvin, 196
Savannah, Georgia, 71, 150, 206
"scalawags," 3, 8, 9, 178, 183–84, 191, 197, 220; in 1860, 182; and abolition, 235; and class, 224–

27; leadership, 221–23; moderate, 211, 212; and national Republican Party, 235; negative image of, 178, 220; origins, 3; as outsiders, 235; primacy in state Republican Party, 182; and post-war violence, 225; and poverty, 224–27; as radicals, 235; reaction to presidential restoration, 8; regional breakdown, 223; as slur, 220; socio-economic background, 182, 221; as wartime unionists, 182, 197, 229–35. *See also* Republican Party; Unionists
Scotland, 268
Scott, Sutton S., 19
Scott's Monthly, 127
Scruggs, Ella, 169
Seaver, William, 139–40
secession: in Alabama, 28, 34, 37–38, 165; blamed on North, 37–38; in South Carolina, 37, 38, 39; and women, 34, 37–40, 41–42, 45
Second Baptist Church (Marion, Alabama), 268
Second Colored Baptist Church (Marion, Alabama), 263
Second Colored Baptist Church (Montgomery, Alabama), 266
"Second Reconstruction," 10, 269, 271
Sedgwick, John 56, 58, 60, 62, 66
segregation, 10
Seibels, John J., 24, 26, 27; opposition to secession, 15; and state Democratic Party convention of 1859, 19, 21; support for Stephen A. Douglas, 18
Seip, Terry L., 2–3, 6, 191–219
Selby, Walter, 226, 231
Seligman, James, 151
Seligman, Joseph, 151, 161n5
Seligman, William, 151, 161n5
Selma, Alabama, 24, 25, 38, 202; Battle of, 2, 4, 80–81, 86, 158, 170; in Civil Rights Era, 10; civilians impressed, 79; controversy regarding Forrest statue, 11; destruction after battle, 83–84, 85–86, 172; Stephen A. Douglas visits, 26; Nathan Bedford Forrest hopes to stop Wilson before reaching, 78; Nathan Bedford Forrest retreats to, 79; and Freedmen's Bureau, 246–47, 252, 257n62; and industry, 4, 71–72; Jewish population, 151, 160; and Abraham Lincoln's assassination, 170–71; and Naval Iron Foundry, 71; and northern immigration, 183; and religion, 259, 266, 267; significance of capture, 83; targeted by William T. Sherman, 76; and wartime population, 72
Selma, Battle of, 2, 4, 80–81, 86, 158, 170; casualties, 81; significance, 83
Selma Daily Messenger, 241, 251, 252
Selma Evening Reporter, 79
Selma Federal Union, 171
Selma Rebel, 171
Selma to Montgomery March, 270
Selma University, 266–67, 268
Semmes, Paul, 62, 66, 70n24
Semmes, Raphael, 2
Serbs, 179
Seven Days Battles, 149, 153, 162n14
Seven Pines, Battle of, 153
Severance, Ben H., 2, 55–70
Seward, William Henry, 172, 173
Sheehan-Dean, Aaron, 108
Sheets, Christopher C., 221, 222
Sheffield, Alabama, 163n25
Sheridan, Philip, 71, 94
Sherman, William Tecumseh, 203, 205, 208, 232; and Atlanta Campaign, 4, 204, 240; and O. O. Howard, 240; and March to the Sea, 71, 99, 201, 205–6, 233, 240; on George Thomas, 75–76
Shiloh, Battle of, 95, 155, 196
Ship Island, Mississippi, 152–53, 170
Shorter, John Gill, 158
Siloam Baptist Church (Marion, Alabama), 261–63
Simons, William, 230
Simpson, Wyatt, 229
Sioux City, Iowa, 194
Sixteenth Street Baptist Church (Birmingham, Alabama), 268–69
Slave Code, 249
slaves and slavery, 163n27: and African customs, 260–61; as cause of war, 178; and Confederacy, 228–29; and emancipation, 168, 172–73, 176n25, 228–29, 259–60; and Abraham Lincoln, 259; and music, 260–61; purchasing freedom, 264; refusals to work, 6; and

religion, 60, 258–64; and secession, 3, 40–41, 46; and slave holders, 5, 40–41, 46, 157, 222, 262–63; and slave holding women, 40–41, 46; and soldiers motivations in enlisting, 92–93; testify to masters' unionism, 224; treatment of, 262
Slidell, John, 94
Slough, R. H, 165, 170, 248–49, 250
Smith, Giles, 205
Smith, J. F., 259
Smith, Thomas, 259
Smith, William Hugh, 9, 191, 197, 208–9, 222, 234
Smith, William, 234
Smyrl, Thomas, 98, 99, 100–101, 102
soldiers, 4; and American Revolution, 91; African Americans, 170, 234; and camp life, 119; casualties, 7; and class, 90, 97, 103, 107–8, 120, 122n2; and comrades, 102, 103; and courtship, 118; and defense of homeland, 98, 114; and desertion, 6, 101, 129, 197, 228, 234; as diehard Rebels, 96–97, 103, 114; and divorce, 107, 121; and draft resistance, 227, 228; and duty, 96, 97, 101, 103; and families, 5, 98–99, 101–3, 107–8, 114, 117–21, 129; and gender identity, 107–8, 114–15, 117–18; and generals, 2; hatred of North, 93–94, 97, 98, 99, 103; and home front privation, 119–20; and honor, 96, 97, 101, 103, 114; and ideology, 90–94, 97–98, 101, 102, 103, 107–8; and illness, 116; and independence, 92, 98–99, 103, 107; and liberty, 91–92, 96, 97, 98, 99, 103; and Abraham Lincoln, 93, 97, 170; and masculinity, 35, 95–96, 107, 114; and morale, 90, 96–97; motivations to enlist and fight, 2, 35, 68, 91–103, 155, 160, 200–201; and nationalism, 90–92, 97, 103, 109; as percentages of state population, 2; and politics, 94; and religion, 94–95, 97, 99–100, 103; and slavery, 92–93, 97, 103, 108, 129; and substitution, 129–30; and Twenty Negro Law, 129; as veterans, 107–8; and war-weariness, 97, 102–3, 120; women's roles in mobilizing, 35, 43–44, 96
Solomons, Alexander, 151
Souls of Black Folk, The (book), 260
South and North Railroad, 181

South Carolina, 10, 41, 150, 162n9, 241; and 160 Democratic convention, 23; and secession, 37, 38, 39; and Jewish population, 152, 156; and Reconstruction, 181
South Carolina troops: Kershaw's brigade, 62
Southern Claims Commission, 220
Southern Fire Arms Company, 19
Southern Rights Oppositionist Party, 32n30
Southern Rights Party, 16
Southern, Alfred, 229
Spanish Fort, Alabama, 170
"Spartan motherhood," 5, 43
Spaulding, James Reed, 136–37, 142, 147n55
Spencer, Bella Zilfa, 198, 201, 203, 208, 210–11
Spencer, George E., 3, 9; and African Americans, 209, 211, 212; ambitions, 192–95, 196, 205, 211; background, 192–93, 213n3; as carpetbagger, 184, 191–92; in Civil War, 196–209, 217n30, 232; comments on Alabama after war, 209–10; and cotton, 198, 209; death of wife, 211; decides to settle in Alabama, 208; and Democrats, 194, 195; on Grenville Dodge's staff, 196–200, 203; and election of 1870, 191; enters politics, 192; and 1st Alabama Cavalry, 200–209, 217n30; as first-generation Republican, 192, 193; and illness, 204; and intelligence gathering in war, 198–200; in Iowa, 192–94; as land speculator, 193–95, 213–14n8, 214n10; and March to the Sea, 205–6; marriage, 198; moves to California, 210; and Nevada mining, 198; and patronage, 191; personality suited for war, 200; and pillaging, 206, 232; political style, 193–94; promotion, 200; prospecting for gold, 195; and radical stance, 209, 212; relationship with Phillip Dale Roddey, 198; and Republican Party in Alabama after war, 211; reputation, 191–92; and scalawags, 212; undermines own party, 184, 191; and unionists, 192, 197, 211, 212, 232; and U. S. Senate, 184, 211 in Utah Territory, 195–96
Spirit Lake, Minnesota, 194
Spotsylvania Court House, Battle of, 96, 149, 154
Sprague, William, 209, 210
Spring Hill, Tennessee, 77
Sprott, Samuel, 96
St. Clair County, Alabama, 232, 234

St. Elmo (novel), 127, 130, 133, 143n11–12
St. Joseph, Missouri, 196
St. Louis, Missouri, 26, 154, 163n25, 201, 203, 206
St. Phillip Street Church (Selma, Alabama), 266
St. Wilfred's Episcopal Church (Marion, Alabama), 259
Stanton, Edwin M., 75
states' rights, 10, 18, 24, 41; as rationale for secession, 178
Stay Act, 252, 253
"Steal Away to Jesus" (song), 260
Stephens, Alexander, 38, 140–41, 147n61
Stephens, James, 92, 94
Stevens, Isaac, 24
Stevens, Nicholas, 227
Stevens, Thaddeus, 180
Stevens, William J., 267
Steward, Thomas, 268
Stewart, A. P., 92
Stewart, George, 64
Stewart, Jacob, 233
Stickney, William A., 259
Stimson, Henry L., 271
Stoneman, George, 73
Stones River, Battle of. *See* Murfreesboro, Battle of
Storey, Margaret, 109, 221, 224, 225, 236n7; and motivations for unionism, 47n3; and percentages of unionists in Alabama, 6, 34, 238n59
Storrs, Ella, 260, 261, 273n10
Streight, Abel, 5, *167*, 199
Strickton, J., 241
Strom, H. S., 98
Strudwick, Osmund, 65
Stuart, Chales E., 30
Stutts, Henry, 221, 225
Sumter (Confederate ship), 2
Suttle, Isaac, 262
Swayne, Noah, 240
Swayne, Wager, 242; accomplishments, 254–55; background, 240–41; and courts, 248–51, 252, 254; criticized by opponents, 253; as head of Freedmen's Bureau in Alabama, 7, 9, 240–54; and labor contracts, 245–48, 253–54; and Mobile, 248–50; and Montgomery, 242–43; and Lewis Parsons, 243, 246, 248–51; and Robert Patton, 251–52; racial views, 241, 243; recruits agents, 243; removed from office, 253; and Republican Party, 253; reputation, 241, 253; and vagrancy laws, 245–46, 253
Swindel, Jesse, 226

Talladega, Alabama, 151, 172
Talladega County, Alabama, 110–11
Tammany Hall, 180
Taylor, Grant, 98–103
Taylor, Malinda, 98–99, 102
Taylor, Richard, 4, 74, 79, 84, 172
Teer, Ide, 102
Tennessee, 1, 8, 25, 26, 150; and military operations, 73, 75–76, 196–97; and unionists, 233, 234
Tennessee River, 4, 56, 75, 163n25, 196–97, 231
Tennessee troops: 3rd Cavalry, 1
Tennessee Valley, 224, 225, 228, 230–32, 233–34
Terrell, E., 267
Teters, Kristopher A., 2, 4, 6, 90–106
Texas, 23, 150
Thane, Robert S., 29
Thayer, John, 196
Thirteenth Amendment, 7, 251, 261
Thomas, Ella Gertrude Clanton, 131
Thomas, Emory, 71
Thomas, George H., 72, 73, 75; bans *Macaria*, 131; and Selma, 71, 76, 85
Thompson, James Monroe, 96
Thompson, M. E., 39–40, 41, 43, 45
Thornton, J. Mills, 30, 224
Tichenor, Isaac, 158
Times of London, 166
Todd, Alexander "Ellick," 40
Tombigbee River, 76
Toney, Edmonia, 169
Toombs, Robert, 129, 140
tourism, 10
Treadwell, E. W., 101
Treadwell, Mattie, 101
Trent Affair, 94
Treviño, Jennifer Ann Newman, 5, 34–54
Tubb, John, 262
Tuscaloosa, Alabama, 77, 209, 226, 229; and Reconstruction, 9, 210–11; and University of Alabama, 58, 268
Tuscaloosa County, Alabama, 226, 228
Tuscumbia, Alabama, 198, 199, 232, 234

Tuscumbia Valley, 201
Tuskegee, Alabama, 44, 46n1
Tuskegee Institute, 268–69
Twain, Mark, 145n27
twenty-slave exemption, 129, 229

U. S. Christian Commission, 231
U. S. Military Academy, 2, 58, 75
U. S. Supreme Court, 16, 152, 153, 240
U. S. War Department, 240
Uncle Tom's Cabin (novel), 127
Unconditional Unionism, 3
Underwood, Theoron, 225
Underwood, William, 225
Union Baptist Church (Perry County, Alabama), 267
Union Leagues, 7, 230
Union raids: in Alabama, *167*, 172, 233
Union Springs, Alabama, 113, 241
Union Springs Times (Alabama), 253
Unionists, 3, 6–7, 8, 9, 34, 47n3, 82, 169, 173, 182, 197, 200, 235n3, 238n59, 239n104; Alabama's, 34, 47n3, 109, 168, 169, 171, 192, 211–12, 223-24, 231, 236n7; after Appomattox, 210; as anti-elites, 224–25, 227; arrested, 227–28; avoid military service, 222–23, 228–29; behind Union lines, 231; John Bell, 165; William Bibb, 168; and class, 221–27; and Confederate relatives, 223; and conscription, 221–22, 225, 228–31, 234; dangers of Unionism, 221–24, 234–35; and Grenville Dodge, 197; and employment, 232–33; in 1st Alabama Cavalry, 200–201; flee state, 233, 234; and foreign origins, 223; Virginia French, 125, 126; and guerrillas, 197, 228, 229, 231, 232, 233, 234; hated by Confederates, 227, 233–34; R. S. Heflin, 222; intimidated, 227, 229–30; and Andrew Johnson, 173, 209, 234; and Abraham Lincoln, 168, 169, 171, 174; locations of, 223, 225; and loyalty oaths, 228; and Northern origins, 223; outspokenness, 227; Thomas M. Peters, 223; post-war violence, 234; and poverty, 224–27, 229; publications, 169, 171, 222; and reconciliation, 234; as refugees, 231; and religion, 231–32; and Republican Party postwar, 220–21, 227;

as scouts and spies, 233, 234; and George Spencer, 192, 197, 211; Tennessee Valley, 27, 225; as Tories, 197, 203, 230, 234; and torture, 224; in Union army, 230–31; women, 230, 231. *See also* "scalawags"
Uniontown, Alabama, 263, 264, 267, 268
Uniontown Baptist Association, 267–68
Uniontown Baptist Church, 264, 267
United Confederate Veterans, 149, 154
Unites States troops: 4th Cavalry, 81–83; 74th Colored Infantry, 170; 7th Reserve Corps, 252
University of Alabama, 4, 19, 58, 268
Uplifting the People (book), 258
Upton, Emory, 63–64, 77, 78, 80
Utah Territory, 195

Vanderbilt University, 1
Vandever, William, 204, 208
Vann, Lizzie, 101
Vann, Samuel King, 98, 101, 102
Varon, Elizabeth, 43
Vaughan, Paul Turner, 95
Veasy, James, 261
Vicksburg, Mississippi, 99
Vicksburg, Siege of, 94, 95, 196
Victor, O. J., 127
Vincent's Crossroads, Mississippi, 202–3
Virgin Islands, 271
Virginia, 4, 38, 71, 264
Virginia troops, 59, 61, 108; Mahone's brigade, 62

Walker, Leroy Pope, 19, 23
Wallace, George C., 270
Wallace, Lew, 196
Wallace, Samuel M., 222
Warner, J. W., 98
Warner, Willard, 191, 211
Warren County, Iowa, 194
Washington, Booker, T., 268–69, 270
Washington, D. C., 16, 152, 180, 197–98, 208, 271; and Phillips family, 162n9
Waterloo, Alabama, 75
Watertown, New York, 208
Watts, Thomas Hill, 6, 19, 156, 158, 159
Weaver, James B., 198

Webb, C. H., 143n11
Webster, Noah, 42
Weil family, 92, 155, 157
Weil, Heinrich, 155
Weil, Jacob, 92, 155
Weil, Joseph, 155
Welty, Eudora, 143n11
West Point. *See* U. S. Military Academy
West Point, Georgia, 150
West Point Railroad, 4, 202
Wetumpka, Alabama, 29
Wheeler, Joseph, 10, 207
Whetstone, Adam Henry, 91
Whig Party, 6, 25, 224, 235
White Hall, Georgia, 205
White, Alexander, 20
White, Clement, 51n23
White, Kenneth B., 241
White, Martha Todd, 38, 51n23
White, Mingo, 173
Whites, LeeAnn, 35
Wiggins, Sarah Woolfolk, 6, 177–90, 191–92
Wilcox, Cadmus Marcellus, 2; background, 58; brigade, 55–56, 58–67; nickname, 58, 60, 65; after Salem Church, 67; at Salem Church, 59–60, 64, 65, 66; at Stansbury's Hill, 59
Wilcox County, Alabama, 110
Wilderness, the (area of Virginia), 56
Wilderness, Battle of the, 149, 154
Wiley, Bell I., 10, 104n12
William, T. Harry, 10
Williams, Hiram Smith, 90, 100, 101
Williams, James, 92, 95, 96, 97
Williams, Jeremiah H., 56, 64
Williams, Robert A., 99
Willis, Nathan, 266
Williston, South Carolina, 207
Wills, Brian Steel, 2, 71–89
Wilmer, Richard Hooker, 166, 168
Wilmore, Gayraud S., 260
Wilmot Proviso, 15, 16
Wilson, Augusta Jane Evans. *See* Evans, Augusta Jane
Wilson, James Harrison: background, 72; and Battle of Selma, 80–81; and captured orders, 78; and destruction of Selma industry, 83–84; on Nathan Bedford Forrest, 76, 84–85; troops capture Jefferson Davis, 85; preparations for raid, 72–74, 75–76; and raid through Alabama, 2, 4, 7, 71, 76–86, 158, 170–71, 174
Wilson, Lorenzo Madison, 142
Wilson's Raid, 2, 71, 76–86, *167*, 170–71, 174; background to, 72–74, 75–76; importance of, 4; legacy of, 7; and Montgomery, 158, 171; weapons, 76
Winn, Walter, 64
Winslow, Edward F., 83
Winston, John, 19, 24, 29
Winston County, Alabama, 6, 224, 227, 230, 231
Withers, Jones, 2
Wofford, William T., 62
women, 5; and antebellum concerns for family, 112; blame Republicans for war, 41; and Confederate identity, 34–36, 41, 46; and Confederate mobilization, 35, 43–44, 96, 101, 108; and courtship, 118; and domestic production, 116; and divorce, 107, 121; and duty, 40; and flag presentations, 35, 44–45, 46; and gender identity, 107–8, 114–16, 121, 128; and honor, 37, 40; and keeping diaries, 35; and nursing, 5, 42, 131, 133; and opposition to Republicans, 226; and patriarchy, 35; politicization of, 35–36, 45, 108–9, 112–13; and post-war future, 134–36; and religion, 34, 36, 38, 39–40, 41–42, 44, 45, 47n2, 114, 117; and respectability, 107, 121; and role models, 132–33; and secession, 34, 37–40, 41–42, 45, 112–13; and slavery, 40–41, 46, 108; and tobacco, 118; and unionists, 230, 231; and war-weariness, 120; and war work, 35, 42, 45, 46, 53n58, 131, 133; and womanhood, 35, 36, 128, 135
Women's Loyal Leagues, 59n58
Woods, C. R., 242
Woods, James, 101–2
Woodson, Carter G., 260
Woodward, C. Vann, 10, 269
Works Progress Administration, 172

Yale University, 240
Yancey, Sarah Caroline Earle, 30n3

Yancey, William Lowndes: and Alabama Platform, 15; on African Americans, 26; attends Stephen A. Douglas's Montgomery speech, 26; background, 15–16, 30n3; and Democratic Party convention of 1848, 16; and Democratic Party convention of 1856, 16; and Democratic Party convention of 1860, 20–21, 23–24; and Democratic state convention of 1859, 19–21; denials of disunionism, 16, 21, 23, 28; and *Dred Scott* decision, 16; and election of Abraham Lincoln, 15, 26, 28; and Augusta Jane Evans, 129; and federal slave code, 15–16; national speaking tour, 25–27; on Republicans, 26; as revolutionary, 15, 28; role in breakup of party, 3, 15, 28; and "Scarlet Letter," 15; and secession, 15; and Southern Rights Party, 16; supporters oppose Stephen A. Douglas, 17; and Wilmot Proviso, 15; and women, 101; women's views of, 36

Yellowhammer: bird, 1, as nickname for Alabama soldiers, 1–7, 10

York, Taylor, 226

Young Men's Christian Association, 266

Young, Andrew, 270

Yugoslavia, 179